Angelic Wisdom

CONCERNING

The Divine Providence

BY

EMANUEL SWEDENBORG

ORIGINALLY PUBLISHED IN LATIN AT AMSTERDAM 1764

STANDARD EDITION

1949

SWEDENBORG FOUNDATION
INCORPORATED
NEW YORK

Organized in 1850 as
The American Swedenborg Printing and Publishing Society

Printed in the United States of America

TRANSLATOR'S NOTE

The same aims and methods have been followed in this translation as in the translation of the *Apocalypsis Explicata*. The defects in previous translations of Swedenborg have arisen mainly from too close an adherence to cognate words and to the Latin order of words and phrases. This is a formal rather than an essential faithfulness to the original. To convey to the English reader the *meaning* of the original with the utmost attainable accuracy and fulness and clearness has been the aim and effort in this translation.

The very full index to this edition is the work of Mr. George W. Colton.

J. C. AGER.

March 22, 1899.

CONTENTS.

        long as the evils in the external man are not put away,
        since these obstruct........................(n. 111).

(iv.)   The evils in the external man can be put away by the Lord
        only through man's instrumentality..........(n. 114).

(v.)   Therefore man ought as if of himself to put away evils from
        the external man..............................(n. 118).

(vi.)   Then the Lord cleanses man from the lusts [of evil] in the
        internal man, and from the evils themselves in the ex-
        ternal.......................................(n. 119).

(vii.) It is the unceasing effort of the Lord's Divine providence
        to conjoin man with Himself and Himself with man,
        that He may be able to bestow upon man the happinesses
        of eternal life; and this can be done only so far as evils
        with their lusts are put away................(n. 123).

        1. The Lord in no wise acts upon any particular thing
           in man singly without acting simultaneously up-
           on all things of man ....(n. 124).

        2. The Lord acts from inmosts and from outmosts
           simultaneously....................(n. 124[4]).

IT IS A LAW OF THE DIVINE PROVIDENCE THAT MAN SHOULD NOT BE COM-
    PELLED BY EXTERNAL MEANS TO THINK AND WILL, AND THUS TO
    BELIEVE AND LOVE, THE THINGS OF RELIGION, BUT SHOULD GUIDE
    HIMSELF, AND SOMETIMES COMPEL HIMSELF........(n. 129–153).

(i.)   No one is reformed by miracles and signs, because they
        compel.......................................(n. 130).

(ii.)   No one is reformed by visions or by conversations with
        the dead, because they compel ....(n. 134).

(iii.) No one is reformed by threats and punishments, because
        they compel..................................(n. 136).

        1. The external cannot compel the internal, but the
           internal can compel the external.... (n. 136[2]).

        2. The internal is so averse to compulsion by the ex-
           ternal that it turns itself away.......(n. 136[3]).

        3. External enjoyments allure the internal to consent,
           and also to love...................(n. 136[5]).

        4. A compelled internal and a free internal are possi-
           ble.............................(n. 136[9]).

(iv.)   No one is reformed in states that do not spring from ration-
        ality and liberty............................(n. 138).

        1. In a state of fear.......................(n. 139).

        2. In a state of misfortune.................(n. 140).

THE LAWS OF PERMISSION ARE ALSO LAWS OF THE DIVINE PROVIDENCE
(n. 234–274).

Some things enumerated that belong to permission, and yet are in accord with the laws of Divine providence, by which a merely natural man confirms himself in favor of nature against God, and in favor of human prudence against Divine providence .... (see n. 236–240).

CONTENTS

ANGELIC WISDOM CONCERNING THE DIVINE PROVIDENCE.

THE DIVINE PROVIDENCE IS THE GOVERNMENT OF THE LORD'S DIVINE LOVE AND DIVINE WISDOM.

1. To understand what the Divine providence is, and that it is the government of the Lord's Divine love and Divine wisdom, it is important to know what has already been said and shown respecting the Divine love and the Divine wisdom in the work on that subject, which is as follows: In the Lord Divine love is of Divine wisdom, and Divine wisdom is of Divine love (n. 34–39). Divine love and Divine wisdom must necessarily have being and existence in other things created by them (n. 47–51). All things of the universe are creations from Divine love and Divine wisdom (n. 52, 53, 151–156). All things of the universe are recipients of Divine love and Divine wisdom (n. 55–60). Before the angels the Lord appears as a sun; and the heat that goes forth therefrom is love, and the light that goes forth therefrom is wisdom (n. 83–88, 89–92, 93–98, 296–301). The Divine love and the Divine wisdom that go forth from the Lord make one (n. 99–102). The Lord from eternity, who is Jehovah, created the universe and all things thereof from Himself, and not from nothing (n. 282–284, 290–295). These things are treated of in the work entitled *Angelic Wisdom concerning the Divine Love and the Divine Wisdom*.

2. From these things, in connection with what is set forth in the same work respecting creation, it can be clearly seen that what is called Divine providence is the government of the Lord's Divine love and Divine wisdom. But as creation was

1

the subject there treated of, and not the conservation of the state of things after creation, which is the Lord's government, the latter shall now be considered. The subject of this chapter will be the conservation of the union of Divine love and Divine wisdom or of Divine good and Divine truth in things created; and this shall be set forth in the following order:—

(1) The universe, with each thing and all things therein, was created from Divine love by means of Divine wisdom.

(2) Divine love and Divine wisdom go forth from the Lord as a one.

(3) In a certain image this one is in every created thing.

(4) The end of the Divine providence is that every created thing, in general and in particular shall be such a one; and if it is not, that it shall become such.

(5) Good of love is good only so far as it has become joined with truth of wisdom; and truth of wisdom is truth only so far as it has become joined with good of love.

(6) Good of love that has not become joined with truth of wisdom is not good in itself, but is apparent good; and truth of wisdom that has not become joined with good of love is not truth in itself, but is apparent truth.

(7) The Lord does not suffer any thing to be divided; consequently it must be in good and also in truth, or it must be in evil and also in falsity.

(8) That which is in good and also in truth is something; but that which is in evil and also in falsity is not any thing.

(9) The Lord's Divine providence causes both the evil and the falsity to be serviceable in the way of equilibrium, of relation, and of purification, and thus in the conjunction of good and truth in others.

3. (1) *The universe, with each thing and all things therein, was created from Divine love by means of Divine wisdom.* In the work on *The Divine Love and the Divine Wisdom* it has been shown that the Lord from eternity, who is Jehovah, is, in His essence, Divine love and Divine wisdom, and that He has created the universe and all things of it from Himself; and from this it follows that the universe, with each thing and all things of it, was created from the Divine love by means of the Divine wisdom. In the same work it has also been shown that love can do nothing apart from wisdom, and that wisdom can do nothing apart from love. For love apart from wisdom, or will apart from understanding, cannot think anything, nor can it see or feel anything, or even say anything; so neither can love apart from wisdom, or will apart from understanding, do anything. In like manner wisdom apart from love, or understanding apart from will, cannot think anything, or see or feel anything, or even say anything; so neither can wisdom apart from love, or understanding apart from will, do anything. For when, in such instances, love is taken away, there is no longer any willing and thus no doing. As this is true of man's doing anything, much more was it true of God, when He who is love itself and wisdom itself created and made the universe and all things thereof. [2] That the universe, with each thing and all things of it, was created from the Divine love by means of the Divine wisdom can be confirmed by all things submitted to sight in the world. Select any particular object and examine it with some wisdom, and you will be convinced. Take a tree, or its seed, its fruit, its flower, or its leaf, gather up the wisdom that is in you, examine the object with a good microscope, and you will see wonderful things; while the interiors that you do not see are still more wonderful. Observe the order in its development, how the tree grows from seed even to new seed, and consider whether there is not at every successive step a continual endeavor to propagate itself further; for the final thing to which it aims is seed, in which its reproductive power exists anew. And if you are willing to think spiritually, which you can do if you wish, will you not now see wisdom here? Moreover, if you are willing to go far enough in spiritual thought, will you not see also that this power is not from the seed, nor from the sun of the world, which is pure fire, but is in the seed from God the Creator, whose wisdom is infinite; and in it not only at the moment it was created, but continually afterwards?

For maintenance involves perpetual creation, as permanence involves a perpetual springing forth. It is the same as if you should withdraw willing from doing, for then work would stop; or as if you should withdraw thought from speech, for then speech would stop, or as if you should withdraw effort from movement, for then movement would stop; in a word, if you should withdraw the cause from the effect the effect would perish; and so on. [3] In fact, every such created thing is endowed with power; but power acts not from itself, but from Him who bestowed the power. Examine any other object on the earth, as a silkworm, a bee, or any other little creature; look at it first naturally, afterwards rationally, and at length spiritually, and if you are able to think deeply, you will be astonished at it all; and if you will let wisdom speak within you, you will say in amazement, "Who can fail to see the Divine in these things? All things are of the Divine wisdom." Still more will you wonder if you examine into the uses of all created things, how in their order they follow on even to man, and from man to the Creator from whom they are; and how upon the conjunction of the Creator with man both the connection of all things, and if you are willing to acknowledge it, the conservation of all things, depend. In what follows it will be seen that Divine love created all things, but nothing apart from Divine wisdom.

4. (2) *Divine love and Divine wisdom go forth from the Lord as a one.* This, too, is clear from what has been shown in the work on *The Divine Love and the Divine Wisdom,* especially from the following: In the Lord *Esse* and *Existere* are one distinctly (n. 14–16). In the Lord infinite things are one distinctly (n. 17–22). Divine love is of Divine wisdom, and Divine wisdom is of Divine love (n. 34–39). Without a marriage with wisdom love is unable to effect any thing (n. 401–403). Love does nothing except in conjunction with wisdom (n. 409, 410). Spiritual heat and spiritual light in their going forth from the Lord as a Sun make one, just as Divine love and Divine wisdom in the Lord are one (n. 99–102). From what has been shown in these places, the truth of this proposition is evident. But as it is not known how two things distinct from each other can act as a one, I wish to show here that a one is impossible apart from a form, the form itself making the one; and next, that the form makes a one the more perfectly as the things entering into the form are distinctly different and yet united. [2] *A one is impossible apart from a form, the form itself making the one.* Any one who thinks intently can see clearly that a one is impossible apart from a form, and if it exists it is a form; for whatever has existence derives from form that which is called quality, and that which is called predicate, also that which is called change of state, also that which is called relativity, and the like; consequently that which is not in a form has no power to affect; and what has no power to affect has no reality. It is the form that gives all these things; and as all the things that are in a form, when the form is perfect, have a mutual regard for each other, as link has to link in a chain, therefore it follows that it is the form that makes the one, and thus the subject, of which quality, state, power to affect, and anything that accords with the perfection of the form, can be predicated. [3] Every object seen by the eyes in the world is such a one; also every object not seen by the eyes, whether in interior nature or in the spiritual world. Man is such a one, human society is such a one, the church is such a one, also the whole angelic heaven before the Lord; in a word, the created universe, not only in general but also in every particular, is such a one. But in order that each thing and all things may be forms, it is necessary that He who created all things should be Form itself, and that all things that are created in forms should be from Form itself. This, therefore, is what has been shown in the work on *The Divine Love and the Divine Wisdom*, as follows: Divine love and Divine wisdom are substance and are form (n. 40–43). Divine love and Divine wisdom are form in itself, thus the Very and the Only (n. 44–46). In the Lord Divine love and Divine wisdom are one (n. 14–22). They go forth from the Lord as a one (n. 99–102, and elsewhere). [4] *The form makes a one the more perfectly as the things entering into the form are distinctly different and yet united.* Unless the understanding is raised up it can scarcely comprehend this, since the appearance is that a form can make a one only through likenesses of uniformity in the things that make up the form. On this subject I have often talked with angels, who said that this is an arcanum their wiser ones perceive clearly, and the less wise obscurely; yet it is a truth that a form is the more perfect as the things that constitute it are distinctly different, and yet have become united each in its own way. This they showed by the societies in the heavens, which taken together constitute the form of heaven; also by the angels of each society, in that the form of the society is more perfect in proportion as each angel is more distinctly his own, and therefore free, and thus loves his companions as if from himself and from his own affection. They illustrated it also by the marriage of good and truth, in that the more distinctly these are two, the more perfectly they can make a one; and the same is true of love and wisdom; while what is not distinct is mixed up, giving rise to every imperfection of form. [5] Furthermore, how perfectly distinct things are united and thus make a one, they showed by many things, especially by the things that are in the human body, where innumerable parts are thus distinct and yet united, distinct by their coverings and united by their ligaments, showing that it is the same with love and all things of it, and with wisdom and all things of it, which are perceived only as a one. More respecting this can be seen in the work on *The Divine Love and the Divine Wisdom* (n. 14–22), and in the work on *Heaven and Hell* (n. 56, 489). This has been adduced because it is of angelic wisdom.

5. (3) *In a certain image this one is in every created thing.* That the Divine love and the Divine wisdom, which are a one in the Lord and go forth from Him as a one, are in every created thing in a certain image can be seen from what is shown throughout the work on *The Divine Love and the Divine Wis-*

dom, and especially from what is said in n. 47–51, 55–60, 282–284, 290–295, 313–318, 319–326, 349–357, where it is shown that the Divine is in every created thing, because God the Creator, who is the Lord from eternity, produced from Himself the sun of the spiritual world, and through that sun all things of the universe, consequently that that sun, which is from the Lord, and in which the Lord is, is not only the first substance but is also the only substance from which all things are; and since this is the only substance, it follows that it is in every created thing, but with infinite variety according to uses. [2] Now since Divine love and Divine wisdom are in the Lord, and since Divine fire and brightness are in that sun from Him, and spiritual heat and spiritual light are from that sun, and these two make a one, it follows that in a certain image this one is in every created thing. Because of this all things in the universe have relation to good and truth, and, in fact, to their conjunction, or what is the same, all things in the universe have relation to love and wisdom and to their conjunction, since good belongs to love and truth to wisdom; for love calls all that pertains to it good, and wisdom calls all that pertains to it truth. That there is a conjunction of these in every created thing will be seen in what follows.

6. Many admit that there is an only substance which is the first substance and the source of all things, but what kind of a substance it is they do not know. They believe it to be so simple that nothing is simpler; that it may be compared to a point with no dimension; and that from an infinite number of such the forms of dimension came into existence. This, however, is a fallacy originating in the idea of space; for the idea of space makes the least to appear such. But the truth is that the simpler and purer any thing is, the more and the fuller it is. It is for this reason that the more deeply any object is examined, the more wonderful, perfect, and beautiful are the things seen in it; and thus that the most wonderful, perfect, and beautiful of all are in the first substance. This is true, because the first substance is from the spiritual sun, which, as has been said, is from the Lord, and in which the Lord is, therefore that sun is itself the only substance; and as this substance is not in space it is the all in all, and is in the greatest and the least things of the created universe. [2] Since that sun is the first and only substance, from which all things are, it follows that infinitely more things are in that substance than can appear in the substances that spring from it, which are called substantiate [or composite], and at length material. These things cannot appear in those substances, because they descend from that sun by degrees of a twofold kind, in accordance with which all perfections decrease. For this reason, as said above, the more deeply any thing is examined, the more wonderful, perfect, and beautiful are the things that are seen. This has been said to show that in a certain image the Divine is in every created thing, but becomes less and less apparent in its descent through the degrees, and still less apparent when a lower degree has become separated from a higher by the closing up of the higher, and by becoming itself choked up with earthy matters. This, however, must needs seem obscure, unless one has read and understood what has been presented in the work on *The Divine Love and the Divine Wisdom*, respecting the spiritual sun (n. 83–172), respecting degrees (n. 173–281), and respecting the creation of the universe (n. 282–357).

7. (4) *The end of the Divine providence is that every created thing, in general and in particular, shall be such a one; and if it is not, that it shall become such.* That is, that in every created thing there shall be something both from the Divine love and from the Divine wisdom; or what is the same, that in every created thing there shall be good and truth, that is, a conjunction of good and truth. Since good is of love and truth is of wisdom (as has been said above, n. 5), in the following pages the terms good and truth will be used throughout instead of love and wisdom, and the marriage of good and truth, instead of the union of love and wisdom.

8. From a preceding article it is evident that the Divine love and the Divine wisdom, which in the Lord are one, and which go forth as one from the Lord, in a certain image are in every thing created by Him. And now something shall be said specifically about that oneness or union that is called the marriage of good and truth. That marriage is (1) In the Lord Himself; for Divine love and Divine wisdom, as has been said, are a one in Him. (2) It is from the Lord; for in every thing that goes forth from Him love and wisdom are fully united, these two going forth from the Lord as a sun, the Divine love as the heat, and the Divine wisdom as the light. (3) These are, indeed, received by the angels as two, but are made one in them by the Lord; and the same is true of men of the church. (4) Because of this influx of love and wisdom from the Lord as a one into angels of heaven and men of the church, and because of the reception of these by angels and men, the Lord is called in the Word the "Bridegroom" and the "Husband," and heaven and the church are called the "bride" and the "wife." (5) Therefore, so far as heaven and the church in general or an angel of heaven and a man of the church individually are in that union, that is, in the marriage of good and truth, they are an image and likeness of the Lord, because good and truth are a one in the Lord, and, in fact, are the Lord. (6) In heaven and in the church in general, or in an angel of heaven or a man of the church, love and wisdom are a one when the will and the understanding, and thus good and truth, make a one, or what is the same, when charity and faith make a one, or what is still the same, when doctrine from the Word and a life according to it make a one. (7) How these two make a one in man and in all things belonging to him has been shown in the work on *The Divine Love and the Divine Wisdom*, in Part Five, where the creation of man and especially the correspondence of the will and understanding with the heart and lungs are treated of (n. 358–432).

9. How these make a one in things below man or outside of him, both those in the animal kingdom and those in the vegetable kingdom, will be told further on. Here three things must be premised: *First*, In the universe and in each thing and all things of it, which the Lord created, there was a marriage of good and truth. *Second*, After creation, this marriage was severed in man. *Third*, It is the end of Divine providence that what is severed shall become one, and thus the marriage of good and truth be restored. As these three things are fully shown in the work on *The Divine Love and the Divine Wisdom*, further proof is unnecessary. Moreover, any one can see from reason that as there was by creation a marriage of good and truth in every created thing, and as this marriage was afterwards severed, the Lord must be continually working to restore it, and therefore its restoration, and the consequent conjunction of the created universe with the Lord through man, must be the end of Divine providence.

10. (5) *Good of love is good only so far as it has become joined with truth of wisdom; and truth of wisdom is truth only so far as it has become joined with good of love.* Good and truth derive this from their origin. Good has its origin in the Lord, and likewise truth, for the Lord is good itself and truth itself; and in Him these two are one. For this reason in angels of heaven and in men on earth good is good in itself only so far as it has become joined with truth; and truth is truth in itself only so far as it has become joined with good. It is acknowledged that every good and every truth is from the Lord; since, therefore, good makes one with truth, and truth with good, it follows that for good to be good in itself, and for truth to be truth in itself, they must make one in the recipient, that is, in an angel of heaven or a man on the earth.

11. It is acknowledged that all things in the universe have relation to good and truth, for by good is meant that which universally embraces and involves all things of love, and by truth that which universally embraces and involves all things of wisdom. But it is not yet acknowledged that good is not any thing until it has become joined with truth, and that truth is not any thing until it has become joined with good. There is an appearance, indeed, that good is something apart from truth, and that truth is something apart from good, and yet

they are not; since love (all things of which are called goods)
is the being (*esse*) of a thing, and wisdom (all things of which
are called truths) is the coming forth (*existere*) of a thing from
that *esse*, as has been shown in the work on *The Divine Love
and the Divine Wisdom* (n. 14–16); and just as *esse* is nothing
apart from *existere*, and *existere* is nothing apart from *esse*, so
good is nothing apart from truth, and truth is nothing apart
from good. So again, what is good unless related to something? Can it be called good, since no affection or perception
can be predicated of it? [2] The thing in connection with
good that affects and causes itself to be perceived and felt has
relation to truth, since it has relation to what is in the understanding. Say to any one, not that this or that is good, but
simply "the good," is "the good" any thing? Good is something because of this or that which is perceived as one with
good. This is united with good nowhere but in the understanding; and every thing of the understanding has relation to
truth. It is the same with willing. To will, apart from knowing, perceiving, and thinking what one wills, is not any thing;
but together with these it becomes something. All willing is
of love, and has relation to good; and all knowing, perceiving,
or thinking is of the understanding, and has relation to truth.
From this it is clear that to will is nothing, but to will this or
that is something. [3] It is the same with every use, because
a use is a good. Unless a use is determined to something with
which it may be a one it is not a use, and thus it is not any
thing. It is from the understanding that use derives its something to which it may be determined; and that from the understanding which is conjoined or adjoined to the use has
relation to truth; and it is from that that the use derives its
quality. [4] From these few things it is clear that good apart
from truth is not any thing; and that truth apart from good is
not any thing. When it is said that good with truth and truth
with good are something, it follows from this that evil with
falsity and falsity with evil are not any thing; for the latter
are opposite to the former, and opposition destroys, and in this

case destroys that something. But more about this in what
follows.

12. There may be a marriage, however, of good and truth
in the cause, and there may be a marriage of good and truth
from the cause in the effect. A marriage of good and truth in
the cause is a marriage of will and understanding, that is, of
love and wisdom. There is such a marriage in every thing
that a man wills and thinks, and in all his conclusions and intentions therefrom. This marriage enters into and produces
the effect. But in producing the effect the good and the truth
appear distinct, because the simultaneous then produces what is
successive. For instance, when a man is willing and thinking
about his food and clothing and dwelling place, about his business or employment, or his relations with others, at first he wills
and thinks, or forms his conclusions and purposes, about these
at the same time; but when these have been determined into
effects, one follows the other; nevertheless, in will and thought
they continue to make one. In these effects uses pertain to
love or to good, while means to the uses pertain to the understanding or to truth. Any one can confirm these general truths
by particulars, provided he clearly perceives what has relation
to good of love and what has relation to truth of wisdom, and
also how these are related in the cause and how in the effect.

13. It has often been said that love makes the life of man;
but this does not mean love separate from wisdom or good separate from truth in the cause, since love separate, or good separate is not any thing; therefore the love that makes man's inmost life, the life that is from the Lord, is love and wisdom
together; and the love that makes the life of man as being a
recipient is also love, not separate in the cause, but only in the
effect. For love can be understood only from its quality, and
its quality is wisdom; and its quality or wisdom can exist only
from its being (*esse*) which is love, and it is from this that
they are one. It is the same with good and truth. Since, then,
truth is from good, as wisdom is from love, the two taken together are called love or good; for love in its form is wisdom,

and good in its form is truth, and form is the source and the only source of quality. From all this it is now evident that good is not in the least good except so far as it has become joined with its truth, and that truth is not in the least truth except so far as it has become one with its good.

14. (6) *Good of love that has not become joined with truth of wisdom is not good in itself, but is apparent good; and truth of wisdom that has not become joined with good of love is not truth in itself, but is apparent truth.* The truth is that no good that is good in itself can exist unless it has become joined with its truth; nor can truth that is truth in itself exist unless it has become joined with its good. Nevertheless, there is good separated from truth, and truth separated from good. This is found in hypocrites and flatterers, in evil persons of every kind, and in such as are in natural good and in no spiritual good. All these are able to do what is good to the church, to the country, to society, to fellow-citizens, to the needy, the poor, the widow, and the orphan; they can also understand truths, and from their understanding can think about truths, and from their thought can talk about them and teach them; nevertheless these goods and truths in them are not interiorly, that is, not in themselves, goods and truths, but they are outwardly and thus only apparently goods and truths, for they look only to self and the world, and not to good itself and truth itself, consequently they are not from good and truth, and therefore are of the mouth and the body only, and not of the heart. [2] They may be likened to gold and silver spread over dross or rotten wood or dung; and such truths when uttered may be likened to a breath that passes away, or to a delusive light that vanishes, though outwardly they appear like genuine truths. These truths so appear in those that utter them, while to those who hear and accept them, not knowing what they are, they may seem to be quite different. For every one is affected by what is external according to his own internal; and a truth, by whatever mouth it is uttered, enters into another's hearing and is taken up by the mind according to the state and quality of the mind. Nearly the same is true of those that are in natural good by inheritance, and in no spiritual good. For the internal of every good and of every truth is spiritual, and the spiritual dispels falsities and evils, while the natural by itself favors them; and favoring evils and falsities is not in accord with doing good.

15. Good can be separated from truth, and truth from good, and when separated may still appear to be good and truth, for the reason that man has the ability to act that is called liberty, and the ability to understand that is called rationality. It is by the abuse of these powers that man can seem in externals to be different from what he is in internals; and in consequence, that a bad man can do what is good and speak what is true, or a devil feign himself an angel of light. But on this see what has been said in the work on *The Divine Love and the Divine Wisdom,* as follows : The origin of evil is from the abuse of the capacities peculiar to man that are called rationality and liberty (n. 264–270). These two capacities are in the evil as well as in the good (n. 425). Love without a marriage with wisdom, or good without a marriage with truth, is unable to effect any thing (n. 401). Love does nothing except in conjunction with wisdom or the understanding (n. 409). Love makes wisdom or the understanding to be reciprocally conjoined to it (n. 410–412). Wisdom or the understanding, from the power given it by love, can be raised up, and can perceive and receive such things as belong to light out of heaven (n. 413). Love can in like manner be raised up, and can receive such things as belong to heat out of heaven, provided it loves wisdom, its marriage partner, in that degree (n. 414, 415). Otherwise love draws down wisdom or the understanding from its elevation, that it may act as one with itself (n. 416–418). Love is purified in the understanding when they are raised up together (n. 419–421). When love has been purified by wisdom in the understanding, it becomes spiritual and celestial; but when love has been defiled in the understanding it becomes sensual and corporeal (n. 422–424). It is the same with

charity and faith and their conjunction as with love and wisdom and their conjunction (n. 427–430). What charity is in
the heavens (n. 431).

16. (7) *The Lord does not suffer any thing to be divided ;
consequently it must be in good and also in truth, or it must be
in evil and also in falsity.* The Lord's Divine providence
chiefly has for its end that man should be in good and also in
truth, and for this it works; for thereby man is his own good
and his own love, and also his own truth and his own wisdom;
for thereby man is man, since he is then an image of the Lord.
But inasmuch as man can be, while he is living in the world,
in good and in falsity at the same time, also in evil and in
truth at the same time, and even in evil and in good at the
same time, and thus be as it were a double man, and inasmuch
as this division destroys that image, and thereby destroys the
man, the Lord's Divine providence, in each and every particular of it, has as its end that this division shall not be. And
since it is better for a man to be in evil and in falsity at the
same time than to be in good and in evil at the same time, the
Lord permits this, not as being what He wills, but because,
in view of the end which is salvation, He cannot prevent it.
That it is possible for a man to be in evil and in truth at the
same time, and that the Lord in view of the end, which is salvation, cannot prevent this, comes from man's ability to have
his understanding raised up into the light of wisdom, and to
see truths or acknowledge them when he hears them, while his
love remains below. For man is thus able to be in heaven
with the understanding, while with the love he is in hell; and
this cannot be denied to man, because the two capacities, rationality and liberty, cannot be taken from him; for these are what
make him to be a man, and differentiate him from the beasts,
and only by means of these can he be regenerated and thus
saved. For by means of these a man is able to act according
to wisdom, and is also able to act according to a love that is
not of wisdom; by means of these he is able also from wisdom
above to view the love below, and thus to view his thoughts,

intentions, affections, and in consequence the evils and falsities and the goods and truths of his life and doctrine; and without a knowledge and recognition of these in himself he cannot be reformed. These two capacities have been treated of above, and more will be said about them in what follows. This is why man can be in good and also in truth, and in evil and also in falsity, and in alternations of these.

17. In this world a man can enter only with difficulty into either conjunction or union, that is, of good and truth, or of evil and falsity; for so long as he is living in the world, he is held in a state of reformation or of regeneration; but after death every man comes into one or the other, because then he can no longer be reformed and regenerated; he then remains such as his life, that is, such as his ruling love, has been in this world. If, therefore, his life has been a life of the love of evil, every truth that he has acquired in the world from a teacher, from preaching, or from the Word, is taken away, and when truth has been taken away, he imbibes such falsity as agrees with his evil, as a sponge imbibes water. On the other hand, if his life has been a life of the love of good, all the falsity that he has gathered in the world from hearing and from reading, but has not confirmed in himself, is removed; and in its place truth agreeing with his good is given him. This is meant by these words of the Lord:—

Take the talent from him, and give it to him that hath the ten talents; for unto every one that hath shall be given, that he may have abundance; but from him that hath not shall be taken away even that which he hath (*Matt.* xxv. 28, 29; xiii. 12; *Mark* iv. 25; *Luke* viii. 18; xix. 24–26).

18. After death every one must be in good and also in truth, or must be in evil and also in falsity, for the reason that good cannot be conjoined with evil, nor can good be conjoined with the falsity of evil, nor evil with the truth of good; for these are opposites, and opposites fight each other until one destroys the other. Those who are in evil and also in good are meant by these words of the Lord to the church of the Laodiceans in the *Apocalypse:*—

I know thy works, that thou art neither cold nor hot; would that thou wert cold or hot. So because thou art lukewarm, and neither cold nor hot, I will spew thee out of My mouth (iii. 15, 16);

and also by these words of the Lord:—

No man can serve two masters; for he will either hate the one and love the other, or he will cling to the one and neglect the other (*Matt.* vi. 24).

19. (8) *That which is in good and also in truth is something; but that which is in evil and also in falsity is not any thing.* It may be seen above (n. 11), that what is in good and also in truth is something; and from this it follows that what is in evil and also in falsity is not any thing. Not being any thing, means to have no power and no spiritual life. Those who are in evil and also in falsity, and all such are in hell, have indeed power with one another; for an evil person is able to do evil, and does it in a thousand ways. And yet only from evil is he able to do evil to the evil; and not in the least is he able to do evil to the good; and if, as is sometimes the case, he does evil to those who are good, it is by a conjunction with their evil. [2] This is the source of temptations, which are infestations by the evil who are with men, and consequent combats by means of which the good can be freed from their evils. As the evil have no power, so before the Lord the entire hell is not only as nothing, but in respect to power is absolutely nothing, as I have seen proved by abundant experience. And yet, what is wonderful, the wicked all believe themselves to be powerful, while the good all believe themselves to be destitute of power. The reason is that the evil attribute all things to their own power, and thus to shrewdness and cunning, and attribute nothing to the Lord; while the good attribute nothing to their own prudence, but all things to the Lord who is Almighty. Evil and falsity together are not any thing, for the reason also that there is no spiritual life in them; and this is why the life of the infernals is not called life, but death; since, therefore, all that is any thing must be ascribed to life, nothing [that is real] can be ascribed to death.

2

20. Those who are in evil and also in truth may be likened to eagles that soar aloft, but drop when deprived of the use of their wings; for thus the men do after death, when they have become spirits, who have understood truths, have talked about them, and have taught them, and yet have not looked to God at all in their life. Such by means of the things in their understanding raise themselves on high, and sometimes enter the heavens and feign themselves angels of light; but when deprived of truths and cast out, they fall down to hell. Moreover, eagles signify rapacious men who are endowed with intellectual sight; and wings signify spiritual truths. As just said, these are such as have not looked to God in their life. To look to God in the life means nothing else than thinking this or that evil to be a sin against Him, and for that reason not doing it.

21. (9) *The Lord's Divine providence causes both the evil and the falsity to be serviceable in the way of equilibrium, of relation, and of purification, and thus in the conjunction of good and truth in others.* From what has been said it can be seen that the Lord's Divine providence continually labors to unite truth with good, and good with truth in man, because such union is the church and is heaven; for there is such a union in the Lord and in all things that go forth from the Lord. From that union heaven is called a marriage, and the church is called a marriage, and in consequence the kingdom of God is likened in the Word to a marriage. From that union the Sabbath in the Israelitish Church was the most holy thing of worship, for it signified that union. For the same reason in each and in all things of the Word there is a marriage of good and truth (respecting which see the *Doctrine of the New Jerusalem concerning the Sacred Scripture,* n. 80–90). The marriage of good and truth is from the marriage of the Lord with the church; and this is from the marriage of love and wisdom in the Lord; for good pertains to love, and truth to wisdom. From all this it can be seen that the unceasing object of the Divine providence is to unite good to truth and truth **to good in man,** for thus man is united to the Lord.

22. But inasmuch as many have sundered or are sundering this marriage, especially by the separation of faith from charity, since faith is of truth and truth is of faith, and charity is of good and good is of charity, and inasmuch as they thereby conjoin evil and falsity in themselves, and have thus become or are becoming opposite [to good and truth], the Lord provides that such shall still be of service for the conjunction of good and truth in others, as means of equilibrium, relation and purification

23. The conjunction of good and truth in others is provided by the Lord, by means of the *equilibrium* between heaven and hell; for there is a constant exhalation from hell of evil and falsity together, while from heaven there is a constant exhalation of good and truth together. In this equilibrium every man is held as long as he lives in the world; and by means of it he is held in freedom to think, to will, to speak, and to do, and in this it is possible for him to be reformed. (Respecting this spiritual equilibrium, from which man has freedom, see the work on *Heaven and Hell*, n. 589–596, and n. 597–603.)

24. The conjunction of good and truth is provided by the Lord by means of *relation*; since the quality of a good is known only by its relation to what is less good, and by its contrariety to evil. From this comes all power to perceive and to feel, since from this comes the quality of these powers; for thereby every thing enjoyable is perceived and felt from the less enjoyable and by means of what is not enjoyable, every thing beautiful from the less beautiful and by means of the unbeautiful; and likewise every good, which is of love, from the less good and by means of evil; and every truth, which is of wisdom, from the less true and by means of falsity. In every matter, from the greatest to the least of it, there must be variety; and when there is variety also in its opposite from its least to its greatest, and there is equilibrium between them, then there is relation according to degrees on both sides; and the perception and sensation of the thing either increase or diminish. But an opposite, as we should know, may take away perceptions and sensations or may exalt them; when it mingles itself it takes away; but when it does not mingle itself it exalts; and for this reason the Lord exactly separates good and evil in man, that they may not be mingled, just as He separates heaven and hell.

25. In others the conjunction of good and truth is provided by the Lord by means of *purification,* which is effected in two ways, one by temptations, and the other by fermentations. *Spiritual temptations* are nothing else than combats against the evils and falsities that are exhaled from hell and affect man. By these combats man is purified from evils and falsities, and good is conjoined to truth in him, and truth to good. *Spiritual fermentations* are effected in many ways, both in the heavens and on the earth; but in the world it is not known what they are or how they are effected. For there are evils and falsities together that do a work, when introduced into societies, like that of leaven put into meal, or ferments into new wine, by which heterogeneous things are separated and homogeneous things are conjoined, and purity and clearness are the result. These are meant by these words of the Lord:—

The kingdom of heaven is like unto leaven, which a woman took and hid in three measures of meal, till it was all leavened (*Matt.* xiii. 33; *Luke* xiii. 21).

26. From the conjunction of evil and falsity in those who are in hell the Lord provides these uses; for the Lord's kingdom, which is not only over heaven, but also over hell, is a kingdom of uses; and the Lord provides that there shall be there no person by whom, or no thing by means of which, some use is not accomplished.

THE LORD'S DIVINE PROVIDENCE HAS AS ITS END A HEAVEN
FROM THE HUMAN RACE.

27. By long-continued intercourse with angels and spirits
it has been made known and proved to me that heaven is not
made up of angels created such from the beginning, and that
hell did not originate in any devil created an angel of light
and cast down from heaven, but that both heaven and hell are
from the human race,—heaven from those who are in the love
of good and in the consequent understanding of truth, and
hell from those who are in the love of evil and in the consequent understanding of falsity. (On this subject see what has
been shown in the work on *Heaven and Hell*, n. 311–316;
also in the little work on the *Last Judgment*, n. 14–27; and
*Continuation concerning the Last Judgment and the Spiritual
World*, from beginning to end.) [2] Now since heaven is from
the human race, and heaven is an abiding with the Lord to
eternity, it follows that this was the Lord's end in creation;
and since heaven was the end in creation this is the end of
His Divine providence. The Lord did not create the universe
for His own sake, but for the sake of those with whom He is
to be in heaven; since spiritual love is such that it wishes to
give its own to another; and so far as it can do this, it is in
its being (*esse*), in its peace, and in its blessedness. Spiritual
love derives this from the Lord's Divine love, which is such
infinitely. From this it follows, that the Divine love and the
Divine providence therefrom have as their end a heaven consisting of men who have become or are becoming angels, upon
whom the Lord is able to bestow all the blessings and felici-
ties that belong to love and wisdom, and to communicate these
from Himself in them. Nor can He do this in any other way;
for there is in them from creation an image and likeness of
Himself; the image in them is wisdom, and the likeness in
them is love; and the Lord in them is love united to wisdom
and wisdom united to love; or, what is the same, is good
united to truth, and truth united to good. (This union was

treated of in the preceding chapter.) [3] But since it is not known what heaven is in general or in many, and what it is in particular or in the individual, what it is in the spiritual world and what it is in the natural world, and yet this knowledge is most important, because heaven is the end of the Divine providence, I will try to present the subject with some clearness, in the following order:—

(1) Heaven is conjunction with the Lord.

(2) From creation man has an ability to be more and more nearly conjoined with the Lord.

(3) The more nearly a man is conjoined with the Lord the wiser he becomes.

(4) The more nearly a man is conjoined with the Lord the happier he becomes.

(5) The more nearly a man is conjoined with the Lord the more distinctly does he seem to himself as if he were his own, and the more clearly does he recognize that he is the Lord's.

28. (1) *Heaven is conjunction with the Lord.* It is not from the angels but from the Lord that heaven is heaven, for the love and wisdom in which angels are and which make heaven, are not from the angels but from the Lord, and in fact, are the Lord in them. And since love and wisdom are the Lord's and are the Lord in heaven, and love and wisdom constitute the life of angels, it is clear that their life is the Lord's life, and in fact, is the Lord. The angels themselves confess that they live from the Lord. All this makes clear that heaven is conjunction with the Lord. But since conjunction with the Lord is various, and consequently heaven is not the same to one as to another, it follows further that heaven is according to the conjunction with the Lord. In the following chapter it will be seen that the conjunction is more and more near, or more and more remote. [2] Here something shall be said about that conjunction, how it is effected, and what it is. It is a conjunction of the Lord with angels, and of angels with the Lord, and is therefore reciprocal. The Lord flows into the life's love of the angels, and the angels receive the Lord in wisdom,

and thereby in turn conjoin themselves with the Lord. But
it must be clearly understood that while to the angels the appearance is that they conjoin themselves with the Lord by
means of wisdom, in fact it is the Lord who conjoins them
with Himself by means of wisdom; for their wisdom is from
the Lord. It is the same if it is said that the Lord conjoins
Himself with angels by means of good, and the angels in turn
conjoin themselves with the Lord by means of truth, for all
good pertains to love, and all truth to wisdom. [3] But as
this reciprocal conjunction is an arcanum that few can understand without explanation, I will try to unfold it, as far as possible, by means of such things as are adapted to the comprehension. In the treatise on *The Divine Love and the Divine
Wisdom* (n. 404, 405), it has been shown how love conjoins
itself with wisdom, namely, through an affection for knowing, from which comes an affection for truth, and through an
affection for understanding, from which comes a perception
of truth, and through an affection for seeing what is known
and understood, from which comes thought. Into all these
affections the Lord flows, for they are derivations from the
life's love of every one; and this influx is received by the
angels in the perception of truth and in thought, for in these
the influx becomes apparent to them, but not in the affections.
[4] Since, then, perceptions and thoughts appear to the angels
as if they were theirs, although they are from affections that
are from the Lord, there is this appearance that the angels
conjoin themselves reciprocally with the Lord, although it is
the Lord who conjoins them with Himself; for perceptions and
thoughts are products of the affection, for the affection, which
pertains to the love, is their soul. For no one can perceive or
think anything apart from affection, and every one perceives
and thinks according to affection. All this makes clear that
the reciprocal conjunction of angels with the Lord is not from
the angels, but is as if it were from them. Such also is the conjunction of the Lord with the church, and of the church with
the Lord, which is called the celestial and spiritual marriage.

29. All conjunction in the spiritual world is effected by means of looking. When any one there is thinking about an-other from a desire to speak with him, the other immediately becomes present, and they see each other face to face. It is the same when any one is thinking about another from an affection of love; but this affection produces conjunction, while the other produces presence only. This is peculiar to the spiritual world, for the reason that all there are spiritual beings; in the natural world, in which all are material beings, it is otherwise. With men in the natural world the same takes place in the affections and thoughts of their spirit; but inasmuch as there are spaces in the natural world, while in the spiritual world the spaces are merely appearances, that which takes place in the thought of every one's spirit, in the spiritual world takes place actually. [2] This has been said to make known how the conjunction of the Lord with angels is effected, and how the apparent reciprocal conjunction of angels with the Lord is effected. For all angels turn their faces to the Lord, and the Lord's look is upon the forehead, because the forehead corresponds to love and its affections, while angels behold the Lord with the eyes, because the eyes correspond to wisdom and its perceptions. Nevertheless angels do not from themselves turn their faces to the Lord, but the Lord turns them to Himself; and He turns them by influx into their life's love, and through that love enters into the perceptions and thoughts; and thus He turns them about. [3] Such a circle of love to thoughts and from thoughts to love from love, is in all things of the human mind. This circle may be called the circle of life. About this something may be seen in the work on *The Divine Love and the Divine Wisdom*, as the following: Angels constantly turn their faces to the Lord as a sun (n. 129–134). All the interior things of the angels, both of mind and of body, are likewise turned to the Lord as a sun (n. 135–139). Every spirit, of whatever quality, turns himself likewise to his ruling love (n. 140–145). Love conjoins itself to wisdom, and causes wisdom to be reciprocally conjoined with it (n. 410–412).

Angels are in the Lord, and the Lord is in them; and because angels are recipients the Lord alone is heaven (n. 113–118).

30. The Lord's heaven in the natural world is called the church; and an angel of that heaven is a man of the church who is conjoined with the Lord, and who becomes an angel of the spiritual heaven after he leaves this world. From this it is clear that what has been said of the angelic heaven applies equally to the human heaven that is called the church. That reciprocal conjunction with the Lord which makes heaven in man is revealed by the Lord in these words:—

Abide in Me and I in you. He that abideth in Me and I in him, the same beareth much fruit; for apart from Me ye can do nothing (*John* xv. 4, 5, 7).

31. From all this it can be seen that the Lord is heaven not only in general in all there, but also in particular in each one there. For each angel is a heaven in the least form; and heaven in general consists of as many heavens as there are angels. This can be seen in the work on *Heaven and Hell* (n. 51–58). This being so, let no one cherish the mistaken idea that enters into the first thought of many, that the Lord dwells among the angels in heaven, or is with them like a king in his kingdom. In respect to their sight He is above them in the sun there; but in respect to the life of their love and wisdom He is in them.

32. (2) *From creation man has an ability to be more and more nearly conjoined with the Lord.* This can be seen from what has been set forth respecting degrees in the third part of the work on *The Divine Love and the Divine Wisdom*, and especially from the following: There are three discrete degrees or degrees of height in man from creation (n. 230–235). These three degrees are in every man from birth; and as they are opened, man is in the Lord and the Lord in man (n. 236–241). All perfections increase and ascend along with degrees, and according to them (n. 199–204). From all this it is clear that from creation man has an ability to be more and more nearly conjoined with the Lord through degrees. [2] But it is necessary to know fully what degrees are, and that there are two kinds, discrete degrees, that is, degrees of height; and continuous degrees, that is, degrees of breadth, also how they differ; and to know that every man by his creation and consequently by birth has three discrete degrees or degrees of height; also that man comes into the first degree, which is called the natural, when he is born, and may develop this degree in himself continuously until he becomes rational; also that he comes into the second degree, which is called the spiritual degree, if he lives according to the spiritual laws of order, which are Divine truths; and finally that he can come into the third degree, which is called the celestial, if he lives according to celestial laws of order, which are Divine goods. [**3**] These degrees the Lord opens in man according to his life, actually in this world, but not perceptibly and sensibly till after he leaves this world; and as they are opened and afterwards perfected man is more and more nearly conjoined with the Lord. This conjunction by continued approach may go on increasing to eternity, and with the angels it does increase to eternity. And yet no angel is able to attain to or to touch upon the first degree of the Lord's love and wisdom, because the Lord is infinite and an angel is finite, and there can be no relation between what is infinite and what is finite. As no one is able without a knowledge of these degrees to understand the state of man, and the state of his elevation and approach to the Lord, they have been treated of in detail in the work on *The Divine Love and the Divine Wisdom* (n. 173–281), which may be referred to.

33. It will now be told briefly how a man can be more nearly conjoined with the Lord, and then how the conjunction appears more and more near. *How man is more and more nearly conjoined with the Lord:*—This is effected not by knowledge alone, nor by intelligence alone, nor even by wisdom alone, but by a life conjoined with these. Man's life is his love, and love is manifold. In general, there is a love of evil and a love of good. The love of evil is a love of committing adultery, taking revenge, defrauding, blaspheming, de-

priving others of their goods. In thinking about these things
and in doing them the love of evil has a sense of pleasure and
delight. The derivatives of this love, which are its affections,
are as many as are the evils into which it has determined
itself; and the perceptions and thoughts of this love are as
many as are the falsities that favor these evils and confirm
them. These falsities make one with the evils, as the understanding makes one with the will; they are not separated from
each other, for one is of the other. [2] Since, then, the Lord
flows into the life's love of every one, and through its affections into the perceptions and thoughts, and not the reverse,
as has been said above, it follows that the Lord can conjoin
Himself more nearly only so far as the love of evil with its
affections, which are lusts, has been set aside. And as these
have their seat in the natural man, and as whatever a man
does from the natural man is felt as if done from himself, so
man ought as if from himself to put away the evils of that
love; and so far as this is done by man the Lord draws nearer
and conjoins Himself with him. Any one can see from reason
that lusts with their enjoyments block the way and close the
doors before the Lord, and that these can not be cast out by
the Lord so long as man himself holds the doors closed, and
by pressing and pushing from without prevents their being
opened. That man himself ought to open them is clear from
the Lord's words in the *Apocalypse:*—

Behold I stand at the door and knock; if any one hear My voice and
open the door, I will come in to him, and will sup with him and he with
Me (iii. 20).

[3] From this it is evident that so far as one shuns evils as
diabolical and as obstacles to the Lord's entrance, he is more
and more nearly conjoined with the Lord, and he the most
nearly who abominates them as so many dusky and fiery devils; since evil and the devil are one, and the falsity of evil
and Satan are one. For as the Lord's influx is into the love
of good and into its affections, and through these affections
into the perceptions and thoughts (and these are all truths by

derivation from the good in which the man is), so the influx of the devil, that is, of hell, is into the love of evil and into its affections, which are lusts, and through these into the perceptions and thoughts (and these are all falsities by derivation from the evil in which the man is). [4] *How that conjunction appears more and more near:*—The more fully evils in the natural man are put aside by shunning them and turning away from them, the more nearly is man conjoined with the Lord. And as love and wisdom, which are the Lord Himself, are not in space (since affection, which belongs to love, and thought, which belongs to wisdom, have nothing in common with space), so the Lord appears to be nearer in the measure of the conjunction by love and wisdom; and on the other hand, more remote in the measure of the rejection of love and wisdom. In the spiritual world there is no space, but there distance and presence are appearances in accordance with similarities and dissimilarities of affections; for the reason, as has been said before, that affections, which belong to love, and thoughts, which belong to wisdom, and which in themselves are spiritual, are not in space. On this subject see what has been set forth in the work on *The Divine Love and the Divine Wisdom* (n. 7–10, 69–72, and elsewhere). [5] The Lord's conjunction with a man in whom evils have been put away, is meant by these words of the Lord:—

The pure in heart shall see God (*Matt.* v. 8);

and by these:—

He that hath My commandments and doeth them, I will make My abode with him (*John* xiv. 21, 23).

"To have the commandments" is to know, and "to do them" is to love; for it is also there said: "He that doeth My commandments, he it is that loveth Me."

34. (3) *The more nearly a man is conjoined with the Lord the wiser he becomes.* As from creation and thus from birth there are three degrees of life in man (of which just above, n. 32), so there are preëminently three degrees of wisdom in him.

These are the degrees that are opened in man in the measure
of conjunction. They are opened in the measure of love, since
love is conjunction itself. Yet the ascent of love according to
degrees is perceived by man only in an obscure way while the
ascent of wisdom is clearly perceived in such as know and see
what wisdom is. The degrees of wisdom are perceived for the
reason that love enters through the affections into the perceptions and thoughts, and these present themselves to the internal sight of the mind, which corresponds to the external sight
of the body. It is owing to this that wisdom is manifest, but
not so much the affection of love that produces it. It is with
this as with all things that are actually done by man. It is
noticed how the body does them; but not how the soul does
them. So also it is seen how one meditates, perceives, and
thinks; but how the soul of these activities, which is an affection for good and truth, produces the meditation, perception,
and thought, is not seen. [2] There are three degrees of wisdom, the natural, the spiritual, and the celestial. While man
lives in the world he is in the natural degree of wisdom. This
degree may then be perfected in him to its highest point, but
it cannot enter the spiritual degree, because that degree is not
continued into the natural degree by continuity, but is conjoined with it by correspondences. After death man is in the
spiritual degree of wisdom; and this degree is also such that
it may be perfected to the highest point, but it cannot enter
the celestial degree of wisdom, for that degree is not continued into the spiritual by continuity, but it is conjoined with it
by correspondences. From all this it can be seen that wisdom
can be elevated in a triplicate ratio, and in each degree in a
simple ratio to its highest point. [3] One who comprehends
the elevation and perfecting of these degrees can in some
measure perceive the truth of what is said of angelic wisdom, .
that it is ineffable, and so ineffable that a thousand ideas in
the thought of angels from their wisdom can present but a
single idea in the thought of men from their wisdom, the other
nine hundred and ninety-nine ideas of angelic thought not

being able to gain entrance, because they are supernatural. That this is so it has often been granted me to know by living experience. But, as said above, no one can come into that ineffable wisdom of the angels except through conjunction with the Lord and in the measure of that conjunction, for the Lord alone opens the spiritual degree and the celestial degree, and opens them in those only who are wise from Him; and those are wise from the Lord who cast out the devil, that is, evil, from themselves.

35. But let no one believe that a man has wisdom because he knows many things, and perceives them in some light, and is able to talk about them intelligently, unless this is conjoined with love; for it is love through its affections that produces wisdom; and wisdom not conjoined with love is like a meteor vanishing in the air, and like a falling star. But when wisdom is conjoined with love it is like the abiding light of the sun, and like a fixed star. A man has a love of wisdom so far as he turns away from the diabolic crowd, which are the lusts of evil and falsity.

36. The wisdom that comes to perception is a perception of truth from an affection for it, especially a perception of spiritual truth. For there is civil truth, moral truth, and spiritual truth. Those who have a perception of spiritual truth from an affection for it have also a perception of moral and of civil truth; for of these perceptions the affection for spiritual truth is the soul. I have sometimes talked with angels about wisdom; and they said that wisdom is conjunction with the Lord, because the Lord is wisdom itself; and that he comes into that conjunction who casts out hell from himself, and comes into it to the extent that he casts out hell. They said that they represent wisdom to themselves as a palace, magnificent and highly adorned, the ascent to which is by twelve steps; and that only from the Lord through conjunction with Him can any one reach the first step; and he ascends in the measure of the conjunction; and as he ascends, he perceives that no one is wise from himself, but only from the Lord, and that the things in

which a man is wise, compared with the things in which he is
not wise, are as a few drops of water to a great lake. The
twelve steps to the palace of wisdom signify goods conjoined
with truths and truths conjoined with goods.

37. (4) *The more nearly a man is conjoined with the Lord
the happier he becomes.* About the degrees of happiness the
same may be said as has been said above (n. 32 and 34), about
the degrees of life and of wisdom in the measure of conjunction with the Lord. For happiness, that is, beatitudes and
pleasures, are exalted as the higher degrees of the mind, which
are called spiritual and celestial, are opened in man; and after
his life in the world these degrees are enlarged to eternity.

38. No one who is in the pleasures of the lusts of evil can
know anything about the pleasures of affections for good in
which the angelic heaven is; for these two kinds of pleasure
are directly opposite to each other in internals, and therefore
interiorly are opposite in externals; although they differ little
on the mere surface. For every love has its own pleasures,
even the love of evil in those who are in lusts, such as the
love of committing adultery, taking revenge, defrauding, stealing, doing cruel deeds, and in the most wicked even the love
of blaspheming the holy things of the church, and of chatter-
ing venomously against God. The love of ruling from love of
self is the fountain head of these pleasures. They are from
the lusts that beset the interiors of the mind; and from the
interiors they flow down into the body, and there excite the
unclean things that titillate the fibers; and thus bodily pleasure springs from the mind's pleasure in accord with the lusts.
[2] What kinds of unclean things there are that titillate the
bodily fibers of such persons it is granted to every one after
death to know in the spiritual world. They are in general cadaverous, excrementitious, stercoraceous, reeking, and urinous
things, for the hells of such abound in these unclean things.
That these are correspondences can be seen in the work on
The Divine Love and the Divine Wisdom (n. 422–424). But
after they have entered hell these filthy pleasures are turned

into direful things. All this has been said that it may be understood what the happiness of heaven is, and the nature of it, which will now be considered. For every thing is known from its opposite.

39. The joys, satisfactions, pleasures, and delights, in a word, the happinesses of heaven, cannot be described in words, although in heaven they are perceptible to the feeling; for what is perceptible to the feeling only cannot be described, because it does not fall into ideas of thought, and thus not into words; for it is the understanding alone that sees; and it sees the things that pertain to wisdom or truth, and not the things that pertain to love or good. For this reason these happinesses are inexpressible; nevertheless they are exalted in a like degree with wisdom. Their varieties are infinite, and each is ineffable. This I have heard and perceived. [2] And yet these happinesses enter as man puts away the lusts of love of evil and falsity as if of himself, although from the Lord; for these happinesses are the happinesses of the affections for good and truth, and are the opposites of the lusts of the love of evil and falsity. The happinesses of affections of the love of good and truth begin from the Lord, thus from the inmost; and they pour themselves forth therefrom into lower things even to the lowest, and thus fill the angel, making him to be as it were wholly a delight. Such happinesses in infinite variety are in every affection for good and truth, especially in an affection for wisdom.

40. The pleasures of the lusts for evil and the pleasures of affections for good cannot be compared; because the devil is inwardly in the pleasures of lusts for evil, and the Lord is inwardly in the pleasures of affections for good. If a comparison must be made, the pleasures of lusts for evil can only be compared to the lewd pleasures of frogs in ponds, or of snakes in putrid places; while the pleasures of affections for good may be compared to the delights of the mind in gardens and flower-beds. For the same things that affect frogs and snakes affect those in the hells who are in the lusts for evil; and the same things that affect the mind in gardens and flower-beds affect those in the heavens who are in affections for good; for, as has been said above, corresponding unclean things affect the evil, and corresponding clean things affect the good.

41. From all this it can be seen that the more nearly any one is conjoined with the Lord the happier he becomes. But this happiness is rarely manifest in the world; for man is then in a natural state, and the natural does not communicate with the spiritual by continuity but by correspondences; and this communication is felt only in a certain quiet and peace of mind, that especially follows combats against evils. But when man puts off the natural state and enters the spiritual state, which he does after his departure from the world, the happiness described above gradually manifests itself.

42. (5) *The more nearly a man is conjoined with the Lord the more distinctly does he seem to himself as if he were his own, and the more clearly does he recognize that he is the Lord's.* There is an appearance that the more nearly one is conjoined with the Lord the less he is his own. It so appears to all who are evil; and it so appears also to those who believe from their religion that they are not under the yoke of the law, and that no one can do good from himself. For all such are unable to see otherwise than that not to be one's own means not to be allowed to think and will evil, but only good; and as those who are conjoined with the Lord are neither willing nor able to think and will evil, all such conclude from the appearance to themselves, that this is not to be one's own. This, however, is the exact opposite of the truth.

43. There is infernal freedom and there is heavenly freedom. To think and will evil, and to speak and do it so far as civil and moral laws do not hinder, is from infernal freedom. But to think and will good, and to speak and do it so far as opportunity is granted, is from heavenly freedom. Whatever a man thinks, wills, speaks, and does from freedom seems to him to be his own; for every one's freedom is wholly from his love. For this reason, those who are in a love of evil have no

3

other perception than that infernal freedom is freedom itself; while those who are in a love of good perceive that heavenly freedom is freedom itself, and consequently its opposite is slavery both to the good and to the evil. Yet every one must confess that either the one or the other of these is freedom; for there cannot be two kinds of freedom, in themselves opposite and each freedom in itself. Furthermore, every one must confess that to be led by good is freedom, and to be led by evil is slavery; because to be led by good is to be led by the Lord, and to be led by evil is to be led by the devil. Since, then, everything that a man does from freedom appears to him to be his own, for it is of his love, and to act from one's love is to act from freedom, as has been said above, so it follows that it is conjunction with the Lord that makes a man seem to himself to be free and therefore his own; and the nearer the conjunction with the Lord is the more free he seems, and thus the more his own. He appears to himself *more distinctly* as if he were his own, because the Divine love is such that it wills its own to be another's, thus to be the man's or the angel's. Such is all spiritual love, and pre-eminently the Divine love. Moreover, the Lord in no case compels any one; for anything to which one is compelled does not appear to be his own; and what does not appear to be one's own cannot come to be of his love, and thus be appropriated to him as his. Therefore man is led by the Lord continually in freedom and is also reformed and regenerated in freedom. But of this more will be said in what follows; something may also be seen above (n. 4).

44. The more distinctly a man appears to himself to be as if he were his own the more clearly he recognizes that he is the Lord's, because the more nearly he is conjoined with the Lord the wiser he becomes (as has been shown above, n. 34–36); this truth wisdom teaches and recognizes; and the angels of the third heaven, because they are the wisest of the angels, also perceive it and call it freedom itself; but to be led by themselves they call slavery. And this, they say, is the reason: that the Lord does not flow immediately into what belongs to their perception and thought from wisdom, but into their affections of love for good, and through these into the former; that they have a perception of the influx in the affection from which they have wisdom; and that then all that they think from wisdom appears to be as if from themselves, and therefore as if it were their own; and that by this a reciprocal conjunction is established.

45. As the end of the Lord's Divine providence is a heaven from the human race, it follows that its end is the conjunction of the human race with Himself (see n. 28–31); also that its end is for man to be more and more nearly conjoined with Him (see n. 32, 33), for thus man possesses heaven more interiorly; also that its end is for man by that conjunction to become wiser (see n. 34–36); also to become happier (see n. 37–41), because it is from wisdom and according to it that man has heaven, and by means of it also has happiness; and finally, that its end is for man to appear to himself more distinctly to be his own, and yet to recognize more clearly that he is the Lord's (see n. 42–44). All these things are of the Lord's Divine providence; for they all are heaven, which it has for its end.

THE LORD'S DIVINE PROVIDENCE LOOKS IN EVERY THING THAT IT DOES TO WHAT IS INFINITE AND ETERNAL.

46. It is known in the Christian world that God is Infinite and Eternal; for in the doctrine of the Trinity that has its name from Athanasius it is said that God the Father is Infinite, Eternal, and Omnipotent; likewise God the Son, and God the Holy Spirit; and yet there are not three that are Infinite, Eternal, and Omnipotent, but One. From this it follows that as God is Infinite and Eternal, nothing but what is Infinite and Eternal can be predicated of God. But what the Infinite and Eternal is the finite cannot comprehend, and yet it can. The finite cannot comprehend it because it cannot contain the infinite; and it can comprehend it because there are abstract ideas by means of which the existence of things can be seen, if not the nature of them. Such ideas are possible respecting the Infinite; as that God because He is Infinite, that is, the Divine because it is Infinite, is Being (*esse*) itself, is Essence itself and Substance itself, is Love itself and Wisdom itself, or Good itself and Truth itself, and therefore is the Itself, yea, is Man Himself; and when the Infinite is said to be the All, that Infinite Wisdom is Omniscience, and that Infinite Power is Omnipotence. [2] And yet such ideas as these fall into obscurity of thought, and perhaps, from their incomprehensibility, into denial, unless those things that thought derives from nature are withdrawn from the idea, especially those that it derives from the two properties of nature, space and time; for these must needs limit ideas and cause abstract ideas to be as nothing. But if these can be withdrawn in man as they are in an angel, the Infinite may be comprehended by means of such ideas as are enumerated just above, and also from this that man is something because he was created by an Infinite God who is the All; also that man is a finite substance because he was created by an Infinite God who is Substance Itself; also, that man is wisdom, because he was created by an Infinite God who is Wisdom itself, and so on. For unless the Infinite God were the All, and were Substance itself and Wisdom itself, man would not be anything; consequently either a nonentity or merely an idea of being, according to those visionaries that are called idealists. [3] From what has been shown in the work on *The Divine Love and the Divine Wisdom*, it is clear that the Divine Essence is love and wisdom (n. 28–39); that the Divine love and the Divine wisdom are substance itself and form itself, and are the Very and the Only (n. 40–46); and that God created the universe and all things thereof from Himself and not from nothing (n. 282–284). From this it follows that every created thing, and especially man, and the love and wisdom in him, are something, and not merely an idea of being. For unless God were Infinite there could be no finite; and unless the Infinite were the All there could not be any thing; and unless God had created all things from Himself there would be nullity or nothing.   In a word, *we are because God is.*

47. As the Divine providence is here treated of, and it is here to be shown that in every thing it does it looks to the Infinite and Eternal, and as this cannot be clearly set forth except in some order, the order shall be as follows:—

(1) The Infinite in itself and the Eternal in itself is the same as the Divine.

(2) The Infinite and Eternal in itself must needs look to what is infinite [and eternal] from itself in things finite.

(3) The Divine providence, in every thing it does, looks to what is infinite and eternal from itself, especially in saving the human race.

(4) An image of the Infinite and Eternal is presented in an angelic heaven from a saved human race.

(5) Looking to what is Infinite and Eternal in the formation of the angelic heaven, that it may be before the Lord as one man, which is an image of Himself, is the inmost of the Divine providence.

48. (1) *The Infinite in itself and the Eternal in itself is the same as the Divine.* This can be seen from what has been shown in many places in the work on *The Divine Love and the Divine Wisdom.* That the Infinite in itself and the Eternal in itself is the Divine is in accord with the angelic idea, the angels understanding by the Infinite nothing else than the Divine being (*esse*), and by the Eternal the Divine manifestation (*existere*). Men also are able to see that the Infinite in itself and Eternal in itself is the Divine, and are not able to see it. Those can see it who think of the Infinite not from space, and of the Eternal not from time; but those who think of what is infinite and eternal from space and time can not see it. Therefore it can be seen by those who think in a higher, that is, in an interior way in the rational, but can not be seen by those who think in a lower, that is, in an exterior way.

[2] It can be seen by those who call to mind that an infinity of space is impossible, also an infinity of time, which is an eternity from which [things have been]; because infinity is without end, either first or last, that is, without limits; and who also consider that an Infinite from itself is impossible, because *from itself* supposes limit and beginning or a prior from which it is; therefore it is unmeaning to speak of the Infinite and Eternal from itself, for this would be like saying being (*esse*) from itself, which is a contradiction; for an Infinite from itself would be an Infinite from an Infinite, and *Esse* from itself would be *Esse* from an *Esse;* and this Infinite and *Esse* would either be the same with *The Infinite* or would be finite. From these and like reasons, which can be seen interiorly in the rational, it is evident that there is an Infinite in itself and an Eternal in itself; and that this Infinite and Eternal is the Divine from which are all things.

49. I know that many will say to themselves, How can one comprehend interiorly in his rational any thing apart from space and apart from time, and not only that this is, but also that it is the All and the Very, from which all things are? But consider interiorly whether love or any affection of it, or wisdom or any perception of it, or even thought, is in space and in time; and you will find that it is not. And since the Divine is love itself and wisdom itself, it follows that the Divine cannot be conceived of as in space and in time; so neither can the Infinite. For a clearer perception of this, carefully decide whether thought is in time and space. Suppose thought to go on for ten or twelve hours, may not this length of time seem to be no more than one or two hours, or may it not seem to be one or two days? The apparent duration is according to the state of affection from which the thought springs. If it is an affection of gladness in which there is no thought about time, ten or twelve hours of thought seem no more than one or two; but if it is an affection of sorrow in which time is attended to, the reverse will be true. All this makes clear that time is only an appearance in accordance with the state of affection from which the thought springs. The same is true of thought about distance in space, either when walking or when making a journey.

50. As angels and spirits are affections that belong to love, and thoughts from affection, they are consequently not in space and time, but only in the appearance of them. To them there is an appearance of space and time, in accordance with their states of affection and thoughts therefrom. When, therefore, an angel thinks from affection about another with a determinate wish to see him or speak with him, he is instantly present before him. [2] From this it is that with every man there are spirits present that are in like affection with himself, evil spirits with one who is an affection for a like evil, and good spirits with one who is an affection for like good; and they are as really present as if the man were included in their society. Space and time have nothing to do with that presence; because affection and the thought from it are not in space and time; and spirits and angels are affections and thoughts therefrom. [3] That this is so, it has been granted me to know from a living experience of several years, and from having talked with many after their death, with some in Europe and its various kingdoms, and with some in Asia and Africa and their various kingdoms; and they all were near me. If there were space and time with them, a journey and time to make it would have intervened. [4] In fact, this is known to every man from an intuition in himself or in his mind, which has been proved to me by this, that no one thought of any distance in space when told that I had spoken with some one who had died in Asia, Africa, or Europe; as, for example, with Calvin, Luther, Melancthon, or with some king, ruler, or priest in a distant land; nor did any thought even arise, How could he speak with those who lived so far away, or how could they come and be with him, when lands and seas intervened? This has made clear to me also that no one thinks from space and time when thinking of those who are in the spiritual world. Nevertheless, that there is an appearance of space and time there may be seen in the work on *Heaven and Hell* (n. 162–169, 191–199).

51. From all this it can now be seen that the Infinite and Eternal, thus the Lord, must be thought of apart from space and time, and that such thought is possible; also that those have such thought who think interiorly in the rational; and that then the Infinite and Eternal is the same as the Divine. Thus do angels and spirits think. From thought abstracted from time and space a comprehension of the Divine Omnipresence and the Divine Omnipotence, also of the Divine from eternity, is possible, but none at all from thought to which an idea from space and time clings. From all this it is clear that God from eternity can be thought about, but in no wise nature from eternity; consequently the creation of the universe by God can be thought about, but in no wise creation from nature; for space and time are properties of nature, but the Divine is apart from space and time. That the Divine is apart from space and time can be seen in the work on *The Divine Love and the Divine Wisdom* (n. 7–10, 69–72, 73–76, and elsewhere).

52. (2) *The Infinite and Eternal in itself must needs look to what is infinite and eternal from itself in things finite.* By the Infinite and Eternal in itself the Divine Itself is meant, as has been shown in the preceding article; by things finite all things created by the Divine, especially men, spirits, and angels, are meant, and to look to what is infinite and eternal from Itself is to look to the Divine, that is, Itself, in these, as a man looks at his image in a mirror. That this is so has been shown in many places in the work on *The Divine Love and the Divine Wisdom,* especially where it has been shown that in the created universe there is an image of man, and this is an image of what is infinite and eternal (n. 317, 318), thus an image of God the Creator, that is, the Lord from eternity. But let it be understood that the Divine in itself is in the Lord, while the Divine from itself is the Divine from the Lord in created things.

53. But that this may be more fully understood it shall be illustrated. The Divine can look only to the Divine; and it can look to this nowhere but in things created by Itself. That this is true is evident from this, that one can look to another only from what is his own in himself. He that loves another looks to him from his own love in himself; and he that is wise looks to another from his own wisdom in himself. He may see that the other loves him or does not love him, and is wise or not wise, but this he sees from the love and wisdom in himself; and therefore he conjoins himself with the other so far as the other loves him as he loves the other, or so far as the other is wise as he is wise; for thus they make one. [2] It is the same with the Divine in itself, for the Divine in itself is not able to look to itself from another, that is, from a man or a spirit or an angel; for there is nothing in them of the Divine in itself from which [all things are], and to look to the Divine from another in whom there is nothing of the Divine would be to look to the Divine from what is not Divine, which is not possible. For this reason the conjunction of the Lord with a man or a spirit or an angel is such that every thing that has relation to the Divine is not from them, but from the Lord. For it is known that all the good and all the truth that any one has is from the Lord and not from himself, and that no one can even mention the Lord, or His names, "Jesus," and "Christ," except from Him. [3] From this, then, it follows, that the Infinite and Eternal, which is the same as the Divine, looks to all things in the finite infinitely, and conjoins Itself with them in accordance with the degree of reception of wisdom and love in them. In a word, the Lord can have an abode in man or angel and dwell with them, only in His own, and not in what is their own *(proprium)*, for that is evil; and if it were good it would still be finite, which in itself and from itself cannot contain the Infinite. All this makes clear that it is impossible for a finite being to look to the Infinite; but it is possible for the Infinite to look to what is infinite from Himself, in finite beings.

54. There is an appearance that the Infinite cannot be conjoined with the finite, because there is no possible ratio between them, and because the finite cannot contain what is infinite; nevertheless, such a conjunction is possible, both because the Infinite created all things from Himself (as is shown in the work on *The Divine Love and the Divine Wisdom*, n. 282–284), and because the Infinite in things finite can look only to what is infinite from Himself, and with finite beings this infinite from Himself can appear as if it were in them, whereby a ratio between the finite and the infinite is provided, not from the finite, but from the infinite in the finite; and by this also the finite being becomes capable of containing what is infinite, not the finite being in himself, but as if in himself from what is infinite from itself in him. But of this more in what now follows.

55. (3) *The Divine providence, in all that it does, looks to what is infinite and eternal from itself, especially in saving the human race.* The Infinite and Eternal in itself is the Divine itself, or the Lord in Himself, while the Infinite and Eternal from itself is the Divine going forth, that is, the Lord in others created from Himself, thus in men and in angels; and this Divine is the same as the Divine providence. For by means of the Divine from Himself the Lord provides that all things may be held together in the order in which and into which they were created. And as this is the work of the Divine that goes forth, it follows that all this is the Divine providence.

56. That the Divine providence in every thing that it does looks to what is infinite and eternal from itself, can be seen from this, that every created thing goes forth from a First, which is the Infinite and Eternal, to things last, and from things last to the First from which *(a quo)*, as has been shown in the work on *The Divine Love and the Divine Wisdom*, where the creation of the universe is treated of. And as the First from which *(a quo)* is inmostly in all progression, it follows that the Divine that goes forth, that is, the Divine providence, in all that it does, looks to some image of the Infinite and Eternal. This it looks to in all things, but in some things obviously to perception, in others not. It presents that image obviously to perception in the variety of all things, and in the fructification and multiplication of all things. [2] *An image of the Infinite and Eternal in the variety of all things,* is apparent in this, that there is no one thing that is the same as another, nor can there be to eternity. In the faces of men this is evident to the eye from the beginning of their creation; consequently it is evident from their minds, of which their faces are types; also from their affections, perceptions, and thoughts, for these constitute the mind. For this reason in the entire heaven there are no two angels or no two spirits that are the same; nor can there be to eternity. The same is true of every visible object in the two worlds, the natural and the spiritual. From all this it can be seen that variety is infinite and eternal. [3] *An image of the Infinite and Eternal in the fructification and multiplication of all things,* is evident in the vegetable kingdom from the ability implanted in seeds, and in the animal kingdom from prolification, especially the propagation of fishes, which, if fructified and multiplied to the extent of their ability, would within a century fill the entire space of the world and even of the universe. From this it is clear that in that ability an endeavor to an infinite self-propagation lies hidden. And as fructifications and multiplications have not failed from the beginning of creation, nor will ever fail to eternity, it follows that in that ability there is also an endeavor to an eternal self-propagation.

57. The same is true of men in regard to their affections which belong to their love, and their perceptions which belong to their wisdom. The variety of both of these is infinite and eternal; so, too, their fructification and their multiplication, which are spiritual. No man enjoys affection or perception so like another's as to be the same; nor can such ever be. Moreover, affections may be fructified and perceptions multiplied without end. That knowledge is inexhaustible is known. This ability to fructify and multiply without end, that is, infinitely and eternally, men have in natural things, the spiritual angels in spiritual things, and the celestial angels in celestial things. Not only are affections, perceptions, and knowledges such in general; but also every single thing in them, even the least, in particular. They are such because they have their existence from the Infinite and Eternal in itself by means of what is infinite and eternal from itself. But inasmuch as the finite has in itself nothing of the Divine, there is in man or angel no such thing as his own, not even the least, for a man or an angel is finite, and purely a receptacle, in itself dead; and whatever is living in him is from the Divine going forth conjoined with him by contiguity, and appearing to him as if it were his. That this is so will be seen in what follows.

58. The Divine providence looks to what is infinite and eternal from itself especially in saving the human race, because the Divine providence has as its end a heaven from the human race (as has been shown above, n. 27–45); and because this is its end it follows that the reformation and the regeneration of man, thus his salvation, is what the Divine providence especially looks to, for from those that have been saved or regenerated heaven exists. Since to regenerate man is to unite good and truth in him, or love and wisdom, as they are united in the Divine that goes forth from the Lord, it is to this that the Divine providence especially looks in saving the human race. The image of the Infinite and Eternal is in man exclusively in the marriage of good and truth. That this is accomplished in mankind by the Divine that goes forth is known from the fact that there have been those who when filled with the Divine that goes forth, which is called the Holy Spirit, have prophesied, of whom in the Word; and there are those who, when enlightened, behold Divine truths in the light of heaven; this can be especially seen in angels, who sensibly perceive the presence, the influx, and the conjunction; but angels also recognize that this conjunction is nothing more than what may be called an adjunction.

59. It has not heretofore been known that the Divine providence in its whole progress with man looks to his eternal state.

It can look to nothing else because the Divine is Infinite and Eternal, and the Infinite and Eternal, that is, the Divine, is not in time, and therefore all future things are present to it; and the Divine being such, it follows that there is what is eternal in each and every thing that it does. But those who think from time and space scarcely perceive this, not only because they love temporal things, but also because they think from what is present in the world and not from what is present in heaven, for that is to them as far away as the end of the earth. But when those who are in the Divine think from what is present, they think also from what is eternal because they think from the Lord, saying within themselves, What is that which is not eternal? Is not the temporal relatively nothing, and does it not become nothing when it is ended? It is not so with what is eternal; that alone Is; for its being (*esse*) has no end. To think thus when thinking from what is present is to think at the same time from what is eternal; and when a man so thinks, and at the same time so lives, the Divine going forth in him, that is, the Divine providence, looks in its entire progress to the state of his eternal life in heaven, and leads towards it. That in every man, both in the evil and in the good, the Divine looks to what is eternal, will be seen in what follows.

60. (4) *An image of the Infinite and Eternal is presented in the angelic heaven.* Among the things we need to know about is the angelic heaven; for every one who has any religion thinks about it, and wishes to go there. But heaven is granted only to those who know the way to it and walk in that way. And that way can to some extent be known by knowing the character of those who constitute heaven, also by knowing that no one becomes an angel, that is, comes into heaven, unless he carries with him from the world what is angelic; and in what is angelic there is present a knowledge of the way from walking in it, and a walking in the way through a knowledge of it. Moreover, in the spiritual world, there are actually ways that lead to every society of heaven and to every society of hell;

and there each one as if from himself sees his own way. He
sees it because there is a way there for every love; and the love
opens the way and leads one to his fellows. Other ways than
the way of his love no one sees. From this it is clear that angels are nothing but heavenly loves, for otherwise they would
not have seen the ways leading to heaven. But this can be
more fully seen when heaven is described.

61. Every man's spirit is affection and thought therefrom;
and as every affection is from the love and every thought is
from the understanding, every spirit is his own love, and his
own understanding therefrom. For this reason, when a man is
thinking solely from his own spirit, which he does when medi-
tating at home by himself, he thinks from the affection which
belongs to his love. From this it is clear that when a man becomes a spirit, as he does after death, he is an affection of his
own love, and is no other thought than what belongs to his
affection. He is an evil affection, which is a lust, if his love
has been a love of evil; and he is a good affection if his love
has been a love of good; and every one has a good affection so
far as he has shunned evils as sins; and every one has an evil
affection so far as he has not so shunned them. And inasmuch
as all spirits and angels are affections, the entire angelic heav-
en is evidently nothing but the love of all affections of good,
and the consequent wisdom of all perceptions of truth. And
as every good and truth is from the Lord, and the Lord is love
itself and wisdom itself, it follows that the angelic heaven is
His image. And as the Divine love and the Divine wisdom in
their form are Man, it also follows that the angelic heaven cannot be otherwise than in such a form. But of this more will
be said in the following chapter.

62. The angelic heaven is an image of the Infinite and Eternal because it is an image of the Lord, and the Lord is the Infinite and Eternal. An image of His Infinite and Eternal is
manifest in this, that heaven is made up of myriads of myriads
of angels; and that it is made up of as many societies as there
are general affections of heavenly love; and that each angel in

eack society is distinctly his own affection; and that the form
of heaven, which before the Lord is as one, just as a man is
one, is from so great a number of affections in general and in
particular; and that this form is perfected to eternity according to the increase of numbers, for the greater the number of
those that enter into the form of the Divine love, which is the
form of forms, the more perfect the unity becomes. From all
this it is very clear that an image of the Infinite and Eternal
is presented in the angelic heaven.

63. From the idea of heaven given by this brief description
it is evident that it is an affection from the love of good that
makes heaven in man. But who at the present day knows
this? Who knows even what the affection from the love of
good is, or that affections from the love of good are innumerable, in fact, infinite? For, as has been said, every angel is
distinctly his own affection; and the form of heaven is the
form of all the affections of the Divine love there. To unite
all affections into this form is possible only to Him who is love
itself and also wisdom itself, and who is at once Infinite and
Eternal, for what is infinite and eternal is in every thing of
the form, the infinite in the conjunction and the eternal in the
perpetuity; and if what is infinite and eternal were withdrawn
from it it would dissolve away in an instant. Who else can
combine affections into a form? Who else can even unite a
single part of it? For a single part can be united only from a
universal idea of all, and the universal of all only from a particular idea of each part. That form is composed of myriads
of myriads; and myriads enter it each year, and will continue
to enter into it to eternity. All children enter into it; and as
many adults as are affections from a good of love. From all
this again an image of the Infinite and Eternal can be seen in
the angelic heaven.

64. (5) *Looking to what is infinite and eternal in the formation of the angelic heaven, that it may be before the Lord as one
man, which is an image of Himself, is the inmost of the Divine
providence.* That the entire heaven is as one man before the

Lord and likewise each society of heaven, and that it is from this that each angel is a man in complete form, and this because God the Creator, who is the Lord from eternity, is Man, may be seen in the work on *Heaven and Hell* (n. 59–86); also, that in consequence there is a correspondence of all things of heaven with all things of man (n. 87–102). That the entire heaven is as one man has not been seen by me; since the entire heaven can be seen by no one except the Lord; but that an entire society of heaven, greater or smaller, appears as one man, has several times been seen by me; and it was then said that the greatest society, which is heaven in its entire aggregate, so appears, but only before the Lord; and that this is the reason why every angel is in complete form a man.

65. As in the Lord's sight the entire heaven is as one man, so heaven is divided into as many general societies as there are organs, viscera, and members in a man; and each general society is divided into as many less general or particular societies as there are larger divisions in each of the viscera and organs. From this it is evident what heaven is. And since the Lord is the very Man, and heaven is His image, to be in heaven is called being in the Lord. That the Lord is the very Man can be seen in the work on *The Divine Love and the Divine Wisdom* (n. 11–13, 285–589).

66. From all this the arcanum, which may be called angelic, can in some measure be seen, namely, that every affection for good and at the same time for truth is in its form a man; for whatever goes forth from the Lord, by its derivation from His Divine love is an affection for good, and by its derivation from His Divine wisdom is an affection for truth. The affection for truth that goes forth from the Lord appears in angel and in man as a perception and consequent thought of truth, for the reason that attention is given to the perception and thought, and little to the affection from which these spring, although they go forth from the Lord as one with affection for truth.

67. Since, then, man by creation is a heaven in the least form, and consequently an image of the Lord, and since heaven consists of as many affections as there are angels, and each affection in its form is a man, it follows that it is the continual aim of the Divine providence that man may become a heaven in form and consequently an image of the Lord, and since this is effected by means of the affection for good and truth, that he may become such an affection. This, therefore, is the continual aim of the Divine providence. But its inmost is that man may be in this or that place in heaven, or in this or that place in the Divine heavenly man; for thus is he in the Lord. This is accomplished, however, only with those whom the Lord can lead to heaven. And as the Lord foresees this, He also provides continually that man may become such; for thereby every one who permits himself to be led to heaven is prepared for his own place in heaven.

68. It has been said above that heaven is divided into as many societies as there are organs, viscera, and members in Man, and in these no part can be in any place but its own. Consequently as angels are such parts of the Divine heavenly Man, and none become angels except such as have become men in the world, it follows that the man who permits himself to be led to heaven is continually prepared by the Lord for his own place; and this is done by means of such an affection for good and truth as corresponds with it. Moreover, every angel-man when he leaves this world is assigned to his place. This is the inmost of the Divine providence respecting heaven.

69. On the other hand, the man who does not permit himself to be led and assigned to heaven is prepared for his own place in hell. For of himself man tends continually to the lowest part of hell, but he is continually withdrawn by the Lord; and he who cannot be withdrawn is prepared for a certain place there, to which also he is assigned immediately after he leaves this world; and this place there is opposite to a certain place in heaven; for hell is the opposite of heaven. Therefore as the angel-man, according to his affection for good and truth, is allotted his own place in heaven, so the devil-man, according

4

to his affection for evil and falsity, is allotted his own place in hell. For these two opposites, arranged in like position over against each other, are held in connection. This is the inmost of the Divine providence respecting hell.

THERE ARE LAWS OF THE DIVINE PROVIDENCE THAT ARE
UNKNOWN TO MEN.

70. That there is a Divine providence is known, but what it is is not known. This is not known because the laws of the Divine providence are arcana heretofore concealed in the wisdom of angels, but now to be revealed, that what belongs to the Lord may be ascribed to Him, and what does not belong to man may not be ascribed to any man. For many in the world attribute all things to themselves and their own prudence; and what they can not attribute to that they call accidental or casual, not knowing that human prudence is nothing, and that accidental and casual are idle words. [2] It is said that the laws of the Divine providence are arcana heretofore hidden in the wisdom of angels. This is because in the Christian world the understanding, for religion's sake, has been closed in respect to Divine things, and consequently it has become in such things so obtuse and resistant that man has not been able because he has not been willing, or has not been willing because he has not been able, to understand anything more about the Divine providence than simply that it exists, and to reason whether it exists or not, and also whether it is only universal or also particular. When for religion's sake the understanding is closed in respect to Divine things it can go no further than this. [3] But since there has been in the church an acknowledgment that man is unable from himself to do good that is in itself good, and unable from himself to think truth that is in itself truth, and since these are one with the Divine providence (because believing the one depends upon believing the other) it is necessary, lest the one be affirmed and the other denied and thus both perish, that what the Divine providence is be explicitly revealed. But this cannot be revealed unless the laws by which the Lord cares for and rules the things of man's will and understanding are disclosed. For the laws of Divine providence are what make known its nature; and only he who knows its nature can acknowledge it, for then he sees it. For this reason the laws of Divine providence, heretofore hidden in the wisdom of angels, are now revealed.

IT IS A LAW OF THE DIVINE PROVIDENCE THAT MAN SHOULD ACT FROM FREEDOM IN ACCORDANCE WITH REASON.

71. Everyone knows that man has the freedom to think and will just as he pleases, but not the freedom to say whatever he thinks, or to do whatever he wills; therefore the freedom that is here meant is spiritual freedom, and not natural freedom, except when the two make one. For thinking and willing are spiritual, but speaking and doing are natural. Moreover, these are clearly distinguished in man; for a man is able to think what he does not speak, and to will what he does not do; which makes clear that the spiritual and the natural in man are discriminated; consequently man can pass from one to the other only through a boundary, such a boundary as may be likened to a door that must be unfastened and opened. This door stands open as it were in those who think and will from reason in accordance with the civil laws of the government and the moral laws of society; for such say what they think and do as they will; but the door stands shut as it were in those who think and will in opposition to those laws. Whoever attends to his volitions and consequent actions will notice that such a boundary intervenes, and sometimes frequently in a single conversation or a single action. This has been premised to make clear that to act from freedom in accordance with reason means to think and will freely and thus to speak and do freely what is in accordance with reason.

72. But as few are aware that this can be a law of Divine providence, for the reason chiefly that this gives a man freedom also to think evil and falsity (although the Divine providence is continually leading him to think and will what is good and true), that this may be clearly seen the subject must be considered step by step, which shall be done in the following order:—

(1) Man possesses reason and freedom, or rationality and liberty; and these two faculties are in man from the Lord.

(2) Whatever a man does from freedom, whether it be of reason or not, provided it is in accordance with his reason, appears to him to be his.

(3) Whatever a man does from freedom in accordance with his thought is appropriated to him as his, and remains.

(4) It is by means of these two faculties that man is reformed and regenerated by the Lord; and without them he cannot be reformed or regenerated.

(5) By means of these two faculties man can be so far reformed and regenerated as he can be led by means of them to acknowledge that every thing good and true that he thinks and does is from the Lord, and not from himself.

(6) By means of these two faculties the conjunction of the Lord with man and the reciprocal conjunction of man with the Lord are effected.

(7) The Lord preserves these two faculties in man inviolate and as sacred in the whole course of His Divine providence.

(8) Therefore it is [a law] of the Divine providence that man should act from freedom in accordance with reason.

73. (1) *Man possesses reason and freedom, or rationality and liberty, and these two faculties are in man from the Lord.* That man has the faculty of understanding which is rationality and the faculty of thinking, willing, speaking, and doing what he understands, which is liberty, and that these two faculties are in man from the Lord, has been treated of in the work on *The Divine Love and the Divine Wisdom* (n. 264–270, 425; also above, n. 43, 44). But as many doubts may arise respecting either of these when they are made a subject of thought, at the outset I will merely advance something respecting the freedom to act in accordance with reason that is in man. [2] First, however, it must be known that all freedom is a property of love, insomuch that love and freedom are one. And as love is the life of man, freedom also belongs to his life. For every enjoyment that man has is from his love; no enjoyment is possible from any other source; and acting from love's enjoyment is acting from freedom; for a man is led by enjoyment as a thing is borne along by the current of a river. Since, then, there are numerous loves, some harmonious and some discordant, it follows that there are likewise numerous kinds of freedom; but in general three, natural, rational, and spiritual. [3] *Natural freedom* every one has by inheritance. From it man loves nothing but self and the world; his first life is nothing else. And as from these two loves all evils spring, and thus it comes that evils belong to the love, it follows that thinking and willing evils is man's natural freedom; and when he has confirmed evils in himself by reasonings he does evils from freedom in accordance with his reason. Thus his doing evils is from his faculty that is called liberty; and his confirming them is from his faculty that is called rationality. [4] A man's desire, for example, to commit adultery, to defraud, to blaspheme, to take revenge, is from the love into which he is born; and when he confirms these evils in himself, and thereby makes them allowable, then, from the enjoyment of the love of them, he as it were freely in accordance with reason thinks and wills them, and, so far as civil laws do not prevent, speaks and acts accordingly. It is from the Lord's Divine providence that man is permitted to do this, because he has freedom or liberty. Man is in this kind of freedom by nature, because of inheritance; and all those are in it who by means of reasonings have confirmed it in themselves from the enjoyment of love of self and the world. [5] *Rational free-*

dom is from the love of reputation with a view to honor or gain. The enjoyment of this love lies in appearing externally as a moral man; and because man loves such a reputation, he does not defraud, commit adultery, take revenge, or blaspheme; and because he makes this a matter of reason, he acts from freedom in accordance with his reason in sincere, just, chaste, and friendly ways; and furthermore, from this reason he can advocate such conduct. But if his rational is merely natural and not also spiritual, such freedom is merely external freedom, not internal freedom; for he does not love these goods in the least inwardly, but only outwardly for the sake of his reputation, as has been said, and for this reason the good deeds that he does are not in themselves good. He may even assert that these things ought to be done for the public welfare; but this he says not from any love for the public welfare, but from a love for his own honor or gain. His freedom, therefore, derives nothing from a love for the public welfare, neither does his reason, since this assents to his love. Consequently, this rational freedom is a more internal natural freedom. This freedom, too, by the Lord's Divine providence remains with every one. [6] *Spiritual freedom* is from a love for eternal life. Into that love and its enjoyment no one comes except he that thinks evils to be sins and in consequence does not will them, and at the same time looks to the Lord. As soon as one does this he is in that freedom. For one's ability not to will evils because they are sins, and not to do them for that reason, comes from the more internal or higher freedom which is from his more internal or higher love. At first such a freedom does not seem to be freedom, and yet it is; and afterwards it so appears, and then man acts from freedom itself, in accordance with reason itself, in thinking, willing, speaking, and doing what is good and true. This freedom increases as natural freedom decreases and becomes subservient; and it conjoins itself with rational freedom and purifies it. [7] Any one may come into this freedom if he is but willing to think that life is eternal, and that the temporary enjoyment and bliss of life in time are but as a fleeting shadow, compared with the never ending enjoyment and bliss of a life in eternity; and this a man can think if he wishes, because he has rationality and liberty, and because the Lord, from whom these two faculties are derived, continually gives the ability.

74. (2) *Whatever a man does from freedom, whether it be of reason or not, provided it is in accordance with his reason, appears to him to be his.* What rationality and liberty, which are peculiar to man, are, can be most clearly understood by a comparison of man with beasts. For beasts have no rationality or ability to understand, and no liberty or ability to will freely; consequently they have no understanding or will, but in place of understanding they have knowledge, and in place of will they have affection, both of which are natural. And as they do not possess these two faculties, they have no thought, but in place of thought they have an internal sight which makes one by correspondence with their external sight. [2] Every affection has its mate which is like a spouse; affection from natural love has knowledge, affection from spiritual love understanding, and affection from celestial love wisdom. For an affection without its mate as a spouse is not any thing; it is as being (*esse*) without coming forth (*existere*), or as substance without form, of which nothing can be predicated. Therefore, in every thing created there is something that is referable to the marriage of good and truth, as has been shown above in many places. In beasts there is a marriage of affection and knowledge, the affection in them pertaining to natural good, and knowledge to natural truth. [3] Since, then, affection and knowledge in beasts act completely as one, and their affection cannot be raised above their knowledge nor their knowledge above their affection, but whenever raised are both raised together, and since they have no spiritual mind, into which, or into the light and heat of which, they can be raised, therefore they have no capacity to understand, that is, rationality, and no capacity to will freely, that is, liberty; they have merely natural affection with its knowledge. The natural affection that they possess is an affection for providing themselves food, shelter, and offspring, and for escaping or avoiding injury, with all requisite knowledge of these things. Such being the state of their life, they have no ability to think, This I wish or do not wish; this I know or do not know; or still less, this I understand, and this I love; but from their affection by means of their knowledge they are borne along without rationality or liberty. They are so borne along, not from the natural world, but from the spiritual. For there is nothing in the natural world unconnected with the spiritual world. From that world is every cause that produces an effect. Something on this subject may be seen below (n. 96).

75. With man it is otherwise. He has not only affection from natural love, but also affection from spiritual love, and affection from celestial love. For the human mind is of three degrees, as shown in Part Third of the work on *The Divine Love and the Divine Wisdom.* Consequently a man can be raised up from natural knowledge into spiritual intelligence and from that into celestial wisdom; and from these two, intelligence and wisdom, he can look to the Lord, and thus be conjoined with Him, whereby he lives forever. But this exaltation in respect to affection would not be possible unless man had from rationality an ability to raise the understanding, and from liberty an ability to will this. [2] By means of these two faculties man has the ability to reflect within himself upon those things that he perceives outside of himself by means of the bodily senses. He also has the ability to think above about what he is thinking below. For one can say: This I have thought and this I now think; also: This I have willed and this I now will; or again: This I understand to be true, this I love because it is such; and so on. From this it is clear that man thinks also above thought, seeing it as if beneath him. This ability man has from rationality and from liberty, from rationality this capacity for higher thought, from liberty the capacity to will, from affection to so think. For without the liberty so to think he would not have the will, and conse-

quently not the thought. [3] For this reason those that have
no wish to understand any thing except what pertains to the
world and its nature, and no wish to understand what moral
and spiritual good and truth are, cannot be raised from knowledge into intelligence, still less into wisdom; for they have
closed up these capacities, and therefore make themselves to
be men no further than having an ability to understand, if
they will, and an ability to so will, from the rationality and
liberty implanted in them. From these two faculties man is
able to think, and to speak from thought; in all other things
men are not men but beasts; and some, from the abuse of these
faculties are worse than beasts.

76. From an unobscured rationality any one can see or
comprehend that it is only from an appearance that it is his
that man can be in any affection for knowing, or in any affection for understanding. For every enjoyment and pleasure,
and therefore every thing of the will, is from affection, which
belongs to love. Who can wish to know any thing or to understand any thing, unless he has some pleasure from affection?
And who can possess this pleasure of affection unless that
which moves the affection appears to be his? If nothing were
his, but everything another's, in other words, if any one from
his own affections should pour something into the mind of
another who had no affection for knowing and understanding
as if from himself, would the other receive it, or even possess
the ability to receive it? Would he not be like what is called
a dullard and a stock? [2] From this it is clearly evident
that although every thing that man perceives, and thinks and
knows therefrom, and wills and does in accordance with the
perception, flows into him, nevertheless it is made by the
Lord's Divine providence to appear to be man's; for otherwise,
as has been said, the man could receive nothing, and therefore
he could be endowed with no understanding or wisdom. It is
acknowledged that every thing good and true is the Lord's
and not man's, and yet that it appears to man to be his; and
because every thing good and true so appears, all things of the

church and of heaven, consequently all things of love and wisdom, and of charity and faith, so appear, and yet nothing of
these is man's. Unless it appeared to man that he perceived
these things as if from himself, he could not receive them
from the Lord. From all this the truth of the matter can be
seen, namely, that whatever one does from freedom, whether
it be of reason or not, provided it is in accordance with his
reason, appears to him to be his.

77. With his faculty called rationality who is not able to
understand that this or that good is useful to society, and that
this or that evil is harmful to it; for example, that justice,
sincerity, and the chastity of marriage, are useful to society,
and that injustice, insincerity, and adulterous relations with
the wives of others, are harmful to it; consequently, that these
evils in themselves are injuries, and that the goods in themselves are benefits? Who therefore is not able, if he will, to
make these distinctions matters of reason? He has rationality, and he has liberty; and so far as he, for these reasons,
shuns these evils in himself, are his rationality and liberty uncovered and made manifest, and so far do they regulate, and
give perception and ability; and so far as this is done man
looks to these goods as a friend looks to his friends. [2] From
all this man is able afterwards from his faculty which is called
rationality to draw conclusions about such goods as are useful
to society in the spiritual world, and about the evils that are
harmful there, if in place of evils he understands sins, and in
place of goods works of charity. This a man is able, if he will,
to make a matter of his reason also, since he has rationality
and liberty. And so far as he shuns these evils as sins, are
his rationality and liberty uncovered and made manifest, and
so far they regulate and give perception and ability; and so far
as this is done, he looks to the goods of charity as neighbor
looks to neighbor, from mutual love. [3] Since, then, it is the
Lord's will, for the sake of reception and conjunction, that
whatever a man does freely in accordance with reason should
appear to him to be his, and this is in accordance with reason

itself, it follows that man is able from his reason to will this on the ground that it constitutes his eternal happiness; and by the Lord's Divine power, when it is invoked, he is able to do it.

78. (3) *Whatever a man does from freedom in accordance with his thought is appropriated to him as his, and remains.* This is because man's own (*proprium*) and his freedom make one. Man's own belongs to his life; and what a man does from his life he does from freedom. Again, man's own belongs to his love, for every one's life is his love; and what a man does from his life's love he does from freedom. From his freedom man acts in accordance with his thought, for the reason that whatever belongs to one's life or love becomes a subject of thought and is confirmed by his thought; and when it has been confirmed he does it from freedom in accordance with his thought. [2] For whatever a man does, he does from the will by means of the understanding; and freedom belongs to the will, and thought to the understanding. Moreover, from freedom man is able to act contrary to reason, also to act in accordance with reason and not from freedom; but what is so done is not appropriated to the man; it belongs merely to his lips and body, not to his spirit and heart. But whatever is from his spirit and heart, when it comes to be also of the lips and body, is appropriated to him. That this is so could be shown by many illustrations; but this is not the place for them. [3] To be appropriated to man means to enter into his life, and to become a part of his life, consequently to become his own. Yet there is nothing, as will be shown in what follows, that is man's own, it merely seems to him as if it were. Here it needs only to be said that every good that a man does from freedom in accordance with reason is appropriated to him as his, because in the thinking, the willing, the speaking, and the doing, it appears to him to be his; nevertheless, the good is not man's but the Lord's in man (as may be seen above, n. 76). How evil is appropriated to man will be seen in the proper place.

79. It is said that whatever one does from freedom in accordance with his thought remains, since nothing that a man has appropriated to himself can be eradicated; for it has come to be of his love and at the same time of his reason, or of his will and at the same time of his understanding, and consequently of his life. It can be removed, but it cannot be eliminated; and when removed it is as it were transferred from the center to the circumference, and there it stays. This is what is meant by its remaining. [2] For instance, if a man in his boyhood and youth has appropriated to himself a certain evil by doing it from the enjoyment of his love, like fraud or blasphemy or revenge or whoredom, as these things have been done from freedom in accordance with his thought, he has appropriated them to himself; but if he afterwards repents of them, shuns them, and looks upon them as sins that must be hated, and thus refrains from them from freedom in accordance with reason, then the good things to which those evils are opposed are appropriated to him. These goods then constitute the center and remove the evils toward the circumferences further and further, to the extent that he loathes and turns away from them. Nevertheless, they cannot be so cast out as to be said to be extirpated, although by such removal they may appear to be extirpated, which is effected by man's being withheld from evils and held in goods by the Lord. This is true both of all man's inherited evil and of all his actual evil. [3] Moreover, I have seen this proved by experience with some in heaven who thought themselves to be free from evils because they were held in good by the Lord. But lest these should believe the good in which they were to be their own, they were let down from heaven and again let into their evils, until they acknowledged that from themselves they were in evils, but from the Lord were in goods. After this acknowledgment they were led back into heaven. [4] Let it be understood, therefore, that these goods are appropriated to man only in the sense that they are always the Lord's in man; and that so far as man acknowledges this the Lord grants that the good may appear to man to be his, that is, that it may appear to man that he loves the neighbor or has charity as if from himself, that he believes or has faith as if from himself, that he does good and understands truths and thus is wise as if from himself. From all this any one who is enlightened can see the nature and strength of the appearance in which the Lord wills man to be; and this the Lord wills for the sake of man's salvation; for without this appearance no one could be saved. On this subject see what has been shown above (n. 42–45).

80. Nothing that a man merely thinks, nor even that which he thinks to will, is appropriated to him, unless at the same time he so far wills it as to do it if opportunity offers. This is because when man so does anything he does it from the will through the understanding, or from the affection of the will through the thought of the understanding; but so long as it is a matter of thought alone it cannot be appropriated, because the understanding does not then conjoin itself with the will, or the thought of the understanding with the affection of the will, but the will with its affection conjoins itself with the understanding and its thought, as has been shown in many places in Part Fifth of the work on *The Divine Love and the Divine Wisdom*. This is meant by the words of the Lord:—

Not that which entereth into the mouth maketh the man unclean; but that which goeth out of the heart through the mouth, this maketh the man unclean (*Matt.* xv. 11; also 17, 18, 19).

In the spiritual sense "the mouth" means thought, because thought speaks by means of the mouth; while "the heart" means in that sense, affection which belongs to the love. When a man thinks and speaks from that affection he makes himself unclean. Again in *Luke* (vi. 45) "the heart" signifies affection which pertains to the love or will, and "the mouth" signifies thought which pertains to the understanding.

81. Again, such evils as a man believes to be allowable, even though he does not do them, are appropriated to him; since whatever is made allowable in the thought comes from the will, for there is then consent. When, therefore, a man believes any evil to be allowable, he releases it from internal restraint; and is withheld from doing it only by external restraints, which are fears. And because his spirit then favors that evil, whenever external restraints are removed he does it as allowable and in the mean time continually does it in his spirit. But respecting this, see the *Doctrine of Life for the New Jerusalem* (n. 108–113).

82. (4) *It is by means of these two faculties that man is reformed and regenerated by the Lord ; and without them he cannot be reformed and regenerated.* The Lord teaches that

Except a man be born again he cannot see the kingdom of God (*John* iii. 3, 5, 7).

But very few know what it is to be born again or regenerated, for the reason that it has not been known what love and charity are, nor, therefore, what faith is; for if one does not know what love and charity are, he cannot know what faith is, since charity and faith make one, like good and truth, and like affection which belongs to the will and thought which belongs to the understanding. Respecting this union, see the work on *The Divine Love and the Divine Wisdom* (n. 427–431); also *The Doctrine of the New Jerusalem* (n. 13–24); and above (n. 3–20).

83. No one can come into the kingdom of God unless he has been born again, for the reason that man by inheritance from his parents is born into evils of every kind, but with an ability to become spiritual by the removal of those evils; and unless he becomes spiritual he cannot come into heaven. From being natural to become spiritual is to be born again or regenerated. But to know how man is regenerated these three things must be considered: what his first state is, which is a state of damnation; what his second state is, which is a state of reformation, and what his third state is, which is a state of regeneration. [2] *Man's first state, which is a state of damnation,* every one has by inheritance from his parents; for man is thereby born into the love of self and love of the world, and from these as fountains, into evils of every kind. It is by the enjoyments of these loves that he is led; and these enjoyments cause him not to know that he is in evils; for no enjoyment of a love is felt otherwise than as a good: consequently unless a man is regenerated he knows no otherwise than that to love himself and the world above all things is goodness itself; and to rule over all, and to possess the wealth of all, is the highest good. Moreover, this is the source of all evil; for a man then from love looks to no one but himself; or if from love he looks to another, it is as a devil looks to a devil, or a thief to a thief, when they act together. [3] Those who, from the enjoyment of these loves confirm in themselves these loves and the evils flowing from them, remain natural and become corporeal-sensual, and in their own thought, which is the thought of their spirit, are insane. Nevertheless, while they remain in the world they are able to speak and act rationally and wisely, because they are men, and in consequence possess rationality and liberty; but even this they do from love of self and the world. After death, when they become spirits, they are incapable of any other enjoyment than that which they had in spirit while in the world; and that enjoyment is the enjoyment of infernal love, which is then turned into what is undelightful, painful, and terrible; and this is what is meant in the Word by torment and hell-fire. All this makes clear that man's first state is a state of damnation, and that those are in it who do not permit themselves to be regenerated. [4] *Man's second state, which is the state of reformation,* is that in which he begins to think about heaven with reference to the joy of heaven, and from this about God, who is to him the source of heavenly joy. But at first this thought springs from the enjoyment of love of self, which enjoyment is to him heavenly joy. And as long as the enjoyment of that love reigns, together with the enjoyments of the evils that flow from it, he must needs think that he draws near to heaven by pouring out prayers, listening to preaching, going to the Holy Supper, giving to the poor, helping the needy, spending money on churches, contributing to hospitals, and so on. A man in this state knows no otherwise than that he is saved by mere thought about those things which religion teaches, whether it be what is called faith, or what is called faith and charity. He has no other idea than that he is saved by so thinking, because he gives no thought to the evils that he finds enjoyment in, and as long as their enjoyments remain the evils remain. The enjoyments of evil are from lust for them that continually inspires them, and also when no fear prevents, brings them forth. [5] So long as evils continue in the lusts of their love, and the consequent enjoyments, there is no faith, charity, piety or worship except in mere externals, which to the world seem real, and yet are not. These may be compared to water issuing from an impure fountain, which no one can drink. Man continues in the first state as long as he thinks from religion about heaven and about God, and yet gives no thought to evils as sins; but he comes into the second state, or the state of reformation, when he begins to think that there is such a thing as sin; and still more when he thinks that this or that is a sin, and when he examines it in himself to some extent, and refrains from willing it. [6] *Man's third state, which is a state of regeneration,* takes up and continues the former state. It begins when man refrains from evils as sins, and it progresses as he shuns them, and is perfected as he fights against them; and as he from the Lord conquers them he is regenerated. With one who is regenerated the order of life is reversed; from being natural he becomes spiritual; for when the natural is separated from the spiritual it is contrary to order, while the spiritual is in accordance with order. Consequently the regenerate man acts from charity; and whatever belongs to his charity he makes to be of his faith also. Yet he becomes spiritual only so far as he is in truths; for man is regenerated only by means of truths and a life in accordance with them; for by means of truths he knows what life is, and by means of the life he does the truths, and thus he conjoins good and truth, which is the spiritual marriage in which heaven is.

85. By means of these two faculties, called rationality and liberty, man is reformed and regenerated, and without them he cannot be reformed and regenerated, for it is by means of rationality that he is able to understand and know what is evil and what is good, and thus what is false and what is true; and it is by means of liberty that he is able to will what he understands and knows. But so long as enjoyment from the love of evil rules he is not able to will freely what is good and true and to make these to be of his reason, and cannot therefore appropriate them to himself. For, as shown above, it is that which a man does from freedom in accordance with reason that is appropriated to him as his; and unless good and truth are appropriated as his, man is not reformed and regenerated. Again, man does not act from an enjoyment of the love of good and truth until the enjoyment from the love of evil and falsity has been removed; for two kinds of enjoyment from love that are opposites are not possible at the same time. Acting from an enjoyment of love is acting from freedom; and since reason favors the love, this is also acting in accordance with reason.

86. As the evil man as well as the good man has rationality and liberty, so the evil man as well as the good man is able to understand truth and do good; but while the good man is able to do this from freedom in accordance with reason, the evil man is not; because the evil man is in the enjoyment of the love of evil, while the good man is in the enjoyment of the love of good. Consequently the truth that the evil man understands and the good that he does are not appropriated to him, while to the good man good and truth are appropriated, and without appropriation as one's own there is no reformation nor regeneration. For in the wicked, evils with falsities are as it were in the center, while goods with truths are in the circumferences; but in the good, goods with truths are in the center and evils with falsities are in the circumferences; and in both cases that which is at the center flows out even to the circumferences, as heat from a central fire, or as cold from a central frigidity. Thus in the evil the goods in the circumferences are defiled by the evils at the center; while in the good, the evils in the circumferences are moderated by the goods at the center. This is why evils

5

do not damn the regenerate man, and goods do not save the unregenerate man.

87. (4) *By means of these two faculties man can be so far reformed and regenerated as he can be led by means of them to acknowledge that every thing good and true that he thinks and does is from the Lord, and not from himself.* It has been told just above what reformation is and what regeneration is, also that man is reformed and regenerated by means of the two faculties, rationality and liberty; and since it is by means of these that this is done, something further shall be said about them. It is from rationality that man has the ability to understand, and from liberty that he has the ability to will, in both cases as if from himself. Nevertheless, none but a regenerate man has the ability to will good from freedom, and thus do it in accordance with reason. An evil man is able from freedom to will evil only, and to do evil in accordance with the thought that he makes by confirmations to appear rational. For evil can be confirmed as easily as good; although evil is confirmed by means of fallacies and appearances, which become falsities when they are confirmed; and when anything has been confirmed it appears to be in harmony with the reason.

88. Every one who has any thought from interior understanding can see that the power to will and the power to understand are not from man, but are from Him who possesses Power itself, that is, Power in its essence. Consider what this source of Power is. Is it not from Him who has it in its very potency, that is, who has it in Himself, and thus from Himself? Power in itself, therefore, is Divine. Every power must have a supply that must be imparted to it, and thus a determination from what is more internal or higher than itself. The eye has no power to see from itself, nor has the ear power to hear from itself, nor the mouth to speak from itself, nor the hand to act from itself; the supply and consequent determination must be from the mind. Nor has the mind from itself the power to think and to will one thing or another apart from something more internal or higher that determines the mind to it. It is the same with the power to understand and the power to will; these can come only from Him who has in Himself the power to will and the power to understand. [2] All this makes clear that these two faculties called rationality and liberty are from the Lord and not from man; and as they are from the Lord, it follows that man wills and understands nothing whatever from himself, but only as if it were from himself. Any one can be convinced that this is true who knows and believes that the volition of every good and the understanding of every truth are not from man but from the Lord. The Word teaches in *John* (iii. 27; xv. 5) that

A man can receive nothing from himself, and can do nothing from himself.

89. Since, then, all willing is from love and all understanding is from wisdom, it follows that the power to will is from the Divine love, and the power to understand from the Divine wisdom, and thus both are from the Lord, who is Divine love itself and Divine wisdom itself; and from this it follows that to act from freedom in accordance with reason is from no other source. And as freedom, like love, is inseparable from willing, so all action is in accordance with reason. But there is in man an interior and an exterior willing; and he can act in accordance with the exterior and not at the same time in accordance with the interior, as the hypocrite or flatterer does; and yet such exterior willing is from freedom, since it is from a love of appearing to be something else from what one is, or it is from a love of some evil that one has in mind from a love of the interior will. And yet, as just said, an evil man is unable to do any thing from freedom in accordance with his reason except what is evil. From freedom in accordance with reason he has no ability to do good. He can do good, to be sure, but not from that interior freedom which is his own freedom, the freedom from which his exterior freedom takes its quality of not being good.

90. It is said that man can be so far reformed and regenerated as he can be led by means of these two faculties to acknowledge that every thing good and true that he thinks and does is from the Lord and not from himself. It is only by means of these two faculties, that man can acknowledge this, because these faculties are from the Lord and are the Lord's in man, as is clear from what has already been said. It therefore follows that man can make this acknowledgment from the Lord, but not from himself, nevertheless he can do it as if it were done from himself; this the Lord gives to every one. He may believe it to be from himself and yet when he is wise he will acknowledge that it is not from himself. Otherwise the truth that man thinks and the good that he does are not truth and good in themselves, for man is in them and not the Lord; and the good that man has in it, provided it has salvation as its end, is a meritorious good; but the good that has the Lord in it is not meritorious.

91. But very few are able to apprehend intelligently that acknowledgment of the Lord, and an acknowledgment that all that is good and true is from the Lord, are what cause a man to be reformed and regenerated. For it may be thought, What does that acknowledgment do, since the Lord is omnipotent and wills to save all? And therefore is He not able and willing to do this, provided He is moved to mercy? But such thought is not from the Lord; nor is it from any interior sight of the understanding, that is, from any enlightenment. Therefore what this acknowledgment effects shall be briefly stated. [2] In the spiritual world, where spaces are nothing but appearances, presence is caused by wisdom and conjunction by love; and *vice versa*. There can be an acknowledgment of the Lord from wisdom, and there can be an acknowledgment of the Lord from love. Acknowledgment of the Lord from wisdom, which regarded in itself is nothing but knowledge, is effected by doctrine; while acknowledgment of the Lord from love is effected by a life in accordance with doctrine. This produces conjunction, but the other presence. And for this reason those that reject doctrine concerning the Lord remove themselves from Him; and as such also reject life,

they separate themselves from Him; while those that reject
life and not doctrine are present, although separated. They
are like friends who talk with one another, but have no love
for one another. Or they are like two persons, one of whom
speaks to the other as a friend, and yet hates him as an enemy.
[3] That this is true is acknowledged in the common belief
that he who teaches well and lives well is saved, but he who
teaches well and lives wickedly is not saved; also that he who
does not acknowledge God cannot be saved. All this makes
clear what that religion is that merely thinks about the Lord
from faith, as it is called, but does not do anything from
charity. So the Lord says:—

Why call ye Me Lord, Lord, and do not the things that I say? Every
one that cometh to Me and heareth My sayings and doeth them, is like
a man building a house and laid a foundation upon the rock. But he
that heareth and doeth not, is like a man that built a house upon the
earth without a foundation (*Luke* vi. 46–49).

92. (6) *By means of these two faculties the conjunction of
the Lord with man and the reciprocal conjunction of man with
the Lord are effected.* Conjunction with the Lord and regeneration are one, for so far as any one is conjoined with the Lord
he is regenerated. Therefore all that has been said above of
regeneration may be said of conjunction; and what is here said
of conjunction may be said of regeneration. That there is a
conjunction of the Lord with man, and a reciprocal conjunction
of man with the Lord, He Himself teaches in *John:*—

Abide in Me and I in you. He that abideth in Me and I in him, the
same beareth much fruit (xv. 4, 5).
At that day ye shall know that ye are in Me and I in you (xiv. 20).

[2] Any one can see from reason alone that there is no conjunction of minds unless it is reciprocal, and that the reciprocation is what conjoins. If one loves another and is not loved
in return, then as one approaches the other withdraws; but
if he is loved in return, then as one approaches the other approaches, and conjunction takes place. Moreover, love wills

to be loved; this is implanted in it; and so far as love is loved in return, it is in itself and in its enjoyment. This makes clear that when the Lord loves man and is not loved in return by man, the Lord approaches and man withdraws; thus the Lord continually wills to draw near to man and to enter into him, and man turns back and goes away. This is true of those that are in hell; but with those that are in heaven there is a mutual conjunction. [3] Since the Lord wills conjunction with man in order to save him, He provides that there shall be in man something reciprocal. The reciprocal in man is this, that the good which he wills and does from freedom, and the truth which, from that willing, he thinks and speaks in accordance with reason, appear to be from himself, and this good in his will and this truth in his understanding appear to be his. To man they even appear to be from himself and to be his precisely as if they were his, with no difference whatever. Take notice whether any one by any sense perceives it to be otherwise. Respecting this appearance as if from oneself, see above (n. 74–87); and respecting appropriation as one's own (n. 78–81). The only difference is that man ought to acknowledge that he does good and thinks truth not from himself but from the Lord, and consequently that the good he does and the truth he thinks are not his. To so think from some love in the will, because such is the truth, is what causes conjunction; for thus man looks to the Lord, and the Lord looks on man.

93. The nature of the difference between those who believe all good to be from the Lord and those who believe good to be from themselves it has been permitted me both to hear and see in the spiritual world. Those who believe good to be from the Lord turn the face to Him, and receive the enjoyment and the blessedness of good. But those who believe good to be from themselves look to themselves and think in themselves that they are meritorious. And because they look to themselves they are able to perceive the enjoyment of their own good only, which is not the enjoyment of good but the enjoyment of evil. For what is man's own (*proprium*) is evil; and the enjoyment of evil when perceived as good is hell. Those that have done good and have believed it to be from themselves, if after death they do not receive this truth that all good is from the Lord, mingle with infernal genii, and at length come to be one with them; while those that receive this truth are reformed. But none receive it except those who have looked to God in their life. Looking to God in their life is nothing else than shunning evils as sins.

94. The conjunction of the Lord with man and the reciprocal conjunction of man with the Lord is effected by loving the neighbor as oneself and loving the Lord above all things. To love the neighbor as oneself consists solely in not acting insincerely or unjustly towards him, not holding him in hatred or burning with revenge against him, not reviling or defaming him, not committing adultery with his wife, and not doing other like things against him. Who cannot see that those who do such things do not love the neighbor as themselves? But those who do not do such things for the reason that they are evils against the neighbor and also sins against the Lord, act sincerely, justly, kindly, and faithfully in relation to the neighbor; and as the Lord does likewise, a reciprocal conjunction is effected. And when there is reciprocal conjunction, whatever a man does to the neighbor he does from the Lord; and whatever he does from the Lord is good. Then it is not the person but the good in the person that is the neighbor to him. To love the Lord above all things consists solely in doing no evil to the Word for the reason that the Lord is in the Word, or to the holy things of the church for the reason that the Lord is in the holy things of the church, or to the soul of any one, for the reason that every one's soul is in the Lord's hand. Those who shun these evils as monstrous sins love the Lord above all things. But this none can do except those who love the neighbor as themselves, for the two are joined together.

95. Because there is a conjunction both of the Lord with man and of man with the Lord, there are two tables of the law, one for the Lord and the other for man. So far as man

keeps the law of his table as if from himself, so far the Lord
enables him to keep the laws of His table. But the man who
does not keep the laws of his own table, all of which refer to
love to the neighbor, can not keep the laws of the Lord's table,
all of which refer to love to the Lord. How can a murderer, a
thief, an adulterer or a false witness, love the Lord? Does not
reason declare that being such and loving God involves a contradiction? Is not the devil such? Can the devil do other
than hate God? But when a man turns away from murder,
adultery, theft, and false witness as infernal, then he can love
the Lord; for he then turns his face from the devil to the Lord;
and when he turns his face to the Lord love and wisdom are
given him. These enter man by the face, and not by the back
of the neck. As conjunction with the Lord is effected in this
way and in no other way, these two tables are called a covenant; and a covenant is between two.

96. (7) *The Lord preserves these two faculties in man inviolate and as sacred in the whole course of His Divine providence.*
This is because without these two faculties man would not possess understanding and will, and thus would not be man; also
because without these two faculties man could not be conjoined
with the Lord, and thus could not be reformed and regenerated; also because without these two faculties man could not
have immortality and eternal life. That this is so can be seen
indeed from a knowledge of what liberty and rationality are
(which are the two faculties here meant), as given in the preceding pages; but not clearly unless the above propositions are
presented to view as conclusions; these therefore must be made
clear. [2] *Without these two faculties man would not possess
will and understanding, and thus would not be man.* For man
has will from no other source than being able to will freely as
if from himself; and to will freely as if from himself is from a
faculty continually given him by the Lord that is called liberty.
And man has understanding from no other source than being
able to understand as if from himself whether a thing is in
harmony with reason or not: and to understand whether a thing

is in harmony with reason or not is from the other faculty continually given to man by the Lord that is called rationality. In man these two faculties are conjoined, like the will and the understanding in this respect, that man has the ability to understand because he has the power to will; for willing is not possible apart from understanding; understanding is its consort or mate, without which it cannot exist. This is why along with the faculty called liberty the faculty called rationality is given; and why if you take away willing from understanding you understand nothing. [3] Moreover, in the measure of your willing you have the ability to understand, provided the aids that are called knowledges are present and are also opened, for these are like tools to the workman. It is said that you have the ability to understand in the measure of your willing, that is, in the measure of your love to understand, for the will and love act as one. This indeed may seem absurd; but it seems so only to those who do not love and therefore do not wish to understand; and those who do not wish to understand say that they cannot. But who those are that are unable to understand, and who those are that are able to understand with difficulty, will be told in a subsequent article. [4] No proof is needed to show that unless man possessed a will from the faculty that is called liberty, and an understanding from the faculty that is called rationality, he would not be a man. Beasts do not have these faculties. There is an appearance that beasts also are able to will and to understand, but they are not. Natural affection, which in itself is desire, with its mate, knowledge, is what alone leads and moves beasts to do what they do. There is, it is true, something of the civil and moral in their knowledge; but this is not above their knowledge because they have no spiritual which gives perception of the moral, and consequently have no ability to think analytically about it. They can, indeed, be taught to do something; but this is only something natural that adds itself to their knowledge and also to their affection, and is reproduced either through the sight or through the hearing; but in no wise becomes a matter of thought

still less of reason in them. But something respecting this may
be seen above (n. 74). [5] *Without these two faculties man could
not be conjoined with the Lord, and thus could not be reformed
and regenerated.* This has been shown above. For the Lord
has His residence in man, both in the evil and in the good, in
these two faculties; and it is by means of them that He conjoins Himself with every man. It is from this that an evil man
as well as a good man has the ability to understand, and in consequence has in potency the will of good and the understanding of truth; that he does not have them actually is owing to
the abuse of these faculties. That the Lord has His residence
in every man in these faculties is from the inflow of His will,
in that He wills to be received by man and to have an abode
in him and to give him the happy things of eternal life. All
this belongs to the Lord's will, for it belongs to His Divine
love. It is this will of the Lord that causes the appearance in
man that what he thinks, speaks, wills and does is his own.
[6] That it is the inflow of the Lord's will that does this can
be established by many things from the spiritual world. Sometimes the Lord so fills an angel with His Divine that the angel
does not know that he is not the Lord. Thus were the angels
filled that were seen by Abraham, Hagar, and Gideon, and
therefore they called themselves Jehovah, of whom in the
Word. Again, one spirit can be so filled by another as not to
know but that he is the other. This I have often seen. Furthermore it is known in heaven that the Lord does every thing
by willing it, and that whatever He wills is done. All this
makes clear that it is by means of these two faculties that the
Lord conjoins Himself with man and causes man to be reciprocally conjoined with Him. But how man is reciprocally conjoined by means of these faculties, and how he is consequently
reformed and regenerated by means of them, has been told
above, and more will be said about it further on. [7] *That
man without these two faculties could not have immortality and
eternal life,* follows from what has just been said, that by
means of them there is conjunction with the Lord, also refor-

mation and regeneration; through conjunction man has immortality and through reformation and regeneration he has eternal life. And as by means of these two faculties there is a
conjunction of the Lord with every man, both the evil and the
good, as has been said, therefore every man has immortality.
But eternal life, that is, the life of heaven, is given to him in
whom there is a reciprocal conjunction from inmosts to outmosts. From all this the reasons are evident why the Lord
preserves these two faculties in man inviolate and as sacred,
in the whole course of His Divine providence.

97. (8) *Therefore it is* [*a law*] *of the Divine providence
that man should act from freedom in accordance with reason.*
To act from freedom in accordance with reason, to act from
liberty and rationality, and to act from the will and the understanding, are the same thing; but it is one thing to act from
freedom in accordance with reason, or to act from liberty and
rationality, and it is another thing to act from freedom itself
in accordance with reason itself or to act from liberty itself
and from rationality itself. For a man who does evil from the
love of evil and confirms that evil in himself, acts from freedom in accordance with reason; and yet his freedom is not in
itself freedom, or freedom itself, but it is an infernal freedom
that is in itself slavery; and his reason is not in itself reason,
but is either a spurious or a false reason, or what is made to
appear by confirmations to be reason. Nevertheless they are
both of the Divine providence; for if the freedom to will evil,
and to make it appear by confirmations to be in accordance
with reason were taken away from the natural man, liberty
and rationality, and will and understanding with them, would
perish, and he would have no ability to be withdrawn from
evils and reformed, and thus conjoined with the Lord and live
forever. Consequently the Lord guards freedom in man, as
man guards the apple of his eye. And yet by means of freedom, the Lord continually withdraws man from evils; and so
far as He is able to withdraw him by means of freedom, He implants what is good by means of freedom. Thus in the place of

infernal freedom, the Lord gradually endows man with heav-enly freedom.

98. It has been said above that every man possesses the faculty to will that is called liberty, and the faculty to under-stand that is called rationality; but it should be well under-stood that these faculties are, as it were, innate in man, for his human itself is in them. But, as has just been said, it is one thing to act from freedom in accordance with reason, and an-other thing to act from freedom itself in accordance with rea-son itself. Only such as have suffered themselves to be regen-erated by the Lord act from freedom itself in accordance with reason itself; all others act from freedom in accordance with thought to which they give the semblance of reason. And yet every man, unless born foolish or excessively stupid, is able to attain to reason itself, and through it to freedom itself. But there are numerous reasons why every man does not do this that will be made known in what follows. Here it will only be told who those are to whom freedom itself or liberty itself, together with reason itself or rationality itself, cannot be given; and to whom they can scarcely be given. [2] Liberty itself and rationality itself cannot be given to those that are born foolish, or to those who have become foolish, so long as they remain so. They cannot be given to those born stupid and gross, or to any who have become so from the torpor of idle-ness, or from any disease that has perverted or wholly closed the interiors of the mind, or from the love of a beastly life. [3] Liberty itself and rationality itself cannot be given to those in the Christian world who wholly deny the Lord's Di-vinity and the holiness of the Word, and have maintained this denial confirmed in them to the end of life; for this is meant by the sin against the Holy Spirit which is not forgiven either in this age or in the age to come (*Matt.* xii. 31, 32). [4] Neither can liberty itself and rationality itself be given to those who attribute all things to nature and nothing to the Divine, and who have made this to be their belief by reasonings from things visible; for such are atheists. [5] Liberty itself and

rationality itself can scarcely be given to those who have
strongly confirmed themselves in falsities of religion, for a
confirmer of falsity is a denier of truth. But they can be
given to those who, whatever their religion may be, have not
so confirmed themselves (on which see what is presented in
*The Doctrine of the New Jerusalem concerning the Sacred
Scripture*, n. 91–97). [6] Infants and children cannot come
into liberty itself and rationality itself until they are grown
up; for the interiors of the mind in man are opened gradually; and in the mean time they are like seeds in unripe fruit,
that cannot sprout in the soil.

99. It has been said that liberty itself and rationality itself
cannot be given to those that have denied the Lord's Divinity
and the holiness of the Word, or to those that have confirmed
themselves in favor of nature against the Divine, and scarcely
to those that have strongly confirmed themselves in falsities
of religion. Yet none of these have lost the faculties themselves. I have known atheists who have become devils and
satans to understand the arcana of wisdom as well as angels,
but only while they heard them from others; and when they returned into their own thoughts they did not understand, for
the reason that they had no desire to. But they were shown
that they, too, might have the desire if they were not misled
by the love and consequent enjoyment of evil; and this they
understood when they heard it, and even asserted that they
might, but that they had no wish to be able, since this would
make them unable to will what they had willed, which was
evil, from enjoyment in its lust. I have often heard such wonderful things in the spiritual world, by which it has been fully
proved to me that every man possesses liberty and rationality; and that every one can come into liberty itself and rationality itself provided he shuns evils as sins. But a mature man
who does not come into liberty itself and rationality itself in
the world can in no wise come into them after death; for his
state of life then remains forever such as it had been in the
world.

IT IS A LAW OF THE DIVINE PROVIDENCE THAT MAN SHOULD
AS IF FROM HIMSELF PUT AWAY EVILS AS SINS IN THE EX-
TERNAL MAN; AND THE LORD IS ABLE IN THIS WAY AND IN
NO OTHER TO PUT AWAY EVILS IN THE INTERNAL MAN, AND
SIMULTANEOUSLY IN THE EXTERNAL.

100. Any one is able to see from reason alone that the Lord,
who is good itself and truth itself, cannot enter into man unless the evils and falsities in him are put away; for evil is the
opposite of good, and falsity is the opposite of truth, and two
opposites can in no wise be commingled, but when one draws
near to the other a combat takes place, which lasts till one
gives way to the other; and the one that yields departs, and
the other takes its place. In such opposition are heaven and
hell, or the Lord and the devil. Can any one think in a rational
way that the Lord can enter where the devil reigns, or that
heaven can be where hell is? From the rationality granted to
every sane man can he not see that for the Lord to enter the
devil must be cast out? or for heaven to enter, hell must be
put away? [2] This opposition is meant by Abraham's words
from heaven to the rich man in hell:—

Between us and you there is a great gulf fixed; that those wishing to
pass from this side to you may not be able, nor can those on that side
pass over to us (*Luke* xvi. 26).

Evil itself is hell, and good itself is heaven; or what is the
same, evil itself is the devil, and good itself is the Lord; and
the man in whom evil reigns is a hell in the least form; while
the man in whom good reigns is a heaven in the least form.
This being so, how can heaven enter hell when between them
a gulf so great is fixed that there can be no crossing from
one to the other? From all this it follows that hell must by
all means be put away to make it possible for the Lord with
heaven to come in.

101. But many, especially such as have confirmed themselves in a faith separated from charity, do not know that when

they are in evils they are in hell; they do not even know what evils are, for the reason that they give no thought to evils, saying that as they are not under the yoke of the law they are not condemned by the law, and that, as they are unable to contribute anything to their salvation, they are unable to put away any evil from themselves; and furthermore are unable to do any good from themselves. These are such as neglect to think about evil, and because of this they are continually in evil. Such are meant by the goats spoken of by the Lord in *Matthew* (xxv. 32, 33, 41–46), as may be seen in *The Doctrine of the New Jerusalem concerning Faith* (n. 61–68), of whom it is said:—

Depart from me, ye cursed, into the eternal fire which is prepared for the devil and his angels (verse 41).

[2] For those who give no thought to the evils in themselves, that is, do not examine themselves and afterwards refrain from evils, must needs be ignorant of what evil is, and must needs love it from enjoyment in it; for he who does not know what evil is loves it, and he who fails to think about it is continually in it. Like a blind man he does not see it. For it is the thought that sees good and evil, as it is the eye that sees the beautiful and the unbeautiful; and he who so thinks and wills evil as to believe that evil does not appear before God, or that if it does appear it is forgiven, is in evil, since he is thus led to think that he is free from evil. If such abstain from doing evils they do not abstain because these are sins against God, but because they fear the laws or the loss of reputation; and they still do them in their spirit, for it is the spirit of man that thinks and wills; consequently what a man thinks in his spirit in this world, that he does after he leaves this world when he becomes a spirit. [3] In the spiritual world into which every man comes after death, it is not asked what your belief has been, or what your doctrine has been, but what your life has been, that is, whether it has been such or such; for it is known that as one's life is such is his belief, and even his doctrine; for the life makes doctrine for itself, and belief for itself.

102. From what has now been said it can be seen that it is a law of the Divine providence that evils should be put away by man; for unless they are put away the Lord cannot be conjoined with man, and cannot from Himself lead man into heaven. But as it has not been known that man ought as if of himself to put away the evils in the external man, and unless man does this as if of himself the Lord cannot put away the evils that are in man's internal, these things shall be presented to the reason in its own light in the following order:—

(1) Every man has an external and an internal of thought.

(2) The external of man's thought is in itself of the same character as its internal.

(3) The internal cannot be cleansed from the lusts of evil so long as the evils in the external man are not put away, since these obstruct.

(4) The evils in the external man can be put away by the Lord only through man's instrumentality.

(5) Therefore man ought as if of himself to put away evils from the external man.

(6) Then the Lord cleanses man from the lusts of evil in the internal man and from the evils themselves in the external.

(7) It is the unceasing effort of the Lord's Divine providence to conjoin man with Himself, and Himself with man, that He may be able to bestow upon man the happinesses of eternal life; and this can be done only so far as evils with their lusts are put away.

103. (1) *Every man has an external and an internal of thought.* The same is here meant by the external and internal of thought as by the external and internal man, and by this nothing else is meant than the external and internal of the will and understanding; for the will and understanding are what constitute man, and as these two manifest themselves in the thoughts, the terms external and internal of thought are used. Since, then, it is the spirit of man and not his body that wills and understands and therefore thinks, it follows that this external and internal are the external and internal of man's spirit. The action of the body, whether in words or deeds, is only an effect from the internal and external of man's spirit, since the body is mere obedience.

104. Every man of mature age has an external and an internal of thought, and therefore an external [and an internal] of will and understanding, or an external and an internal of the spirit, which is the same as the external and the internal man; and this is evident to any one who observes carefully another's thoughts and intentions as exhibited in his words or acts, and also his own thoughts when in company and when he is alone. For one can talk with another in a friendly way from external thought, and yet be at enmity with him in internal thought. From external thought together with its affection a man can talk about love towards his neighbor and love to God, when in his internal thought he cares nothing for the neighbor and has no fear of God. From external thought together with its affection a man can talk about the justice of civil laws, the virtues of moral life, and matters of doctrine and spiritual life; and yet when alone by himself he may from internal thought and its affection speak against the civil laws, the virtues of moral life, and matters of doctrine and spiritual life; and this is done by those who are in the lusts of evil, but who wish it to appear before the world that they are not in them. [2] Moreover, many think to themselves, when they hear others talking, whether these are interiorly in themselves thinking in accord with the thoughts they are expressing, whether or not they are to be believed, and what their intentions are. It is well known that flatterers and hypocrites have a double thought; for they are able to keep things to themselves and to guard against disclosing their interior thought; and some can conceal it more and more deeply, and as it were block up the doors lest it appear. That both exterior and interior thought are possible to man is also clearly evident from his being able from his interior thought to look upon his exterior thought, and also to reflect upon it, and to judge of it whether it is evil or not evil

6

That the mind of man is such is due to the two faculties that man has from the Lord, called liberty and rationality. Unless man had from these an external and an internal of thought he would not be able to perceive and see any evil in himself and be reformed; in fact, he would not be able to speak, but only to utter sounds like a beast.

105. The internal of thought is from the life's love and its affections and the perceptions therefrom; the external of thought is from the contents of the memory, which are serviceable to the life's love as confirmations and as means to further its ends. From infancy to early manhood man is in the external of thought from an affection for knowing, which then constitutes its internal; also there exhales from his life's love, which is innate from his parents, something of lust and inclination therefrom. But afterwards the way he lives determines his life's love; and its affections with the perceptions therefrom constitute the internal of his thought; while the life's love determines the love of the means; and the enjoyment of this and the knowledges thereby called forth from the memory constitute the external of his thought.

106. (2) *The external of man's thought is in itself of the same character as its internal.* That man from head to foot is of the same character as his life's love has been shown above. In the first place, therefore, something must here be said about the life's love in man; for this must precede any consideration of the affections associated with perceptions which constitute man's internal, and of the enjoyments of affections associated with thoughts which constitute his external. Loves are manifold; but two of them, heavenly love and infernal love, are like lords and kings. Heavenly love is love to the Lord and love towards the neighbor; and infernal love is love of self and of the world. These two kinds of love are opposite to each other as hell and heaven are; for those who are in the love of self and the world have no good will for any but themselves; while those who are in love to the Lord and in love towards the neighbor have good will for all. These two loves are the life's loves of

man, but with much variety. Heavenly love is the life's love
of those whom the Lord leads, and infernal love is the life's
love of those whom the devil leads. [2] But the life's love of
no one can exist without derivations, which are called affections.
The derivations of infernal love are affections for evil and falsity, which, strictly speaking, are lusts; and the derivations of
heavenly love are affections for good and truth, which, strictly
speaking, are dilections. Of infernal love there are as many
affections, or strictly speaking, lusts, as there are evils; and of
heavenly love there are as many affections, or strictly speaking, dilections, as there are goods. Love dwells in its affections
like a lord in his realm, or like a king in his kingdom. The
dominion or sovereignty of these loves is over the things of the
mind, that is, the things of man's will and understanding, and
thence of the body. The life's love, by means of its affections
and perceptions therefrom, and its enjoyments and thoughts
therefrom, rules the entire man,—the internal of his mind by
means of affections and perceptions therefrom, and the external by means of the enjoyments of the affections and thoughts
therefrom.

107. The form of this rule can in some measure be seen by
comparisons. Heavenly love with its affections for good and
truth and perceptions therefrom, together with its enjoyments
from these affections and thoughts therefrom, may be likened
to a tree distinguished for its branches, leaves, and fruits. The
life's love is the tree; the branches with the leaves are affections
for good and truth with their perceptions; and the fruits are
the enjoyments of affections with their thoughts. But infernal
love with its affections for evil and falsity, which are lusts,
together with the enjoyment of these lusts and thoughts therefrom, may be likened to a spider with its surrounding web.
The love itself is the spider, the lusts of evil and falsity with
their interior subtleties are the net-like threads nearest the spider's seat; and the enjoyments of these lusts with their deceitful devices are the remoter threads, where the flies are caught
on the wing, and are ensnared and eaten.

108. The conjunction of all things of the will and understanding, that is, of the mind of man with his life's love, is made evident by these comparisons, and yet not made rationally evident. The conjunction is made rationally evident in this way. There are every where three things together that make one; these are called end, cause, and effect; here the life's love is the end, the affections with their perceptions are the cause, and the enjoyment of the affections with their thoughts are the effect; for just as the end through the cause enters into the effect, so does the love through its affections come to its enjoyments, and through its perceptions to its thoughts. The effects themselves are in the mind's enjoyments and their thoughts, whenever these enjoyments belong to the will and the thoughts to the understanding therefrom, that is, whenever the agreement is complete. Then the effects belong to the spirit, and if they do not come into bodily act, still they are as if in act when there is agreement. Furthermore, they are then together in the body, and dwell there with the life's love of the man, and aspire to action, which takes place when nothing hinders. Such are lusts of evil and the evils themselves in those who in their spirit make evils allowable. [2] Now as the end conjoins itself with the cause, and through the cause with the effect, so does the life's love conjoin itself with the internal of thought, and through this with its external. This makes clear that the external of man's thought is in itself of the same character as its internal; for the end imparts itself wholly to the cause, and through the cause to the effect; for there is nothing essential in the effect except what is in the cause, and through the cause in the end. And as the end is thus the very essential which enters into the cause and the effect, so cause and effect are called mediate and outmost ends.

109. Sometimes the external of man's thought does not appear to be in itself of the same character as the internal; but this is because the life's love with its surrounding internals places a vicar below itself, which is called the love of means, and enjoins upon it to take heed and watch that nothing from its lusts appear. This vicar, therefore, from the cunning of its chief, which is the life's love, talks and acts in accord with the civil requirements of the country, the moral requirements of reason, and the spiritual requirements of the church. Some do this so craftily and ingeniously that no one sees that they are not such as their speech and act indicate; and at last, from the habit of concealment, they scarcely know otherwise themselves. All hypocrites are such; and such are the priests who at heart care nothing for the neighbor and do not fear God, and yet preach about love of the neighbor and the love of God; such are the judges who give judgment according to bribes and friendship, while they show a pretended zeal for justice, and from reason talk of judgment; such are the merchants who are insincere and fraudulent at heart, while they act sincerely for the sake of gain; and such are adulterers, when from the rationality that every man has they talk about the chastity of marriage; and so on. [2] But when these same persons strip this love of means—this vicar of their life's love—of the garments of purple and fine linen with which they have invested it, and clothe it in its domestic garb, they then think, and sometimes with their dearest friends whose life's love is similar, they speak from their thought in a wholly opposite way. It might be supposed, when from their love of means they have talked so justly, sincerely, and piously, that the character of the internal of their thought was not in the external of their thought, and yet it was. There is hypocrisy in such; there is a love of self and the world in them, and the cunning of that love is to secure reputation for the sake of honor or gain, in respect to outmost appearances. This character of the internal is in the external of their thought when they so speak and act.

110. But in those who are in heavenly love the internal and the external of thought, or the internal and the external man, make one when they speak; nor do such know any difference between these. Their life's love, with its affections for good and the perceptions for truth belonging thereto, is like a soul in their thoughts, and in what they speak and do from them. If they are priests they preach from love towards the neighbor and from love to the Lord; if judges they judge from genuine justice; if merchants they act from genuine sincerity; if married they love their wives from genuine chastity; and so on. The life's love of such has also its love of means as its vicar, which it teaches and leads to act from prudence, and clothes with garments of zeal both for truths of doctrine and for goods of life.

111. (3) *The internal cannot be cleansed from the lusts of evil so long as the evils in the external man are not put away, since these obstruct.* This follows from the preceding statement, that the external of man's thought is in itself of the same character as its internal; and that the two cohere like things that are not only one within the other but also one from the other; consequently one cannot be set aside unless the other is also. It is so with every thing external that is from an internal, and with every thing posterior that is from a prior, and with every effect that is from a cause. [2] Since, then, lusts with their subtleties constitute in the evil the internal of thought, and the enjoyments of lusts together with their devices constitute their external of thought, and the latter and the former are joined together as one, it follows that the internal cannot be cleansed from lusts so long as the evils in the external man are not put away. It should be understood that man's internal will is that which is in the lusts, and the internal understanding is that which is in the subtleties, and that the external will is that which is in the enjoyments of the lusts, and the external understanding is that which is in the devices from the subtleties. Anyone can see that lusts and their enjoyments make one, and that the subtleties and devices make one; also that these four are in one series, and together make as it were one bundle; and from this again it is clear that the internal, which consists of lusts, can be cast out only by the putting away of the external, which consists of evils. Lusts through their enjoyments produce evils; but when evils are believed to be allowable, which comes from the agreement of will and understanding, the enjoyments and the evils then make one. It is acknowledged that this agreement is equivalent to doing the thing; and this is what the Lord says:—

Whosoever looketh on another's woman to lust after her hath committed adultery with her already in his heart (*Matt.* v. 28).

It is the same with other evils.

112. From all this it can now be seen that evils must surely be put away from the external man that man may be cleansed from the lusts of evil; for until this is done there is no possible exit for lusts; and if there is no exit the lusts remain within and breathe out enjoyments from themselves, and so they urge men on to the consent, thus to the doing. Through the external of thought the lusts enter the body; when therefore there is consent in the external of thought the lusts are at once present in the body; and the enjoyment that is felt is there. That as the mind is such is the body, thus the whole man, may be seen in the work on *The Divine Love and the Divine Wisdom* (n. 362–370). This may be made clear by comparisons and also by examples. [2] *By comparisons:* Lusts with their enjoyments may be likened to fire; the more a fire is fed the more it burns; and the freer the course given it the further it spreads, until in a city it consumes the houses, and in a forest the trees. In the Word the lusts of evil are likened to fire, and their evils to its burning. Moreover, in the spiritual world, lusts of evil with their enjoyments appear like fires; infernal fire is nothing else. Lusts may also be likened to floods and inundations of water when dikes or dams give way. They may also be likened to gangrenous sores and ulcers, which, if they run their course or are not cured, bring death to the body. [3] *By examples:* It is made clear that unless the evils in the external man are put away the lusts and their enjoyments grow and multiply. The more a thief steals the more he loves to steal, till at last he cannot refrain; so with the defrauder, the more he defrauds. The same is true of hatred and revenge, of luxury and intemperance, of whoredom

and blasphemy, and the like. Every one knows that the love
of ruling from the love of self increases as rein is given to it;
equally the love of possessing from love of the world; these
seem to be without limit or end. All this makes clear that so
far as the evils in the external are not put away their lusts
multiply, and that lusts increase to the extent that evils have
loose rein.

113. Man is not able to perceive the lusts of his evil; he
does perceive their enjoyments, although he does not think
much about them; for the enjoyments divert the thoughts and
banish reflection. Consequently, unless one knew from some
other source that his lusts are evils he would call them good,
and from freedom in accordance with the reason of his thought
he would give expression to them; and when he does that he
appropriates them to himself. So far as he confirms evils as
allowable he enlarges the court of the ruling love, which is his
life's love. Lusts are what constitute its court; for they are
like its ministers and attendants, through which it governs
the exteriors that constitute its kingdom. But as is the king
such are the ministers and attendants, and such the kingdom.
When a king is a devil his ministers and attendants are insanities, and the people of his kingdom are falsities of every kind,
which his ministers (whom they call wise although they are
insane), cause, by means of reasoning from fallacies and by
means of illusions, to appear as truths, and cause to be acknowledged as truths. Can such a state in man be changed
except by putting away the evils in the external man? For
thereby the lusts that cling to the evils are put away. Otherwise no exit is open for the lusts; for they are shut in like a
besieged city, or like a closed ulcer.

114. (4) *The evils in the external man can be put away by
the Lord only through man's instrumentality.* In all Christian
churches the doctrine has been accepted that before man approaches the holy communion he shall examine himself, shall
see and acknowledge his sins, and shall do the work of repentance by refraining from evils and by rejecting them because

they are from the devil; and otherwise his sins are not forgiven, and he is damned. The English hold the doctrine of
faith alone, and yet in their exhortation to the holy communion they plainly teach self-examination, acknowledgment, confession of sins, repentance, and renewal of life; and those who
fail to do this are threatened in these words that unless they
repent the devil will enter into them as he did into Judas, and
will fill them with all iniquity, and destroy both body and soul.
The Germans, the Swedes, and the Danes, who also hold the
doctrine of faith alone, have the same teaching in their exhortation to the holy communion, threatening also that all such
will be subject to infernal punishments and to eternal damnation for mixing the holy and the profane. This is read by the
priest with a loud voice before those who are about to come
to the Holy Supper, and is listened to by them with full acknowledgment that it is so. [2] And yet when these same
persons listen on the same day to the preaching of faith alone,
and at the same time that the law does not condemn them because the Lord fulfilled it for them, and that they are not able
from themselves to do any good except what is meritorious,
and thus works have nothing saving in them, but faith only,
they return home entirely forgetful of their former confession,
and discarding it so far as they give their thought to the preaching about faith alone. Which of these, then, is true; this or
that? For two things contrary to each other cannot both be
true, as on the one hand, that without self-examination, recognition, acknowledgment, confession, and renunciation of sins,
thus without repentance, there is no forgiveness of sins, thus
no salvation, but eternal damnation; and on the other hand
that such things contribute nothing to salvation, because the
Lord by the passion of the cross has made full satisfaction for
all the sins of men, for those who have faith; and that those
who have faith only, with confidence that it is true, and with a
trust in the imputation of the Lord's merit, are without sins,
and appear before God like those with washed and bright faces.
From all this it is clear that it is the common religion of all

the churches in the Christian world that man should examine himself, should see and acknowledge his sins, and afterwards refrain from them; and that otherwise there is not salvation, but damnation.   Moreover, that this is the veritable Divine truth is evident from the passages in the Word, where man is commanded to repent; as the following:—

Jesus said, Bring forth therefore fruits worthy of repentance. Even now is the axe laid unto the root of the tree; every tree therefore that bringeth not forth good fruit is hewn down, and cast into the fire (*Luke* iii. 8, 9).

Jesus said, Except ye repent ye shall all perish (*Luke* xiii. 3, 5).

Jesus preached the gospel of the kingdom of God. Repent ye and believe the gospel (*Mark* i. 14, 15).

Jesus sent forth His disciples, and they went out and preached that men should repent (*Mark* vi. 12).

Jesus said to the apostles that repentance and remission of sins should be preached unto all nations (*Luke* xxiv. 47).

John preached the baptism of repentance for the remission of sins (*Mark* i. 4; *Luke* iii. 3).

Think of this with some understanding; and if you have religion you will see that repentance from sins is the way to heaven, that faith separate from repentance is not faith, and that those who are not in faith because they do not repent are in the way to hell.

115. Those who are in faith separate from charity, and have confirmed themselves in it from Paul's saying to the Romans,

That a man is justified by faith apart from the works of the law (*Rom.* iii. 28),

adore this saying like men who adore the sun; and they become like those who fix their eyes steadily on the sun, by which the sight is so blurred that they can see nothing in ordinary light. For they do not see that "the works of the law" there mean, not the commandments of the Decalogue, but the rituals described by Moses in his books, which are there always called "the law." Lest, therefore, it should be thought that the commandments are meant Paul explains by saying,

Do we then make void the law through faith; God forbid; yea, we establish the law (verse 31 of the same chapter).

Those who have confirmed themselves by this saying in faith separate from charity, from gazing at this passage as at the sun, fail to see where Paul enumerates the laws of faith as being the very works of charity; and what is faith without its laws? Nor do they notice where he enumerates evil works, and declares that those who do them cannot enter into heaven. This shows clearly how great is the blindness that has been induced by a wrong understanding of this single passage.

116. Evils in the external man can be put away only by man's instrumentality, because it is of the Lord's Divine providence that whatever man hears, sees, thinks, wills, speaks, and does, seems to him to be wholly his own. Without this appearance (as has been shown above, n. 71–95, and in subsequent numbers) there could be in man no reception of Divine truth, no determination towards doing good, no appropriation of love and wisdom or of charity and faith, and therefore no conjunction with the Lord, consequently no reformation and regeneration and thus salvation. Without this appearance repentance from sins, and faith even, are evidently impossible. It is also evident that without this appearance a man would not be a man, but would be devoid of natural life like a beast. Let any one who will consult his reason and see, when a man thinks about good and truth, spiritual, moral, or civil, whether there is any other appearance than that he thinks from himself; let him then accept this doctrinal, that everything good and true is from the Lord and nothing from man; and will he not acknowledge this consequence, that man must do good and think truth as if of himself, and yet must acknowledge that he does it from the Lord; and furthermore, that man must put away evils as if of himself and yet must acknowledge that he does it from the Lord?

117. Many are not aware that they are in evils, inasmuch as they do not do them outwardly because they fear the civil laws and the loss of reputation, and thus from custom and habit fall into the way of shunning evils as detrimental to their honor and profit. But when evils are not shunned from a religious principle, on the ground that they are sins and antagonistic to God, the lusts of evil with their enjoyments still remain, like impure waters confined and stagnant. Let such examine their thoughts and intentions, and they will find these lusts, provided they know what sins are. [2] This is the state of many who have confirmed themselves in faith separate from charity, who, believing that the law does not condemn them, do not even think about sins; and some question whether there are any sins in them, or if there are, whether they are sins before God, since they have been pardoned. In a like state also are natural moralists, who believe that civil and moral life with its prudence accomplishes everything and Divine providence nothing. Such also are those who strive with great eagerness after a reputation and name for honesty and sincerity for the sake of honor or gain. But those who are of this character, and who have also despised religion, become after death spirits of lusts, appearing to themselves as if they were men, but to others at a distance like treacherous forms (*priapi*); and like birds of night they see in the dark and not in the light.

118. (5) *Therefore man ought as if of himself to put away evils from the external man.* This has already been proved by what has been said. It may also be explained in three articles in the *Doctrine of Life for the New Jerusalem, first,* That no one can shun evils as sins, so as to turn away from them interiorly, except by combats against them (n. 92–100); *secondly,* That man ought to shun evils as sins and fight against them as if of himself (n. 101–107); *thirdly,* That if one shuns evils for any reasons whatever except that they are sins he does not shun them, but only prevents their appearing before the world (n. 108–113).

119. (6) *Then the Lord cleanses man from the lusts [of evil] in the internal man, and from the evils themselves in the external.* The Lord cleanses man from the lusts of evil when the man, as if of himself, puts away the evils, for the reason, that the Lord cannot cleanse him until he does this because the evils are in the external man and the lusts of evil in the internal man, and the two are connected like roots and trunk; consequently until the evils are put away no opening is possible, for the evils obstruct and close the door; and the door can be opened by the Lord only by man's instrumentality, as has been shown just above   When, therefore, man as if of himself opens the door, the Lord roots out the lusts and the evils together.   Another reason is, that the Lord acts into man's inmost, and from the inmost into consequent things even to outmosts; while man is simultaneously in outmosts. Therefore so long as man from himself holds the outmosts closed there can be no cleansing, but only such operation by the Lord in man's interiors as the Lord carries on in hell (the man who is both in lusts and in evils being a form of hell) and this operation is only an arrangement to prevent one thing from destroying another, and to prevent the violation of good and truth. The Lord continually solicits and urges man to open the door to Him, as is clear from His words in the *Apocalypse:*—

Behold, I stand at the door and knock; if any one hear My voice and open the door, I will come in to him and will sup with him and he with Me (iii. 20).

120. Of the interior state of his mind or of his internal man, man knows nothing whatever. Although there are infinite things there, not one of them comes to man's cognizance. For the internal of man's thought, or his internal man, is his spirit itself; and in it there are things as infinite and numberless as there are in his body, and even more innumerable; for man's spirit is a man in its form, and all things belonging to it correspond with all things of man in the body. And just as man has no knowledge from any sensation of the manner in which his mind or his soul operates in all things of the body, conjointly and severally, so neither does he know in what manner the Lord operates in all things of his mind or soul, that is, in all things of his spirit. The operation is unceasing; in it man has no part, and yet the Lord can cleanse man from no lust of evil in his spirit or internal man so long as man holds his external closed. Man holds his external closed by means of evils, every one of which seems to him as a single thing, and yet in every one there are infinite things; and when man puts away an evil as a single thing the Lord puts away the infinite things in it. This is what is meant by the Lord's then cleansing man from the lusts of evil in the internal man, and from evils themselves in the external.

121. Many believe that man is cleansed from evils by merely believing what the church teaches; others by his doing good; others by his knowing, talking about, and teaching the things of the church; others by his reading the Word and pious books; others by his attending churches, listening to sermons, and especially by coming to the Holy Supper; others by his renouncing the world and devoting himself to piety; and others by his confessing himself guilty of all sins; and so on. Yet none of these cleanse man in the least unless he examines himself, sees his sins, acknowledges them, condemns himself for them, and repents by refraining from them; and all this he must do as if of himself, but with acknowledgment from the heart that he does it from the Lord. [2] Until this is done the things that have been mentioned above do not help at all, for they are either meritorious or hypocritical; and those who do them appear in heaven before angels like beautiful harlots, smelling badly from their corruption, or like ill-favored women so painted as to appear handsome, or like masked actors and mimics on the stage, or like apes in human clothing. But when evils have been put away the things enumerated above belong to the love of those who do them; and such appear in heaven before the angels as beautiful human beings, and partners and companions of the angels.

122. But it must be well understood that when a man wishes to repent he must look to the Lord alone; if he looks to God the Father only he cannot be cleansed; nor if he looks to the Father for the sake of the Son, nor if he looks to the Son as merely a man. For there is one God, and that one is the Lord, His Divine and Human being one person, as shown in the *Doctrine of the New Jerusalem concerning the Lord*. In order that man in repenting might look to the Lord alone He instituted the Holy Supper, which confirms the remission of sins in those who repent. It confirms this because in that Supper or communion every one is kept looking to the Lord alone.

123. (7) *It is the unceasing effort of the Lord's Divine providence to conjoin man with Himself and Himself with man, that He may be able to bestow upon man the happinesses of eternal life ; and this can be done only so far as evils with their lusts are put away*. That it is the unceasing effort of the Lord's Divine providence to conjoin man with Himself and Himself with man, and that this conjunction is what is called reformation and regeneration, and that from it man has salvation, has been shown above (n. 27–45). Who does not see that conjunction with God is life eternal and salvation ? Every one sees it who believes that men are from creation images and likenesses of God (*Gen*. i. 26, 27), and who knows what an image and likeness of God is. [2] Who that is possessed of sound reason, when he thinks from his rationality and is willing to think from his liberty, can believe that there are three Gods, equal in essence, and that Divine Being (*Esse*) or Divine Essence can be divided ? That there is a Trine in the one God can be conceived and comprehended, as one can comprehend that there are soul, body, and outgoing of life from these in an angel or in a man. And as it is in the Lord alone that this Trine in One is possible, it follows that conjunction must be with the Lord. Make use of your rationality together with your liberty of thinking and you will see this truth in its light; but first grant that there is a God, and a heaven and eternal life. [3] Since, then, God is one, and man was made from creation an image and likeness of Him, and since by means of infernal love and its lusts and their enjoyments man has come into the love of all evils, and has thereby destroyed in himself the image and likeness of God, it follows that it is the unceasing effort of the

Lord's Divine providence to conjoin man with Himself and Himself with man, and thus make man to be an image of God. It also follows, that this is to the end that the Lord may bestow upon man the happinesses of eternal life; for such is Divine love. [4] But the Lord cannot bestow these upon man, nor make him an image of Himself, unless man, as if of himself, puts away sins in the external man; for the reason that the Lord is not only Divine love but is also Divine wisdom; and Divine love does nothing except from its own Divine wisdom and in accordance with it. And it is in accordance with his Divine wisdom that man cannot be conjoined with the Lord, and thus reformed, regenerated, and saved, unless it is permitted him to act from freedom in accordance with reason (for by this man is man). And whatever is in accordance with the Lord's Divine wisdom belongs also to His Divine providence.

124. To this I will add two arcana of angelic wisdom, from which it can be seen what the Divine providence is: first, that the Lord in no wise acts upon any particular thing in man singly without acting simultaneously upon all things; secondly, that the Lord acts from inmosts and from outmosts simultaneously. *The Lord in no wise acts upon any particular thing in man singly without acting simultaneously upon all things of man,* for the reason that all things of man are in such connection, and through this connection in such a form that they do not act as many but as a one. It is acknowledged that in respect to his body man is in such a connection, and through this connection in such a form. The human mind also is in a like form from a connection of all things in it; for the human mind is the spiritual man, and is actually the man. From this it is that man's spirit, which is his mind in his body, is in its entire form a man; consequently man after death is just as much a man as he was in the world, with this difference only, that he has cast off the coverings that formed his body in the world. [2] Since, then, the human form is such that all the parts make a general whole, which acts as one, it follows that one part cannot be moved out of its place and changed in state except with the consent of the rest; for if one were removed from its place and changed in state, the form which acts as one would suffer. This makes clear that the Lord in no wise acts upon any particular thing without acting simultaneously upon all. Thus does the Lord act upon the entire angelic heaven, since the entire angelic heaven in the Lord's sight is as one man. Thus, too, does He act upon each angel, because each angel is a heaven in the least form. Thus also does He act upon each man, primarily upon all things of his mind, and through these upon all things of his body; for the mind of man is his spirit, and in the measure of its conjunction with the Lord is an angel, while the body is obedience. [3] But it should be clearly understood that the Lord also acts upon every particular in man singly, and even most singly, but simultaneously through all things of his form; and yet He does not change the state of any part or of any particular thing except harmoniously with the whole form. But on this more will be said in what follows; where it will be shown that the Lord's Divine providence is universal because it is in particulars, and that it is particular because it is universal. [4] *The Lord acts from inmosts and from outmosts simultaneously.* This is true for the reason that in this and in no other way can all things and each thing be held together in connection; for intermediates are connected in unbroken series from inmosts even to outmosts, and in outmosts they are together; for in the outmost there is a simultaneous presence of all things from the first, as has been shown in Part Third of the work on *The Divine Love and the Divine Wisdom.* It was for this reason also that the Lord from eternity, or Jehovah, came into the world, and there put on and assumed Humanity in outmosts, that He might be from firsts and in outmosts together; and thus from firsts through outmosts might rule the whole world and thereby save the men whom He is able to save in accordance with the laws of His Divine providence, which are also the laws of His Divine wisdom. And thus it is, as acknowledged in the Christian world, that no mortal could have been saved unless the Lord had come into the world (see the

7

Doctrine of the New Jerusalem concerning Faith, n. 35). And
this is why the Lord is called "The First and the Last."

125. These angelic arcana have been premised to make com-
prehensible the operation of the Lord's Divine providence in
conjoining man with the Lord, and the Lord with man. This
operation is not upon any particular of man by itself, except as
it is simultaneously upon all things of man; and this is done
from his inmost and from his outmosts simultaneously. The
inmost of man is his life's love; his outmosts are the things
that are in the external of his thought; and his intermediates
are the things that are in the internal of his thought. The
quality of these in the evil man has already been shown. From
this again it is clear that the Lord cannot act from inmosts and
outmosts simultaneously except in connection with man, for in
outmosts man and the Lord are together, consequently as man
acts in outmosts, which are under his control, being within the
realm of his freedom, so the Lord acts from man's inmosts and
upon the unbroken series to outmosts. The things that are in
man's inmosts and in the series from inmosts to outmosts are
wholly unknown to man; and therefore he knows nothing whatever of the way in which the Lord works there or what He
does; but as these things are so closely connected as to be
a one with outmosts it is unnecessary for man to know more
than that he must shun evils as sins and look to the Lord. In
this and in no other way can his life's love, which from birth
is infernal, be put away by the Lord, and a heavenly life's love
be implanted in its place.

126. When a heavenly life's love has been implanted by the
Lord in place of an infernal life's love, affections for good and
truth are implanted in place of the lusts of evil and falsity;
and the enjoyments of affections for good are implanted in
place of the enjoyments of the lusts of evil and falsity; and
the goods of heavenly love are implanted in place of the evils
of infernal love. Then prudence is implanted in place of cunning, and wise thoughts in place of crafty thoughts. Thus man
is born again and becomes a new man. What kinds of good

succeed in place of evils can be seen in the *Doctrine of Life for the New Jerusalem* (n. 67–73, 74–79, 80–86, 87–91); also that so far as a man shuns and turns away from evils as sins he loves the truths of wisdom (n. 32–41); and so far he has faith and is spiritual (n. 42–52).

127. It has been shown above from the exhortations read in all Christian churches before the holy communion that the common religion of the whole Christian world teaches that man must examine himself, see his sins, acknowledge them, confess them before God, and refrain from them; and that this is repentance, remission of sins, and consequently salvation. This can be seen also from the Faith that takes its name from Athanasius, and that has been accepted in the whole Christian world; at the end of which are these words:—

The Lord will come to judge the living and dead; at whose coming those that have done good shall enter into life eternal, and those that have done evil into eternal fire.

128. Who does not know from the Word that a life after death is allotted to every one according to his deeds? Open the Word, read it, and you will see this clearly; but while doing this, exclude from your thoughts faith and justification by it alone. As evidence that the Lord teaches this everywhere in His Word, take these few examples:—

Every tree that bringeth not forth good fruit is hewn down and cast into the fire. Therefore by their fruits ye shall know them (*Matt.* vii. 19, 20).

Many will say to Me in that day, Lord, have we not prophesied by Thy name, and in Thy name done many mighty works? And then will I profess unto them, I do not know you; depart from Me, ye that work iniquity (*Matt.* vii. 22, 23).

Every one that heareth My words and doeth them, I will liken him to a prudent man who built his house upon a rock; and every one that heareth these sayings of Mine and doeth them not, shall be likened unto a foolish man who built his house upon the ground without a foundation (*Matt.* vii. 24, 26; *Luke* vi. 46–49).

[2] The Son of man shall come in the glory of His Father, and then He shall render unto every man according to his deeds (*Matt.* xvi. 27).

The kingdom of God shall be taken away from you and shall be given to a nation bringing forth the fruits thereof (*Matt.* xxi. 43).

Jesus said, My mother and My brethren are these who hear the Word of God and do it (*Luke* viii. 21).

Then shall ye begin to stand without and to knock at the door, saying, Lord, open unto us; but He shall answer and say to them, I know ye not whence ye are; depart from Me, all ye workers of iniquity (*Luke* xiii. 25–27).

They that have done good shall go forth unto the resurrection of life, and they that have done evil unto the resurrection of judgment (*John* v. 29).

[**3**] We know that God heareth not sinners; but if anyone worship God and do His will, him He heareth (*John* ix. 31).

If ye know these things, blessed are ye if ye do them (*John* xiii. 17).

He that hath My commandments and doeth them, he it is that loveth Me, and I will love him and will come to him, and make My abode with him (*John* xiv. 15, 21–24).

Ye are My friends if ye do whatsoever I command you. I have chosen you that ye may bring forth fruit, and that your fruit may abide (*John* xv. 14, 16).

[**4**] The Lord said to John, To the angel of the Ephesian church write, I know thy works; I have against thee that thou hast left thy first charity. Repent, and do the first works; if not I will remove thy lampstand out of its place (*Apoc.* ii. 1, 2, 4, 5).

To the angel of the church of the Smyrneans write, I know thy works (*Apoc.* ii. 8, 9).

To the angel of the church at Pergamum write, I know thy works, repent (*Apoc.* ii. 12, 13, 16).

To the angel of the church in Thyatira write, I know thy works and charity, and thy last works to be more than the first (*Apoc.* ii. 18, 19).

To the angel of the church in Sardis write, I know thy works, that thou hast a name and that thou livest, and art dead. I have not found thy works perfect before God; repent (*Apoc.* iii. 1–3).

To the angel of the church in Philadelphia write, I know thy works (*Apoc.* iii. 7, 8).

To the angel of the church of the Laodiceans write, I know thy works; repent (*Apoc.* iii. 14, 15, 19).

I heard a voice from heaven saying, Write, Blessed are the dead who die in the Lord from henceforth; their works do follow them (*Apoc.* xiv. 13).

A book was opened, which is the book of life; and the dead were judged, all according to their works (*Apoc.* xx. 12, 13).

Behold, I come quickly; and My reward is with Me, to give to every man according to his work (*Apoc.* xxii. 12).

Thus far the New Testament. [5] Still more numerous are the evidences in the Old Testament, from which I will quote this one only:—

Stand in the gate of Jehovah, and proclaim there this word, Thus saith Jehovah of Hosts, the God of Israel: Amend your ways and your doings; trust ye not in lying words, saying, The temple of Jehovah, the temple of Jehovah, the temple of Jehovah are these. Will ye steal, murder, and commit adultery, and swear falsely, and then come and stand before Me in this house, upon which My name is named, and say, We are delivered, while ye do these abominations? Is this house become a den of robbers? Behold I, even I, have seen it, saith Jehovah (*Jer.* vii. 2–4, 9–11).

IT IS A LAW OF THE DIVINE PROVIDENCE THAT MAN SHOULD NOT BE COMPELLED BY EXTERNAL MEANS TO THINK AND WILL, AND THUS TO BELIEVE AND LOVE, THE THINGS OF RELIGION, BUT SHOULD GUIDE HIMSELF, AND SOMETIMES COMPEL HIMSELF.

129. This law of the Divine providence follows from the two preceding, namely, that man should act from freedom in accordance with reason (n. 71–99); and that he should do this from himself and yet from the Lord, therefore as if from himself (n. 100–128). And as being compelled is not from freedom in accordance with reason, and not from oneself, but is from what is not freedom, and from another, so this law of the Divine providence follows in order after the two former. Everyone admits, moreover, that it is impossible to compel any one to think what he is not willing to think, and to will what his thought forbids him to will, thus to believe what he does not believe, and wholly so what he is unwilling to believe; or to love what he does not love, and wholly so what he is unwilling to love. For a man's spirit or mind has full liberty in thinking, willing, believing, and loving. It has this liberty by influx from the spiritual world, which does not compel (for man's spirit or mind is in that world), and not by influx from the natural world, which is received only when it acts in harmony with spiritual influx. [2] A man may be forced to say that he thinks and wills and believes and loves the things of religion; but he does not think, will, believe, and love them unless they are matters of affection and consequent reason with him, or come to be so. Also, a man may be compelled to speak in favor of religion and to do what it inculcates; but he cannot be compelled to favor it in his thought from any belief in it, or to favor it in his will from any love for it. Moreover, in kingdoms where justice and judgment are guarded, men are compelled not to speak against religion, and to do nothing in opposition to it, and yet no one can be compelled to favor it in his thought and will. For it is within every one's freedom to think in harmony with hell and to will in favor of hell, and also to favor heaven in thought and will. But the reason teaches what hell is and what heaven is, and what the abiding condition is in the one and in the other; and it is from the reason that the will has its preference and choice. [3] From all this it can be seen that the external can not compel the internal. Nevertheless, this is sometimes done; but that it is pernicious will be shown in this order:—

(1) No one is reformed by miracles and signs, because they compel.

(2) No one is reformed by visions or by conversations with the dead, because they compel.

(3) No one is reformed by threats and punishments, because they compel.

(4) No one is reformed in states that do not spring from rationality and liberty.

(5) To compel oneself is not contrary to rationality and liberty.

(6) The external man must be reformed by means of the internal, and not the reverse.

130. (1) *No one is reformed by miracles and signs, because they compel.* It has been shown above that man has an internal and an external of thought, and that the Lord flows into

man through the internal of thought into its external, and thus
teaches and leads him; also that it is of the Lord's Divine
providence that man should act from freedom in accordance
with reason. Both of these would perish in man if miracles
were wrought and man were thereby driven to believe. That
this is true can be seen rationally in this way. It cannot be denied that miracles induce a belief and powerfully persuade that
what is said and taught by him who does the miracles is true,
and that this at first so occupies man's external thought as to
bind and fascinate it, as it were. But by this man is deprived
of his two faculties called rationality and liberty, and thus of
the ability to act from freedom in accordance with reason; and
then the Lord can no longer flow in through the internal into
the external of his thought, except merely to leave the man to
confirm by his rationality what he has been made through the
miracle to believe. [2] The state of man's thought is such as
to enable him from the internal of his thought to see any matter in the external of his thought as in a sort of mirror; for,
as has been said above, a man is able to see his own thought,
which would not be possible except from a more internal
thought. And when he thus sees a matter as in a mirror he
can turn it this way and that, and shape it until it appears to
him beautiful; and if the matter is a truth it may be likened
to a virgin or a youth, beautiful and living. But when one
cannot turn it this way and that, and shape it, but can simply
believe it from the persuasion induced by the miracle, it may
be likened, if it is a truth, to a virgin or a youth carved from
stone or wood, in which there is no life. It may also be likened to an object that is constantly before the sight, and being
alone seen conceals every thing that is on either side of it and
behind it. Or it may be likened to a sound continually in the
ear that takes away the perception of harmony from many
sounds. Such blindness and deafness are induced on the human mind by miracles. It is the same with every thing confirmed that is not looked into with some rationality before it
is confirmed.

131. From all this it can be seen that a faith induced by miracles is not faith but persuasion; for there is nothing rational in it, still less anything spiritual; for it is only an external without an internal. The same is true of every thing that a man does from such a persuasive faith, whether he acknowledges God, worships Him at home or in churches, or does good deeds. When a miracle alone leads a man to acknowledgment, worship, and piety, he acts from the natural man and not from the spiritual. For a miracle imparts faith through an external way and not through an internal way, thus from the world and not from heaven; and the Lord enters into man through no other than an internal way, which is through the Word, and doctrine and preachings from the Word. And as miracles close this way, at this day no miracles are wrought.

132. That miracles are such can be seen very clearly from the miracles wrought before the people of Judah and Israel. Although these had seen so many miracles in the land of Egypt, and afterwards at the Red Sea, and others in the desert, and especially on Mount Sinai when the law was promulgated, yet only a month afterwards, while Moses tarried on that mountain, they made themselves a golden calf and acknowledged it as Jehovah who led them forth out of the land of Egypt (*Exod.* xxxii. 4–6). So again, from the miracles afterwards wrought in the land of Canaan; and yet the people relapsed so many times from the prescribed worship. And again, from the miracles that the Lord wrought before them when He was in the world; and yet they crucified Him. [2] Miracles were wrought among them because the men of Judah and Israel were wholly external men, and were led into the land of Canaan merely that they might represent the church and its internals by means of the externals of worship, a bad man equally with a good man being able to represent; for externals are rituals, and all of their externals were significative of spiritual and celestial things. Aaron even, although he made the golden calf and commanded the worship of it (*Exod.* xxxii.

2–5, 35), could represent the Lord and His work of salvation.
And because they could not be brought by the internals of
worship to represent those things they were brought to it and
even driven and forced to it by miracles. [3] They could not
be brought to it by the internals of worship because they did
not acknowledge the Lord, although the whole Word that was
in their possession treats of Him alone; and he that does not
acknowledge the Lord is unable to receive any internal of
worship. But when the Lord had manifested Himself, and
had been received and acknowledged in the churches as the
eternal God, miracles ceased.

133. But the effect of miracles on the good and on the evil
is different. The good do not desire miracles, but they believe
in the miracles recorded in the Word. And when they hear
anything about a miracle they give thought to it only as an
argument of no great weight that confirms their faith; for
they think from the Word, thus from the Lord, and not from
the miracle. It is not so with the evil. They may be driven
and compelled to a belief by miracles, and even to worship and
piety, but only for a short time; for their evils are shut in;
and the lusts of their evils and the enjoyments therefrom continually act upon their external of worship and piety; and in
order to get out of their confinement and break away they
reflect upon the miracle, and at length call it a trick or artifice,
or a work of nature, and thus go back to their evils. And he
who returns to his evils after he has worshiped profanes the
goods and truths of worship; and the lot after death of those
who commit profanation is the worst of all. Such as these are
meant by the Lord's words (*Matt.* xii. 43–45), that their last
state becomes worse than the first. Furthermore, if it is need-
ful to work miracles for the sake of those who do not believe
from miracles in the Word, they must be wrought for all such
continually and visibly. All this makes clear why miracles
are not wrought at this day.

134a. (2) *No one is reformed by visions or by conversations
with the dead, because they compel.* Visions are of two kinds,

Divine and diabolical. Divine visions are produced by means of representations in heaven, and diabolical visions by means of magic in hell. There are also fantastic visions, which are delusions of an abstracted mind. *Divine visions*, which are produced (as has been said) by means of representations in heaven, are such as the prophets had, who were not in the body but in the spirit when they were in these visions; for visions can not appear to any one in the waking states of the body. When, therefore, they appear to the prophets they are said to have been "in the spirit," as is evident from the passages that follow. *Ezekiel* says:—

Moreover, the spirit lifted me up, and brought me in the vision of God, in the spirit of God, into Chaldea, to them of the captivity. So the vision that I had seen went up over me (xi. 1, 24).

Again, that the spirit lifted him up between the earth and the heaven, and brought him in the visions of God to Jerusalem (viii. 3, *seq.*).

In like manner he was in the vision of God or in the spirit when he saw the four living creatures which were cherubim (i. and x.).

As also when he saw the new temple and the new earth, and the angel measuring them (xl.–xlviii.).

That he was then in the visions of God he says (xl. 2, 26); and in the spirit (xliii. 5). [2] In a like state was Zechariah,

When he saw a man riding among the myrtle trees (*Zech.* i. 8, *seq.*);

When he saw four horns (i. 18); and a man in whose hand was a measuring line (ii. 1–3, *seq.*);

When he saw a lampstand and two olive trees (iv. 1, *seq.*);

When he saw the flying roll and the ephah (v. 1, 6);

When he saw four chariots coming out from between two mountains, and horses (vi. 1, *seq.*).

In a like state was Daniel,

When he saw four beasts coming up from the sea (*Dan.* vii. 1, *seq.*);

When he saw the combat between a ram and a he-goat (viii. 1, *seq.*).

That he saw these things in the vision of his spirit is stated (vii. 1, 2, 7, 13; viii. 2; x. 1, 7, 8); and that the angel Gabriel was seen by him in vision (ix. 21). [3] John, also, was in the vision of the spirit when he saw what he described in the *Apocalypse:*—

As when he saw seven lampstands, and in their midst the Son of man (i. 12–16);

When he saw a throne in heaven, and One sitting upon the throne, and four animals which were cherubim round about it (iv.);

When he saw the book of life taken by the Lamb (v.);

When he saw horses going out from the book (vi.);

When he saw seven angels with trumpets (viii.);

When he saw the pit of the abyss opened, and locusts going out of it (ix.);

When he saw the dragon, and its combat with Michael (xii.);

When he saw two beasts, one rising up out of the sea and the other out of the earth (xiii.);

When he saw a woman sitting upon a scarlet colored beast (xvii.);

And Babylon destroyed (xviii.);

When he saw a white horse and Him who sat upon it (xix.);

And when he saw the new heaven and the new earth; and the Holy Jerusalem coming down out of heaven (xxi.).

And when he saw the river of the water of life (xxii.).

That he saw these things in the vision of the spirit is said (i. 10; iv. 2; v. 1; vi. 1; xxi. 1, 2). [4] Such were the visions that appeared to them from heaven, not before the sight of the body but before the sight of the spirit. Such visions do not take place at the present day; if they did they would not be understood, because they are produced by means of representations, each one of which is significative of the internal things of the church and the arcana of heaven. Moreover, it was foretold by *Daniel* (ix. 24) that they would cease when the Lord came into the world. But *diabolical visions* have sometimes appeared, induced by enthusiastic and visionary spirits, who from the delirium that possessed them called themselves the Holy Spirit. But these spirits have now been gathered up by the Lord and cast into a hell separate from the hells of others. All this makes clear that by no other visions than those in the Word can one be reformed. There are also *fantastic visions :* but these are mere delusions of an abstracted mind.

134b. That no one is reformed by conversations with the dead is evident from the Lord's words respecting the rich man in hell and Lazarus in Abraham's bosom; for the rich man said :—

I pray thee, father Abraham, that thou wouldst send Lazarus to my father's house, for I have five brethren, that he may testify unto them, lest they also come unto this place of torment. Abraham said unto him, They have Moses and the Prophets, let them hear them. But he said, Nay, father Abraham, but if one come to them from the dead they will repent. He answered him, If they hear not Moses and the Prophets, neither will they be persuaded if one rise from the dead (*Luke* xvi. 27–31).

Conversation with the dead would have the same effect as miracles, of which just above, namely, man would be persuaded and forced into a state of worship for a short time. But as man is thus deprived of rationality, and at the same time evils are shut in, as said above, this spell or internal bond is loosed, and the evils that have been shut in break out, with blasphemy and profanation. But this takes place only when some dogma of religion has been imposed upon the mind by spirits, which is never done by any good spirit, still less by any angel of heaven.

135. Nevertheless, conversation with spirits is possible (though rarely with the angels of heaven); and this has been granted to many for ages back. And when it is granted the spirits speak with man in his mother tongue, and only a few words. But those who speak by the Lord's permission never say any thing that takes away the freedom of the reason, nor do they teach; for the Lord alone teaches man, but mediately by means of the Word when in a state of enlightenment, of which hereafter. That this is true it has been granted me to know by personal experience. For several years I have talked with spirits and with angels; nor has any spirit dared or any angel wished to tell me any thing, still less to instruct me, about any matter in the Word, or about any matter of doctrine from the Word; but I have been taught by the Lord alone, who was revealed to me, and who has since appeared and now appears constantly before my eyes as a Sun in which He is, in the same way that He appears to the angels, and has enlightened me.

136. (3) *No one is reformed by threats and punishments, because they compel.* It is admitted that the external cannot compel the internal, but that the internal can compel the external; also that the internal is so averse to compulsion by the external that it turns itself away. It is also admitted that external enjoyments allure the internal to consent and love; and it may be known that a compelled internal and a free internal are possible. But although all these things are admitted they nevertheless need illustration; for many things when they are heard, being true, are at once perceived to be so, and are therefore assented to; but unless they are also corroborated by reasons they may be disproved by arguments from fallacies, and at last denied. Therefore the things just stated as admitted must be taken up and rationally confirmed. [2] First: *The external cannot compel the internal, but the internal can compel the external.* Who can be compelled to believe and to love? One can no more be compelled to believe than to think that a thing is so when he thinks that it is not so; and one can no more be compelled to love than to will what he does not will; for belief belongs to thought, and love belongs to the will. But the internal may be compelled by the external not to speak ill of the laws of the kingdom, the moralities of life, and the sanctities of the church; thus far the internal may be compelled by threats and punishments; and it is so compelled and ought to be. This internal, however, is not the strictly human internal, but is an internal that man has in common with beasts; and beasts can be compelled. The human internal has its seat above this animal internal. It is this human internal that is here meant, and that cannot be compelled. [3] Secondly: *The internal is so averse to compulsion by the external that it turns itself away.* This is because the internal wishes to be in freedom, and loves freedom, for freedom belongs to man's love or life, as has been shown above; consequently when freedom feels itself to be compelled it withdraws as it were within itself and turns itself away, and looks upon compulsion as its enemy; for the love that constitutes man's life is irritated, and causes the man to think that in this respect he is not his own, and therefore does not live for himself. Man's internal is such from the law of the Lord's Divine providence that man should act from freedom in accordance with reason. [4] From this it is clear that to compel men to Divine worship by threats and punishments is pernicious. But there are some who suffer themselves to be compelled in respect to religion, and some who do not. Of those who suffer themselves to be so compelled there are many within the papal jurisdiction; but this takes place with those in whose worship there is nothing internal, but all is external. Of those who do not suffer themselves to be compelled there are many of the English nation; and as a consequence of this there is in their worship an internal, and what there is in the external is from their internal. In regard to their religion their interiors appear in spiritual light like bright clouds; while the interiors of the former, in respect to religion, appear in the light of heaven like dark clouds. These appearances are presented to sight in the spiritual world, and will be seen by any one who wishes to see them when he comes into that world after death. Furthermore, compelled worship shuts in evils, which evils then lie hidden like fire in wood under ashes, which is continually kindling and spreading till it breaks out in flames; while worship not compelled, but spontaneous, does not shut evils in, and in consequence they are like fires that blaze up quickly and are gone. All this makes clear that the internal is so averse to compulsion that it turns itself away. The internal can compel the external, because the internal is like a master, and the external like a servant. [5] Thirdly: *External enjoyments allure the internal to consent, and also to love.* There are two kinds of enjoyments, enjoyments of the understanding and enjoyments of the will; those of the understanding are also enjoyments of wisdom, and those of the will are also enjoyments of love; for wisdom belongs to the understanding, and love to the will. And inasmuch as the enjoyments of the body and its senses, which are external enjoyments, act as one with the internal enjoyments which belong to the understanding and the will, it follows that while the internal is so averse to compulsion by the external as to turn itself away from it, it also looks with such favor on enjoyments in the external as even to turn itself to it; thus on the part of the understanding there is consent, and on the part of the will there is love. [6] In the spiritual world all children are led by the Lord into angelic wisdom, and through that into heavenly love, by means of things enjoyable and pleasing; first by means of beautiful things in their homes, and by means of pleasing things in gardens; then by means of representatives of spiritual things, which affect the interiors of their minds with pleasure; and finally by means of truths of wisdom, and so by means of goods of love. Thus this is done continuously by means of enjoyments in their order; first by means of the enjoyments of the love of the understanding and of its wisdom; and finally by the enjoyments of the will's love, which becomes their life's love; and to this all other things that have entered by means of enjoyments are held subordinate. [7] This takes place because everything of the understanding and will must be formed by means of what is external before it is formed by the means of what is internal; since everything of the understanding and will is first formed by means of what enters through the senses of the body, especially through the sight and hearing; and when the first understanding and first will have been formed, the internal of thought looks upon these as the externals of its thought, and either conjoins itself with them or separates itself from them. It conjoins itself with them if they are delightful to it, and it separates itself from them if they are not. [8] But it must be clearly understood that the internal of the understanding does not conjoin itself with the internal of the will, but that the internal of the will conjoins itself with the internal of the understanding, and makes the conjunction to be reciprocal; but this is done by the internal of the will, and not in the least by the internal of the understanding. This is the reason why man cannot be reformed by means of faith alone, but only by means of the will's love, which makes a faith for itself. [9] Fourthly: *A compelled internal and a free internal are possible.* A compelled internal is possible in such as are in external worship only and in no internal worship; for their internal consists in thinking and willing that to which the external is compelled. Such is the state of those who worship men living and dead, and thus worship idols, and whose faith is based on miracles. In such no internal is possible except what is at the same time external. A compelled internal is also possible in such as are in the internal of worship. It may be an internal compelled by fear or an internal compelled by love. Those have an internal compelled by fear who are in worship from a fear of the torment of hell and its fire. Such an internal, however, is not the internal of thought before treated of, but is the external of thought, and is here called an internal because it belongs to thought. The internal of thought before treated of cannot be compelled by any fear; but it can be compelled by love and by a fear of losing love. In its true sense the fear of God is nothing else. To be compelled by love and a fear of losing it is to compel oneself. That compelling oneself is not contrary to liberty and rationality will be seen below.

137. All this makes clear what compelled worship is and what worship not compelled is. Compelled worship is corporeal, lifeless, darkened, and sad; corporeal because it is of the body and not of the mind, lifeless because there is no life in it, darkened because there is no understanding in it, and sad because there is no enjoyment of heaven in it. But worship not compelled, when it is genuine, is spiritual, living, clear, and joyful; spiritual because there is spirit from the Lord in it, living because there is life from the Lord in it, clear because there is wisdom from the Lord in it, and joyful because there is heaven from the Lord in it.

138. (4) *No one is reformed in states that do not spring from rationality and liberty.* It has been shown above that nothing is appropriated to man except what he does from freedom in accordance with reason. This is because freedom belongs to the will and reason to the understanding; and when man acts from freedom in accordance with reason he acts from the will by means of his understanding; and whatever is done in a conjunction of these two is appropriated. Since, then, it is the Lord's will that man should be reformed and regenerated, that he may have eternal life or the life of heaven, and no one can be reformed and regenerated unless good is so appropriated to his will as to be as if it were his, and truth is so appropriated to his understanding as to be as if it were his, and since nothing can be appropriated to any one except what is done from freedom of the will in accordance with the reason of the understanding, it follows that no one is reformed in states that do not spring from liberty and rationality. These states are many, but in general they may be referred to the following, namely: *states of fear, of misfortune, of disordered mind, of bodily disease, of ignorance, and of blindness of the understanding.* Something shall be said of each state in particular.

139. No one is reformed in a *state of fear,* because fear takes away freedom and reason, or liberty and rationality; for while love opens the interiors of the mind fear closes them; and when they are closed man thinks but little, and only of what then presents itself to the mind or the senses. Such is the effect of all fears that take possession of the mind. [2] It has been shown above that man has an internal and an external of thought; fear can in no wise take possession of the internal of thought; this is always in freedom because in its life's love; but it can take possession of the external of thought, and when it does this the internal of thought is closed; and when that is closed man can no longer act from freedom in accordance with his reason, and therefore cannot be reformed. [3] The fear that takes possession of the external of thought and closes the internal is chiefly a fear of the loss of honor or gain. The internal of thought is not closed by a fear of civil punishments or of external ecclesiastical punishments, because such laws only prescribe penalties for those who speak and act contrary to the civil interests of the kingdom and the spiritual interests of the church, and not for those who merely think in opposition to them. [4] A fear of infernal

8

punishments may take possession of the external of thought, but only for a few moments or hours or days; it is soon brought back to its freedom from the internal of thought, which belongs strictly to its spirit and its life's love, and is called the thought of the heart. [5] But a fear of the loss of honor and gain takes possession of the external of man's thought; and when it does this it closes the internal of thought from above against influx from heaven, and makes it impossible for man to be reformed. This is because every man's life's love from his birth is a love of self and the world; and the love of self makes one with the love of honor, and the love of the world makes one with the love of gain. When, therefore, a man has gained honor or wealth, from a fear of losing them he strengthens with himself the means that are serviceable to him for honor and gain, whether civil or ecclesiastical, both of which are means of power. One who has not yet gained honor and wealth does the like if he desires them; but he does it from a fear of the loss of reputation on their account. [6] It is said that that fear takes possession of the external of thought, and closes the internal from above against the influx from heaven. The internal is said to be closed when it completely makes one with the external, for it is not then in itself but in the external. [7] But inasmuch as the loves of self and the world are infernal loves, and are the fountain heads of all evils, it is clear what the internal of thought is in itself in those in whom these loves are the loves of the life, or in whom these loves rule, namely, that it is full of the lusts of evils of every kind. This is not known to those who from a fear of the loss of dignity and wealth are strongly persuaded respecting the religion they accept, especially if the religion involves their worship as deities, and also as having supreme power over hell. Such may seem to be in a blaze of zeal for the salvation of souls, and yet this may be from an infernal fire. As such a fear especially takes away rationality itself and liberty itself, which are heavenly in their origin, it is evidently a hindrance to man's ability to be reformed.

140. No one is reformed in a *state of misfortune*, if he thinks of God and implores His aid only in that state, because that is a compelled state; consequently as soon as he comes into a free state he goes back to his former state, in which he had thought little or nothing about God. It is otherwise with those who in their former free state had feared God. By "fearing God" is meant fearing to offend Him, "offending God" meaning to sin. This fear is not a matter of fear but of love, for when one loves another does he not fear to do him wrong? And does he not fear this the more, the more he loves? Without such a fear love is insipid and superficial, a mere matter of the thought and not at all of the will. By "states of misfortune" are meant states of despair from danger, as in battles, duels, shipwrecks, falls, fires, threatened or unexpected loss of wealth or of office and thus of honors, and other like things. To think of God only when in such dangers is not from God but from self. For the mind is then as it were imprisoned in the body; thus not at liberty, and therefore not in rationality; and apart from these no reformation is possible.

141. No one is reformed in *unhealthy mental states*, because these take away rationality, and consequently the freedom to act in accordance with reason. For the mind may be sick and unsound; and while a sound mind is rational a sick mind is not. Such unhealthy mental states are melancholy, a spurious or false conscience, hallucinations of various kinds, grief of mind from misfortunes, and anxieties and mental suffering from a vitiated condition of the body. These are sometimes regarded as temptations, but they are not. For genuine temptations have as their objects things spiritual, and in these the mind is wise; but these states have as their objects natural things, and in these the mind is unhealthy.

142. No one is reformed in a *state of bodily disease*, because the reason is not then in a free state; for the state of the mind depends upon the state of the body. When the body is sick the mind is also sick, because of its separation from the world if for no other reason. For when the mind is removed from

the world it may think about God, but not from God, for it
does not possess freedom of reason. Man has freedom of reason by his being midway between heaven and the world, and
by his ability to think from heaven or from the world, also
from heaven about the world, or from the world about heaven.
So when a man is sick, and is thinking about death and the
state of his soul after death, he is not in the world; but in
spirit he is withdrawn; and in this state alone no one can be
reformed; but if before he fell sick he had been reformed this
can then be strengthened. [2] It is the same with those who
give up the world and all business there, and give themselves
solely to thoughts about God, heaven, and salvation; but of
this more elsewhere. As a consequence, if these persons had
not been reformed before their sickness, if they die they afterwards become such as they were before the sickness. It is
therefore vain to think that any can repent or receive any faith
during sickness, for in such repentance there is nothing of action, and in such faith nothing of charity; thus both belong
wholly to the lips and not at all to the heart.

143. No one is reformed in a *state of ignorance*, because all
reformation is effected by means of truths and a life according
to them; consequently those who are ignorant of truths cannot be reformed; but if they desire truths from an affection for
truths, after death in the spiritual world they are reformed.

144. Neither can any one be reformed in a *state of blindness
of the understanding*. These, too, are ignorant of truths, and
consequently of life; for the understanding must teach truths,
and the will must do them; and when the will does what the
understanding teaches its life comes into harmony with the
truths. But when the understanding is blinded the will also
is closed up; and from a freedom that is in accord with its
reason it does only the evil that has been confirmed in the understanding, which is falsity. The understanding is blinded
not only by ignorance but also by a religion that teaches a
blind faith, also by false doctrine. For as truths open the understanding so falsities close it; they close it above but open it

below; and an understanding that is opened only below cannot
see truths, but can merely confirm whatever it wills, especially
falsity. The understanding is also blinded by the lusts of evil.
As long as the will is in these it moves the understanding to
confirm them; and so far as the lusts of evil are confirmed
the will cannot be in affections for good and to see truths from
them, and thus be reformed. [2] When one, for example, is
in the lust of adultery, his will, which is in the enjoyment of
his love, moves his understanding to confirm it, saying, "What
is adultery? Is there anything wicked in it? Is there not a
like thing between husband and wife? Cannot offspring be
born from adultery as well as from marriage? Cannot a woman
admit more than one without harm? What has the spiritual
to do with this?" So thinks the understanding that is then
the will's harlot, and that has become so stupid from debauch-
ery with the will as to be unable to see that conjugial love is
the spiritual heavenly love itself, an image of love of the Lord
and of the church, and derived from that love, and thus is in
itself holy, is chastity itself, purity, and innocence; also that it
makes men to be loves in form, since consorts can love each
other mutually from inmosts, and thus form themselves into
loves; while adultery destroys this form, and with it the image
of the Lord, and, what is horrible, the adulterer mingles his
life with the husband's life in his wife, since a man's life is in
his seed. [3] Because this is profane hell is called adultery,
and heaven on the other hand is called marriage. Moreover,
the love of adultery communicates with the lowest hell, while
love truly conjugial communicates with the inmost heaven;
and the organs of generation in either sex correspond to societies of the inmost heaven. All this has been presented to make
known how blinded the understanding is when the will is in
the lust of evil; and that no man can be reformed in a state of
blindness of the understanding.

145. (5) *To compel oneself is not contrary to rationality and
liberty.* It has been shown already that man has an internal
of thought and an external of thought, and that these are dis-

tinct like what is prior and what is posterior, or like what is
higher and what is lower; and because they are so distinct
they can act separately and can act conjointly. These act
separately when from the external of his thought a man speaks
and acts in one way while interiorly he thinks and wills in another way; and these act conjointly when a man speaks and
acts as he interiorly thinks and wills. The latter is generally
true of the sincere, the former of the insincere. [2] Inasmuch
as the internal and the external of the mind are so distinct,
the internal can even fight with the external, and can force it
by combat into compliance. Combat arises when a man thinks
that evils are sins and therefore resolves to refrain from them;
for when he refrains a door is opened, and when it is opened
the Lord casts out the lusts of evil that have occupied the internal of thought, and implants affections for good in their
place. This is done in the internal of thought. But as the
enjoyments of the lusts of evil that occupy the external of
thought cannot be cast out at the same time, a combat arises
between the internal and the external of thought, the internal
wishing to cast out these enjoyments because they are enjoyments of evil and not in accord with the affections for good in
which the internal now is, and to bring in, in place of these
enjoyments of evil, enjoyments of good that are in accord.
The enjoyments of good are what are called goods of charity.
From this contrariety a combat arises; and when this becomes
severe it is called temptation. [3] Since, then, a man is a man
from the internal of his thought, for this is a man's very spirit,
it is clear that when a man compels the external of his thought
to acquiescence or to an acceptance of the enjoyments of his
affections, which are goods of charity, he is compelling himself.
This evidently is not contrary to rationality and liberty, but is
in accord with them, for rationality excites the combat and
liberty carries it on. Moreover, liberty itself with rationality
has its seat in the internal man, and from that in the external. [4] When, therefore, the internal conquers, as it does
when the internal has reduced the external to acquiescence

and compliance, the Lord gives man liberty itself and ration
ality itself; for the Lord then withdraws man from infernal
freedom, which in itself is slavery, and brings him into heavenly freedom, which is in itself real freedom, and bestows upon him fellowship with the angels. That those who are in sins
are servants, and that the Lord makes free those who accept
truths from Him through the Word He teaches in *John* (viii.
31–36).

146. This may be illustrated by the example of a man who
has had a sense of enjoyment in fraud and secret theft, and
who now sees and internally acknowledges that these are sins,
and therefore wishes to refrain from them. When he refrains
a combat of the internal man with the external arises. The
internal man has an affection for sincerity, while the external
still finds an enjoyment in defrauding; and as this enjoyment
is the direct opposite of the enjoyment of sincerity it only
gives way when it is compelled; and it can be compelled only
by combat. But when the victory has been gained the external man comes into the enjoyment of the love of what is sincere, which is charity ; afterwards the enjoyment of defrauding
gradually becomes unenjoyable to him. It is the same with
other sins, as with adultery and whoredom, revenge and hatred,
blasphemy, and lying. But the hardest struggle of all is with
the love of rule from the love of self. He who subdues this
easily subdues all other evil loves, for this is their head.

147. It shall also be stated briefly how the Lord casts out
the lusts of evil which occupy the internal man from birth,
and how He imparts in their stead affections for good whenever a man as if from himself puts away evils as sins. It has
been shown before that man has a natural mind, a spiritual
mind, and a celestial mind; and that so long as a man is in the
lusts of evil and in their enjoyments he is in the natural mind
alone, and the spiritual mind is closed. But as soon as a man
after examination acknowledges evils to be sins against God,
because they are contrary to Divine laws, and resolves in consequence to refrain from them, the Lord opens his spiritual

mind and enters into his natural mind through affections for truth and good, and He also enters into the rational, and from it arranges in order the things that are contrary to order below it in the natural. This is what appears to man as combat; and in those that have indulged much in the enjoyments of evil it appears as temptation, for there is grief of mind when the order of his thoughts is being reversed. And as there is a combat against the things that are in the man himself and that he feels to be his own, and as one can fight against himself only from an interior self and from freedom there, it follows that the internal man then fights against the external, and fights from freedom, and compels the external to obedience. This, therefore, is compelling one's self; and this, evidently, is not contrary to liberty and rationality, but in accordance with them.

148. Furthermore, every man wishes to be free, and to put away from himself non-freedom or servitude. Every boy subject to a teacher wishes to be his own master, and thus free; the same is true of every servant under his master, and every maidservant under her mistress. Every maiden wishes to leave her father's house and to marry, that she may act freely in her own house; every youth who desires employment or to be in business or to perform the duties of some office, while he is subject to others longs to be released, so as to be at his own disposal. All such who willingly serve for the sake of liberty compel themselves; and when they compel themselves they act from freedom in accordance with reason, but from an interior freedom, from which exterior freedom is looked upon as a servant. This has been presented to show that it is not contrary to rationality and liberty to compel oneself.

149. Man does not wish in like manner to come out of spiritual servitude into spiritual liberty, for the reason, first, that he does not know what spiritual servitude is and what spiritual liberty is; he does not possess the truths that teach this; and without truths, spiritual servitude is believed to be freedom, and spiritual freedom to be servitude. Another reason is that

the religion of the Christian world has closed up the under-standing, and faith alone has sealed it; for both of these have placed around themselves, like a wall of iron, the dogma that theological matters transcend the comprehension, and cannot therefore be reached by any exercise of the reason, and are for the blind, not for those that see. In this way have the truths been hidden that teach what spiritual liberty is. A third reason is, that few examine themselves and see their sins; and he who does not see his sins and refrain from them is in the freedom of sin, which is infernal freedom, in itself bondage; and from this to see heavenly freedom, which is freedom itself, is like seeing day when immersed in thick darkness, or like seeing what is from the sun above when under a dark cloud. For these reasons it is not known what heavenly freedom is, and that the difference between it and infernal freedom is like the difference between what is alive and what is dead.

150. (6) *The external man must be reformed by means of the internal, and not the reverse.* By the internal and external man the same is meant as by the internal and external of thought, which have been frequently defined above. The reformation of the external by means of the internal means that the internal flows into the external, and not the reverse. It is admitted in the learned world that there is an influx of the spiritual into the natural, and not the reverse; and it is admitted in the church that the internal man must be first cleansed and renewed and thereby the external. This is admitted because it is taught by the Lord and declared by the reason. It is taught by the Lord in these words :—

Woe unto you, hypocrites; for ye cleanse the outside of the cup and of the platter, but within they are full from extortion and excess. Thou blind Pharisee, cleanse first the inside of the cup and of the platter, that the outside of them may become clean also (*Matt.* xxiii. 25, 26).

[2] That reason declares this has been abundantly shown in the work on *The Divine Love and the Divine Wisdom.* For what the Lord teaches He gives man ability to perceive rationally, and this in two ways; in one, man sees in himself that a

thing is so as soon as he hears it; in the other, he understands it by means of reasons. His seeing it in himself is in his internal man; his understanding it by means of reasons is in the external man. Does not every one see it in himself when he hears that the internal man must be cleansed first, and the external by means of it? But one who does not receive a general idea of this subject by influx from heaven may be misled when he consults the external of his thought; from that alone no one sees otherwise than that the external works of charity and piety, apart from internal works, are what save. So in other things; as that sight and hearing flow into thought, and that smell and taste flow into perception, thus the external into the internal, when, nevertheless, the contrary is true. The appearance that things seen and heard flow into the thought is a fallacy; for it is the understanding that sees in the eye and hears in the ear, and not the reverse. So in everything else.

151. But it shall now be told briefly how the internal man is reformed, and the external by means of it. The internal man is not reformed merely by knowing, understanding, and being wise, consequently not by thought alone; but by willing that which knowledge, understanding, and wisdom teach. When a man from his knowledge, understanding, and wisdom sees that there is a heaven and a hell, and that all evil is from hell, and all good is from heaven, if he ceases to will evil because it is from hell, and wills good because it is from heaven, he is in the first stage of reformation, and is at the threshold from hell into heaven. When he goes further and wills to refrain from evils he is in the second stage of reformation, and is outside of hell, but not yet in heaven; he sees heaven above him. Man must have such an internal in order to be reformed; and yet he is not reformed unless the external is reformed as well as the internal. The external is reformed by means of the internal when the external refrains from the evils that the internal does not will because they are infernal, and still more when the external for this reason shuns evils and fights against them. Thus willing is the internal and doing is the external; for unless one does that which he wills there is within a failure to will, and finally the willing ceases. [2] From these few statements it can be seen how the external man is reformed by means of the internal. This is what is meant by the Lord's words to Peter :—

Jesus said, If I wash thee not thou hast no part with Me. Peter said unto Him, Lord, not my feet only, but also my hands and my head. Jesus said unto him, He that hath bathed needeth not save to wash his feet, but is clean every whit (*John* xiii. 8–10).

"To wash" means spiritual washing, which is to cleanse from evils; "washing the head and the hands" means to cleanse the internal man; and "washing the feet" means to cleanse the external man. That when the internal man has been cleansed the external must be cleansed is meant by this, "He that hath bathed needeth not save to wash his feet." That all cleansing from evils is from the Lord is meant by this, "If I wash thee not thou hast no part with Me." That among the Jews washing represented cleansing from evils, and this is what "washing" signifies in the Word, and "washing the feet" signifies the cleansing of the natural or external man, has been shown in the *Arcana Cœlestia*, in many places.

152. Since man has an internal and an external, and both must be reformed that the man may be reformed, and since no one can be reformed unless he examines himself, sees and acknowledges his evils, and afterwards refrains from them, it follows that not only the external but also the internal must be examined. If the external alone is examined, a man sees only what he has actually done, as that he has not committed murder, adultery, or theft, has not borne false witness; and so on. Thus he examines the evils of his body, and not the evils of his spirit. Nevertheless, one cannot be reformed unless the evils of the spirit are examined, for after death man lives a spirit, and all the evils that are in the spirit remain. The spirit is examined only by man's attending to his thoughts, especially his purposes, for purposes are thoughts from the will; that is where evils are in their origin and in their root,

that is, in their lusts and in their enjoyments; and unless
these are seen and acknowledged the man is still in evils, although in externals he has not committed them. That to think
from purpose is to will and to do is clear from the Lord's
words:—

Everyone that looketh on another's woman to lust after her hath committed adultery with her already in his heart (*Matt.* v. 28).

Such is the examination of the internal man, whereby the external man is essentially examined.

153. I have often wondered, that although it is known by
the whole Christian world that evils must be shunned as sins,
and that otherwise they are not remitted, and unless they are
remitted there is no salvation, yet this is known by scarcely
one among thousands. Inquiry was made about this in the
spiritual world, and it was found to be so. This is known by
everyone in the Christian world from the exhortations read
before those who come to the Holy Supper, for it is openly
declared in these; nevertheless when they are asked whether
they know this, they answer that they do not, and that they
have never known it. This is because they have not thought
about it, and because most of them have thought only of faith,
and of salvation by it alone. I have also wondered that faith
alone so closes the eyes that when those who have confirmed
themselves in it are reading the Word they see nothing that
is there said about love, charity, and works. It is as if they
had daubed faith over all things of the Word, as one might so
smear a manuscript with red lead that nothing underneath it
would appear. Or if anything does appear, it is absorbed by
faith and is said to be faith.

IT IS A LAW OF THE DIVINE PROVIDENCE THAT MAN SHOULD
BE LED AND TAUGHT BY THE LORD FROM HEAVEN BY
MEANS OF THE WORD AND BY MEANS OF DOCTRINE AND
PREACHINGS FROM THE WORD, AND THIS TO ALL APPEAR-
ANCE AS IF BY HIMSELF.

154. The appearance is that man is led and taught by himself; but the truth is that he is led and taught by the Lord
alone. Those who confirm in themselves the appearance and
not also the truth are unable to put away from themselves
evils as sins; but those who confirm in themselves both the
appearance and the truth are able to do so, for in appearance
it is man who puts away evils as sins, but in truth it is the
Lord. This latter class can be reformed, the former cannot.
[2] Those who confirm in themselves the appearance and not
also the truth are all interior idolaters, since they are worshipers of self and the world. If they have no religion they
become worshipers of nature and thus atheists; while if they
have a religion they become worshipers of men and also of
images. Such at the present day are meant by those described
in the first commandment of the Decalogue, who worship other
gods. But those who confirm in themselves both the appearance and the truth become worshipers of the Lord; for they
are raised up by the Lord out of what is their own (*proprium*),
which is in the appearance, and are brought into the light in
which is truth and which is truth; and the Lord enables them
to perceive interiorly that they are led and taught by Him,
and not by themselves. [3] To many the rational of both
classes seems to be the same, but it is different. The rational
of those who are both in the appearance and in the truth is a
spiritual rational, while the rational of those who are in the
appearance apart from the truth is a natural rational. This
natural rational may be likened to a garden as it is in the
light of winter, while the spiritual rational may be likened to
a garden as it is in the light of spring. But more about this
in what follows, and in this order:—

(1) Man is led and taught by the Lord alone.

(2) Man is led and taught by the Lord alone through the angelic heaven and from it.

(3) Man is led by the Lord by means of influx, and taught by means of enlightenment.

(4) Man is taught by the Lord by means of the Word, and by means of doctrine and preachings from the Word, thus immediately by the Lord alone.

(5) In externals man is led and taught by the Lord in all appearance as if by himself.

155. (1) *Man is led and taught by the Lord alone.* This flows, as a universal consequent, from all that has been set forth in the work on *The Divine Love and the Divine Wisdom;* from what is there shown respecting the Lord's Divine love and His Divine wisdom in Part First, also respecting the sun of the spiritual world and the sun of the natural world in Part Second; also respecting degrees in Part Third, and also respecting the creation of the universe in Part Fourth; and respecting the creation of man in Part Fifth.

156. That man is led and taught by the Lord alone means that he lives from the Lord alone; for what is led is his life's will, and what is taught is his life's understanding. But this is contrary to the appearance; for man seems to himself to live from himself, while the truth is that he lives from the Lord and not from himself. Since, then, so long as man remains in this world no perception by sensation can be given him that he lives from the Lord alone (because the appearance that he lives from himself is never taken away from him, for without it a man is not a man), therefore this truth must be established by reasons, and these must be confirmed by experience, and finally by the Word.

157. That man lives from the Lord alone, and not from himself, is established by these reasons: There is an only essence, an only substance, and an only form, from which are all the essences, substances, and forms that have been created. That only essence, substance, and form is the Divine love and

the Divine wisdom, from which all things that have relation
to love and wisdom in man are derived. It is also the Good
itself and the Truth itself to which all things have relation.
These are the life, which is the source of the life of all things
and of all things of life. The Only and the Itself is the omnipresent, omniscient, and omnipotent. This Only and Itself is
the Lord from eternity, or Jehovah. [2] First: *There is an
only essence, an only substance, and an only form, from which
have come all the essences, substances, and forms, that have been
created.* This is shown in the work on *The Divine Love and
the Divine Wisdom* (n. 44–46); and in Part Second of that
work it has been shown that the sun of the angelic heaven,
which is from the Lord and in which the Lord is, is that only
substance and form from which are all things that have been
created, and that there is nothing and can be nothing that is
not from that sun. And in Part Third it has been shown that
all things are from that sun by derivations according to degrees. [3] Who does not perceive and acknowledge from his
reason that there is an only essence from which is all essence,
or an only Being (*Esse*) from which is all being (*esse*)? Can any
thing have existence apart from being? And what is the being
from which is all being, unless it is Being itself? And that
which is Being itself is also the only Being and Being in itself.
This being true (and every one perceives and acknowledges, or
can perceive and acknowledge from his reason that it is true),
what else follows than that this Being, which is the Divine
Itself, and is Jehovah, is the all of all things that have being
and existence? [4] The same is true when it is said that there
is an only substance from which are all things. And as substance without form is not anything, it follows also that there
is an only form from which are all things. That the sun of the
angelic heaven is this only substance and form, and how this
essence, substance and form is varied in created things, has
been shown in the work mentioned above. [5] Secondly: *That
only essence, substance and form is the Divine love and the Divine wisdom, from which are all things that have relation to love*

and wisdom in man. This, too, has been fully shown in the work on *The Divine Love and the Divine Wisdom.* Whatever things in man appear to live have relation to the will and the understanding in him; and that these two are what constitute man's life is perceived and acknowledged by every one from his reason. What more is there in life than, This I will, or this I understand, that is, This I love, or this I think? And as that which is loved is willed, and that which is understood is thought, so all things of the will have relation to love, and all things of the understanding to wisdom. And since love and wisdom cannot exist in any one from himself, but only from Him who is Love itself and Wisdom itself, it follows that all this is from the Lord from eternity, that is, Jehovah; if it were not so, man would be Love itself and Wisdom itself, thus God from eternity; and at this human reason itself shudders. Can any thing exist except from what is prior to itself? And can this prior exist except from what is prior to it, and thus finally, except from the First which is in itself? [6] Thirdly: *It is likewise the Good itself and the Truth itself to which all things have relation.* It is accepted and acknowledged by every rational being that God is Good itself and Truth itself, and that every good and truth is from Him; and therefore, that no good or truth can come from any other source than Good itself and Truth itself. This is acknowledged by every rational man as soon as he hears it. When after this it is said that everything of the will and the understanding, or everything of love and wisdom, or everything of affection and thought in a man who is led by the Lord, has relation to good and truth, it follows that every thing that such a man wills and understands, or everything of his love and wisdom, or of his affection and thought, is from the Lord. And from this every one in the church knows that any good or any truth that is from man is not truth and good in itself, but only that which is from the Lord. As this is the truth, it follows that everything that such a man wills and thinks is from the Lord. That no evil man is able to will and to think from any other source will be shown hereafter. [**7**] Fourthly: *These are the life, which is the source of the life of all things and of all things of life.* This has been fully shown in the work on *The Divine Love and the Divine Wisdom.* Moreover, human reason accepts and acknowledges, as soon as it is heard, that the whole life of man belongs to his will and understanding, for if these were to be taken away he would cease to live; or, what is the same, that the whole life of man belongs to his love and thought, for if these were to be taken away he would cease to live. Since, then, everything of the will and understanding, or everything of love and thought in man, is from the Lord, as has just been said, it follows that every thing of his life is from the Lord. [**8**] Fifthly: *This Only and Itself is omnipresent, omniscient and omnipotent.* This, too, every Christian acknowledges from his doctrine, and every Gentile from his religion. And for this reason also every one, wherever he may be, thinks that God is where he is, and prays to God as present. And as every one so thinks and so prays, it follows that there can be no other thought than that God is everywhere, thus omnipresent. The same is true of His omniscience and omnipotence. Consequently, whoever prays in his heart to God implores Him to lead him, because He is able. Thus at such a time every one acknowledges the Divine omnipresence, omniscience, and omnipotence; this he does because he turns his face to the Lord, and this truth then flows in from the Lord. [**9**] Sixthly: *This Only and Itself is the Lord from eternity, or Jehovah.* It has been shown in *The Doctrine of the New Jerusalem concerning the Lord,* that God is one in essence and in person, and that this God is the Lord; also that the Divine Itself, which is called Jehovah the Father, is the Lord from eternity; that the Divine Human is the Son conceived from His Divine from eternity and born in the world, and that the Divine going forth is the Holy Spirit. The expressions, the Itself and the Only are used, because it has been said above that the Lord from eternity, or Jehovah, is Life itself, since He is Love itself and Wisdom itself, or Good itself and Truth itself, from which

9

all things are. That the Lord created all things from Himself, and not from nothing, may be seen in the work on *The Divine Love and the Divine Wisdom* (n. 282–284, 349–357). From all this the truth that man is led and taught by the Lord alone is established by reasons.

158. With the angels, especially the angels of the third heaven, this truth is established, not by reasons alone but also by living perceptions. They perceive the influx of Divine love and Divine wisdom from the Lord. And because they perceive that influx, and from their wisdom know that this inflowing love and wisdom is life, they say that they live from the Lord and not from themselves; and not only do they say this, they love and wish to have it so. Nevertheless, to all appearance, they are as if they lived from themselves; and the appearance is even stronger with them, than with other angels; for as has been shown above (n. 42–45), *The more nearly any one is conjoined with the Lord, the more distinctly does he appear to himself to be his own, and the more clearly does he recognize that he is the Lord's.* It has been granted me now for several years to be in a like perception and appearance, and I have been fully convinced by it that nothing of my will or thought is from myself, but only appears to be from myself; and it has also been granted me to will and to love this. This truth might be established by many other things from the spiritual world; but these two are enough for the present.

159. That the Lord alone has life is made clear by the following passages in the Word :—

I am the Resurrection and the Life; he that believeth in Me, though he die, yet shall he live (*John* xi. 25).

I am the Way, the Truth, and the Life (*John* xiv. 6).

God was the Word. In Him was life, and the life was the light of men (*John* i. 1, 4).

Here " the Word" means the Lord.

As the Father hath life in Himself, so gave He to the Son to have life in Himself (*John* v. 26).

That man is led and taught by the Lord alone is clear from
the following passages : —

Without Me ye can do nothing (*John* xv. 5).

A man can receive nothing except it be given him from heaven (*John*
iii. 27).

A man cannot make one hair white or black (*Matt.* v. 36).

" A hair" signifies in the Word the least of all things.

160. That the life of the evil is from the same source will
be shown in its proper place further on. Here it will merely
be illustrated by a comparison. From the sun of the world
heat and light flow in, flowing alike into trees that bear evil
fruit and into trees that bear good fruit, and they are alike
quickened and grow. It is not the heat in itself, but the forms
into which the heat flows, that cause this diversity. It is the
same with light, which is turned into various colors according
to the forms into which it flows. Some colors are beautiful
and pleasing, and some are ugly and dull ; and yet the light is
the same. The same is true of the influx of spiritual heat,
which in itself is love, and of spiritual light, which in itself is
wisdom, from the sun of the spiritual world. The forms into
which they flow are what cause the diversity, and not that
heat which is love, and that light which is wisdom, in themselves. The forms into which they flow are human minds.
From all this it is clear that man is led and taught by the
Lord alone.

161. But what the life of animals is has been shown above,
namely, that it is a life of merely natural affection with the
knowledge that is its mate ; and that it is a mediate life,
corresponding to the life of those who are in the spiritual
world.

162. (2) *Man is led and taught by the Lord alone through
the angelic heaven and from it.* It is said that man is led by
the Lord through and from the angelic heaven ; that he is led
through the angelic heaven is an appearance ; that he is led
from that heaven is the truth. That he is led through the angelic heaven is an appearance from the Lord's appearing above

that heaven as a sun; that he is led from that heaven is the truth, because the Lord is in that heaven as the soul is in man. For the Lord is omnipresent, and is not in space, as has been shown above; consequently distance is an appearance according to conjunction with the Lord; and conjunction is according to the reception of love and wisdom from the Lord. And as no one can be conjoined with the Lord as He is in Himself, He appears to angels at a distance like a sun; nevertheless He is in the whole angelic heaven, like the soul in man. He is in like manner in every society of heaven, and in every angel therein; for a man's soul is both the soul of the whole and also the soul of every part. [2] But because of the appearance that the Lord rules the whole heaven, and through it the world, from the sun that is from Him and in which He is (respecting which sun see Part Second of the work on *The Divine Love and the Divine Wisdom*), and because every man is permitted to speak from appearance, nor can he do otherwise, so any one who is not in wisdom itself is permitted to think that the Lord rules each thing and all things from His sun; and also that He rules the world through the angelic heaven. From that appearance, moreover, the angels of the lower heavens think; but the angels of the higher heavens, while they speak from appearance, think from the truth, which is that the Lord rules the universe from the angelic heaven, which is from Himself. [3] That the simple and the wise speak alike but do not think alike, may be illustrated by the sun of the world, about which all speak according to appearance, saying that it rises and sets; but while those who are wise use the same language they think of the sun as standing unmoved, which is the truth, while the other is the appearance. Illustrations of this may also be found in the appearances in the spiritual world; for spaces and distances appear there as in the natural world; nevertheless they are appearances that are in accord with the dissimilarity of affections and of thoughts therefrom. The same is true of the Lord's appearance in His sun.

163. How the Lord leads and teaches every man from the angelic heaven shall be told in a few words. In the work on *The Divine Love and the Divine Wisdom*, and above in this work on the *Divine Providence*, and also in the work on *Heaven and Hell*, published in London in 1758, it has been made known from things seen and heard that the whole angelic heaven appears before the Lord as one man, and likewise every society of heaven ; and that it is from this that every angel and spirit is in complete form a man. In the above mentioned works it has also been shown that heaven is not heaven from any thing that is the angels' own, but from the reception by angels of the Divine love and wisdom from the Lord. From this it can be seen that the Lord rules the whole angelic heaven as one man, and inasmuch as that heaven in itself is a man, it is the very image and likeness of the Lord, and the Lord rules heaven as the soul rules its body; and as the whole human race is ruled by the Lord, it is ruled not through heaven but from heaven by the Lord, consequently from Himself, because He is heaven, as has been said before.

164. But this is an arcanum of angelic wisdom, and therefore cannot be comprehended by man unless his spiritual mind has been opened,—such a man, by virtue of his conjunction with the Lord, being an angel. Such a man, from what has already been said, is able to comprehend what here follows : (1) All, both men and angels, are in the Lord and the Lord in them in the measure of their conjunction with Him, or, what is the same, in the measure of their reception of love and wisdom from Him. [2] (2) Each one of these is allotted a place in the Lord, that is, in heaven, according to the quality of his conjunction with or reception of the Lord. [3] (3) Each one in his place has his state distinct from the state of others ; and draws his portion from the common body according to his location, his function, and his need, precisely as each part does in the human body. [4] (4) Every man is initiated into his place by the Lord according to his life. [5] (5) Every one from infancy is introduced into this Divine Man, whose soul

and life is the Lord; and in the Lord, not out of Him, is led
and taught from the Lord's Divine love according to His Divine wisdom. But as man is not deprived of freedom he can
be led and taught only in the measure of his recipiency as if
by himself. [6] (6) Those who receive are borne to their
places through infinite turnings, as if by winding ways, much
as the chyle is carried through the mesentery and its lacteals
into the receptacle, and from this through the thoracic duct
into the blood, and thus to its destination. [7] (7) Those who
do not receive are separated from those that are within the
Divine Man, as excrement and urine are separated from man.
These are arcana of angelic wisdom which man can in some
measure comprehend; but there are many others that he cannot.

165. (3) *Man is led by the Lord by means of influx, and
taught by means of enlightenment.* Man is led by the Lord by
means of influx, for leading and inflowing are predicated of
the love and the will; and man is taught by the Lord by means
of enlightenment, because teaching and enlightening are predicated only of wisdom and the understanding. It is admitted
that every man is led by himself from his love, and by others
according to his love, and not by his understanding. He is led
by his understanding and in accordance with it only when his
love or will forms his understanding; and when this is done
the understanding may also be said to be led; yet even then it
is not the understanding that is led, but the will from which
it is. The term influx is used, because it is a common saying
that the soul flows into the body; also, as has been shown
above, that influx is spiritual and not physical, and a man's
soul or life is his love or will; also, because influx is relatively
like the inflow of the blood into the heart, and from the heart
into the lungs. That there is a correspondence of the heart
with the will, and of the lungs with the understanding, and
that the conjunction of the will with the understanding is like
the inflow of the blood from the heart into the lungs, has been
shown in the work on *The Divine Love and the Divine Wisdom* (n. 371–432).

166. But man is taught by means of enlightenment, since teaching and enlightenment are predicated of the understanding; for the understanding, which is man's internal sight, is illumined by spiritual light, just as the eye or man's external sight is illumined by natural light. Moreover, the two are similarly taught; the internal sight, which is that of the understanding, by spiritual objects; and the external sight, which is that of the eye, by natural objects. There is spiritual light and natural light; these are alike in outward appearance, but internally unlike; for natural light is from the sun of the natural world, and is therefore in itself dead, while spiritual light is from the sun of the spiritual world, and is therefore in itself living. It is spiritual light and not natural light that illumines the human understanding. Natural and rational lumen is from the former, not from the latter. This is called natural and rational lumen because it is spiritual-natural. [2] For in the spiritual world there are three degrees of light, celestial light, spiritual light, and spiritual-natural light. Celestial light is a flaming ruddy light. This is the light of those who are in the third heaven. Spiritual light is a shining white light. This is the light of those who are in the intermediate heaven. Spiritual-natural light is like the light of day in our world. This is the light of those that are in the lowest heaven, also of those that are in the world of spirits, which is intermediate between heaven and hell; but in the world of spirits this light with the good is like summer light on the earth, and with the evil like winter light. [3] It must be understood, however, that none of the light of the spiritual world has any thing in common with the light of the natural world; they differ as what is living and what is dead. From all this it is clear that it is not natural light like that before our eyes that enlightens the understanding, but spiritual light. Of this man is ignorant, because hitherto he has known nothing about spiritual light. That the origin of spiritual light is the Divine wisdom or the Divine truth has been shown in the work on *Heaven and Hell* (n. 126–140).

167. As the light of heaven has now been spoken of, some-thing must also be said about the light of hell. In hell also there are three degrees of light. In the lowest hell the light is like that from burning charcoal; in the middle hell it is like the light from the flame of a hearth fire, while in the uppermost hell it is like the light from candles, and to some like the nocturnal light of the moon. These lights are not natu-ral, they are spiritual, for all natural light is dead, and extin-guishes the understanding; but those that are in hell have the ability to understand that is called rationality, as has been shown above; and rationality itself is from spiritual light, and not at all from natural light. But the spiritual light which these have from rationality is changed into infernal light, as the light of day is changed into the darkness of night. [2] Never-theless, all in the spiritual world, both those in the heavens and those in the hells, see in their light as clearly as man sees by day in his light; and for the reason that every one's eyesight is formed for the reception of the light in which it is. Thus the eyesight of the angels of heaven is formed for the reception of their light; and the eyesight of the spirits of hell for the recep-tion of their light; and this is comparatively like the sight of owls and bats, which see objects at night or in twilight as clearly as other birds see them by day; for their eyes are formed to receive such light. [3] But the difference between these lights is very obvious to those who look from one light into the other; as when an angel of heaven looks into hell he sees nothing there but mere thick darkness; and when a spirit of hell looks into heaven he sees nothing there but thick darkness. This is because heavenly wisdom is like thick darkness to those that are in hell; and on the other hand, the insanity of hell is like thick darkness to those in heaven. From all this it can be seen that the light a man has is such as his understanding is; and that after death every one comes into his own light, not being able to see in any other; and in the spiritual world, where all are spiritual even in respect to their bodies, each one's eyes are formed to see from their light. Each one's life's love makes an understanding for itself, and thus a light; for love is like the fire of life, from which is the light of life.

168. As few know anything about the enlightenment that the understanding of a man who is taught by the Lord is in, something shall be said about it. There is an interior and an exterior enlightenment from the Lord; and there is an interior and an exterior enlightenment from man. By interior enlightenment from the Lord a man perceives at the first hearing whether what is said is true or is not true. Exterior enlightenment is from this in the thought. Interior enlightenment from man is from mere confirmation; and exterior enlightenment from man is from mere knowledge. About each one of these something shall be said. [2] *A man who is rational from interior enlightenment from the Lord* immediately perceives, when he hears them, whether many things are true or not true; for example, that love is the life of faith, that is, that faith lives from love. Also by interior enlightenment man perceives that whatever one loves he wills, and what he wills he does, consequently that to love is to do ; and again, that whatever man believes from love, this too he wills and does, consequently to have faith is to do; also that a wicked man cannot have love of God, thus neither faith in God. By interior enlightenment a rational man perceives as soon as he hears it that God is One; that He is omnipresent; that all good is from Him; also that all things have relation to good and truth; and that all good is from Good itself, and all truth from Truth itself. Man perceives these things and other like things interiorly in himself when he hears them; and he has this perception because he has rationality that is in the light of heaven, which gives enlightenment. [3] *Exterior enlightenment* is an enlightenment of the thought that is from the interior enlightenment; and the thought is in such enlightenment so far as it continues in the perception that it has from interior enlightenment, and also so far as it has knowledges of truth and good; for from these it draws the reasons by means of which it confirms. Thought from this exterior enlightenment sees a thing from both sides; on the one it sees the reasons that confirm, on the other the appearances that invalidate; the latter it disperses, the former it collects. [4] *Interior enlightenment from man* is wholly different. By it man sees a subject on one side and not on the other; and when he has confirmed it he sees it in a light apparently like the light spoken of above, but it is a winter light. For example, a judge who judges unjustly because of gifts or for the sake of gain, when he has confirmed his decision by the laws and by reasons, sees nothing but justice in it. To some the injustice may be evident, but as they do not wish to see it they mystify and blind themselves, and thus do not see. The same is true of a judge who is influenced in his decisions by friendship, or by a desire to gain favor, or by the ties of relationship. [5] Such men regard in the same way every thing that they hear from the lips of a man in authority, or a man of celebrity, or that they have hatched out from their own intelligence. They are rationally blind; for they have their vision from falsities, which they confirm; and falsity closes the sight, while truth opens it. Such see no truth from the light of truth, and no justice from a love of justice, but only from the light of confirmation, which is a delusive light. In the spiritual world they appear like faces without heads, or like faces that resemble human faces behind which there are wooden heads; and they are called rational animals, because they have rationality potentially. Those have *exterior enlightenment from man*, who think and talk from mere knowledge impressed on the memory. Such are scarcely able to confirm any thing from themselves.

169. Such are the differences of enlightenment, and consequently of perception and thought. From spiritual light there is an actual enlightenment; but the enlightenment itself from that light is not manifest to any one in the natural world, because natural light has nothing in common with spiritual light; but this enlightenment has sometimes been manifest to me in the spiritual world, being visible in the case of those who were in enlightenment from the Lord as a luminous appearance around the head glowing with the color of the human face. But in the case of those that were in enlightenment from themselves, this luminous appearance was not about the head, but about the mouth and over the chin.

170. Besides these kinds of enlightenment there is another, by which it is revealed to man in what faith and in what intelligence and wisdom he is; and the revelation is such as to enable him to perceive this in himself. He is admitted into a society where there is genuine faith, also true intelligence and wisdom; and there his interior rationality is opened, and from it he sees the quality of his faith and his intelligence and wisdom, even to an acknowledgment of it. I have seen some of these on their return, and have heard them confessing that they had no faith, although in the world they had supposed their faith to be abundant, surpassing that of others, and their intelligence and wisdom to be the same. These were in faith alone, and in no charity, and were in their own intelligence.

171. (4) *Man is taught by the Lord by means of the Word, and by means of doctrine and preaching from the Word, and thus immediately by the Lord alone.* It has been said and shown above that man is led and taught by the Lord alone and this from heaven, and not through heaven or through any angel there; and as he is led by the Lord alone, it follows that he is led immediately and not mediately. How this is done will now be told.

172. In the *Doctrine of the New Jerusalem concerning the Sacred Scripture* it has been shown that the Lord is the Word, and that all doctrine of the church must be drawn from the Word. Since, then, the Lord is the Word, it follows that the man who is taught from the Word is taught by the Lord alone. But as this is not easily comprehended, it shall be illustrated in the following order: (1) The Lord is the Word because the Word is from Him and treats of Him. (2) Also because it is the Divine truth of the Divine good. (3) Thus to be taught from the Word is to be taught from the Lord. (4) That this is done mediately through preaching does not take away the immediateness. [2] First: *The Lord is the Word because*

the Word is from Him and treats of Him. That the Word is
from the Lord is denied by no one in the church. That the
Word treats of the Lord alone is not denied, indeed, but neither
is it known. This has been set forth in the *Doctrine of the
New Jerusalem concerning the Lord* (n. 1–7, 37–44); also in
the *Doctrine of the New Jerusalem concerning the Sacred
Scripture* (n. 62–69, 80–90, 98–100). Since, then, the Word is
both from the Lord alone and treats of the Lord alone, it follows that when man is taught from the Word he is taught from
the Lord, since the Word is the Divine; and who except the
essential Divine, from whom the Word is and of whom it
treats, can communicate the Divine, and plant it in the heart?
When, therefore, the Lord speaks of His conjunction with the
disciples He says:—

> That they should abide in Him, and His words in them (*John* xv. 7).
> That His words are spirit and life (*John* vi. 63).
> And that He makes His abode with those who keep His words (*John*
> xiv. 20–24).

To think from the Lord, therefore, is to think from the Word,
seemingly through the Word. That all things of the Word
have communication with heaven has been shown in the *Doctrine of the New Jerusalem concerning the Sacred Scripture*, from
beginning to end. And since the Lord is heaven, this means
that all things of the Word have communication with the Lord
Himself. It is true that the angels of heaven have communication; but this, too, is from the Lord. [3] Secondly: *The
Lord is the Word, because it is the Divine truth of the Divine
good.* That the Lord is the Word He teaches in *John* in these
words:—

> In the beginning was the Word, and the Word was with God, and God
> was the Word; and the Word became flesh, and dwelt among us (*John*
> i. 1, 14).

As heretofore this has been understood to mean only that God
taught men through the Word, it has been explained as a hy-
perbolical expression, not meaning that the Lord is the Word
itself; and for the reason that it was unknown that by "the

Word" the Divine truth of the Divine good is meant, or, what is the same, the Divine wisdom of the Divine love. That these are the Lord Himself is shown in Part First of the work on *The Divine Love and the Divine Wisdom ;* and that these are the Word is shown in the *Doctrine of the New Jerusalem concerning the Sacred Scripture* (n. 1–86). [4] How the Lord is the Divine truth of the Divine good shall also be briefly told. Every man is a man not from his face and body but from the good of his love and from the truths of his wisdom; and because it is from these that a man is a man, every man is also his own truth and his own good, or his own love and his own wisdom. Apart from these he is not a man. But the Lord is good itself and truth itself, or, what is the same, He is love itself and wisdom itself; and these are the Word which was in the beginning with God and which was God, and which became flesh. [5] Thirdly : *Thus to be taught from the Word is to be taught by the Lord Himself,* because it is to be taught from good itself and truth itself, or from love itself and from wisdom itself, which are the Word, as has been said. But every one is taught according to the understanding that belongs to his own love; what is beyond this is not permanent. All those who are taught by the Lord in the Word are taught a few truths in the world, but many when they become angels ; for the interiors of the Word, which are Divine spiritual and Divine celestial things, although implanted at the same time, are not opened in man until after his death, thus in heaven, where he is in angelic wisdom, which in comparison with human wisdom, that is, man's former wisdom, is ineffable. That Divine spiritual and Divine celestial things, which constitute angelic wisdom, are present in all things, and in each thing of the Word, may be seen in the *Doctrine of the New Jerusalem concerning the Sacred Scripture* (n. 5–26). [6] Fourthly : *That this is done mediately through preaching does not take away the immediateness.* The Word must needs be taught mediately through parents, teachers, books, and especially the reading of it. Nevertheless it is not taught by these, but by the Lord through them. And this the preachers know, and they say that they do not speak from themselves but from the spirit of God, and that all truth, like all good, is from God. They are able, indeed, to declare the Word, and bring it to the understanding of many, but not to the heart of any one; and what is not in the heart perishes in the understanding; "the heart" meaning man's love. From all this it can be seen that man is led and taught by the Lord alone, and is led and taught immediately by Him when this is done from the Word. This is the arcanum of arcana of angelic wisdom.

173. That by means of the Word they also have light who are not in the church and do not have the Word is shown in the *Doctrine of the New Jerusalem concerning the Sacred Scripture* (n. 104–113). And since man has light through the Word, and from that light has understanding, and as both the evil and the good have understanding, it follows that from the light in its origin there is light in its derivatives, which are perceptions and thoughts respecting all subjects. The Lord says:—

That without Him man can do nothing (*John* xv. 5).

That a man can receive nothing except it has been given him from heaven (*John* iii. 27).

And that the Father in the heavens maketh His sun to rise on the evil and on the good, and sendeth rain on the just and on the unjust (*Matt.* v. 45).

By "the sun," here as elsewhere in the Word, is meant in its spiritual sense the Divine good of the Divine love; and by "rain," the Divine truth of the Divine wisdom. These are given to the evil and the good, to the just and the unjust; for unless they were given no one would have perception and thought. That there is only one life, from which all have life, has been shown above; and perception and thought belong to life, consequently perception and thought are from the same fountain from which life is. That all the light that constitutes the understanding is from the sun of the spiritual world, which is the Lord, has already been fully shown.

174. (5) *In externals man is led and taught by the Lord in all appearance as if by himself.* This takes place in man's externals, but not in internals. How the Lord leads and teaches man in his internals no one knows, as no one knows how the soul operates to cause the eye to see, the ear to hear, the tongue and mouth to speak, the heart to move the blood, the lungs to breathe, the stomach to digest, the liver and pancreas to assort, the kidneys to secrete, and countless other things. These things do not come to man's perception and sensation. The same is true of what is done by the Lord in the interior substances and forms of the mind, which are infinitely more numerous; the Lord's operations in these are not manifest to man. But the effects, which are numerous, are manifest, as well as some of the causes producing the effects. These are the externals wherein man and the Lord are together. And because externals make one with internals (for they cohere in one series), the Lord can arrange things in internals only in accordance with the disposition that is effected by means of man in the externals. [2] Every one knows that man thinks, wills, speaks, and acts to all appearance as if from himself; and every one can see that without this appearance man would have no will or understanding, thus no affection or thought, also no reception of any good and truth from the Lord. This being so, it follows that without this appearance there would be no knowledge of God, no charity or faith, and consequently no reformation or regeneration, and therefore no salvation. From all this it is clear that this appearance is given to man by the Lord for the sake of all these uses, and chiefly that man may have the ability to receive and to reciprocate, whereby the Lord may be conjoined with him and he with the Lord, and that through this conjunction man may live forever. This is the appearance here meant.

IT IS A LAW OF THE DIVINE PROVIDENCE THAT NOTHING OF
THE OPERATION OF THE DIVINE PROVIDENCE SHOULD BE
EVIDENT TO MAN'S PERCEPTIONS OR SENSES, BUT THAT HE
SHOULD, NEVERTHELESS, KNOW ABOUT IT AND ACKNOWL-
EDGE IT.

175. The natural man who does not believe in Divine providence thinks to himself, "What is Divine providence, when
the wicked are advanced to honors and acquire riches more
than the good, and when those who do not believe in a Divine
providence are more successful in many like respects than
those who do? And still further, the unbelieving and impious
can inflict injuries, wrongs, and misfortunes, and sometimes
death, upon the believing and pious, and this by means of de-
ceptions and tricks." Therefore he thinks, "Do I not see from
actual observation as in clear daylight that crafty devices, when
by ingenious shrewdness they can be made to seem trustworthy
and just, prevail over fidelity and justice? What else is there,
then, except necessities, consequences, and things of chance, in
which nothing from a Divine providence is manifest? Do not
necessities belong to nature? Are not consequences the causes
that flow from natural or civil order? And are not things of
chance either from unknown causes or from no cause?" Thus
the natural man thinks to himself, ascribing nothing to God,
but all things to nature; for he that attributes nothing to God
attributes nothing to Divine providence; since God and Divine
providence make one. [2] But the spiritual man speaks or
thinks to himself differently. Although he has in his thought
no perception of the Divine providence in its progress, nor is
made sensible of it by the sight of the eye, still he knows about
it and acknowledges it. Since, then, the appearances and consequent fallacies above mentioned have blinded the understanding, and this can receive no sight until the fallacies that
have blinded it and the falsities that have darkened it are dispelled, and since this cannot be done except by truths, which
have in them the power to dispel falsities, therefore these truths

shall be disclosed, and for the sake of distinctness, in the following order:—

(1) If the operation of the Divine providence were made evident to man's perceptions and senses he would not act from freedom in accordance with reason; nor would anything appear to him to be from himself. It would be the same if he foreknew events.

(2) If man clearly saw the Divine providence he would intrude himself into the order and tenor of its course and would pervert and destroy it.

(3) If man clearly saw the Divine providence either he would deny God or he would make himself to be God.

(4) It is granted man to see the Divine providence in the back and not in the face; also to see it in a spiritual state and not in a natural state.

176. (1) *If the operation of the Divine providence were made evident to man's perceptions and senses he would not act from freedom in accordance with reason ; nor would any thing appear to him to be his. It would be the same if he foreknew events.* It has been made evident to the understanding in its proper chapters above that it is a law of the Divine providence that man should act from freedom in accordance with reason, also that every thing a man wills, thinks, speaks, and does should appear to him to be from himself; also that without this appearance there would be nothing his (*suus*) to any man, nor would he be his own man (*homo suus*); thus he would have no ownhood (*proprium*); and therefore nothing could be imputed to him; and without such imputation it would be a matter of indifference whether he did evil or good, whether he had the faith of God or the persuasion of hell; in a word, he would not be man. [2] It shall now be shown that man would have no liberty to act in accordance with reason, and nothing would appear to him to be from himself, if the operation of the Divine providence were made evident to his perceptions and senses; since, if it were thus made evident he would be led by it; for the Lord leads all by means of His Divine provi-

10

dence, and man leads himself only in appearance, as has also been shown above. Consequently if man were led in accord with a living perception and sensation he would not be conscious of life, but he would be moved to utter sounds and to act much like a carved image. If he were still conscious of life he would be led like one bound hand and foot, or like a beast before a cart. Who does not see that a man would then have no freedom? And if he had no freedom he would have no reason; for every one thinks from freedom and in freedom; and whatever he does not think from freedom and in freedom does not appear to him to be from himself but from another; in fact, if you consider it interiorly you will perceive that he would then have no thought, still less any reason, and therefore would not be a man.

177. The operation of the Lord's Divine providence to withdraw man from evils is continuous. If this continuous operation were evident to man's perceptions and senses, and he were not led as one bound, would he not continually struggle against it, and then either strive with God or mix himself in with Divine providence? If the latter he would also make himself God; if the former he would release himself from restraint and deny God. It is clearly evident that there would then be two powers continually acting against each other, the power of evil from man and the power of good from the Lord; and when two opposites act against each other either one of them conquers or both perish; but in this case if one conquers they both perish, for the evil that belongs to man does not instantly receive good from the Lord, nor does good from the Lord instantly cast out evil from man; if either were done instantly there would be no life left to man. These and many other harmful results would ensue if the operation of the Divine providence were clearly evident to man's perceptions and senses. But this will be shown fully in what follows.

178. A knowledge of future events is not granted to man for the same reason, namely, that he may have the ability to act from freedom in accordance with reason; for it is known that any thing that a man loves he wills to possess in effect, and he leads himself thereto by means of his reason ; also that every thing that a man contemplates in his reason is from a love for it to come into effect by means of his thought. If, therefore, he knew the effect or event by Divine prediction his reason would cease to act, and with it his love; for the love rests with the reason in the effect, and from the effect then begins anew. It is reason's essential delight to see from love the effect in the thought, not after but before the effect is reached, that is, not in the present but in the future. This is the source of what is called Hope, which increases and decreases in the reason as man sees or anticipates the event. The delight is made complete in the event, and thereafter fades away with the thought belonging to it. [2] Thus would it be if the event were foreknown. The mind of man is continually in these three things, called end, cause, and effect. If one of these is lacking, the human mind is not in its life. The affection of the will is the end from which; the thought of the understanding is the cause by which; and the action of the body or the speech of the lips, or the external sensation, is the effect of the end by means of the thought. That the human mind is not in its life when it is in the affection of the will alone, and nothing follows, or when it is likewise merely in the effect, must be clear to any one. Thus the mind has no life from one of these separately, but from the three conjointly. This life of the mind would be diminished and pass away if the event were foretold.

179. As a knowledge of future events takes away the human itself, which is to act from freedom in accordance with reason, a knowledge of the future is granted to no one; nevertheless, every one is permitted to form conclusions about the future from the reason; and in this the reason with all that pertains to it is in its proper life. This is why a man is not permitted to know what his lot will be after death, or to know about any event until he is in it; for if he knew this he would cease to think from his interior self how he must act or must

live in order to come into it; but he would simply think from
his exterior self that he was coming into it; and such a state
closes the interiors of his mind, in which the two faculties of
his life, liberty and rationality, have their chief seat. A longing to know things future is innate with most people; but this
longing has its origin in a love of evil, and is therefore taken
away from those who believe in the Divine providence; and
there is given them a trust that the Lord is directing their lot,
and consequently they have no wish to know beforehand what
it will be, lest they should in some way interfere with the Divine providence. This is taught by the Lord in a variety of
ways in *Luke* (xii. 14–48). [2] That this is a law of the Divine providence can be shown by many things in the spiritual
world. Most persons when they enter that world after death
wish to know their lot; but they are told that if they have
lived well their lot is in heaven, if they have lived wickedly
it is in hell. But as every one fears hell, even the evil, they
ask what they must do and what they must believe to gain
entrance to heaven; and the answer is that while they can do
and believe as they will, they may be sure that in hell good
is not done or truth believed, but only in heaven. " If you
are able, seek to know what is good and what is true, and
think the truth, and do the good." Thus in the spiritual world
as in the natural world all are left to act from freedom in accordance with reason; but as they have acted in this world so
do they in that; for every one's life awaits him, and from this
is his lot; for the lot is in accordance with the life.

180. (2) *If man clearly saw the Divine providence he would
intrude himself into the order and tenor of its course, and would
pervert and destroy it.* To bring this clearly to the perception
of the rational man and of the natural man it must be illustrated by examples in this order: (1) Externals are so connected with internals as to make one in every operation. (2)
Only in certain externals is man associated with the Lord;
and if he were at the same time in the internals he would pervert and destroy the whole order and tenor of the course of

the Divine providence. But, as has been said, this shall be illustrated by examples. [2] First: *Externals are so connected with internals as to make one in every operation.* In illustration of this by examples take certain parts of the human body. In the whole body and in every part there are both externals and internals; the externals are called skins, membranes, and sheaths, the internals are forms variously composed and interwoven of nerve fibers and blood vessels. The surrounding sheath, by continuations from itself, enters into all the interiors even to the inmosts; thus the external, which is a sheath, conjoins itself with all the internals, which are the organic forms, made of fibers and vessels. From this it follows that as the external acts or is acted upon so the internal acts or is acted upon; for there is a perpetual bundling together of them all. [3] Take some general sheath in the body, the pleura, for example, which is the general sheath of the chest, or of the heart and lungs, and examine it with an anatomical eye; or if you have not made anatomy a study, consult anatomists; and you will learn that this general sheath, by various circumvolutions and then by continuations from itself, becoming finer and finer, enters into the inmosts of the lungs, even into the smallest bronchial branches, and into the follicles that are the beginnings of the lungs; not to mention its subsequent progress through the trachea to the larynx towards the tongue. From all this it is evident that there is a constant connection between the outermosts and the inmosts; consequently as the outermost acts or is acted upon so the interiors from the inmosts act or are acted upon. For this reason, when this outermost sheath, the pleura, is congested or inflamed or ulcerated, the lungs labor from their inmosts; and if the disease grows worse all action of the lungs may cease and the man die. [4] It is the same everywhere else in the whole body; as with the peritoneum, which is the general sheath of all the abdominal viscera; also the sheaths surrounding the several organs, as the stomach, liver, pancreas, spleen, intestines, mesentery, kidneys, and the organs of generation in either sex. Take any one of these abdominal viscera, and either examine it yourself and you will see, or ask those skilled in anatomy and you will learn. Take, for instance, the liver, and you will find that there is a connection between the sheath of that organ and the peritoneum, and through the sheath with its inmosts; for there are perpetual extensions from the sheath, with insertions towards the interior parts, and in this way continuations to the inmosts; and by these means all the parts are so bundled together that when the sheath acts or is acted upon the whole form acts or is acted upon in like manner. It is the same with the other organs; and this is because in every form the general and the particular, or the universal and the special, by wonderful conjunction, act as one. [5] It will be shown below that in spiritual forms and in the changes and variations of their state, which have relation to the operations of the will and the understanding, the same order prevails as in natural forms and their operations, which have relation to motion and action. Since, then, man is associated with the Lord in certain external operations, and since no one is ever deprived of the liberty of acting in accordance with reason, it follows that the Lord cannot act otherwise in internals than as He acts with man in externals. If man, therefore, does not shun and turn away from evils as sins, not only does the external of the thought and will become vitiated and destroyed, but the internals of them at the same time; comparatively as the pleura is attacked by its disease called pleurisy, which causes the death of the body. [6] Secondly: *If man should be at the same time in the internals he would pervert and destroy the whole order and tenor of the Divine providence.* This, too, may be illustrated by examples from the human body. If man knew all the workings of both brains into fibers, of fibers into muscles, and of muscles into actions, and from this knowledge were to direct all things as he does his actions, would he not pervert and destroy them all? [7] If a man knew how the stomach digests, how the surrounding viscera absorb each its portion, elaborate the blood, and distribute it for every

operation of life, and if he had the ordering of these things as
he has of external things, such as eating and drinking, would
he not pervert and destroy them all ?   When he is unable to
order the external, that appears like a single thing, without
destroying it by luxury and intemperance, what would he do if
he had also the ordering of the internals, which are infinite ?
This is why the internals, lest man's will should in some way
enter into them and get control of them, are wholly exempt
from his volition, except the muscles, which constitute the
covering; and he does not know even how these act, he only
knows that they act.   [8] It is the same with the other organs;
as, for example, if man were to have the ordering of the interiors of the eye for seeing, of the interiors of the ear for hearing, of the interiors of the tongue for tasting, of the interiors
of the skin for feeling, of the interiors of the heart in its beat-
ing, of the interiors of the lungs in breathing, of the interiors
of the mesentery in distributing the chyle, of the interiors of
the kidneys in their work of secretion, of the interiors of the
organs of generation in propagating, of the interiors of the
womb in perfecting the embryo, and so on, would he not in
numberless ways pervert and destroy in them the order of the
course of the Divine providence?   Every one knows that man
is in the externals; that is, he sees with the eye, hears with
the ear, tastes with the tongue, feels with the skin, breathes
with the lungs, contributes to propagation, and so on.   Is it
not sufficient for him to know about the externals, and to order
them for the health of body and mind?   If he cannot do this,
what would happen if he had also the ordering of the internals?   From all this it is evident that if a man clearly saw
the Divine providence he would intrude himself into the order
and tenor of its course, and would pervert and destroy it.

181.   There is a likeness between the spiritual things of the
mind and the natural things of the body, because all things of
the mind correspond to all things of the body; therefore also
the mind actuates the body in externals, and in general with
complete control.   It moves the eye to see, the ear to hear, the

mouth and the tongue to eat and drink, also to speak, the hands
to act, the feet to walk, the generative organs to propagate.
The mind moves not only the externals to these actions, but
the internals also throughout the whole series, the outmosts
from the inmosts, and the inmosts from the outmosts. Thus
while it is moving the mouth to speak, it simultaneously moves
the lungs, the larynx, the glottis, the tongue, the lips, each one
separately to the performance of its function, also the face to
fitting expression. [2] This makes clear that what has been
said of the natural forms of the body can be said similarly of
the spiritual forms of the mind; and that what has been said
of the natural operations of the body can be said of the spiritual operations of the mind; consequently as man orders the
externals so the Lord orders the internals; thus in one way
when man orders the externals from himself, and in another
way when he orders the externals from the Lord and at the same
time as if from himself. Moreover man's mind in its entire form
is a man; for it is man's spirit; and this after death appears a
man precisely as in the world; consequently there are like things
in body and mind. So what has been said of the conjunction of
externals with internals in the body can also be applied to the
conjunction of externals with internals in the mind, with the
difference only that one is natural and the other spiritual.

182. (3) *If man clearly saw the Divine providence either he
would deny God or he would make himself to be God.* The
merely natural man says to himself, "What is Divine providence? Is it any thing else or more than a phrase that the
common people have learned from the priest? Who sees anything of it? Are not all things in the world done from prudence, wisdom, shrewdness, and cunning? And are not all
other things necessities and consequences? And besides there
are many happenings. Does the Divine providence lie concealed in these? How can it be in frauds and craft? Yet it
is said that the Divine providence does everything. Then make
me see it, and I will believe it. Can any one believe it before
he sees it?" [2] So says the merely natural man; but the

spiritual man speaks otherwise. Because he acknowledges God
he also acknowledges the Divine providence, and moreover, he
sees it. But he cannot make it manifest to any one who thinks
only in nature and from nature; for such a one is unable to lift
his mind above nature and to see in its appearances anything
of Divine providence, or to draw conclusions respecting it from
the laws of nature, which also are laws of the Divine wisdom.
If, therefore, he should clearly see the Divine providence he
would mix it up with nature, and thus would not only enshroud
it in fallacies but would also profane it; and instead of acknowledging it he would deny it; and he who in heart denies the
Divine providence denies God also. [**3**] It must be thought
either that God or that nature governs all things. He who
thinks that God governs all things thinks that they are governed by Love itself and Wisdom itself, thus by Life itself.
But he who thinks that nature governs all things thinks that
they are governed by natural heat and light, and yet these in
themselves are dead, because they are from a sun that is dead.
Does not what is itself living govern what is dead? Can that
which is dead govern anything? If you think that what is
dead can give life to itself you are insane. Life must be from
Life.

183. That if the Divine providence and its operation were
clearly seen by man he would deny God does not appear probable; for it would seem that if it were clearly seen by any one
he could not but acknowledge it, and thus acknowledge God;
yet the contrary is the truth. The Divine providence never
acts in accord with the will's love in man, but constantly against
it; since man, because of his hereditary evil, is always panting
for the lowest hell; but the Lord by His providence is continually leading and drawing him away from it, first to a milder
hell, then out of hell, and finally to Himself in heaven. This
operation of the Divine providence is perpetual. Consequently
if man clearly saw or felt this drawing or leading away he
would grow angry and would regard God as his enemy, and
from the evil of his selfhood (*proprium*) would deny God.

Consequently, lest this be known to man he is kept in a state of freedom from which he knows no otherwise than that he leads himself. [2] But let examples serve for illustration. By inheritance man possesses a desire to become great; he has also a desire to gain riches ; and so far as these loves are unrestrained he longs to become greater and richer, and at length to be greatest and richest; nor would he rest here; he would wish to become greater than God Himself and to possess heaven itself. This passion lies most deeply hidden in hereditary evil, and thus in man's life and in his life's nature. The Divine providence does not instantly take away this evil, for if it were instantly taken away man would cease to live; but providence takes it away so quietly and gradually that man knows nothing about it. This is done by permitting man to act in accordance with the thought that his reason adopts; and then by various means, rational and civil and moral the Divine providence leads him away from the evil; and he is thus led as far away from it as he can be led in freedom. Nor can evil be taken away from any one until it becomes evident and is seen and acknowledged; it is like a wound that does not heal until it is opened. [3] If, then, man were to know and see that the Lord so works by means of His Divine providence against man's life's love, from which he has his chief enjoyment, he could not but go in the opposite direction, become enraged, strive against it, say hard words, and finally from his evil set aside the operation of the Divine providence by denying it and thus denying God; especially if he saw in it an obstacle to his success, and saw himself fallen from honor and stripped of wealth. [4] But it must be known that the Lord never leads man away from seeking honors or from acquiring wealth, but He leads him away from a desire to seek honors for the sake of mere eminence, or for the sake of himself; also from acquiring wealth for the sake of mere opulence, that is, for the sake of riches. And when the Lord leads man away from these He leads him into a love of uses, that he may esteem eminence not for his own sake but for the sake of uses, thus that it may belong to uses, and to himself therefrom, and not to himself and to uses therefrom. The same is true of opulence. That the Lord constantly humbles the proud and exalts the humble He Himself teaches in many places in the Word; and what He there teaches pertains also to His Divine providence.

184. The same is true of other evils that man is in by inheritance, such as adulteries, frauds, revenge, blasphemy, and others like these. None of these could be put away unless a liberty to think and will them were left to man, that so he might put them away as if of himself; and yet he can do this only by acknowledging the Divine providence and praying that the work may be done by it. Except for that liberty, combined with the Divine providence, such evils would be like poison kept in and not expelled, which would soon spread and carry death to the whole system; or they would be like a disease of the heart itself, from which the whole body soon dies.

185. The truth of this cannot be better learned than from the states of men after death in the spiritual world. Most of those there who have become great and rich in the natural world, and in their honors and riches have regarded themselves only, at first talk about God and the Divine providence as if they had acknowledged them in heart. But because they then clearly see the Divine providence, and from it their final lot, which is that they are to come into hell, they join themselves with the devils there, and then not only deny but also blaspheme God; and at last they fall into such madness as to acknowledge the more powerful of the devils as their gods, and desire nothing more ardently than to become gods themselves also.

186. Man would run counter to God, and also deny Him, if he clearly saw the workings of His Divine providence, because man is in the enjoyment of self-love, and that enjoyment constitutes his very life; therefore when he is kept in his life's enjoyment he is in freedom; for freedom and that enjoyment make one. If, therefore, he had a perception of being continually led away from his enjoyment he would be enraged as against one who wished to destroy his life, and would regard him as an enemy. To prevent this the Lord does not manifestly appear in His Divine providence, but by it He leads men as silently as a hidden current or favoring tide bears a vessel; and in consequence man does not know but that he is constantly in his own (*proprium*), for man's freedom and his own make one. From this it is clear that freedom appropriates to man what the Divine providence introduces, but that this would not take place if the Divine providence made itself manifest. To be appropriated is to come to be of the life.

187. (4) *It is granted man to see the Divine providence in the back and not in the face; also to see it in a spiritual state and not in his natural state.* To see the Divine providence in the back and not in the face is to see it after it occurs and not before; and to see it from a spiritual and not from a natural state is to see it from heaven and not from the world. All who receive influx from heaven and acknowledge the Divine providence, and especially those who by reformation have become spiritual, when they see events in some wonderful series see as it were the Divine providence by an interior acknowledgment, and confess it. Such have no wish to see it in the face, that is, before it occurs, fearing that their will might intrude itself into something of its order and tenor. [2] It is otherwise with those who admit into themselves no influx from heaven but only from the world, especially with those who have become natural from the confirmation of appearances in themselves. These see nothing of the Divine providence in the back, or after it occurs; but they wish to see it in the face, or before it occurs; and as the Divine providence works by means, and the means operate through man or through the world, whether they see it in the face or the back they attribute it either to man or to nature, and thus confirm themselves in a denial of it. This they do because their understanding is closed from above and is open only from below, that is, closed towards heaven and open towards the world; and it is not granted to see the Divine providence from the world, but only from heaven.

I have sometimes thought within myself whether such would acknowledge the Divine providence if their understanding were opened from above, and they could see as in clear day that nature in itself is dead, and that human intelligence in itself is nothing, while it is from influx that these both have an appearance of being; and I have perceived that such as have confirmed themselves in favor of nature and of human prudence would not acknowledge this, for the reason that the natural light flowing in from below would immediately extinguish the spiritual light flowing in from above.

189. The man who has become spiritual by the acknowledgment of God, and wise by a rejection of what is his own (*proprium*), sees the Divine providence in the whole world, and in all and each of the things in it. When he looks at natural things he sees it; when he looks at civil matters he sees it; when he looks at spiritual things he sees it; he sees it alike in the simultaneous and the successive relations of things, in ends, in causes, in effects, in uses, in forms, in things great and small. Especially does he see it in the salvation of men, as that Jehovah gave the Word, taught men by it respecting God, heaven and hell, and eternal life, and came Himself into the world to redeem and save men. These things and many others, and the Divine providence in them, man sees from natural light in spiritual light. But the merely natural man sees none of these things. [2] He is like one who sees a magnificent temple, and hears a preacher enlightened in Divine things, and at home declares that he has seen nothing but a house of stone, and has heard nothing but an articulate sound. Or he is like a near-sighted person who goes into a garden remarkable for fruits of every kind, and returning home says that he has seen only trees and woods. When such persons after death have become spirits, and when they are raised up into the angelic heaven, where all things are in forms representative of love and wisdom, they see nothing, not even that they exist; as I have seen tried with many who have denied the Lord's Divine providence.

190. There are many constant things created in order that things not constant may have existence. The constants are the stated changes in the rising and setting of the sun and moon and of the stars; their obscuration by interpositions called eclipses; the heat and light from them; the seasons of the year called spring, summer, autumn, and winter; the times of the day which are morning, noon, evening, and night; also the atmospheres, waters, and lands, viewed in themselves; the vegetative power in the vegetable kingdom; both the vegetative and the prolific in the animal kingdom; also the things that are constantly effected by these when brought into act according to the laws of order. These and many other things exist by creation; and are provided in order that infinitely varied things may have existence; for the varied can have existence only in the constant, the fixed, and the sure. [2] But let examples illustrate. Varieties of vegetation would not be possible unless the rising and setting of the sun, and the resultant heat and light were constant. Harmonies of sound are of infinite variety, but they would be impossible unless the atmospheres were constant in their laws and the ears in their form. Varieties in sight, which are also infinite, would be impossible unless the ether in its laws and the eye in its form were constant. The same is true of color, unless the light were constant. It is the same with thoughts, words, and actions, which are also of infinite variety; these would be impossible unless the organic forms of the body were constant. Must not a house be constant that various things may be done in it by man; or a temple, that in it there may be the varying services, sermons, instruction, and pious meditation? So in other things. [3] As to the changes themselves that go on in the constant, the fixed, and the sure, they progress to infinity and have no end; and yet there is never one exactly the same as another among all the things of the universe or in any one of them, nor can there be in those that are to follow to eternity. Who so directs these changes going on to infinity and eternity that they may be in order but He who created the constant things to the end that the changes might have existence in them? And who can direct the infinite changes of life in men but He who is Life itself, that is, Love itself and Wisdom itself? Without His Divine providence, which is like a continual creation, could men's infinite affections and consequent thoughts, and thus the men themselves, be so arranged as to make a one,—evil affections and thoughts therefrom one devil which is hell, and good affections and thoughts therefrom one Lord in heaven? That the entire angelic heaven is in the Lord's sight as one man, His image and likeness, and that all hell is opposed to it as a monstrous man, has been frequently stated and shown before. These things have now been said because some natural men, even from the constant and fixed things that are necessary to the end that changeable things may have existence in them, find arguments for their madness in favor of nature and of one's own prudence.

MAN'S OWN PRUDENCE IS NOTHING; IT MERELY APPEARS TO BE SOMETHING, AND SHOULD SO APPEAR; BUT THE DIVINE PROVIDENCE, BECAUSE OF ITS MINUTE PARTICULARS, IS UNIVERSAL.

191. That man's own prudence is nothing is wholly contrary to appearance, and therefore contrary to the belief of many; and for this reason, whoever from the appearance holds the belief that human prudence does all things can be convinced of the truth only by reasons drawn from deeper investigation, and these must be gathered from the realm of causes. The appearance is an effect, and the causes disclose its source. In this introduction something shall be said about the general belief on this subject. In opposition to the appearance is the teaching of the church, that love and faith are from God and not from man, likewise wisdom and intelligence, and therefore also prudence, and in general all good and truth. When this teaching is accepted it must be conceded also that man's own prudence is nothing, but only appears to be something. Prudence has no other source than intelligence and wisdom and these two have no other source than the understanding and the thought therefrom about truth and good. Those who acknowledge the Divine providence accept and believe this that has just been said, but not those who acknowledge human prudence alone. [2] Now the truth must be either as the church teaches, that all wisdom and prudence are from God, or as the world teaches, that all wisdom and prudence are from man. Can these be reconciled in any other way than by admitting that what the church teaches is the truth, and that what the world teaches is the appearance? For the church draws its proof from the Word, but the world from man's own (*proprium*), and the Word is from God, while man's own is from man. It is because prudence is from God and not from man that the Christian in his devotions prays that God will lead his thoughts, counsels, and deeds; adding also, because from himself he cannot do this. When, moreover, he sees any one doing good he says that he has been led to it by God; and many other like things. How can any one so speak unless at the time he interiorly believes it? And believing this interiorly is from heaven. But when one thinks within himself and collects arguments in favor of human prudence he can accept the opposite belief, which is from the world. Nevertheless, the internal faith prevails in those who acknowledge God in heart; while the external faith prevails in those who do not acknowledge God in heart, whatever their professions may be.

192. It has been said that one who believes from the appearance that human prudence does all things can be convinced of the truth only by reasons drawn from deeper investigation, which are to be gathered from the realm of causes. In order, therefore, that reasons gathered therefrom may be brought clearly before the understanding they must be presented in their order, which will be as follows:—

(1) All of man's thoughts are from the affections of his life's love; and apart from these there are and can be no thoughts whatever.

(2) The affections of a man's life's love are known to the Lord alone.

(3) By means of His Divine providence the Lord leads the affections of a man's life's love, and at the same time leads his thoughts, from which human prudence is derived.

(4) By means of His Divine providence the Lord combines the affections of the whole human race into one form, which is the human form.

(5) In consequence of this, heaven and hell, which are from the human race, are in such a form.

(6) Those that have acknowledged nature alone and human prudence alone constitute hell; while those that have acknowledged God and His Divine providence constitute heaven.

(7) None of these things could be done except from the appearance to man that he thinks from himself and directs all things from himself.

193. (1) *All of man's thoughts are from the affections of his life's love; and apart from these there are and can be no thoughts whatever.* What in their essence the life's love and the affections and their thoughts are, and what the sensations and actions from these which exist in the body are, has been shown above in this work, and also in the work entitled *Angelic Wisdom concerning the Divine Love and the Divine Wisdom*, particularly in Parts One and Five. Since, then, the causes from which human prudence flows forth as an effect are from these, it is necessary to set forth here something in respect to these; for things written elsewhere cannot be brought into close connection with things written later unless they are repeated and viewed together. [2] Earlier in the present work, and in the one just mentioned on *The Divine Love and the Divine Wisdom*, the following principles are set forth: In the Lord there are Divine love and Divine wisdom; these two are Life itself; from these two man has will and understanding, will from the

11

Divine love and understanding from the Divine wisdom; and
to these two the heart and lungs in the body correspond. From
this it is clear that as the pulsation of the heart together with
the respiration of the lungs governs the whole man in respect
to his body, so the will together with the understanding governs the whole man in respect to his mind. Thus in every
man there are two principles of life, the one natural and the
other spiritual, the natural principle of life being the heart's
pulsation, and the spiritual principle of life the mind's volition; each of these joins to itself its mate, with which it cohabits, and with which it performs the functions of life, the
heart joining with itself the lungs, and the will joining with
itself the understanding. [**3**] Since, then, the soul of the will
is love and the soul of the understanding is wisdom, both of
them from the Lord, it follows that love is every one's life,
and the love is such life as is conjoined with wisdom; or, what
is the same, that the will is every one's life, and the will is
such life as is conjoined with the understanding. But more
on this subject may be seen above in this work, also in the
*Angelic Wisdom concerning the Divine Love and the Divine
Wisdom*, especially in Parts One and Five.

194. In these works it has also been shown that the life's
love produces from itself subordinate loves, which are called
affections, and that these are exterior and interior; also that
these when taken together form as it were one sovereignty or
kingdom, in which the life's love is lord or king. It has also
been shown that these subordinate loves or affections join to
themselves mates, each its own; the interior affections, mates
called perceptions, and the exterior affections, mates called
thoughts; and that each cohabits with its own mate, and dis-
charges the offices of its life; also that the conjunction of each
is like that of life's being (*esse*) with life's going forth (*existere*),
which is such that one is nothing except with the other; for
what is life's being unless it goes forth, and what is life's going
forth except from life's being? Moreover, the conjunction in
the life is like that between tone and harmony, or between tone

and speech, and in general like that between the heart's pulsation and the lungs' respiration, which conjunction is such that
one is nothing without the other, and each becomes something
by conjunction with the other. Either there must be conjunctions in them or conjunctions must be effected by them. Take
tone for example: He is mistaken who thinks that tone is
anything unless there is in it that which makes it distinctive.
Moreover, the tone corresponds with the affection in man; and
because there is always something that is distinctive in it the
affection of one's love can be recognized from his tone when
speaking; and from the variation of it, which is speech, his
thought can be recognized. For this reason the wiser angels
merely from the tone of the voice of one speaking have a perception of his life's loves, together with certain affections derived from them. This has been said to make known that no
affection is possible apart from its thought, nor any thought
apart from its affection. But more on this subject may be seen
in the present work; also in *Angelic Wisdom concerning the
Divine Love and the Divine Wisdom.*

195. Now as the life's love has its delight, and the wisdom
thereof has its enjoyment, likewise every affection (which in
its essence is a subordinate love derived from the life's love,
as a stream from its fountain, as a branch from its tree, or as
an artery from its heart), so every particular affection has its
delight, and every particular perception and thought therefrom
has its enjoyment. And from this it follows that the varieties
of delight and enjoyment constitute man's life. What is life
without delight and enjoyment? It is not anything animate,
but it is inanimate. Lessen these and you will grow cold or
torpid; take them away and you will cease to breathe and will
die. [2] Vital heat is from the delights of the affections, and
from the enjoyment of the perceptions and thoughts. And
since every affection has its own delight, and the thought therefrom its own enjoyment, the source of good and truth can be
seen, also what good and truth are in their essence. Every
one's good is that which is delightful to his affection; and truth

is that which is enjoyable therefrom to his thought. For every one calls that good which, from the love of his will, he feels to be delightful; and he calls that truth which, from the wisdom of his understanding, he perceives to be enjoyable therefrom. Both of these flow from the life's love as water flows from a fountain, or as blood from the heart. Taken together they are like a wave or a breeze in which is the whole human mind. [3] These two, delight and enjoyment, are spiritual in the mind, but natural in the body; and together they constitute man's life. From all this it is clear what it is in man that is called good, and what it is that is called truth; also what it is in man that is called evil, and what it is that is called falsity; for that is evil to him that destroys the delight of his affection, and that is falsity that destroys the enjoyment of his thought therefrom. It is also clear that evil from its delight and falsity from its enjoyment may be called and may be believed to be good and truth. In fact, goods and truths are changes and variations of state in the forms of the mind; but these are perceived and have their life solely by means of their delights and enjoyments. These things have been presented to make known what affection and thought are in their life.

196. Since, then, it is man's mind and not his body that thinks (and it thinks from the delight of its affection), and since man's mind is his spirit, which lives after death, it follows that man's spirit is nothing but affection and the thought therefrom. That no thought is possible apart from affection is clearly evident from the state of spirits and angels in the spiritual world, in that all there think from the affections of their life's love, and the delight of these affections encompasses every one as his atmosphere; and all are joined together in accord with these spheres that exhale from their affections through their thoughts. Moreover, what each one is is recognized from the sphere of his life. From all this it may be seen that every thought is from an affection, and is a form of its affection. It is the same with the will and the understanding; also with good and truth; also with charity and faith.

197. (2) *The affections of a man's life's love are known to the Lord alone.* Man knows his thoughts and consequent intentions, because he sees them in himself; and as all prudence is from these, he also sees that in himself. If, then, his life's love is love of self, he comes into the pride of his own intelligence and ascribes prudence to himself, and collects arguments in its favor, and thus recedes from the acknowledgment of the Divine providence. It is the same when his life's love is love of the world; although in this case he does not recede in the same degree. This shows that these two loves ascribe every thing to man and his prudence, and, when interiorly examined, ascribe nothing to God and His providence. Consequently, when such men happen to hear that the truth is that human prudence is nothing, but that it is the Divine providence alone that governs all things, if they are complete atheists they laugh at it; but if they retain in their memory something of religion, and it is said to them that all wisdom is from God, at the first hearing they assent, although inwardly in their spirit they deny it. Such, especially, are those priests who love themselves more than God, and the world more than heaven; or what is the same, who worship God for the sake of honor and gain, and yet have preached that charity and faith, every good and truth, also all wisdom and even prudence, are from God, and nothing from man. [2] In the spiritual world I once heard two priests disputing with a certain royal ambassador about human prudence, whether it is from God or from man. The dispute grew warm. In heart the three believed alike, namely, that human prudence does all things, and the Divine providence nothing; but the priests, who were then in theological zeal, asserted that nothing of wisdom or prudence is from man; and when the ambassador retorted that then there is nothing of thought from man, they assented to this. And the angels perceiving that the three believed alike, the ambassador was told to put on priestly robes and to believe himself to be a priest, and then to speak. He put them on and believed, and then loudly declared that there could not possibly be anything of wisdom or prudence in

man except from God; and with his accustomed eloquence, full
of rational arguments, he defended this. Afterwards the two
priests were told to lay aside their vestments and to put on the
robes of officers of state, and to believe themselves to be such.
This they did, and at once thought from their interior self, and
spoke from arguments they had inwardly cherished before, in
favor of human prudence and against Divine providence. After
this the three, since they held the same belief, became cordial
friends, and entered together upon the way of one's own prudence, which leads to hell.

198. It has been shown above that no thought is possible
to man except from some affection of his life's love; and that
thought is nothing but the form of affection. Since, then,
man sees his thought, but cannot see his affection, for that he
feels, it follows that it is from sight, which is in the appearance, and not from affection, which comes into feeling and not
into sight, that man concludes that his own prudence does all
things. For affection is evident only through a certain delight
in thought and satisfaction in reasoning about it; and this
satisfaction and delight then make one with the thought in
those who from self-love or love of the world believe in their
own prudence; and thought floats on in its delight like a ship in
the current of a stream, to which the master pays no attention,
regarding only the sail he spreads.

199. Nevertheless, a man may reflect upon a delight of his
external affection while that delight is acting as one with the
delight of some bodily sensation. Nevertheless, he does not
reflect upon the fact that this delight is from a delight of his
affection in his thought. For example: when a fornicator sees
a lewd woman his eye glows with the fire of lasciviousness,
and from that fire he feels a delight in the body. And yet
in his thought he feels no delight of his affection or lust except a certain longing connected with the body. So a robber
in a forest when he sees travellers; or a pirate on the sea when
he sees vessels; and so on. Evidently it is these delights that
rule the man's thoughts and the thoughts are nothing apart

from them; yet they seem to him to be nothing but thoughts; when in fact, thoughts are nothing but affections so composed into forms by his life's love as to be presented in light; for all affection is in heat, and thought is in light. [2] Such are the external affections of thought, which manifest themselves in bodily sensation, but rarely in the thought of the mind. But the internal affections of thought, from which the external affections have their existence, never manifest themselves before man. Of these man knows no more than one sleeping in a carriage knows of the road, or than one feels the revolution of the earth. Considering, then, that man knows nothing of the things that are going on in the interiors of his mind, which are too limitless to be numbered, and yet those few externals that do come within the view of his thought are produced from the interiors, and the interiors are governed by the Lord alone by His Divine providence, and only those few externals by the Lord and man together, how can any one say that his own prudence does all things? If you were to see but one idea of thought laid open you would see wonderful things, more in number than tongue can express. [3] That in the interiors of man's mind there are things too limitless to be numbered is clear from the infinite things in the body, from which nothing comes to sight or feeling except action only in much simplicity; and yet in this thousands of motor or muscular fibers concur, thousands of nerve fibers, thousands of blood-vessels, thousands of lung cells, all of which must co-operate in every action, thousands of cells in the brains and spinal cord, and many more yet in the spiritual man, which is the human mind, in which all things are forms of affections and of their perceptions and thoughts. Does not the soul, which directs the interiors, direct also the actions from them? Man's soul is nothing else than the love of his will and the love therefrom of his understanding. The quality of that love is the quality of the whole man; and that is determined by the way in which the externals are disposed, in which man and the Lord co-operate. Consequently, if man attributes all things to himself and to nature the love of self becomes the soul; but if he attributes all things to the Lord, love to the Lord becomes the soul; and this love is heavenly, while the other is infernal.

200. Since, then, the delights of man's affections, from inmosts through interiors to exteriors, and finally to the outermosts which are in the body, bear man along as a current or breeze bears a ship, and nothing of these is evident to man except what goes on in the outermosts of the mind and of the body, how can man claim as his own what is Divine merely because these few outermosts appear to him to be his? Still less ought he to claim what is Divine as his own, when he knows from the *Word* that a man can of himself "receive nothing except it have been given him from heaven;" and from *Reason*, that this appearance has been granted him in order that he may live as a man, may see what is good and what is evil, may choose one or the other, may appropriate to himself that which he chooses, and may thus be conjoined reciprocally with the Lord, be reformed, regenerated, saved, and may live for ever. That this appearance has been granted to man in order that he may act from freedom in accordance with reason, thus as if from himself, and may not let his hands hang down and wait for influx, has been stated and shown above. From this follows, as already proved, the next proposition to be demonstrated: (3) *By means of His Divine providence the Lord leads the affections of a man's life's love, and at the same time leads his thoughts, from which human prudence is derived.*

201. (4) *By means of His Divine Providence the Lord collects the affections [of the whole human race] into one form, which is the human form.* That this is the universal [end] of the Divine providence will be seen in the next section. Those who ascribe all things to nature also ascribe all things to human prudence; for those who ascribe all things to nature deny God in heart; and those who ascribe all things to human prudence deny in heart the Divine providence; the two are inseparable. And yet both, for the sake of their good name and from fear of losing it, admit in words that the Divine providence is universal, and that its particulars rest with man, and that these particulars in the aggregate are what are meant by human prudence. [2] But reflect within yourself what a universal providence is when the particulars are taken away. Is it anything more than a mere phrase? For that is called universal which is made up of the most particular things taken together, like any general thing that exists from its particulars. So if the most particular things are taken away what is the universal but like a something empty within, thus like a surface with nothing inside, or an aggregate that includes nothing? If it is claimed that the Divine providence is a universal government, while nothing is governed, but things are merely held in connection, and the matters pertaining to the government are conducted by others, how can this be called a universal government? There is no king with such a government; for if any king should permit his subjects to govern all things of his kingdom he would no longer be a king, but would be merely so called; thus he would have the dignity of the mere title, but not of any reality. Government cannot be predicated of such a king, still less universal government. [3] That which is called providence in God is called prudence in a man; and as a king cannot be said to have universal prudence when he has reserved nothing but the title, in order that his kingdom may be called a kingdom and thus be held together, so there cannot be said to be a universal providence when all things are provided by men from their own prudence. The same is true of the terms universal providence and universal government when applied to nature, with the understanding that God created the universe and endowed nature with the power of producing all things from itself. In this case, what else is universal providence than a metaphysical term, which, except as a term, is a nonentity? Of those who attribute all that is produced to nature and all that is done to human prudence, but who still say with the lips that God created nature, there are many who never think about the Divine providence except as an empty term. But the real truth is, that the Divine providence is in the minutest particulars of nature, and in the minutest particulars of human prudence, and that it is from these that it is universal.

202. The Lord's Divine providence is universal from the minutest particulars, in that He created the universe that an infinite and eternal creation from Himself might exist in it; and this creation exists by the Lord's forming a heaven out of men to be before Him as one man, which is His image and likeness. That this heaven formed out of men is such in the Lord's sight, and that this was the end of creation, is shown above (n. 27–45); also that the Divine in all that it does, looks to the infinite and eternal (n. 46–69). The infinite and eternal that the Lord looks to in forming His heaven out of men, is that it shall be enlarged to infinity and to eternity, and that He may thus have a constant abiding place in the end of His creation. This is the infinite and eternal creation that the Lord provided for through the creation of the universe; and He is constantly present in that creation by His Divine providence. [2] Who that knows and believes from the doctrine of the church that God is infinite and eternal (*for it is in the doctrine of all the churches in the Christian world that God the Father, God the Son, and God the Holy Spirit, is infinite, eternal, uncreated, and omnipotent, as may be seen in the Athanasian creed*), can be so devoid of reason as not to admit as soon as he hears it that God cannot do otherwise than look to what is infinite and eternal in the great work of His creation? For what else can He look to when He looks from Himself? This also He looks to in the human race, from which He forms that heaven which is His own. What else, then, can the Divine providence have for its end than the reformation and salvation of the human race? But no one can be reformed by himself by means of his own prudence, but only by the Lord by means of His Divine providence. Thus it follows that unless man were led every moment and fraction of a moment by the Lord, he would depart from the way of reformation and would perish. [3] Every change and variation of the state of the human mind produces some change and variation in the series of things present, and consequently in the things that follow; why not then progressively to eternity ? It is like an arrow shot from a bow, which, if it should depart in the least at its start from the line of aim, would at a distance of a thousand paces or more go far wide of the mark. So would it be if the Lord did not lead the states of human minds every least moment. This the Lord does in accordance with the laws of His Divine providence; and it is in accordance with these laws that it should appear to man that he leads himself; while how he leads himself is foreseen by the Lord with an unceasing adaptation. That laws of permission are also laws of the Divine providence, and that every man can be reformed and regenerated, and that there is no other possible predestination, will be seen in what follows.

203. Since, therefore, every man lives for ever after death, and is allotted a place according to his life, either in heaven or in hell, and since both heaven and hell must exist in a form that will act as a one, as said before, and since no one can be allotted in that form any place but his own, it follows that the human race throughout the whole world is under the Lord's auspices; and that each one, from infancy even to the end of his life, is led by the Lord in the least particulars, and his place foreseen and at the same time provided. [2] From all this it is clear that the Lord's Divine providence is universal because it is in every least particular; and that this is the infinite and eternal creation which the Lord provided for Himself by means of the creation of the universe. Of this universal providence man sees nothing. If he did see it it would appear in his eyes only as one passing sees scattered heaps and accumulated material from which a house is to be built, while the Lord sees it as a magnificent palace, with its work of construction and enlargement constantly going on.

204. (5) *Heaven and hell are in such a form.* That heaven is in the human form has been made known in the work on *Heaven and Hell,* published in London in 1758 (n. 59–102);

also the work on *The Divine Love and the Divine Wisdom;* also in several places in the present treatise. Further evidence will therefore be omitted. Hell also is said to be in the human form; but it is in a monstrous human form, like that of the devil, by whom is meant hell in the whole complex. Hell is in the human form, because those who are there were also born men, and have the two human faculties called liberty and rationality; although they have abused their liberty in willing and doing evil, and their rationality in thinking and confirming evil.

205. (6) *Those that have acknowledged nature alone and human prudence alone constitute hell; while those that have acknowledged God and His Divine providence constitute heaven.* All who lead an evil life interiorly acknowledge nature and human prudence only; the acknowledgment of these is inwardly hidden in all evil, howsoever it may be covered over with goods and truths. These are only borrowed garments, or are like wreaths of perishable flowers, put on lest evil should appear in its nakedness. Because of this general covering it is not known that all who lead an evil life interiorly acknowledge nature alone and human prudence alone, for this is hidden from sight by the covering. But by considering the source and cause of their acknowledgment it can be made clear that it is such. To make this evident it shall be told whence man's own prudence is and what it is; and then whence the Divine providence is and what it is; also who and what those are of each class; and finally, that those who acknowledge the Divine providence are in heaven, and those who acknowledge their own prudence are in hell.

206. *Whence man's prudence is and what it is.* It is from man's own (*proprium*) which is his nature, and is called his soul from his parent. This own is the love of self and the love of the world therefrom, or is the love of the world and the love of self therefrom. It is the nature of the love of self to regard self only, and to regard others as of little or no account; if it gives any consideration to some, it is only so long as they honor and pay court to it. Inmostly in that love, like the endeavor in seed to bring forth fruit or offspring, there lies hidden a desire to become great, and if possible to become a ruler, and still further if possible to become a god. A devil is such, for he is self-love itself; he is such that he adores himself, and favors no one who does not adore him; any other devil like himself he hates, because he wishes to be adored exclusively. As there is no love without its mate, and as the mate of the love or the will in man is called the understanding, when the love of self breathes its own love into its mate, the understanding, this in the mate becomes conceit, which is the conceit of one's own intelligence. This is the origin of one's own prudence. [2] Since, then, the love of self wills to be the sole lord of the world, and thus a god, the lusts of evil, which are derivatives of that love, have their life from it; the same is true of the perceptions belonging to the lusts, which are devices; also of the delights belonging to the lusts, which are evils; also of the thoughts belonging to the delights, which are falsities. They are all like servants and attendants of their lord and obey his every nod, not knowing that they do not act, but are only acted upon. They are acted upon by the love of self through the conceit of their own intelligence. This makes clear how it is that in every evil, from its origin, one's own prudence lies hidden. [3] The acknowledgment of nature alone also lies hidden in it, because it has closed the window of its roof which opens heavenward, as well as the side windows, lest it should see and hear that the Lord alone governs all things, and that nature in itself is dead, and that man's own is hell, and consequently the love of one's own is the devil. Then, with its windows closed it is in darkness, and there it makes a hearth for itself at which it sits with its mate, and they reason together in a friendly way in favor of nature and against God, and in favor of one's own prudence and against the Divine providence.

207. *Whence the Divine providence is and what it is.* It is the Divine operation in man that takes away the love of self;

for, as just said, the love of self is the devil; and lusts and their enjoyment are the evils of his kingdom, which is hell. When that love has been taken away the Lord enters with affections of love of the neighbor, and opens the roof-window, and then the side-windows, and enables man to see that there is a heaven, a life after death, and eternal happiness; and by means of the spiritual light together with the spiritual love then flowing in He enables man to acknowledge that God governs all things by His Divine providence.

208. *Who and what those of each class are.* Those who acknowledge God and His Divine providence are like the angels of heaven, who are averse to being led by themselves and love to be led by the Lord. It is an evidence that they are led by the Lord that they love the neighbor. But those who acknowledge nature and their own prudence are like spirits of hell, who are averse to being led by the Lord and love to be led by themselves. If they have been great men in a kingdom they wish to rule over all things; likewise if they have been primates of the church; if they have been judges they pervert judgment and exercise arbitrary power over the laws; if they have been learned they employ their knowledges to uphold what is man's own (*proprium*) and nature; if they have been merchants they act as robbers; if husbandmen they act as thieves. They are all enemies of God and scoffers at the Divine providence.

209. It is remarkable that when to such heaven is opened, and they are told that they are insane, and this is also made evident to their very perception, which is done by influx and enlightenment, still they shut up heaven to themselves with indignation, and look to the earth, under which is hell. This takes place with those in the spiritual world who are not yet in hell, and who are of this character. This shows how mistaken those are who think, " When I shall have seen heaven and shall have heard angels talking with me I shall acknowledge." Their understanding acknowledges; and yet if the will does not also acknowledge they do not acknowledge; for the will's love inspires the understanding with whatever it desires, and not the reverse; it even destroys in the understanding every thing that is not from itself.

210. (8) *None of these things could be done except from the appearance to man that he thinks from himself and directs all things from himself.* It has been fully shown in what has gone before that man would not be man except for the appearance to him that he lives from himself, and therefore thinks and wills and speaks and acts as if from himself. From this it follows that unless man, as if from his own prudence, directs all things belonging to his employment and life, he cannot be led and directed by the Divine providence; for he would be like one standing with relaxed hands, opened mouth, closed eyes, and breath indrawn, awaiting influx. Thus he would divest himself of humanity, which he has from the perception and sensation that he lives, thinks, wills, speaks, and acts as if from himself; he would also divest himself of his two faculties, liberty and rationality, by which he is distinguished from the beasts. That without this appearance a man would have no capacity to receive and reciprocate, and thus no immortality, has been shown above in the present work, and also in the work on *The Divine Love and the Divine Wisdom.* [2] If, therefore, you wish to be led by the Divine providence use prudence as a servant and minister who faithfully dispenses the goods of his master. This prudence is the talent given to the servants to trade with, of which they must render an account (*Luke* xix. 13–28; *Matt.* xxv. 14–31). Prudence itself appears to man to be his own; and he believes it to be his own so long as he keeps shut up within him the deadliest enemy of God and of Divine providence, the love of self. This has its abode in the interiors of every man from his birth; if you do not recognize it (for it does not wish to be recognized) it dwells securely, and guards the door lest man should open it and the Lord should thereby cast it out. Man opens this door by shunning evils as sins as if from himself, with the acknowledgment that he does it from the Lord. This is the prudence with which the Divine providence acts as one.

211. The Divine providence, in order that man may not perish, works so secretly that scarcely any one knows of its existence. For man's own (*proprium*), which is his will, in no wise acts as one with the Divine providence; man's own has an inborn enmity against it; in fact, man's own is the serpent that seduced the first parents, of which it is said:—

I will put enmity between thee and the woman, and between thy seed and her Seed; and it shall bruise thy head (*Gen.* iii. 15).

"The serpent" is evil of all kinds; its "head" is love of self; "the Seed of the woman" is the Lord; the "enmity," that is put, is between the love belonging to man's own and the Lord, and thus between man's own prudence and the Lord's Divine providence. For man's own prudence is continually raising its head, and the Divine providence is continually putting it down. [2] If man felt this he would be provoked and enraged against God, and would perish; but as long as he does not feel it he may be provoked and enraged against men and with himself, and also against fortune, but this does not destroy him. In this way the Lord by His Divine providence continually leads man in freedom, and the freedom always appears to man to be that which is his own. And to lead man in freedom in opposition to himself, is like raising a heavy and resisting weight from the earth by means of screws, through the power of which the weight and resistance are not felt; or it is like a man in company with an enemy who intends to kill him, which at the time he does not know, and a friend leads him away by unknown paths, and afterwards discloses his enemy's intention.

212. Who does not talk about fortune? And who does not acknowledge it, because he talks about it, and knows something about it from experience? But who knows what it is? That it is something, since it exists and operates, cannot be denied; and a thing cannot exist and operate without a cause; but the cause of this something, that is, of fortune, is unknown. But that fortune be not denied because its cause is unknown, take dice or cards and play, or talk with those who play. Do any such deny fortune? For they play with it and it with them in a wonderful way. Who can succeed against fortune if it is obstinate? Does it not then laugh at prudence and wisdom? While you shake the dice and shuffle the cards, does not fortune seem to know and to direct the turns and movements of the muscles of the hand, to favor one party more than the other from some cause? And can the cause have any other possible source than the Divine providence in outmosts, where by things constant and things inconstant it deals wonderfully with human prudence, and yet conceals itself? [2] It is known that the heathen formerly acknowledged Fortune and built her a temple, also the Italians at Rome. About this fortune, which is as has been said, the Divine providence in outmosts, it has been granted me to learn many things that I am not permitted to disclose; by which it has been made clear to me that it is no illusion of the mind or sport of nature, nor a something without a cause, for that is not anything, but an ocular proof that the Divine providence is in the least particulars of man's thoughts and actions. As the Divine providence is in the least particulars of things so insignificant and trifling, why should it not be in the least particulars of things not insignificant and trifling, as the affairs of peace and war in the world, or of salvation and life in heaven?

213. But I know that human prudence is more able to draw the reason over to its side than the Divine providence is, because the Divine providence does not make itself evident as human prudence does. That there is one only life, which is God, and that all men are recipients of life from Him, as frequently shown before, can be more easily accepted; and yet this is the same thing, for prudence belongs to the life. Who in his reasoning, when he speaks from the natural or external man, does not speak in favor of one's own prudence and in favor of nature? And who in his reasoning, when he speaks from the spiritual or internal man, does not speak in favor of the Divine providence and of God? But to the natural man I say, Pray write two books, one in favor of one's own prudence,

12

the other in favor of nature, and fill them with arguments plausible, probable, likely, and in your judgment valid; and then give them into the hand of any angel; and I know that the angel will write underneath these few words, They are all appearances and fallacies.

THE DIVINE PROVIDENCE LOOKS TO ETERNAL THINGS AND TO TEMPORAL THINGS ONLY SO FAR AS THEY AGREE WITH ETERNAL THINGS.

214. That the Divine providence looks to eternal things, and to temporal things only so far as they make one with eternal things, will be shown in the following order :—

(1) Temporal things relate to dignities and riches, thus to honors and acquisitions in the world.

(2) Eternal things relate to spiritual honors and possessions which pertain to love and wisdom in heaven.

(3) Temporal things and eternal things are separated by man, but are conjoined by the Lord.

(4) The conjunction of temporal things and eternal things is the Lord's Divine providence.

215. (1) *Temporal things relate to dignities and riches, thus to honors and acquisitions in the world.* Temporal things are manifold, but they all relate to dignities and riches. Temporal things mean such as either perish with time, or are merely terminated with man's life in the world; but eternal things mean such as do not perish or terminate with time, thus not with life in the world. And since, as has been said, all temporal things have relation to dignities and riches it is important to know the following, namely, what dignities and riches are and whence they are; what the love of them for their own sake is, and what the love of them for the sake of uses is; that these two loves are as distinct from each other as heaven and hell are; that the difference between these two loves can scarcely be known by man. But of these separately. [2] First:

What dignities and riches are, and whence they are. Dignities
and riches in the most ancient times were wholly different
from what they afterwards gradually became. Dignities in the
earliest times were such only as were accorded by children to
parents ; they were dignities of love, full of respect and veneration, not on account of their birth from them but because of
the instruction and wisdom received from them, which was a
second birth, in itself spiritual, because it was the birth of
their spirit. This was the only dignity in the earliest times ;
for tribes, families, and households then dwelt apart, and
not under general governments as at this day. It was the
father of the family to whom this dignity was accorded. By
the ancients those times were called the golden ages. [3] But
after those times the love of rule from the mere delight of
that love gradually came in ; and because enmity and hos-
tility against those who were unwilling to submit entered at
the same time, tribes, families, and households necessarily
gathered themselves together into general communities, and appointed over themselves one whom they at first called judge, and
afterwards prince, and finally king and emperor. At the same
time they began to protect themselves by towers, earthworks,
and walls. From judge, prince, king, or emperor, as from the
head into the body, the lust of ruling spread like a contagion
to others ; and from this arose degrees of dignity, and also
honors according to them ; and with these the love of self and
the pride of one's own prudence. [4] Then there was a like
change in regard to the love of riches. In the earliest times,
when tribes and families dwelt apart from one another, there
was no other love of riches than a desire to possess the necessaries of life, which they acquired by means of their flocks
and herds, and their lands, fields, and gardens, which furnished them with food. Among their necessaries of life were
also suitable houses, furnished with useful things of every
kind, and also clothing. The parents, children, servants, and
maids in a house, were engaged in the care and labor connected
with all these things. [5] But when the love of rule had

entered and destroyed this commonwealth, the love of possessing wealth beyond their necessities also entered, and grew to such a height that it desired to possess the wealth of all others. These two loves are like blood-relations; for he that wishes to rule over all things also wishes to possess all things; for thus all others become servants, and they alone lords. This is clearly evident from those within the papal jurisdiction, who have exalted their dominion even into heaven to the throne of the Lord, upon which they have placed themselves; they also seek to grasp the wealth of all the earth, and to enlarge their treasuries without end. [6] Secondly: *What the love of dignities and riches for their own sake is, and what the love of dignities and riches for the sake of uses is.* The love of dignities and honors for the sake of dignities and honors is the love of self, strictly, the love of ruling from the love of self; and the love of riches and possessions for the sake of riches and possessions is the love of the world, strictly, the love of possessing the goods of others by any device whatever. But the love of dignities and riches for the sake of uses is the love of uses, which is the same as love of the neighbor; for that for the sake of which man acts is the end from which he acts, and this is first or chief, while all other things are means and are secondary. [7] As to the love of dignities and honors for their own sake, which is the same as the love of self, or, strictly, the same as the love of rule from the love of self, it is the love of one's own (*proprium*), and man's own is all evil. For this reason man is said to be born into all evil, and what he has hereditarily is nothing but evil. What man has hereditarily is his own, in which he is and into which he comes through the love of self, and especially through the love of ruling from love of self; for the man who is in that love looks only to himself, and thus immerses his thoughts and affections in what is his own. Consequently there is in the love of self the love of doing evil; and for the reason that the man loves not the neighbor but himself alone; and he who loves himself alone sees others only as apart from himself, or as insignificant or of no account, and he despises them in comparison with himself, accounting it nothing to inflict evil upon them. [8] And this is why one who is in the love of ruling from the love of self thinks nothing of defrauding the neighbor, committing adultery with his wife, defaming him, breathing revenge against him even to murder, venting his rage against him, and so on. Man becomes such for the reason that the devil himself, with whom he is conjoined and by whom he is led, is nothing else than a love of ruling from the love of self; and he who is led by the devil, that is, by hell, is led into all these evils; and he is led continually by means of the delights of these evils. For this reason all who are in hell wish to do evil to all, while those who are in heaven wish to do good to all. From the opposition between these an intermediate state arises in which man is, and in it he is as it were in equilibrium, which enables him to turn either to hell or to heaven; and so far as he favors the evils of love of self he turns towards hell, but so far as he rejects those evils from himself he turns toward heaven. [9] What and how great the delight of the love of ruling from the love of self is it has been granted me to feel. I was let into it that I might know what it is. It was such as to surpass all the delights that there are in the world; it was a delight of the whole mind from its inmosts to its outmosts; but it was felt in the body only as an agreeable and pleasurable sensation in the swelling breast. It was also granted me to perceive that from that delight, as from their fountain, gushed forth the delights of all evils, as adultery, revenge, fraud, defamation, and evil doing in general. There is a like delight in the love of possessing the goods of others by whatever device, and from that love in the lusts derived from it; yet not in the same degree unless that love is conjoined with the love of self. But in regard to dignities and riches not for their own sake but for the sake of uses, this is not a love of dignities and riches, but a love of uses, to which dignities and riches are serviceable as means; this is a heavenly love. But more on this subject hereafter. [10] Thirdly: *These two loves are distinct from each other as heaven and hell are.* This is clear from what has just been said; to which I will add, that all who are in a love of ruling from a love of self, whoever they are, whether great or small, are in hell as to their spirits; and that all who are in that love are in the love of all evils, and if they do not commit them, in their spirit they believe them to be allowable, and therefore they do them in the body when dignity and honor and fear of the law do not hinder. And what is more, the love of ruling from the love of self inmostly conceals in itself hatred against God, consequently against the Divine things pertaining to the church, and especially against the Lord. If they acknowledge God it is only with the lips; and if they acknowledge the Divine things of the church it is from a fear of the loss of honor. Such a love has inmostly stored up in it hatred against the Lord, for the reason that there is inmostly in it a desire to be God, since it worships and adores itself alone. Therefore if any one honors it so far as to say that it possesses Divine wisdom and is the deity of the world, it heartily loves him. [11] It is not so with the love of dignities and riches for the sake of uses; this is a heavenly love, being the same, as has been said, as love of the neighbor. By *uses* goods are meant; and therefore doing uses means doing goods, and doing uses or goods means serving others and ministering to them. Although such enjoy dignity and wealth they regard them only as a means for performing uses, thus for serving and ministering. Such are meant by these words of the Lord :—

Whosoever will become great among you must be your minister; and whosoever will be first must be your servant (*Matt.* xx. 26, 27).

To such also dominion in heaven is entrusted by the Lord; because to such, dominion is a means for doing uses or goods, thus for serving; and when uses or goods are the ends or loves it is the Lord and not they that rule, for all good is from the Lord. [12] Fourthly: *The difference between these loves can scarcely be made known to man.* For most of those who possess dignity and wealth also perform uses; but they do not know whether they do this for their own sake or for the sake of the uses; and this is still less known because there is more of the fire and ardor of doing uses in love of self and the world than there is in those who are not in the love of self and the world; but the former perform uses for the sake of reputation or gain, thus for the sake of self; while those who perform uses for the sake of uses, or goods for the sake of goods, do this from the Lord, and not from self. [13] The difference between these can scarcely be recognized by man, because man does not know whether he is led by the devil or by the Lord. He that is led by the devil performs uses for the sake of self and the world; but he that is led by the Lord performs uses for the sake of the Lord and heaven; and all who shun evils as sins perform uses from the Lord, while all who do not shun evils as sins perform uses from the devil; since evil is the devil, and use or good is the Lord. In this and in no other way is the difference recognized. In external form they appear alike, but in internal form they are wholly unlike. One is like gold within which is dross, the other is like gold with pure gold within. One is like artificial fruit, which in external form appears like fruit from a tree, although it is colored wax containing within it dust or bitumen; while the other is like excellent fruit, pleasing in taste and smell, and containing seeds within.

216. (2) *Eternal things relate to spiritual honors and possesssions which pertain to love and wisdom in heaven.* As the delights of the love of self, which are also delights of the lusts of evil, are called good by the natural man, and he confirms himself in the idea that they are good, therefore he calls honor and possessions Divine blessings. But when this natural man sees that the evil as well as the good are exalted to honors and advanced to wealth, and still more when he sees the good despised and in poverty, and the evil in glory and opulence, he thinks to himself, "Why is this? It cannot be of the Divine providence. For if that governed all things it would heap honors and possessions upon the good, and would afflict the evil with poverty and contempt, and thus drive the evil to the ac-

knowledgment that there is a God and a Divine providence."
[2] But the natural man, unless enlightened by the spiritual
man, that is, unless he is at the same time spiritual, does not
see that honors and possessions may be blessings and also may
be curses, and that when they are blessings they are from God,
and when they are curses they are from the devil. Also that
honors and possessions may be from the devil is confessed, for
from this he is called the prince of the world. Since, then, it
is not known when honors and possessions are blessings and
when they are curses it shall be told, and in the following
order: (1) Honors and possessions are blessings and they are
curses. (2) When honors and possessions are blessings they are
spiritual and eternal, but when they are curses they are temporal and perishable. (3) Honors and possessions that are
curses, compared with honors and possessions that are blessings,
are as nothing to everything, or as that which in itself is not
to that which in itself is.

217. These three points shall now be illustrated separately.
First: *Honors and possessions are blessings and they are curses.*
General experience testifies that both the pious and the impious, or both the just and the unjust, that is, both the good and
the evil, alike enjoy dignities and possessions, and yet no one
can deny that the impious and unjust, that is, the evil, come
into hell, while the pious and just, that is, the good, come into
heaven. This being true it follows that dignities and riches,
or honors and possessions, are both blessings and curses; blessings to the good and curses to the evil. In the work on *Heaven
and Hell*, published at London in the year 1758 (n. 357–365),
it has been shown that in heaven there are both rich and
poor, and both great and small, and in hell also; which makes
clear that dignities and riches were blessings in the world to
those now in heaven, and were curses in the world to those
now in hell. [2] But why they are blessings and why they are
curses any one may know if he only reflects a little about it
from reason; that is, he may know that they are blessings to
those who do not set their hearts upon them, and curses to

those who do set their hearts upon them. To set the heart upon them is to love oneself in them; and not to set the heart upon them is to love uses in them, and not self. What difference there is between these two loves, and what that difference is has been told above (n. 215); to which must be added that some are led astray by dignities and possessions, and some are not. These lead astray when they excite the loves of man's own (*proprium*), which is love of self. That this is the love of hell, which is called the devil, has also been shown above. But they do not lead astray when they do not excite this love. [3] Both the evil and the good are exalted to honors and advanced to wealth, because the evil equally with the good perform uses; but the evil do this for the sake of honors and profit to their own person, while the good do it for the sake of the honors and profit to the work itself. The good regard the honors and profit pertaining to the work itself as principal motives, and the honors and profit pertaining to their own person as instrumental motives; while the evil regard the honors and profit pertaining to the person as principal motives, and those to the work as instrumental motives. But who does not see that the person and his work and honor are for the sake of the matter which he is administering, and not the reverse? Who does not see that the judge is for the sake of justice, the magistrate for the sake of the common welfare, and the king for the sake of the kingdom, and not the reverse? And therefore every one, in accordance with the laws of the kingdom, is in dignity and honor according to the dignity of the task he is performing. And who does not see that the difference is like that between what is principal and what is instrumental? He that attributes to himself or to his own person the honor belonging to his function appears in the spiritual world, when there is a representation of it, like a man with his body inverted, feet up and and head down. [4] Secondly: *When dignities and possessions are blessings they are spiritual and eternal, and when they are curses they are temporal and perishable.* There are dignities and possessions in heaven as in the world, for there are gov ernments there, and consequently administrations and functions, also business transactions and consequent possessions, since there are societies and communities there. The entire heaven is divided into two kingdoms, one of which is called the celestial kingdom, the other the spiritual kingdom; and each kingdom into societies without number, larger and smaller; all of which, with all who are in them, are arranged according to differences of love and of wisdom therefrom; the societies of the celestial heaven according to the differences of celestial love, which is love to the Lord, and the societies of the spiritual kingdom according to the differences of spiritual love, which is love towards the neighbor. Because these societies are such, and because all who are in them have been men in the world, and therefore retain the loves which they had in the world (with the difference that they are now spiritual, and that the dignities and possessions are now spiritual in the spiritual kingdom and celestial in the celestial kingdom), therefore those who have love and wisdom more than others have dignities and possessions more than others; and these are those to whom dignities and possessions were blessings in the world. [5] From all this it can be seen what spiritual dignities and possessions are, and that they belong to the work and not to the person. A person who is in dignity there is in magnificence and glory like that of kings on earth: and yet they do not regard the dignity itself as anything, but the uses, in the ministration and discharge of which they are engaged. They receive honors, indeed, suited to the dignity of each one; but they do not attribute it to themselves, but to the uses; and because all uses are from the Lord they attribute the honors to the Lord, from whom they come. Such, therefore, are spiritual dignities and possessions, which are eternal. [6] But it is otherwise with those to whom dignities and possessions in the world have been curses. Because they attributed these to themselves and not to the uses, and because they desired to control the uses and not to be controlled by them, and deemed uses to be uses merely so far as they were serviceable to their honor and glory, they are in hell, and are vile slaves there, despised and miserable. And because such dignities and possessions perish they are called temporal and perishable. Of these two classes the Lord thus teaches:—

Lay not not up for yourselves treasures upon the earth, where moth and rust doth consume, and where thieves dig through and steal; but lay up for yourselves treasures in heaven, where neither moth nor rust doth consume, and where thieves do not dig through nor steal; for where your treasure is your heart will also be (*Matt.* vi. 19–21).

[7] Thirdly: *Dignities and possessions that are curses, compared with dignities and possessions that are blessings, are as nothing to everything, or as that which in itself is not to that which in itself is.* Everything that perishes and comes to nothing is inwardly in itself nothing; outwardly indeed it is something, and even seems to be much, and to some it seems to be everything as long as it lasts; but it is not so inwardly in itself. It is like a surface with nothing within it; or like an actor in royal robes when the play is over. But that which remains forever is in itself something perpetually, thus every-thing; and it also is, for it does not cease to be.

218. (3) *Temporal things and eternal things are separated by man, but are conjoined by the Lord.* This is true because all things pertaining to man are temporal, and for this reason man may be called temporal; while all things pertaining to the Lord are eternal, and for this reason the Lord is called Eternal. Temporal things are those that have an end and perish; while eternal things are those that have no end and do not perish. Any one can see that the two can be conjoined only through the Lord's infinite wisdom, and thus can be conjoined by the Lord, but not by man. But to make known that the two are separated by man and are conjoined by the Lord it must be shown in this order: (1) What temporal things are, and what eternal things are. (2) Man is in himself temporal and the Lord is in Himself eternal; and therefore only what is temporal can proceed from man, and only what is eternal from the Lord. (3) Temporal things separate eternal things from themselves,

and eternal things conjoin temporal things to themselves. (4)
The Lord conjoins man with Himself by means of appearances. (5) Also by means of correspondences.

219. But these points must be illustrated and established
one by one. First: *What temporal things are and what eternal
things are.* Temporal things are all things which are proper
to nature, and which are therefore proper to man. The things
proper to nature are especially spaces and times, both having
limit and termination; the things therefrom proper to man are
those that belong to his own will and his own understanding,
and consequently to his affection and thought, and especially
to his prudence; these, it is admitted, are finite and limited.
But eternal things are all such as are proper to the Lord, and
from Him are seemingly proper to man. All things proper to
the Lord are infinite and eternal, thus without time, consequently without limit and without end. Things therefrom
seemingly proper to man are likewise infinite and eternal, yet
nothing of them is man's, but they belong to the Lord alone in
man. [2] Secondly: *Man is in himself temporal, and the Lord
is in Himself eternal ; and therefore only what is temporal can
proceed from man, and only what is eternal from the Lord.* It
has been said above that man in himself is temporal, and the
Lord in Himself eternal. As nothing can proceed from any
one except what is in him, it follows that nothing but what is
temporal can proceed from man, and nothing but what is
eternal from the Lord. For the infinite cannot proceed from
the finite; to say that it can is a contradiction. And yet the
infinite can proceed from the finite, although not from the finite but from the infinite through the finite. Neither, on the
other hand, can the finite proceed from the infinite; to say that
it can is also a contradiction; yet the finite can be produced by
the infinite, but this is creating, not proceeding. On this subject see *Angelic Wisdom concerning the Divine Love and the
Divine Wisdom*, from beginning to end. Consequently, when
what is finite proceeds from the Lord, as is the case in many
things in man, it does not proceed from the Lord, but from

man; and it can be said to proceed from the Lord through man, because it so appears. [**3**] This may be illustrated by these words of the Lord:—

Let your speech be, Yea, yea; Nay, nay; whatever is beyond these is from evil (*Matt.* v. 37).

Such is the speech of all in the third heaven; for they never reason about Divine things whether a thing is so or not so, but they see in themselves from the Lord whether it is so or is not so. Therefore a reasoner reasons about Divine things whether they are so or not, because he does not see them from the Lord, but wishes to see from himself; and what man sees from himself is evil. Nevertheless, the Lord is willing that a man should think and talk about Divine things, and also reason about them for the purpose of seeing a thing to be so or not so; and such thought, speech, or reasoning, provided the end is to see the truth, can be said to be from the Lord in man, although it is from man until he sees the truth and acknowledges it. Meanwhile it is only from the Lord that man has the ability to think, to talk, and to reason; for he has this ability from the two faculties called liberty and rationality, and man has these faculties from the Lord alone. [**4**] Thirdly: *Temporal things separate eternal things from themselves, and eternal things conjoin temporal things to themselves.* That temporal things separate eternal things from themselves means that this is done by man, who is temporal, from the temporal things in himself; and that eternal things conjoin temporal things to themselves means that this is done by the Lord, who is eternal, from the eternal things in Himself, as has been said above. It has been shown in the foregoing pages that there is a conjunction of the Lord with man and a reciprocal conjunction of man with the Lord; but that this reciprocal conjunction of man with the Lord is not from man but from the Lord; also that man's will runs counter to the Lord's will; or, what is the same thing, man's own prudence runs counter to the Lord's Divine providence. From all this it follows that man [when acting] from his temporal things separates from himself the Lord's eternal things, but that the Lord conjoins His eternal things with man's temporal things, that is, Himself with man and man with Himself. As these points have been fully treated heretofore, further confirmation is not necessary. [5] Fourthly: *The Lord conjoins man with Himself by means of appearances.* For the appearance is that it is from himself that man loves the neighbor, does good, and speaks the truth; and except for this appearance man would not love the neighbor, do good, and speak truth, thus would not be conjoined with the Lord. But love, good, and truth are from the Lord; evidently, then, it is by means of appearances that the Lord conjoins man with Himself. But this appearance, and the Lord's conjunction with man, and man's reciprocal conjunction with the Lord by means of it, have been fully treated of above. [6] Fifthly: *The Lord conjoins man with Himself by means of correspondences.* This is done by means of the Word, the literal sense of which consists of pure correspondences. That by means of this sense there is a conjunction of the Lord with man and a reciprocal conjunction of man with the Lord has been shown in the *Doctrine of the New Jerusalem concerning the Sacred Scripture*, from beginning to end.

220. (4.) *The conjunction of temporal things and eternal things in man is the Lord's Divine providence.* But as these things cannot enter even into the first perception of the understanding until they have been arranged in order, and unfolded and made clear according to that order, let them be set forth as follows:—

(1) It is from the Divine providence that by death man puts off what is natural and temporal, and puts on what is spiritual and eternal.

(2) Through His Divine providence the Lord conjoins Himself with natural things by means of spiritual things, and with temporal things by means of eternal things, according to uses.

(3) The Lord conjoins Himself with uses by means of correspondences, and thus by means of appearances, in accordance with the confirmations of these by man.

(4) This conjunction of temporal and eternal things is the Divine providence.

But let these things be brought into clearer light by explanations. [2] First: *It is from the Divine providence that by death man puts off what is natural and temporal, and puts on what is spiritual and eternal.* Natural and temporal things are the extremes and outmosts into which man first enters; and this he does at birth, to the end that he may be able afterwards to be introduced into things more internal and higher. For extremes and outmosts are containants; and these are in the natural world. And this is why no angel or spirit was created such immediately, but were all born first as men, and were thus led into higher things. From this they have extremes and outmosts which in themselves are fixed and established, within which and by which interiors can be held together in connection. [3] But at first man puts on the grosser things of nature; these constitute his body; but by death he puts these off, and retains the purer things of nature which are nearest to spiritual things; and these then become his containants. Furthermore, all interior or higher things are simultaneously in extremes or outmosts, as has already been shown; and consequently the entire working of the Lord is from first principles and from outmosts simultaneously, thus in fulness. But inasmuch as the extremes or outmosts of nature are not receptive of the spiritual and eternal things in conformity to which the human mind was formed, as these are in themselves, and yet man was born to become spiritual and to live for ever, therefore these are put off by man, and he retains only the interior natural things that agree and harmonize with the spiritual and celestial, and serve them as containants. This is accomplished by the rejection of temporal and natural outmosts, which is the death of the body. [4] Secondly: *Through His Divine providence the Lord conjoins Himself with natural things by means of spiritual things, and with temporal things by means of eternal things, according to uses.* Natural and temporal things are not only such as are proper to nature, but also such as are proper to men in the natural world. Both of these man puts off by death, and puts on the spiritual and eternal things that correspond to them. That these are put on in accordance with uses has been abundantly shown heretofore. The natural things that are proper to nature have relation in general to times and spaces, and in particular to the things that are seen on the earth. It is these that man leaves by death, and in place of them he takes on spiritual things, which are similar in outer aspect or appearance, but not in inner aspect and very essence (which also has been treated of above). [5] The temporal things that are proper to men in the natural world have relation in general to dignities and possessions, and in particular to every one's necessities, which are food, clothing, and habitation. These also are put off by death and left behind; and things are put on and received that are similar in outer aspect or appearance, but not in inner aspect and essence. All these have their inner aspect and essence from the uses of temporal things in the world. Uses are the goods that are called the goods of charity. From all this it can be seen that through His Divine providence the Lord conjoins spiritual and eternal things with natural and temporal things according to uses. [6] Thirdly : *The Lord conjoins Himself with uses by means of correspondences, and thus by means of appearances in accordance with the confirmations of these by man.* As this must needs seem obscure to those who have not yet gained a clear notion of what correspondence is and what appearance is, they must be illustrated by example, and thus explained. All things of the Word are pure correspondences of spiritual and celestial things, and because they are correspondences they are also appearances; that is, all things of the Word are the Divine goods of the Divine love and the Divine truths of the Divine wisdom, which in themselves are naked, but in the sense of the letter of the Word are clothed. They therefore appear like a man in clothing that corresponds to the state of his love and wisdom. All this makes evident that when a man confirms appearances it is the same as asserting that the clothes are the man. It is thus that appearances are converted into fallacies. It is otherwise when man is seeking for truths and sees them in the appearances. [7] Since, then, all uses, that is, the truths and goods of charity that a man does to the neighbor, may be done either in accordance with these appearances or in accordance with the truths themselves in the Word, when he does them in accordance with the appearances confirmed in himself he is in fallacies; but when he does them in accordance with truths he does them as he ought. All this makes clear what is meant when it is said that the Lord conjoins Himself with uses by means of correspondences, and thus by means of appearances in accordance with the confirmations of these by man. [8] Fourthly: *This conjunction of temporal and eternal things is the Divine providence.* To set this before the understanding with some clearness let it be illustrated by two examples, one relating to dignities and honors, and the other to riches and possessions. Both of these are, in external form, natural and temporal, but in internal form are spiritual and eternal. Dignities with their honors are natural and temporal when in them man regards himself personally, and not the commonwealth and uses; for then man must needs think interiorly in himself that the commonwealth is for his sake, and not he for the commonwealth's sake. He is like a king who thinks that the kingdom and all the people in it exist for his sake, and not he for the sake of the kingdom and the people. [9] But these same dignities with their honors are spiritual and eternal when man regards himself personally as existing for the sake of the commonwealth and uses, and not that they exist for his sake. When man does this he is in the verity and in the essence of his dignity and honor; but in the former case he is in the correspondence and appearance [of dignity and honor]; and if he confirms these in himself [as the truth] he is in fallacies, and is in conjunction with the Lord only as those are who are in falsities and in evils therefrom; for fallacies are falsities with which evils are conjoined. They have, indeed, promoted uses and good works, but from themselves and not from the Lord; thus they have put themselves in the Lord's place. [**10**] It is the same with riches and possessions, which also may be natural and temporal or spiritual and eternal. They are natural and temporal with those who look solely to them, and to themselves in them, finding in these their sole pleasure and delight. But these same things are spiritual and eternal with those who look to good uses in them, and find in these uses interior pleasure and delight. With such, moreover, the outward pleasure and delight become spiritual, and the temporal becomes the eternal. Therefore such after death are in heaven; and there they live in palaces, the furnishings of which are forms resplendent with gold and precious stones; but these they regard only as externals, resplendent and translucent from their internals which are uses, and from these uses they have essential pleasure and enjoyment; and these in themselves are the happiness and bliss of heaven. The reverse is the lot of such as have looked to riches and possessions solely for their sake and for the sake of self, thus for the sake of externals and not for the sake of internals also; thus according to the way they appear and not according to their essences. When such put off these appearances, which they do at death, they put on the internals belonging to them; and as these are not spiritual they must needs be infernal, for one or the other of these must be in them, since the two cannot exist together. Consequently in place of riches they have poverty, and in place of possessions wretchedness. [**11**] By uses are not meant merely the necessaries of life, which have relation to food, clothing, and habitation for man and for those dependent on him, but also the good of one's country, of society, and of the fellow citizen. Business is such a good when that is the final love, and money is a mediate and subservient love, provided the business man shuns and turns away from frauds and evil devices as sins. It is otherwise when money is the final love, and the business is the mediate and subservient love; for this is avarice, which is the root of evils (respecting which see *Luke* xii. 15, and the parable relating to it, verses 16–21).

MAN IS ADMITTED INTERIORLY INTO TRUTHS OF FAITH AND
INTO GOODS OF CHARITY ONLY SO FAR AS HE CAN BE KEPT
IN THEM UNTIL THE END OF HIS LIFE.

221. It is admitted in the Christian world that the Lord
wills the salvation of all, and that He is almighty; and from
this many conclude that He is able to save every one, and that
He saves those who implore His mercy; especially those who
implore it after the formula of the received faith, that God the
Father will be merciful for the sake of the Son; and particularly if they pray at the same time that they may receive that
faith. But that it is altogether otherwise will be seen in the
last chapter of this work, where it will be explained that the
Lord cannot act contrary to the laws of His Divine providence,
because to act against these would be to act contrary to His
Divine love and His Divine wisdom, thus contrary to Himself.
It will also be seen there that such immediate mercy is impossible, because the salvation of man is effected by means, and
only He who wills the salvation of all, and is at the same time
almighty, in other words, the Lord, is able to lead man in accordance with these means. The means whereby man is led by the
Lord are what are called the laws of the Divine providence;
and among these is this, that man is admitted interiorly into
the truths of wisdom and into the goods of love only so far as
he can be kept in them until the end of his life. But to make
this clear to the reason it shall be explained in the following
order:—

(1) A man may be admitted into the wisdom of spiritual
things, and also into a love for them, and yet not be reformed.

(2) If he afterwards recedes from them, and passes over into
the opposite, he profanes holy things.

(3) There are many kinds of profanation, but this is the
worst kind of all.

(4) Therefore the Lord admits man interiorly into the truths
of wisdom and at the same time into the goods of love only so
far as he can be kept in them until the end of his life.

222. (1) *A man may be admitted into the wisdom of spiritual things, and also into a love for them, and yet not be reformed.* This is because man has rationality and liberty; and by rationality he may be raised up into wisdom almost angelic; and by liberty into a love not unlike angelic love. Nevertheless such as the love is such is the wisdom. When the love is celestial and spiritual the wisdom also becomes celestial and spiritual; but when the love is diabolical and infernal the wisdom is also diabolical and infernal. In outward form, and thus to others, such wisdom may appear to be celestial and spiritual; but in internal form, which is its very essence, it is diabolical and infernal; not as it is out of the man, but as it is within him. To men it does not appear to be such because men are natural and see and hear naturally, and the external form is natural. But to angels it appears such, because angels are spiritual and see and hear spiritually, and the internal form is spiritual. [2] From all this it can be seen that man can be admitted into the wisdom of spiritual things, and also into a love for them, and yet not be reformed, but in that case only into a natural love for them, and not into a spiritual love for them. This is because man has the ability to admit himself into natural love, while the Lord alone can admit into spiritual love; and such as are admitted into that love are reformed, but those who are admitted into natural love alone are not reformed. For such are mostly hypocrites, and very many of them are of the order of Jesuits, who interiorly do not believe in the Divine at all, but play with Divine things outwardly like actors.

223. By much experience in the spiritual world it has been made known to me that man possesses in himself the ability to understand the secrets of wisdom like the angels themselves. For I have seen fiery devils who, while they were hearing the secrets of wisdom, not only understood them but from their rationality talked about them. But as soon as they returned to their diabolical love they ceased to understand them; and in place of them thought opposite things which were insanities, and this they then called wisdom. I have even been permitted to hear them, when they were in a state of wisdom laughing at their own insanity, and when in a state of insanity laughing at wisdom. The man who has been of this character in the world, when after death he becomes a spirit is usually let into alternate states of wisdom and insanity, that he may see the latter from the former. But although from wisdom such see that they are insane, yet when the choice is given them, as is done with every one, they admit themselves into the state of insanity and love it; and then they regard with hatred the state of wisdom. This is because their internal has been diabolical, and their external seemingly Divine. Such are meant by the devils who make themselves angels of light; also by the one at the house of the wedding who was not clothed in a wedding garment, and was cast into outer darkness (*Matt.* xxii. 11–13).

224. Who cannot see that the external springs from the internal, and consequently has its essence from the internal? And who does not know from experience that the external can present an appearance not in accordance with its essence from the internal? For there is evidently such an appearance in the case of hypocrites, flatterers and pretenders. And that a man can externally personate other characters than his own is manifest from players and mimics; for they know how to represent kings, emperors, and even angels, in tone, language, face, and gesture, as if they were such, when yet they are but actors. This has been said to show that man can likewise play the sycophant both in civil and moral matters and in spiritual matters; and it is known, moreover, that many do so. [2] When, therefore, the internal in its essence is infernal, and the external in its form appears spiritual, and yet, as has been said, the external draws its essence from the internal, it may be asked where in the external that essence lies concealed. It does not appear in gesture, in the tone, in the speech, or in the countenance; and yet it is interiorly hidden in all four of these. That it is interiorly hidden in them can be clearly seen from these same in the spiritual world; for when a man comes from the natural world into the spiritual world, as he does at death, he leaves his externals behind with the body, and retains his internals which he had stored up in his spirit; and if his internal had been infernal he then appears like a devil, such as he had been as to his spirit while he lived in the world. Who does not acknowledge that every man leaves externals when he leaves the body, and enters into internals when he becomes a spirit? [**3**] To this I will add that in the spiritual world there is a communication of affections and of consequent thoughts; and therefore no one there can speak otherwise than as he thinks. Also every one's face there is changed and becomes like his affections; so that what he is is apparent even from his face. Hypocrites are sometimes permitted to speak otherwise than as they think; but the tone of their speech is to the ear wholly discordant with their interior thoughts; and the discordance makes them known. This makes clear that the internal is hidden interiorly in the tone, in the speech, in the countenance, and in the gestures, of the external; and this is not perceived by men in the natural world, but is clearly perceived by angels in the spiritual world.

225. From all this it is now clear that so long as a man lives in the natural world he can be admitted into the wisdom of spiritual things, and also into a love for them; and that this can take place and does take place, both with those who are merely natural and with those who are spiritual; but with this difference, that the spiritual are thereby reformed, while the merely natural by the same means are not reformed. With these there may be an appearance that they love wisdom; but they merely love it as an adulterer loves an honorable woman, that is, the same as he would love a courtesan, talking sweetly to her, giving her beautiful garments, but saying to himself privately, She is nothing but a mere harlot, whom I will make believe that I love because she gratifies my lust; but if she should fail to gratify it I would cast her off. The internal man of such is that adulterer; while their external is that woman.

226. (2) *If a man afterwards recedes from these spiritual things and passes over into the opposite he profanes holy things.*

There are several kinds of profanation of what is holy (which will be treated of under the following head), but this kind is the most grievous of all; for profaners of this kind after death come to be no longer men; they live, indeed, but are continually in fantastic hallucinations, seeming to themselves to be flying on high; and while they remain there they sport with fantasies, which are seen by them as real things; and being no longer men, they are not called "he" and "she," but "it." And when they are presented to view in the light of heaven they look like skeletons, some like skeletons of the color of bone, some as fiery skeletons, and others as charred. It is unknown in the world that profaners of this kind become such after death; and it is unknown because the cause is unknown. The essential cause is that when a man has first acknowledged Divine things and believed in them, and afterwards withdraws from and denies them, he mixes together what is holy and what is profane; and when these have been mixed together they cannot be separated without destroying the whole. But to make this more clear to the perception it shall be unfolded in order, as follows: (1) Whatever a man thinks, says, and does from his will, whether good or evil, is appropriated to him, and remains. (2) But the Lord, by His Divine providence, continually foresees and arranges, in order that evil may be by itself and good by itself, and thus the two may be separated. (3) But this cannot be done when at first man acknowledges the truths of faith and lives according to them, and afterwards withdraws from and denies them. (4) He then mixes together good and evil to such an extent that they cannot be separated. (5) And since the good and the evil must be separated in every human being, and cannot be separated in such a one, he is therefore destroyed in respect to every thing truly human.

227. Such are the causes from which this enormity springs; but as ignorance of them causes obscurity, they need to be so explained as to make them clear to the understanding. First: *Whatever a man thinks, says, and does from his will, whether* *good or evil, is appropriated to him, and remains.* This has been shown above (n. 78–81). For man has an external or natural memory, and an internal or spiritual memory. Upon his internal memory each and every thing that he has thought, spoken and done in the world has been inscribed, so completely and particularly that not a single thing is lacking. This memory is the book of man's life, which is opened after death and in accordance with which he is judged. Many other things with regard to this memory, from actual experience, are set forth in the work on *Heaven and Hell* (n. 461–465). [**2**] Secondly: *But the Lord by means of His Divine providence continually foresees and arranges in order that evil may be by itself and good by itself, and thus the two may be separated.* Every man is both in evil and in good, in evil from himself, and in good from the Lord; nor can he live unless he is in both; for if he were in self alone and thus in evil alone he would have nothing of life; and if he were in the Lord alone, and thus in good alone, he would have nothing of life, for in such a state of life he would continually gasp for breath like one suffocated, or like one in the agony of death; while in the former state of life he would become extinct; for evil apart from any good is in itself dead; consequently every man is in both; with the difference that in the one case man is interiorly in the Lord and exteriorly as it were in himself; and in the other case is interiorly in himself, but exteriorly as it were in the Lord; and such a man is in evil, while the former is in good; although each is in both. The evil man is in both for the reason that he is in the good of civil and moral life, and also outwardly in some good of spiritual life, besides being kept by the Lord in rationality and liberty, that he may be capable of being in good. It is by such good that every one, even a bad man, is led by the Lord. From all this it can be seen that the Lord keeps evil and good separate, so that one may be interior and the other exterior, thus providing against their being mixed together. [**3**] Thirdly: *But this cannot be done if man acknowledges the truths of faith and lives according to them, and afterwards withdraws from and denies* *them.* This is clear from what has already been said, first, that all things that a man thinks, says, and does from the will are appropriated to him and remain; and secondly, that the Lord by His Divine providence continually foresees and arranges that good may be by itself and evil by itself, and that the two may be separated. Moreover, they are separated by the Lord after death. From those who are interiorly evil and outwardly good the good is taken away, and thus they are left to their evil. The reverse takes place with those who are interiorly good, but outwardly, like other men, have sought to gain riches, have striven for dignities, have taken delight in various worldly interests, and have favored certain lusts; for with such good and evil have not been mixed together, but have been kept separate like internal and external; thus while in external form they have been in many respects like the evil, they have not been so internally. But with the evil who in external form have presented the same appearance as the good in piety, worship, words, and works, while in internal form they have been evil, the reverse is true; with such also evil is kept separate from good. But in those who have acknowledged the truths of faith and lived according to them, and have afterwards passed over into the opposite and have rejected these truths, and especially if they have denied them, goods and evils are no longer separate, but are mixed together. For such a man has appropriated good to himself, and has also appropriated evil to himself, and thus has joined and mixed them together. [4] Fourthly : *Man then mixes together good and evil to such an extent that they cannot be separated.* This follows from what has just been said. If evil could not be separated from good and good from evil it would be impossible to be either in heaven or in hell. Every human being must be in either one or the other; he cannot be in both; for he would then be at one time in heaven, and at another time in hell; and when in heaven he would be acting in accord with hell, and when in hell he would be acting in accord with heaven; thus he would destroy the life of all about him, heavenly life among the angels, and infernal life among the devils; whereby the life of all would perish. For each one must have his own life; no one lives in another's life, still less in an opposite life. For this reason, in every man after death, when he becomes a spirit or a spiritual man, the Lord separates the good from the evil and the evil from the good; the good from the evil in those who are interiorly in evil; and the evil from the good in those who are interiorly in good; which is according to His words:—

To every one that hath shall be given, that he may have more abundantly; but from him that hath not shall be taken away even that he hath (*Matt.* xiii. 12; xxv. 29; *Mark* iv. 25; *Luke* viii. 18; xix. 26).

[5] Fifthly: *Since good and evil must be separated in every human being, and cannot be separated in such a one, he is therefore destroyed in respect to everything truly human.* Every one has what is truly human from rationality, in being able to see and to know, if he will, what is true and what is good; also in being able from liberty to will, think, say, and do it; as has been shown before. But this liberty with its rationality has been destroyed in those who have mixed good and evil together in themselves; for such from good are unable to see evil and from evil to recognize good, since the two make one; consequently they no longer possess rationality in its capability or power, nor therefore any liberty. For this reason they are like mere fantastic hallucinations, as has been said above; and they no longer appear like men, but like bones covered with some skin; and therefore when referred to they are not called "he" or "she," but "it." Such is the lot of those who in this manner mix together things holy and things profane. But there are other kinds of profanation that are not like this, and these will be considered in a following article.

228. A man who is ignorant of holy things does not thus profane them. For he who is ignorant of them cannot acknowledge them and afterwards deny them. Therefore those who are outside of the Christian world, and who know nothing about the Lord, and about redemption and salvation by Him, do not profane this holiness when they refuse to accept it, or even

when they speak against it. Nor do the Jews themselves profane it because from infancy they are unwilling to accept and
acknowledge it. It would be otherwise if they should accept
and acknowledge it, and afterwards deny it; but this rarely
occurs; although many of them outwardly acknowledge it and
inwardly deny it, and are like hypocrites. But those who profane holy things by mixing them with things profane are such
as first accept and acknowledge them, and afterwards backslide and deny. [2] This does not refer to the acceptance and
acknowledgment of these things in early childhood and boyhood; this every Christian does; for the things belonging to
faith and charity are not then accepted and acknowledged from
any rationality and liberty, that is, in the understanding from
the will, but are accepted only by memory and from confidence
in the teacher; and if the life is according to them it is from a
blind obedience. But when man comes into the exercise of his
rationality and liberty, which he does gradually as he grows into
youth and manhood, if he then acknowledges truths and lives
according to them and afterwards denies them he mixes holy
things with profane things, and from being a man he becomes
such a monster as has been described above. If, however, man
is in evil from the time that he reaches the age of rationality
and liberty, that is, of self-control, and even in early manhood,
but afterwards he acknowledges the truths of faith and lives
according to them, provided he then remains in them until the
end of his life, he does not mix the two; for the Lord then separates the evils of the former life from the goods of the latter
life. This is done with all who repent. But of this more in
what follows.

229. (3) *There are many kinds of profanation of what is
holy, but this is the worst kind of all.* In the most general sense
profanation means all impiety; and therefore profaners mean
all the impious, who in heart deny God, the holiness of the
Word, and the spiritual things of the church therefrom, which
are essentially holy things, and who also speak impiously of
these. But of such we are not now treating, but of those who

profess to believe in God, who assert the holiness of the Word, and who acknowledge the spiritual things of the church; most of whom, however, only with the mouth. Such commit profanation for the reason that what is holy from the Word is in them and with them, and this which is in them and which makes some part of their understanding and will they profane; but in the impious, who deny the Divine and Divine things, there is nothing holy that can be profaned. Such are profaners, and yet they are not profane.

230. The profanation of what is holy is referred to in the second commandment of the Decalogue, "Thou shalt not profane the name of thy God." And the words in the Lord's Prayer, "Hallowed be Thy name," mean that this name must not be profaned. Scarcely any one in the Christian world knows what is meant by "the name of God," and for the reason that no one knows that there are no names in the spiritual world like those in the natural world, but each one there has a name that is in accordance with the quality of his love and wisdom; for as soon as any one enters a society or into association with others, he immediately receives a name that is in accord with his character there. This naming is effected by spiritual language, which is such that it is capable of naming every thing; for each letter in its alphabet signifies a single thing, and the several letters joined into a single word and making a person's name involve the entire state of the thing. This is one of the wonders of the spiritual world. [2] From all this it is clear that in the Word "the name of God" signifies God with every thing that is in Him and that goes forth from Him. And as the Word is the Divine going forth, which is the name of God, and as all the Divine things that are called the spiritual things of the church are from the Word, they, too, are "the name of God." All this makes clear what is meant in the second commandment of the Decalogue:—

Thou shalt not profane the name of God (*Exod.* xx. 7);

and in the Lord's Prayer by

Hallowed be Thy name (*Matt.* vi. 9).

The name of God and of the Lord has a like signification in many places in the Word of both Testaments, as in *Matt.* vii. 22; x. 22; xviii. 5, 20; xix. 29; xxi. 9; xxiv. 9, 10; *John* i. 12; ii. 23; iii. 17, 18; xii. 13, 28; xiv. 14–16; xvi. 23, 24, 26, 27; xvii. 6; xx. 31; besides other places; and very frequently in the Old Testament. [3] He who knows that this is what is signified by "name" can understand what is signified by these words of the Lord:—

He that receiveth a prophet in the name of a prophet shall receive a prophet's reward; and he that receiveth a righteous man in the name of a righteous man shall receive a righteous man's reward. And whosoever shall give to drink unto one of these little ones a cup of cold [water] only in the name of a disciple shall not lose his reward (*Matt.* x. 41, 42).

One who thinks that "the name of a prophet," "of a righteous man," and "of a disciple," here means simply a prophet, a righteous man, and a disciple, recognizes no meaning except that of the letter; nor does he know what "the reward of a prophet" is, or the reward of "a righteous man," or the "reward" for a cup of cold water given to a disciple; nevertheless "the name" and "the reward of a prophet" mean the state and the happiness of those who are in Divine truths; "the name" and "the reward of a righteous man" mean the state and the happiness of those who are in Divine goods; a "disciple" means the state of those who are in some of the spiritual things of the church; and "a cup of cold water" means something of truth. [4] That "name" signifies the nature of the state of love and wisdom, or of good and truth, is made evident also by these words of the Lord:—

He that entereth in by the door is the shepherd of the sheep; to him the porter openeth, and the sheep hear his voice; and he calleth his own sheep by name and leadeth them out (*John* x. 2, 3).

"To call the sheep by name" means to teach and to lead every one who is in the good of charity according to the state of his love and wisdom. "The door" means the Lord, as is evident from the ninth verse:—

I am the door; through Me if any one enter in he shall be saved.

All this makes clear that for any one to be saved the Lord Himself must be approached, and that whoever goes to Him is "a shepherd of the sheep;" but whoever does not go to Him is "a thief and a robber," as is said in the first verse of the same chapter.

231. As profanation of what is holy means profanation by those who know the truths of faith and the goods of charity from the Word, and who in some measure acknowledge them, and does not mean those who are ignorant of these, nor those who from impiety wholly reject them, so what now follows is said of the first class, and not of the others. Of the profanation of such there are several kinds, some lighter and some more grievous; but they may be referred to these seven. The first kind of profanation is committed by those *who make jests from the Word and about the Word, or from the Divine things of the church and about them.* This is done by some from a bad habit, in taking names or expressions from the Word and mixing them with remarks that are hardly becoming, and sometimes foul. This cannot but be joined with some contempt for the Word; yet the Word in all things and in every particular is Divine and holy; for every expression therein conceals in its bosom something Divine, and thereby has communication with heaven. But this kind of profanation is lighter or more grievous according to the acknowledgment of the holiness of the Word and the unbecoming character of the talk into which it is introduced by those who jest about it. [2] The second kind of profanation is committed by *those who understand and acknowledge Divine truths, and still live contrary to them.* Those who only understand profane more lightly, while those who also acknowledge profane more grievously, for the understanding merely teaches, almost like a preacher, and does not from itself conjoin itself with the will; but acknowledgment conjoins itself, for nothing can be acknowledged except by consent of the will. Nevertheless, this conjunction varies, and when one is living contrary to the truths that are acknowledged the profanation is measured by

the conjunction. When, for instance, one acknowledges that
revenge and hatred, adultery and whoredom, fraud and deceit,
defamation and lying, are sins against God, and yet is committing them, he is in this more grievous kind of profanation,
for the Lord says:—

The servant that knoweth his Lord's will and doeth not His will, shall
be beaten with many stripes (*Luke* xii. 47).

And elsewhere:—

If ye were blind ye would have no sin; but now ye say, We see; therefore your sin remaineth (*John* ix. 41).

But it is one thing to acknowledge appearances of truth, and
another to acknowledge genuine truths. Those who acknowledge genuine truths and yet do not live according to them
appear in the spiritual world without the light and heat of
life in voice and speech, as if they were pure idlers. [3] The
third kind of profanation is committed by those *who adapt the
sense of the letter of the Word to the confirmation of evil loves
and false principles*. This is because the confirmation of falsity is a denial of truth, and the confirmation of evil is a rejection of good; and the Word in its bosom is nothing but Divine
truth and Divine good; but in the outmost sense, which is the
sense of the letter, this is not expressed in genuine truths
(except where it teaches about the Lord and the way of salvation itself), but in truths clothed, which are called appearances
of truth; and therefore that sense may be diverted to uphold
many kinds of heresies. But he that upholds evil loves does
violence to Divine goods; and he that upholds false principles
does violence to Divine truths. This violence is called falsification of truth, the other is called adulteration of good. Both
are meant in the word by "bloods." For a spiritual holiness,
which is also called the spirit of truth going forth from the
Lord, is within each of the particulars of the sense of the letter of the Word. This holiness is injured when the Word is
falsified and adulterated. Evidently, then, this is profanation.
[4] A fourth kind of profanation is committed by *those who*

say with the lips pious and holy things, and counterfeit the affections of love for these in tone and in gesture, and yet in heart do not believe and love them. Most of such are hypocrites and Pharisees, from whom after death all truth and good are taken away, and they are then sent into outer darkness. Those who have confirmed themselves by this kind of profanation against the Divine and against the Word, and consequently against the spiritual things of the Word, sit in that darkness dumb, powerless to speak, wishing to babble pious and holy things as they did in the world, but unable to do so. For in the spiritual world every one is compelled to speak as he thinks; while a hypocrite wishes to speak otherwise than as he thinks; from which there exists an opposition in the mouth, owing to which they can only mutter. But the hypocrisy is lighter or more grievous in the measure of the confirmations against God and the outward reasonings in favor of God. [5] The fifth kind of profanation is committed by *those who attribute to themselves what is Divine.* Such are meant by "Lucifer" in the fourteenth chapter of *Isaiah.* "Lucifer" there means Babylon, as is evident from the fourth and twenty-second verses of the same chapter, where, too, the lot of such is described. The same are meant and described also in the seventeenth chapter of the *Apocalypse* by "the harlot sitting on the scarlet-colored beast." Babylon and Chaldea are mentioned in many places in the Word, "Babylon" meaning the profanation of good, and "Chaldea" the profanation of truth; both of these in such as attribute to themselves what is Divine. [6] The sixth kind of profanation is committed by those *who acknowledge the Word and yet deny the Divinity of the Lord.* In the world these are called Socinians, and some of them Arians. The final condition of all such is that they call, not upon the Lord, but upon the Father, and continually pray to the Father; some, indeed, for the sake of the Son, to be admitted into heaven, but without effect, until at last they lose all hope of salvation; and they are then let down into hell among those who deny God. Such are meant by those

Who blaspheme the Holy Spirit, for whom there will be no forgiveness in this age nor in the age to come (*Matt.* xii. 32).

This is because God is one in person and in essence, in whom is the trinity, and this God is the Lord; and since the Lord also is heaven, and consequently those who are in heaven are in the Lord, it follows that those who deny the Divinity of the Lord cannot be admitted into heaven and be in the Lord. That the Lord is heaven, and consequently those who are in heaven are in the Lord, has been shown above. [7] The seventh kind of profanation is committed by those *who first acknowledge Divine truths and live according to them, but afterwards recede and deny them*. This is the worst kind of profanation; for such mix together things holy and things profane, even to the extent that they cannot be separated; nevertheless they must be separated that men may be either in heaven or in hell; and since with such this cannot be done, all that is human, both intellectual and voluntary, is rooted out, and, as has been said before, they come to be no longer men. Nearly the same is true of those who in heart acknowledge the Divine things of the Word and of the church, but immerse them wholly in what is their own (*proprium*), which is the love of ruling over all things; of which much has been said already. For such, when after death they become spirits, are wholly unwilling to be led by the Lord, but wish to be led by themselves; and when loose rein is given to their love they wish to rule not only over heaven but also over the Lord; and as they cannot do this they deny the Lord and become devils. It must be understood that the life's love, which is the ruling love, continues with every one after death, and cannot be taken away. [8] The profane of this sort are meant by the "lukewarm," who are thus described in the *Apocalypse:*—

I know thy works, that thou art neither cold nor hot; would thou wert cold or hot. But because thou art lukewarm, and neither cold nor hot, I will spew thee out of My mouth (iii. 15, 16).

This kind of profanation is thus described by the Lord in *Matthew:*—

14

> When the unclean spirit goeth out of a man he walketh through dry places, seeking rest and finding it not. Then he saith, I will return to the house whence I went forth. When he cometh he findeth it empty and swept and adorned for him. Then he goeth away and taketh to himself seven other spirits worse than himself, and entering in they dwell there; and the latter things of that man become worse than the first (xii. 43–45).

Man's conversion is here described by "the unclean spirit's going out of him;" and his turning back to former evils when goods and truths have been cast out is described by "the return of the unclean spirit with seven others worse than himself into the house adorned for him;" and the profanation of what is holy by a profane person is described by "the last things with that man becoming worse than the first." The same is meant by this in *John:*—

> Jesus said to the man who had been healed at the pool of Bethesda, Sin no more, lest a worse thing befall thee (v. 14).

[9] The Lord's providing against man's acknowledging truths interiorly and afterwards receding and becoming profane is meant by these words:—

> He hath blinded their eyes and hardened their heart, lest they should see with their eyes and understand with their heart, and turn, and I should heal them (*John* xii. 40).

"Lest they should turn and I should heal them" signifies lest they should acknowledge truths and then recede, and thus become profane. For the same reason the Lord spoke in parables, as He Himself declares (*Matt.* xiii. 13). The Jews being forbidden to eat fat or blood (*Lev.* iii. 17; vii. 23, 25), signified that they should not profane what is holy; since "fat" signified Divine good, and "blood" Divine truth. That he who is once converted must continue in good and truth to the end of his life, the Lord teaches in *Matthew:*—

> Jesus said, He that endureth to the end shall be saved (x. 22; also *Mark* xiii. 13).

232. (4) *Therefore the Lord admits man interiorly into the truths of wisdom and at the same time into the goods of love only so far as he can be kept in them even to the end of his life.*

The demonstration of this must proceed by distinct steps, for two reasons; first, because it concerns human salvation; and secondly, because a knowledge of the laws of permission depends upon a knowledge of this law, which will be considered in the next chapter. It concerns human salvation, since, as has just been said, he that acknowledges the Divine things of the Word, and thus of the church, and afterwards recedes from them, profanes holy things most grievously. Therefore to so unfold this arcanum of the Divine providence that the rational man may see it in its own light, it must be set forth in the following order: (1) Good and evil cannot be in man's interiors together, neither, therefore, the falsity of evil and the truth of good together. (2) Good and the truth of good can be brought into man's interiors by the Lord only so far as evil and the falsity of evil there have been removed. (3) If good with its truth were to be brought in before or to a greater extent than evil with its falsity is removed, man would recede from good and return to his evil. (4) When man is in evil many truths may be brought into his understanding, and these may be stored up in his memory, and yet not be profaned. (5) But the Lord by His Divine providence takes the greatest care that the will shall receive from the understanding only so fast as, and to the extent that, man as if of himself removes evils in the external man. (6) If it should receive faster or more, the will would adulterate good and the understanding would falsify truth by mixing them with evils and with falsities. (7) Therefore the Lord admits man interiorly into the truths of wisdom and into the goods of love only so far as he can be kept in them to the end of his life.

233. Therefore, to so unfold this arcanum of the Divine providence that a rational man may see it in its own light, the points that have now been presented must be explained one by one. First: *Good and evil cannot be in man's interiors together, neither, therefore, the falsity of evil and the truth of good together.* The interiors of man mean the internal of his thought, of which he knows nothing until he comes into the spiritual world and its light, which he does after death. In the natural world this can be known only from the delight of his love in the external of his thought, and from evils themselves while he is examining them in himself; for, as has been shown above, the internal of thought in man coheres with the external of thought in so close a connection that they cannot be separated. But of this more will be said. The terms *good* and *truth of good*, also *evil* and *falsity of evil* are used because good cannot exist apart from its truth, nor evil apart from its falsity; for they are bedfellows or consorts; for the life of good is from its truth, and the life of truth is from its good. The same is true of evil and its falsity. [2] That evil with its falsity and good with its truth cannot be in man's interiors together the rational man can see without explanation; for evil is the opposite of good, and good is the opposite of evil, and two opposites cannot exist together. Moreover, there is inherent in all evil a hatred of good, and there is inherent in all good a love of protecting itself against evil and of separating it from itself; from which it follows that one cannot be together with the other; and if they were together there would arise first a conflict and combat, and then destruction; as the Lord also teaches in these words:—

Every kingdom divided against itself is brought to desolation; and every city or house divided against itself standeth not. He that is not with Me is against Me; and he that gathereth not with Me scattereth (*Matt.* xii. 25, 30).

And again:—

No one can serve two masters at the same time; for either he will hate the one and love the other [or he will hold to the one and despise the other] (*Matt.* vi. 24).

Two opposites cannot exist together in one substance or form without its being torn asunder and destroyed. If one should approach and come near to the other they would surely separate like two enemies, one keeping himself within his camp or his fortifications, and the other keeping outside of them. This is true of the evil and of the good in a hypocrite; he is in both, but the evil is within and the good is without, and thus the two are separated and are not mixed together.   From all this it is clear that evil with its falsity and good with its truth cannot exist together.   [**3**] Secondly: *Good and truth of good can be brought into a man's interiors by the Lord only so far as evil and the falsity of evil there have been removed.*   This is a necessary consequence of the foregoing; since, if evil and good cannot exist together good cannot be brought in until evil has been removed.   The term *man's interiors* is used, meaning the internal of thought, which is now under consideration. Either the Lord or the devil must be in these interiors.   The Lord is there after reformation, but the devil is there before it; consequently, so far as man suffers himself to be reformed the devil is cast out; but so far as he does not suffer himself to be reformed the devil remains.   Who cannot see that it is impossible for the Lord to enter so long as the devil is there?   And he is there so long as man keeps the door closed, which is where man and the Lord are together.   That the Lord enters when that door is opened by man's instrumentality He teaches in the *Apocalypse:*—

I stand at the door and knock; if any one hear My voice and open the door, I will come in to him and will sup with him and he with Me (iii. 20).

The door is opened by man's removing evil by shunning and turning away from it as infernal and diabolical; for whether you say evil or the devil it is the same; and on the other hand, whether you say good or the Lord it is the same; for the Lord is within all good, and the devil is within all evil.   This makes clear the truth of this matter.   [**4**] Thirdly: *If good with its truth were to be brought in before or to a greater extent than evil with its falsity is removed, man would recede from good and return to his evil.*   And for this reason, that evil would be the stronger, and the stronger conquers, if not at the time then afterwards.   So long as evil is the stronger, good cannot be brought into the inmost apartments but only into the entrance hall; because evil and good, as has been said, cannot exist together, and what is only in the entrance hall is removed by the enemy that is in the inner rooms; and in consequence there is a receding from good and a return to evil, which is the worst kind of profanation. [5] Furthermore, the essential delight of man's life is to love himself and the world above all things. This delight cannot be removed instantly, but only gradually; and so much as there is of this delight remaining in man so far evil prevails in him. And there is no way in which this evil can be removed except that the love of self become a love of uses, or the love of rule come to have uses as its end and not self; for then uses constitute the head, and the love of self or love of ruling constitutes first the body beneath the head, and then the feet on which it walks. Who does not see that good must constitute the head, and that when it does the Lord is there? Good and use are one. Who does not see that if evil consti-tutes the head the devil is there? And as civil and moral good, and spiritual good also in external form, must be ac-cepted, who does not see that this then constitutes the feet and the soles of the feet, to be walked upon? [6] Since, then, the state of man's life must be reversed, so that what is above shall be below, and this reversal cannot be effected instantly, for the greatest delight of life, which is from love of self and conse-quent love of dominion, can only gradually be weakened and turned into a love of uses, therefore good can be brought in by the Lord no faster or to a greater extent than this evil is re-moved; and if it were man would recede from good and return to his evil. [7] Fourthly: *When man is in evil many truths may be brought into his understanding, and these may be stored up in the memory, and yet not be profaned.* This is because the understanding does not flow into the will, but the will flows into the understanding; and as the understanding does not flow into the will many truths may be received by the understand-ing and stored up in the memory, and not be mixed with the evil of the will, consequently holy things will not be profaned. Moreover, it is incumbent upon every one to learn truths from the Word or from preaching, to lay them up in the memory and to think about them. For from the truths that are in the memory, and that come from it into the thought the understanding must teach the will, that is, must teach the man what to do. Therefore this is the chief means of reformation. When truths are in the understanding only, and from it in the memory, they are not in the man, but outside of him. [8] Man's memory may be compared to the ruminating stomach of certain animals, into which they first receive their food; and so long as it is there it is not within but without the body; but when they draw the food out of the stomach and eat it it becomes a part of their life, and the body is nourished. But man's memory contains spiritual not material foods, that is, truths, which in themselves are knowledges. So far as a man by thinking, or as it were by ruminating, draws these from the memory, his spiritual mind is nourished. The will's love is what longs for, and as it were has an appetite for these, and causes them to be imbibed and to furnish nourishment. If that love is evil it longs for and as it were has an appetite for things unclean; but if good it longs for and has an appetite for things clean; and what is not suitable it separates, dismisses, and casts forth, which is done in various ways. [9] Fifthly: *But the Lord by His Divine providence takes the greatest care that the will shall receive from the understanding only so fast as, and to the extent that, man as if of himself removes evils in the external man.* For what is received by the will comes into the man and is appropriated to him and comes to be of his life; and in the life itself, which man has from the will, evil and good cannot be together, if they were he would perish; but the two can be in the understanding, where they are called falsities of evil and truths of good, yet they are not together; if they were man would be unable from good to see evil or from evil to know good; but they are there distinguished and separated, like a house into inner and outer parts. When an evil man thinks and talks about good things he thinks and speaks exteriorly, but interiorly when he thinks and speaks about evil things: therefore when he says good things his speech comes as it were

from the outer wall of the house. It may be likened to fruit
fair on the surface, but wormy and rotten within; or to the shell
of a dragon's egg. [**10**] Sixthly: *If it should receive faster or
more, the will would adulterate good and the understanding
would falsify truth by mixing them with evils and with falsities therefrom.* When the will is in evil it adulterates good in
the understanding; and good adulterated in the understanding
is evil in the will, for it proves that evil is good, and that good
is evil; evil does this with all good which is opposite to itself.
Evil also falsifies truth, for the truth of good is opposite to
falsity of evil; and this is done by the will in the understanding,
and not by the understanding from itself. In the Word adulterations of good are depicted by adulteries and falsifications
of truth by whoredoms. These adulterations and falsifications
are effected by reasonings from the natural man, which is in evil,
also by confirmations drawn from the appearances of the sense
of the letter of the Word. [**11**] The love of self, which is the
head of all evils, surpasses all other loves in its ability to adulterate goods and falsify truths; and it does this by a misuse of
the rationality that every man, both the evil man and the good
man, has from the Lord. By its proofs it can even make evil
to appear wholly like good, and falsity like truth. What can it
not do when it can prove by a thousand arguments that nature
created itself, and that it then created men, beasts, and plants
of all kinds; also that by influx from its inner self nature
causes men to live, to think analytically, and to understand
wisely? Self-love excels in its ability to prove whatever it will
because its outer surface is a kind of splendor of light variegated in different colors. This splendor is the glory of being
wise that pertains to that love, and also thereby of being emi-
nent and dominant. [**12**] But when it has established these
principles this love becomes so blind as not to see but that man
is a beast, and that man and beast think in the same way, and
even that if a beast could speak it would be a man in another
form. If it can be led by any persuasion to believe that something of man lives after death, it is then so blind as to believe

that the same is true of the beast; and that this something that
lives after death is only a subtle exhalation of life, like a vapor,
which still settles back to its corpse; or that it is something
vital without sight, hearing, or speech, thus is blind, deaf, and
dumb, flitting about and thinking; besides many other insanities, with which nature itself, which in itself is dead, inspires
the fancy. This the love of self does, which viewed in itself is
the love of one's own (*proprium*); and man's own in respect to
its affections, which are all natural, is not unlike the life of a
beast; while in respect to its perceptions, because they are from
these affections, it is not unlike a bird of night. Consequently
whoever continually immerses his thoughts in what is his own
cannot be raised out of natural into spiritual light and see any·
thing of God, of heaven, and of the eternal life. Because this
love is such, and nevertheless excels in its ability to confirm
whatever it pleases, it has also a like ability to adulterate the
goods of the Word, and to falsify its truths, while from a kind
of necessity it is kept in a confession of them. [**13**] Seventhly:
*Therefore the Lord admits man interiorly into the truths of wis-
dom and into the goods of love only so far as he can be kept in
them to the end of his life.* This the Lord does that man may
not fall into that most grievous kind of profanation of what is
holy which has been treated of in this chapter. It is because
of this danger that the Lord permits evils of life and many
heresies in worship. Of the permissions of these something
will be seen in the sections following.

THE LAWS OF PERMISSION ARE ALSO LAWS OF THE DIVINE PROVIDENCE.

234. There are no laws of permission by themselves or
apart from the laws of the Divine providence, but the two are
the same; therefore God is said to permit, which does not mean
that He wills, but that on account of the end, which is salvation, He cannot avert. Whatever is done for the sake of the

end, which is salvation, is according to the laws of the Divine providence. For the Divine providence, as has been said before, is constantly moving in a way diverse from and contrary to man's will, continually intent upon its end; and in consequence, at every movement of its operation or at every step of its progress, where it observes man to be swerving from that end, it guides, bends, and directs him according to its laws, by leading him away from evil and leading him to good. That this cannot be done without the permission of evil will be seen in what follows. Moreover, nothing can be permitted without a reason, and the reason can be found only in some law of the Divine providence, which law teaches why it is permitted.

235. One who does not acknowledge the Divine providence at all does not in his heart acknowledge God, but acknowledges nature in place of God, and human prudence in place of the Divine providence. This does not appear to be true, because man can think in one way or another, and can talk in one way or another. From his inner self he is able to think and talk in one way, and from his outer self in another way. He is like a hinge that can let the door turn either way, one way when one is entering, and the other when going out; or like a sail by which a vessel can be turned either way in its course, as the master sets it. Those that have confirmed themselves in favor of human prudence to such an extent as to deny the Divine providence, so long as they are in that thought of theirs, give heed to nothing else, whatever they may be seeing, hearing, or reading; nor are they able to do so, because they receive nothing from heaven, but only from themselves. And because they draw conclusions from appearances and fallacies only, and see nothing else, they can swear that it is so. Moreover, if they acknowledge nature alone they may be angry with the defenders of Divine providence; provided they are not priests, for they regard this as a matter belonging to the teaching or function of the priesthood.

236. We will now enumerate some things that belong to permission and yet are in accord with the laws of Divine providence, by which a merely natural man confirms himself in favor of nature against God, and in favor of human prudence against Divine providence. For example: When he reads in the Word that the wisest of mankind, Adam and his wife, suffered themselves to be seduced by a serpent, and that God did not avert this by His Divine providence; that their first son Cain killed his brother Abel, and that God did not withhold him at the time by speaking with him, but only after the deed, by cursing him; that the Israelitish nation worshiped a golden calf in the desert, and acknowledged it as the God who led them out of the land of Egypt, and yet Jehovah saw this from Mount Sinai near by and did not seek to prevent it; also that David numbered the people, and in consequence a plague was sent upon them, by which so many thousands of men perished, and that God, not before but after the deed, sent Gad the prophet to David and denounced punishment; that Solomon was permitted to establish idolatrous worship, and many kings after him were permitted to profane the temple and the holy things of the church; and finally, that that nation was permitted to crucify the Lord. In these and many other things in the Word one who acknowledges nature and human prudence sees nothing but what is contrary to Divine providence; therefore he can use these things as arguments for rejecting it, if not in his outer thought which is nearest to speech, still in that inner thought which is remote from it.

237. Every worshiper of himself and of nature confirms himself against the Divine providence when he sees in the world so many impious persons, and so many of their impieties, and at the same time the glorying of some in these impieties, and yet no punishment of such by God on this account. And he confirms himself against the Divine providence still further when he sees that plots, devices, and frauds are successful even against the pious, just, and sincere; and that injustice triumphs over justice in the courts and in business. Especially does he confirm himself in this when he sees the impious exalted to honors and to high offices in church and state, also abounding in wealth, and living in luxury and magnificence; while on the other hand he sees the worshipers of God despised and poor. He also confirms himself against Divine providence when he reflects that wars are permitted, and the consequent slaughter of so many men, and the plundering of so many cities, nations, and families; also that victories are on the side of prudence, and sometimes not on the side of justice; and that it makes no difference whether the commander is an upright man or not; besides other things like these; all of which are permissions according to the laws of the Divine providence.

238. The same natural man confirms himself against Divine providence when he considers the religious conditions of various peoples; as that there are some who are wholly ignorant of God; some who worship the sun and moon; some also who worship monstrous idols, graven images, and even dead men; still further when he sees the Mohammedan religion accepted by so many empires and kingdoms, and the Christian religion only in Europe, the smallest division of the habitable globe, and there it is divided; and that there are some in it who claim for themselves Divine power, and wish to be worshiped as gods, and that the dead are invoked; also that there are some who place salvation in certain phrases which they should think and talk about, making no account of the good works they should do; also that there are few who live their religion; besides the heresies, of which there have been many; also some that exist at this day, as those of the Quakers, the Moravians, the Anabaptists, and others; also that Judaism still continues. From these things he who denies Divine providence concludes that religion in itself is nothing, but is necessary because it serves as a restraint.

239. To these arguments others can be added at this day by which those who think interiorly in favor of nature and human prudence alone may still further confirm themselves; as that the whole Christian world has acknowledged three Gods, not knowing that God is one in person and in essence, and that

the Lord is this one God; also that it has not hitherto been
known that in every particular of the Word there is a spiritual
sense, and that its holiness is from this; also that it has not
been known that to shun evils as sins is the Christian religion
itself; and that it has not been known that man lives a man
after death. For men can say to themselves and to one another, Why does the Divine providence, if there is any, now
first reveal such things?

240. All the things that have been mentioned in sections
236, 237, 238, and 239, have been presented to the end that it
may be seen that each and all things that take place in the
world, both with the evil and with the good, belong to the Divine providence; consequently that the Divine providence is
in the smallest particulars of man's thoughts and actions, and
therefore is universal. But as this cannot be seen from the
things presented unless each one is explained by itself they
shall be briefly explained in the order in which they were presented, beginning with section 236.

241. (1.) *The wisest of mankind, Adam and his wife, suffered themselves to be seduced by a serpent, and God did not
avert this by His Divine providence.* This is so, inasmuch as
by Adam and his wife the first of all mankind that were created on this earth are not meant, but the men of the Most
Ancient Church; and their new creation or their regeneration
is thus described. Their new creation itself, that is, their regeneration, is described in the first chapter of *Genesis* by the
creation of heaven and earth; their wisdom and intelligence
by the garden of Eden; and the end of that church by their
eating from the tree of knowledge. For the Word in its bosom
is spiritual, containing arcana of Divine wisdom; and that it
may contain these it is written throughout wholly by correspondences and representatives. This makes clear that the men
of that church, who were in the beginning the wisest of men,
but in the end, from the conceit of their own intelligence, became the worst, were not seduced by any serpent, but by the
love of self; and it is this that is meant by "the serpent's

head" that the Seed of the woman, that is, the Lord, should bruise. [2] Who is not able to see from reason that other things are meant than those that are there related historically in the letter? For who can comprehend how the world could have been created in the way there described? Therefore the learned strenuously try to explain the contents of that first chapter, and at length confess that they do not understand it. And the same is true of what follows, that two trees, a tree of life and a tree of knowledge, were placed in their garden or paradise, the latter as a cause of stumbling; also, that from the mere eating of this tree they so far transgressed that not only they but the whole human race, their posterity, became subject to damnation; furthermore, that they could have been seduced by a serpent; besides other things there stated; as that the wife was created from the rib of the husband; that after their fall they acknowledged their nakedness and covered it with fig-leaves, and that coats of skin were given them for bodily coverings; and that cherubim were placed with a flaming sword to guard the way to the tree of life. [3] All these things are representatives, depicting the establishment of the Most Ancient Church, its condition, its change, and finally its destruction. The arcana involved in all these things, which are contained in the spiritual sense that is in every particular of the story, may be found explained in the *Arcana Cœlestia* on *Genesis* and *Exodus*, published at London; and it can there be seen that "the tree of life" means the Lord in respect to His Divine providence; and "the tree of knowledge" means man in respect to his own prudence.

242. (2) *Their first son Cain killed his brother Abel, and God did not withhold him at the time by speaking with him, but only after the deed, by cursing him.* As Adam and his wife, as has been said above, mean the Most Ancient Church, so Cain and Abel, their first sons, mean the two essentials of the church, which are love and wisdom, or charity and faith, "Abel" meaning love and charity, and "Cain" wisdom or faith; strictly, wisdom separated from love, or faith separated from charity; and wisdom as well as faith when so separated is such that it not only rejects love and charity, but even annihilates them; and thus it kills its brother. That faith separate from charity does this is well known in the Christian world, as may be seen in the *Doctrine of the New Jerusalem concerning Faith.* [2] The cursing of Cain involves the spiritual state into which those come after death who separate faith from charity or wisdom from love. And yet, that wisdom or faith might not perish in consequence, a mark was put upon Cain to prevent his being slain; for love cannot exist apart from wisdom, or charity apart from faith. These things have nearly the same representation as the eating from the tree of knowledge; and this is why it properly follows the description of Adam and his wife. Moreover, those who are in faith separated from charity are in their own intelligence; while those who are in charity and in faith therefrom are in intelligence from the Lord, thus in the Divine providence.

243. (3) *The Israelitish nation worshiped a golden calf in the wilderness and acknowledged it as the God who led them out of the land of Egypt; and yet Jehovah saw this from Mount Sinai near by, and did not seek to prevent it.* This took place in the desert of Sinai near the mountain. Jehovah's not withholding them from that abominable worship is in accordance with all the laws of the Divine providence heretofore set forth, as well as with those that follow. This evil was permitted them lest they should all perish. For the sons of Israel were led out of Egypt that they might represent the Lord's church; and this they could not represent unless Egyptian idolatry had first been rooted out of their hearts; and this could not have been done without its having been left for them to act in accord with what was in their hearts, that this might thereby be removed by means of severe punishment. What is further signified by that worship, and by the threat that they should be wholly rejected and that a new nation should be raised up by Moses, may be seen in the *Arcana Cœlestia* on the thirty-second chapter of *Exodus*, where these things are treated of.

244. (4) *David numbered the people, and in consequence a plague was sent upon them, by which so many thousands of men perished ; and God, not before but after the deed, sent Gad the prophet to David, and denounced punishment upon him.* Whoever confirms himself against the Divine providence may have various thoughts and reflections about this also, especially why David was not admonished in advance, and why the people were so severely punished for the king's transgression. His not having been admonished in advance is in accordance with the laws of Divine providence already set forth, especially the two explained from n. 129 to 153, and from n. 154 to 174. This severe punishment of the people on account of the king's transgression, and the smiting of seventy thousand with the plague, was not for the king's sake but for the people's sake. For it is said,

Again the anger of Jehovah was kindled against Israel; therefore He moved David against them, saying, Go, number Israel and Judah (2 *Sam.* xxiv. 1).

245. (5) *Solomon was permitted to establish idolatrous worship.* This was done that he might represent the Lord's kingdom or the church, with all the varieties of religion in the whole world; for the church instituted with the nation of Israel and Judah was a representative church; therefore all the judgments and statutes of that church represented the spiritual things of the church, which are its internals; that people itself representing the church, the king representing the Lord, David representing the Lord who was to come into the world, and Solomon the Lord after His coming. And because the Lord after the glorification of His Human had power over heaven and earth (as He Himself says *Matt.* xxviii. 18), so Solomon His representative appeared in glory and magnificence, and possessed wisdom above all the kings of the earth, and also built the temple. Furthermore, Solomon permitted and set up the worship of many nations, by which the various religions in the world were represented. His wives, seven hundred in number, and his concubines, who numbered three hundred (1 *Kings* xi. 3), had a like signification, for a "wife" in the Word signifies the church, and a "concubine" a religion. This makes clear why it was granted to Solomon to build the temple, which signified both the Lord's Divine Human (*John* ii. 19, 21) and also the church; and why he was permitted to establish idolatrous worship, and to marry so many wives. That by "David," in many places in the Word, the Lord who was to come into the world is meant, can be seen in the *Doctrine of the New Jerusalem concerning the Lord* (n. 43, 44).

246. (6) *Many kings after Solomon were permitted to profane the temple and the holy things of the church.* This was because the people represented the church, and their king was their head; and as the nation of Israel and Judah was such that they could no longer represent the church, for they were idolaters at heart, they gradually fell away from representative worship by perverting all things of the church, till at last it was devastated. This was represented by the profanations of the temple by the kings, and by their idolatries; and the essential devastation of the church was represented by the destruction of the temple itself, and by the carrying away of the people of Israel, and by the captivity of the people of Judah in Babylonia. Such was the cause; and whatever is done from any cause is done from the Divine providence according to some law of it.

247. (7) *That nation was permitted to crucify the Lord.* This was because the church with that nation had been wholly devastated, and had become such that not only they did not know and acknowledge the Lord, but they even hated Him; and yet all things that they did to Him were done in accordance with the laws of His Divine providence. That the passion of the cross was the last temptation or the last combat, by which the Lord fully conquered the hells and fully glorified His Human may be seen in the *Doctrine of the New Jerusalem concerning the Lord* (n. 12–14); and in the *Doctrine of the New Jerusalem concerning Faith* (n. 34, 35).

15

248. This is an explanation of the things enumerated above (in n. 236), which are some of the things from the Word by which a natural man who is a reasoner can confirm himself against the Divine providence. For whatever such a man sees, hears, or reads, as has been said, he can employ as an argument against the Divine providence. There are few, however, who confirm themselves against the Divine providence from such things as are in the Word; but many do so from things that take place before their eyes, such as are mentioned in n. 237, which will now likewise be explained.

249. (1) *Every worshiper of himself and of nature confirms himself against the Divine providence when he sees in the world so many impious persons, and so many of their impieties, and at the same time the glorying of some in these impieties, and yet no punishment of such by God.* All impieties and also the glorying in them are permissions, the causes of which are laws of the Divine providence. Every man can freely, yea, most freely, think as he wishes, as well against God as for God; and he that thinks against God is rarely punished in the natural world, because there he is always in a state to be reformed; but he is punished in the spiritual world. This takes place after death, because he can then no longer be reformed. [2] That the laws of Divine providence are the causes of permissions is clear from its laws that have been set forth above, when they are recalled and examined; which are these: Man should act from freedom in accordance with reason (see above, n. 71–99); Man should not be compelled by external means to think and will, and thus to believe and love, the things of religion, but should guide himself and sometimes compel himself (see n. 129–153); Man's own prudence is nothing, it merely appears to be something, and ought to appear as if it were; but the Divine providence, because of its minute particulars, is universal (n. 191–213); The Divine providence looks to eternal things, and to temporal things only so far as they make one with eternal things (n. 214–220); Man is admitted interiorly into truths of faith and into goods of charity only so far as he can be kept in them until the end of his life (n. 221–233). [**3**] That the causes of permissions are laws of the Divine providence will also be made clear from what is to follow, as from this: Evils are permitted for the sake of the end, which is salvation. Also from this: The Divine providence is unceasing, both with the evil and with the good. And finally from this: The Lord cannot act contrary to the laws of His Divine providence, for to act contrary to them would be acting contrary to His Divine love and to His Divine wisdom, thus contrary to Himself. When these laws are considered together they make clear the reasons why impieties are permitted by the Lord, and are not punished so long as they are in the thought, and rarely even while they are in the purpose and thus in the will, but not in the act. And yet its own punishment follows every evil; it is as if its punishment were inscribed upon the evil, and this punishment the wicked man endures after death. [**4**] By what has now been set forth that which was stated above (in n. 237) is also explained, namely, *The worshiper of himself and of nature confirms himself against the Divine providence still further when he sees that plots, devices, and frauds are successful even against the pious, just, and sincere; and that injustice triumphs over justice in the courts and in business.* All the laws of Divine providence are necessities; and as they are the causes of the permission of these things it is clear that if man is to live as a man, to be reformed and to be saved, these things can be taken away from him by the Lord only by means,—by the Word, and especially by the commandments of the Decalogue,—with those who acknowledge all kinds of murder, adultery, theft, and false witness as sins; but with those who do not acknowledge such things to be sins, by means of the civil laws and fear of their punishments, also by means of moral laws, and the fear of the loss of reputation, and thereby of honor and wealth. By these means the Lord leads the evil, but only away from doing these things, not from thinking and willing them; while by the former means He leads the good, not only away from doing these things, but also from thinking and willing them.

250. (2) *The worshiper of himself and of nature confirms himself against the Divine providence when he sees the impious exalted to honors and to high offices in church and state, also abounding in wealth and living in luxury and magnificence, while he sees the worshipers of God despised and poor.* The worshiper of himself and of nature believes dignities and wealth to be the highest and the only happiness that can be granted, thus happiness itself; and if he has any thought of God from a sense of worship instilled in infancy he calls them Divine blessings; and so long as he is not puffed up by them he thinks that there is a God, and even worships God. But there lies hidden in the worship what he is himself then ignorant of, an aspiration to be raised up by God to still higher dignities, and to still greater wealth; and when he reaches these his worship tends more and more to outward things, even until it falls away, and at length he despises and denies God; and he does the same if he is cast down from the dignity and opulence on which he has set his heart. What, then, are dignities and wealth to the wicked but stumbling-blocks? [2] But to the good they are not so, because they do not set their hearts on them, but on the uses or the goods in the performance of which dignities and wealth are of service as means. Therefore only he that is a worshiper of himself and nature can confirm himself against Divine providence because of the advancement of the impious to honors and wealth and to high offices in church and state. Moreover, what is dignity greater or less? And what is opulence greater or less? In itself is it anything but an imaginary something? Is one person more fortunate or happier than another? Does a great man, or even a king or emperor, after a single year, regard the dignity as anything more than something common, which no longer exalts his heart with joy, but may even become worthless to him? Are such by virtue of their dignities in any greater degree of happiness than those who are in less dignity, or even in the least, like farmers and

even their servants? These, when all goes well with them, and
they are content with their lot, may have a greater measure of
happiness. What is more restless at heart, more frequently
provoked, more violently enraged, than self-love; and this as
often as it is not honored according to the pride of its heart,
and as often as anything does not succeed according to its wish
and whim? What, then, is dignity, if it does not pertain to
some matter or use, but an idea? And can there be such an
idea in any thought except thought about self and the world,
which essentially in itself is that the world is everything and
the eternal nothing: [3] Something shall now be said about
the Divine providence, why it permits the impious in heart to
be raised to dignities and enriched with possessions. The impious or wicked can perform uses equally with the pious or good,
and even with greater zeal, for they have regard to themselves
in the uses, and to the honors as the uses; therefore to whatever height the love of self climbs the lust of performing uses
for the sake of its own glory burns in it. With the pious or
good there is no such fire, unless unconsciously kindled by some
feeling of honor. Thus the Lord governs the impious in heart
who are in places of dignity, by the glory of their name, and
incites them to the performance of uses to the community or
country, to the society or city in which they dwell, and to their
fellow-citizen or neighbor with whom they are associated. This
is the Lord's government, which is called the Divine providence
with such; for the Lord's kingdom is a kingdom of uses; and
where there are but few who perform uses for the sake of uses
He causes the worshipers of self to be raised to the higher
offices, in which each one is incited to do good by means of his
own love. [4] Suppose an infernal kingdom in the world (although there is none such) where none but the loves of self
rule (and the love of self is itself the devil), would not every
one perform uses from the fire of self-love and for the splendor
of his own glory, to a greater extent than in any other kingdom? But there the public good would be in every mouth,
but his own good in every heart. And as each one would look

to his own chief for his advancement (for each one would aspire to become greatest), could such a man see that there is a
God ? A smoke like that of a conflagration would surround
him, through which no spiritual truth in its own light could
pass. I have seen that smoke about the hells of such. Light
your lamp and search, and see how many there are in the kingdoms of the present day who aspire to dignities and who are not
loves of self and the world. Will you find fifty in a thousand
who are loves of God, and among these some, perhaps, who aspire to dignities ?   Since, then, there are so few who are loves
of God, and so many who are loves of self and the world, and
since the latter loves from their fire perform uses more than
the loves of God from theirs, how can anyone confirm himself
[against the Divine providence] because the evil are in eminence and opulence more than the good? [5] This is shown
in these words of the Lord:—

> The Lord commended the unjust steward because he had done wisely;
> for the sons of this age are in their own generation wiser than the sons of
> light. And I say unto you, Make to yourselves friends out of the mam-
> mon of unrighteousness, that when ye fail they may receive you into the
> eternal tabernacles (*Luke* xvi. 8, 9).

The meaning of this in the natural sense is clear; but in the
spiritual sense "the mammon of unrighteousness" means the
knowledges of truth and good possessed by the evil, which they
employ solely in acquiring for themselves dignities and wealth;
out of these knowledges the good, or "the sons of light," must
make to themselves friends; and these are what will receive
them into the eternal tabernacles.   That many are loves of self
and the world, and that few are loves of God, the Lord also
teaches in these words:—

> Wide is the gate and broad is the way that leadeth to destruction, and
> many be they that enter in thereby; but narrow and straitened is the
> way that leadeth unto life, and few be they that find it (*Matt.* vii. 13, 14).

That dignities and wealth are either curses or blessings, and
with whom they are the one or the other, may be seen above
(n. 217).

251. (3) *The worshiper of himself and of nature confirms himself against Divine providence when he reflects that wars are permitted, and the consequent slaughter of so many men, and the plundering of their wealth.* It is not from the Divine providence that wars exist, for they are connected with murders, plunderings, violence, cruelties, and other terrible evils, which are directly opposed to Christian charity; and yet they must needs be permitted, because, since the time of the most ancient people, meant by Adam and his wife (of whom above, n. 241), the life's love of man has become such that it wills to rule over others, and finally over all; also to possess the wealth of the world, and finally all wealth. These two loves cannot be kept bound, for it is according to the Divine providence that every one be allowed to act from freedom in accordance with reason (see above, n. 71–99); furthermore, without permissions man cannot be led from evil by the Lord, and thus be reformed and saved. For unless evils were permitted to break out man would not see them, and therefore would not acknowledge them, and thus could not be led to resist them. For this reason evils cannot be prevented by any providence; for if they were they would remain shut in, and like the diseases called cancer and gangrene would spread about and consume all that is vital in man. [2] For man from birth is like a little hell, between which and heaven there is perpetual discordance. No man can be withdrawn from his hell by the Lord unless he sees that he is in hell and wishes to be led out; and this cannot be done without permissions, the causes of which are laws of the Divine providence. For this reason there are wars, lesser and greater, the lesser between the possessors of estates and their neighbors, and the greater between the rulers of kingdoms and their neighbors. Between the lesser and greater there is no difference, except that the lesser are kept within bounds by the laws of the nation, and the greater by the laws of nations; also that while both the lesser and greater wish to transgress their laws, the lesser cannot, and the greater can, although not beyond its abilities. [3] There are many other reasons stored up in the

treasury of Divine wisdom why the Lord does not check the
greater wars, with their kings and commanders, connected as
they are with murders, depredations, violence, and cruelties,
neither in their beginning nor in their progress, but only at the
close, when the power of one or the other has become so reduced that he is in danger of destruction. Some of these reasons have been revealed to me, and among them is this: that
all wars, however much they may belong to civil affairs, represent in heaven the states of the church, and are correspondences.
Such were all the wars described in the Word, and such also
are all wars at this day. The wars described in the Word are
those that the children of Israel waged with various nations, as
the Amorites, the Ammonites, the Moabites, the Philistines,
the Syrians, the Egyptians, the Chaldeans, and the Assyrians;
and when the children of Israel, who represented the church,
departed from their commandments and statutes and fell into
the evils signified by those nations, they were punished by some
nation, because each nation with which the children of Israel
waged war signified some particular kind of evil. For example, when they profaned the holy things of the church by foul
idolatries they were punished by the Assyrians and Chaldeans,
because "Assyria" and "Chaldea" signify the profanation of
what is holy. What was signified by their wars with the Philistines may be seen in the *Doctrine of the New Jerusalem concerning Faith* (n. 50–54). [4] Like things are represented by
the wars of the present day, wherever they occur; for all things
that take place in the natural world correspond to spiritual
things in the spiritual world, and every thing spiritual has relation to the church. It is not known in this world what kingdoms in Christendom answer to the Moabites and Ammonites,
what to the Syrians and Philistines, or what to the Chaldeans
and Assyrians, and the others with whom the children of Israel
waged war; and yet there are those that do answer to them.
Moreover, what the quality of the church upon earth is and
what the evils are into which it falls, and for which it is punished by wars, cannot be seen at all in the natural world; be-

cause in this world externals only are evident, and these do not constitute the church; but this is seen in the spiritual world, where internals are manifest, in which the church itself is; and there all are conjoined in accordance with their various states. The conflicts of these in the spiritual world correspond to wars; which are governed by the Lord on both sides correspondentially, in accordance with His Divine providence. [5] That in this world wars are governed by Divine providence the spiritual man acknowledges, but the natural man does not, except when a festival is appointed on account of a victory that he may return thanks on his knees to God that He has given the victory, also by a few words before going into battle. But when he returns into himself he ascribes the victory either to the prudence of the general or to some measure or occurrence in the midst of the battle, which they had not thought of, from which nevertheless came the victory. [6] That the Divine providence that is called fortune is in the least particulars of even trivial things may be seen above (n. 212); and if in these you acknowledge the Divine providence you must certainly acknowledge it in the affairs of war. Also the successes and favorable occurrences of war are called in common language the fortune of war; and this is Divine providence, especially in the plans and preparations of the general, even although he then and afterwards may ascribe it all to his own prudence. And let him do this if he will, for he is in full liberty to think in favor of the Divine providence or against it, and even in favor of God and against Him; but let him know that no part whatever of the plan or preparation is from himself; it all flows in either from heaven or from hell,—from hell by permission, from heaven by providence.

252. (4) *The worshiper of himself and of nature confirms himself against Divine providence when he reflects according to his perception that victories are on the side of prudence, and sometimes not on the side of justice; and that it makes no difference whether the commander is an upright man or not.* Victories seem to be on the side of prudence, and sometimes not on the side of justice, because man judges from the appearance, and favors one side more than the other, and that which he favors he is able to confirm by reasonings; nor does he know that in heaven there is a spiritual justice to a cause and in the world a natural justice, as has just been said, and that these are conjoined by means of a connection between things past and things future that are known only to the Lord.   [2] It makes no difference whether the commander is an upright man or not, for the same reason as was set forth above (n. 250), namely, that the wicked perform uses equally with the good, and the evil from their fire with more ardor than the good, especially in wars, because the evil man is more crafty and shrewd in contriving devices; and from a love of glory he takes more delight than a good man in killing and plundering those whom he knows and declares to be his enemies; for a good man is prudent and zealous only in defending, and rarely is prudent and zealous in any degree in attacking.   It is the same as with spirits of hell and angels of heaven; the spirits of hell attack, while the angels of heaven defend themselves.   From this comes the conclusion that it is allowable for any one to defend his country and his fellow-citizens against invading enemies, even by means of wicked commanders, but that it is not allowable to become an enemy without cause.   A cause that looks to glory alone is in itself diabolical, for it is of the love of self.

253. Thus far have been explained the things presented above (in n. 237), by which the merely natural man confirms himself against Divine providence.   The things that follow (in n. 238), relating to the state of religion in various nations, that also may serve the merely natural man as arguments against Divine providence, shall now be explained.   For the natural man says in his heart, How can so many discordant religions exist, instead of one true religion over all the earth, if the Divine providence has as its end a heaven from the human race (as shown above, n. 27–45)?   But listen, I pray: All the human beings that are born, however many and in whatever religion, can be saved, provided they acknowledge God and live according to the commandments in the Decalogue, which are not to kill, not to commit adultery, not to steal, and not to bear false witness, for the reason that doing such things is contrary to religion, and thus contrary to God. Such fear God and love the neighbor; they fear God in the thought that to do such things is contrary to God; and they love the neighbor in the thought that to kill, to commit adultery, to steal, to bear false witness, and to covet the neighbor's house or wife is against the neighbor. Because such in their life look to God, and do not do evil to the neighbor, they are led by the Lord; and those who are led are also taught in accordance with their religion, about God and about the neighbor; for those who so live love to be taught, while those who live otherwise do not; and because they love to be taught, when after death they become spirits they are instructed by the angels and gladly accept such truths as are in the Word. Something about these may be seen in the *Doctrine of the New Jerusalem concerning the Sacred Scripture* (n. 91–97, and n. 104–113).

254. (1) *The merely natural man confirms himself against the Divine providence when he considers the religious condition of various peoples—that there are some who are totally ignorant of God, and some who worship the sun and moon, and some who worship idols and graven images.* Those who draw arguments from these things against the Divine providence are ignorant of the arcana of heaven, which are innumerable, and with scarcely one of which man is acquainted, among which is this, that man is not taught immediately from heaven but mediately (see above, n. 154–174). And because man is taught mediately, and the Gospel could not reach through missionaries all that dwell in the whole world, and yet religion could be communicated in various ways even to the nations that occupy the remote parts of the earth, therefore this has been accomplished by the Divine providence. For no man gets his religion from himself, but through another, who has either learned directly from the Word, or by transmission from others who have

learned it, that there is a God, that there are a heaven and a
hell, that there is a life after death, and that in order to become happy God must be worshiped. [2] That a religion was
spread throughout the world from the Ancient Word, and afterwards from the Israelitish Word, may be seen in the *Doctrine of the New Jerusalem concerning the Sacred Scripture*
(n. 101–103); and that if there had been no Word there could
have been no knowledge of God, of heaven and of hell, of the
life after death, still less of the Lord, see the same work (n.
114–118). When a religion has been once implanted in a nation the Lord leads that nation according to the precepts and
dogmas of its own religion; and He has provided that there
shall be in every religion precepts like those in the Decalogue;
as, that God must be worshiped, His name must not be profaned, a sacred day must be observed, parents must be honored,
and there must be no murder, adultery, theft, or false witness.
The nation that regards these precepts as Divine and lives according to them from a religious motive is saved (as has been
said just above, n. 253). Moreover, most nations remote from
Christendom regard these not as civil but as Divine laws, and
hold them sacred. That man is saved by a life according to
these precepts may be seen in the *Doctrine of the New Jerusalem [concerning Life] from the Commandments of the Decalogue,* from beginning to end. [3] Among the arcana of heaven
is this also: The angelic heaven before the Lord is as one man,
whose soul and life is the Lord; and this Divine Man is a man
in complete form, not only in respect to external members and
organs, but also in respect to internal members and organs,
which are many, and even with respect to the skins, membranes, cartilages, and bones; but in that Man all these are
spiritual, not material. And it has been provided by the Lord
that those also who could not be reached by the Gospel, but
only by a religion, should also be able to have a place in that
Divine Man, that is, in heaven, constituting those parts that
are called skins, membranes, cartilages, and bones, and that
they, like others, should be in heavenly joy. For it matters

not whether they are in joy like that of the angels of the highest
heaven or in joy like that of the angels of the lowest heaven;
for every one who comes into heaven enters into the highest
joy of his heart; he can bear no higher joy, for he would be
suffocated thereby. [4] This may be compared to a peasant
and a king. A peasant may be in a state of the highest joy
when he goes about with a new suit of coarse wool, and sits
down to a table on which is pork, a bit of beef, cheese, beer,
and common wine, and would be oppressed at heart if like
a king he were clothed in purple and silk, gold and silver,
and a table were placed before him covered with delicacies and
costly dishes of many kinds, with noble wine. From this it is
clear that there is heavenly happiness for the last as well as
for the first, for each in his degree; so also for those who are
outside of the Christian world, provided they shun evils as sins
against God because they are contrary to religion. [5] There
are a few who are wholly ignorant of God. That if such have
lived a moral life they are taught by angels after death and
receive in their moral life something spiritual, can be seen
in the *Doctrine of the New Jerusalem concerning the Sacred
Scripture* (n. 116). So with those who worship the sun and
moon, believing God to be there; as they do not know otherwise this is not imputed to them as a sin; for the Lord says,

If ye were blind (that is, if ye did not know) ye would have no sin
(*John* ix. 41).

But there are many, even in the Christian world, who worship
idols and graven images. This indeed is idolatrous, and yet
not with all; for there are some to whom graven images are
serviceable as a means of awakening thought about God; for it
is from an influx from heaven that those who acknowledge God
wish to see Him; and as these are not able, like the interiorly
spiritual, to lift their minds above sensual things, their thought
of God is aroused by the graven thing or image. Those who
do this and do not worship the graven image itself as God, if
they live according to the precepts of the Decalogue from a re-

ligious motive, are saved. [6] From all this it is clear that as
the Lord desires the welfare of all He has provided also that
every one may have some place in heaven if he lives well.
That before the Lord heaven is as one man, and thus heaven
corresponds to each and all things in man, and also that there
are those who answer to skins, membranes, cartilages, and bones,
may be seen in the work on *Heaven and Hell*, published at
London in the year 1758 (n. 59–102); and in the *Arcana Cœlestia* (n. 5552–5569); also above (n. 201–204).

255. (2) *The merely natural man confirms himself against
the Divine providence when he sees the Mohammedan religion
accepted by so many empires and kingdoms.* That this religion
is accepted by more kingdoms than the Christian religion may
be a stumbling-block to those who think about the Divine providence and who at the same time believe that only those who
are born Christians, that is, those where the Word is, and by it
the Lord is known, can be saved. But the Mohammedan religion is not a stumbling-block to those who believe that all things
belong to the Divine providence. Such inquire how this is, and
they find out; it is in this, that the Mohammedan religion acknowledges the Lord as the Son of God, as the wisest of men,
and as a very great prophet who came into the world to teach
men; a great part of the Mohammedans make Him greater than
Mohammed. [2] To make it fully clear that this religion was
raised up by the Lord's Divine providence to destroy the idolatries of many nations it shall be set forth in a certain order.
First, then, respecting the origin of idolatry. Previous to that
religion the worship of idols was common throughout the world.
This was because the churches before the coming of the Lord
were all representative churches. Such was the Israelitish
church. In that church the tabernacle, Aaron's garments, the
sacrifices, all things belonging to the temple at Jerusalem, and
the statutes, were representative. Among the ancients there
was a knowledge of correspondences (which includes a knowledge of representatives), the essential knowledge of the wise;
and this was especially cultivated in Egypt, and from it their

hieroglyphics were derived. From that knowledge they knew the signification of animals of every kind, also the signification of all kinds of trees, and of mountains, hills, rivers, fountains, and also of the sun, the moon, and the stars. And as all their worship was representative, consisting of pure correspondences, they worshiped on mountains and hills, and also in groves and gardens, and they consecrated fountains, and in their adoration of God they turned their faces to the rising sun; moreover they made graven images of horses, oxen, calves, lambs, and even birds and fishes, and serpents; and at home and elsewhere they placed these in an order in conformity to the spiritual things of the church to which they corresponded, or which they represented. They also placed like things in their temples, to call to remembrance the holy things which they signified. [3] After a time, when the knowledge of correspondences had been lost, their posterity began to worship the graven images themselves, as holy in themselves, not knowing that their fathers of ancient time had seen no holiness in them, but that they merely represented and thus signified holy things, according to correspondences. From this the idolatries arose which filled the whole world, Asia with the neighboring islands, Africa, and Europe. To extirpate all these idolatries it came to pass, under the Lord's Divine providence, that a new religion arose, adapted to the genius of Orientals, in which there was something from the Word of both Testaments, and which taught that the Lord came into the world, and that He was the greatest prophet, the wisest of men, and the Son of God. This was done through Mohammed, from whom that religion was called the Mohammedan religion. [4] Under the Lord's Divine providence this religion was raised up and adapted to the genius of Orientals, as has been said, to the end that it might destroy the idolatries of so many nations, and give them some knowledge of the Lord before they entered the spiritual world. And this religion would not have been accepted by so many kingdoms, and would have been powerless to extirpate idolatries, if it had not been adapted and suited to the ideas of thought and to the life of them all. It did not acknowledge the Lord as the God of heaven and earth, because Orientals acknowledged God as the Creator of the universe, and were unable to comprehend how He could come into the world and assume the Human; even as Christians do not comprehend this, and consequently in their thought separate His Divine from His Human, and place the Divine near the Father in heaven, and His Human they know not where. [5] From all this it can be seen that the Mohammedan religion arose under the Lord's Divine providence; and that all of that religion who acknowledge the Lord as the Son of God, and at the same time live according to the commandments of the Decalogue (which they also have), by shunning evils as sins, come into a heaven that is called the Mohammedan heaven. This heaven, too, is divided into three heavens, a highest, a middle, and a lowest. In the highest heaven are those who acknowledge the Lord to be one with the Father, and thus to be Himself the only God; in the second heaven are those who give up their many wives, and live with one wife; and in the lowest those who are being initiated. More about this religion may be seen in the *Continuation concerning the Last Judgment and concerning the Spiritual World* (n. 68–72), where the Mohammedans and Mohammed are treated of.

256. (3) *The merely natural man confirms himself against the Divine providence when he sees that the Christian religion is accepted only in the smaller division of the habitable globe called Europe, and is there divided.* The Christian religion is accepted only in the smaller division of the habitable globe called Europe because it was not adapted to the genius of the Orientals, like the Mohammedan religion, which is a mixed religion, as has been shown just above; and a religion that is not adapted is not accepted. For example, a religion that makes it unlawful to marry more than one wife is not accepted but is rejected by those who for ages back have been polygamists. The same is true of other ordinances of the Christian religion. [2] Nor does it matter whether a smaller or a greater part of the world has accepted that religion, provided there are peoples

that have the Word; for even those have light therefrom who
are outside of the church and do not have the Word, as is shown
in the *Doctrine of the New Jerusalem concerning the Sacred
Scripture* (n. 104–113); and what is wonderful, where the Word
is read reverently and the Lord is worshiped from the Word
the Lord with heaven is present. This is because the Lord is
the Word, and the Word is Divine truth which makes heaven;
therefore the Lord says:—

Where two or three are gathered together in My name, there am I in
the midst of them (*Matt.* xviii. 20).

This may take place with the Word in many parts of the habitable world with Europeans, because their commerce extends
over the whole earth, and everywhere the Word is read by
them, or there is teaching from the Word. This seems like a
fabrication, and yet it is true. [3] The Christian religion is
divided for the reason that it is from the Word, and the Word
is written throughout wholly by correspondences, and the correspondences are in great part appearances of truth, enclosed
within which, however, genuine truths lie hidden. And as the
doctrine of the church must be drawn from the sense of the
letter of the Word, and that sense is such, there must needs
spring up in the church disputes, controversies, and dissensions,
especially in regard to the understanding of the Word, but not
in regard to the Word itself and in regard to the Lord's Divine
itself; for it is everywhere acknowledged that the Word is holy,
and that Divinity belongs to the Lord; and these two are the
essentials of the church. Also for this reason those who deny
the Lord's Divinity, who are called Socinians, have been ex-
communicated by the church; and those who deny the holiness
of the Word are not regarded as Christians. To this I will add
a noteworthy fact in regard to the Word, from which it may be
concluded that the Word interiorly is the Divine truth itself,
and inmostly is the Lord. [4] Whenever any spirit opens the
Word, and rubs his face or his clothing against it, his face or
clothing shines from the mere rubbing, as brightly as the moon

16

or a star, and this in the sight of all whom he meets. This is a proof that nothing exists in the world more holy than the Word. That the Word is written throughout wholly in correspondences, may be seen in the *Doctrine of the New Jerusalem concerning the Sacred Scripture* (n. 5–26). That the doctrine of the church must be drawn from the sense of the letter of the Word and established by it (see n. 50–61 of the same work). That heresies may be extorted from the sense of the letter of the Word, but that it is destructive to confirm them (n. 91–97). That the church is from the Word, and is such as its understanding of the Word is (76–79).

257. (4) *The merely natural man confirms himself against the Divine providence by the fact that in many of the kingdoms where the Christian religion is accepted there are some who claim for themselves Divine power, and wish to be worshiped as gods, and that the dead are invoked.* They say, indeed, that they have not arrogated to themselves Divine power, and do not wish to be worshiped as gods; and yet they declare that they can open and close heaven, remit and retain sins, and therefore save and condemn men; and this is Divinity itself. For the Divine providence has for its end nothing else than reformation and consequent salvation; this is its unceasing operation with everyone; and salvation can be accomplished only through an acknowledgment of the Divinity of the Lord, and a confidence that the Lord effects salvation when man lives according to His commandments. [2] Who cannot see that this is the Babylon described in the *Apocalypse;* also that it is the Babylon spoken of here and there in the prophets? It is also the "Lucifer" spoken of in *Isaiah* xiv., as is evident from the verses of that chapter in which are these words:—

Thou shalt take up this proverb against the king of Babylon (verse 4);
And then I will cut off from Babylon name and remnant (verse 22);

from which it follows that Babylon there is Lucifer, of whom it is said:—

How art thou fallen from heaven, O Lucifer, son of the morning! And thou saidst in thy heart, I will ascend into the heavens; I will exalt my

throne above the stars of God; and I will sit upon the mount of the con-
gregation, in the sides of the north; I will ascend above the heights of the
clouds; I will become like the Most High (verses 12–14).

That they invoke the dead and pray to the dead for help is
known. They may be said to invoke the dead, inasmuch as
invocation of the dead was established by a papal bull confirming the decree of the Council of Trent, in which it is plainly
declared that the dead are to be invoked. Yet every one knows
that God alone should be invoked, and not any dead person.
[**3**] It shall now be told, however, why the Lord has permitted
such things. It cannot be denied that He has permitted them
for the sake of the end, which is salvation. For it is known
that apart from the Lord there is no salvation; and it was for
this reason necessary that the Lord should be preached from
the Word, and that the Christian church should by that means
be established. But this could be done only by an advance
guard who would do this with zeal; and none would do this
except those who were in an ardor resembling zeal that was from
the fire of self-love. By such a fire they were at first stirred
up to preach the Lord and to teach the Word; and it was because of this their primeval state that

Lucifer was called the son of the morning (verse 12).

But as they saw that they could gain dominion by means of the
holy things of the Word and the church, the love of self, by
which they were first stirred up to preach the Lord, broke forth
from within, and finally exalted itself to such a height that
they transferred to themselves the whole of the Lord's Divine
power, leaving nothing. [**4**] This could not have been prevented by the Lord's Divine providence; for if it had been prevented they would have publicly taught that the Lord is not
God, and that the Word is not holy, and would have made
themselves Socinians or Arians, and thus would have destroyed
the whole church, which, whatever may be the character of its
rulers, continues to exist with the submissive people; for all
those of this religion who approach the Lord and shun evils as

sins are saved, consequently there are many heavenly societies
of such in the spiritual world. It has also been provided that
among them there should be a nation that has not passed under the yoke of such domination, and that holds the Word to
be holy; this is the noble French nation. But what has been
done? [5] When the love of self exalted its dominion even to
the Lord's throne, set Him aside, and placed itself thereon,
that love, which is Lucifer, could not but profane all things of
the Word and the church. That this might be prevented, the
Lord by His Divine providence took care that they should withdraw from the worship of Himself, and should invoke the dead,
should pray to images of the dead, should kiss their bones, and
bow down at their tombs, should forbid the reading of the Word,
should place holy worship in masses not understood by the
common people, and sell salvation for money; because if they
had not done these things they would have profaned the holy
things of the Word and of the church. For only those who
have a knowledge of holy things can profane them, as has been
shown in a preceding paragraph. [6] So to prevent their profaning the most Holy Supper they were permitted, under the
Lord's Divine providence, to divide it, and to give the bread to
the people and drink the wine themselves, for the wine in the
Holy Supper signifies holy truth and the bread holy good; but
when these are separated the wine signifies profaned truth and
the bread adulterated good; and still further, they were permitted to make it corporeal and material, and to adopt this as the
primary principle of religion. Any one who turns his mind to
these several things and considers them with some enlightenment of mind can see the wonderful activities of the Divine
providence in guarding the holy things of the church, in saving
all that can be saved, and in snatching from the fire, as it were,
those who are willing to be rescued.

258. (5) *The merely natural man confirms himself against
the Divine providence by the fact that among those who profess
the Christian religion there are some who place salvation in
certain phrases which they should think and talk about, making*

no account of the good works they should do. That such are
those who make faith alone saving, and not a life of charity,
and therefore those who separate faith from charity, is shown
in the *Doctrine of the New Jerusalem concerning Faith ;* and
there it is also shown that such are meant in the Word by
"Philistines," by the "dragon," and by "goats." [**2**] Such
doctrine also has been permitted under the Divine providence
in order that the Divine of the Lord and the holiness of the
Word might not be profaned. The Divine of the Lord is not
profaned when salvation is placed in the words, "That God the
Father may be merciful for the sake of His Son, who endured
the cross and made satisfaction for us;" for in this way the
Divine of the Lord is not approached, but the Human, which
is not acknowledged as Divine. Nor is the Word profaned,
for they pay no attention to the passages where love, charity,
doing, and works are mentioned. They claim that these are
all included in a belief in the formula just quoted; and those
who confirm this say to themselves, "The law does not con
demn me, so neither does evil; and good does not save me,
because the good from me is not good." These, therefore, are
like those who have no knowledge of truth from the Word, and
thus cannot profane it. But belief in the above statement is
confirmed by those only who from the love of self are in the
pride of their own intelligence. Such are not Christians at
heart, but only wish to seem so. It shall now be explained
how the Lord's Divine providence is, nevertheless, unceasingly
working for the salvation of those in whom faith separate
from charity has become a matter of religion. [**3**] It is of the
Lord's Divine providence that, although that faith has come to
to be a matter of religion, yet every one knows that it is not
that faith that saves, but a life of charity with which faith acts
as one; for in all churches where that religion is accepted it is
taught that there is no salvation unless man examines himself,
sees his sins, acknowledges them, repents, refrains from them,
and enters on a new life. This is proclaimed with great zeal
in the presence of all who are coming to the Lord's Supper;

and to this is added, that unless they do this they mix what is holy with what is profane, and hurl themselves into eternal damnation; and in England it is taught even that unless they do this the devil will enter into them as he entered into Judas, and will destroy them both soul and body. From all this it is clear that even in the churches where the doctrine of faith alone has been adopted every one is still taught that evils must be shunned as sins. [4] Furthermore, every one who is born a Christian knows also that evils must be shunned as sins, because the Decalogue is placed in the hands of every boy and every girl, and is taught them by parents and teachers; also all citizens of the kingdom, especially the common people, are examined by a priest from the Decalogue alone, recited from memory, as to their knowledge of the Christian religion; and are counselled to do the things there commanded. It is then never said by any leader that they are under the yoke of law, or that they cannot do the things commanded because they can do no good from themselves. Moreover, the Athanasian Creed has been accepted throughout the Christian world, and what is said in it at the end is acknowledged, namely, that the Lord shall come to judge the living and the dead, and then those that have done good shall enter into life eternal, and those that have done evil into everlasting fire. [5] In Sweden, where the religion of faith alone has been adopted, it is also plainly taught that a faith separate from charity or without good works is impossible. This is found in a certain appendix concerning things to be kept in remembrance, attached to all their psalm books,* called "Hindrances or Stumbling-blocks of the Impenitent (*Obotfardigas forhinder*)." In it are these words: "They that are rich in good works thereby show that they are rich in faith, since when faith is saving it operates these through charity; for justifying faith never exists alone and separate from good works, just as there can be no good tree without fruit, or a sun without light and heat, or water without moisture." [6] These few statements are made to show

---

* This appendix was omitted in the revision of the psalm book made in 1819.

that although a religion of faith alone has been adopted, goods of charity, which are good works, are nevertheless everywhere taught; and that this is of the Lord's Divine providence, that the common people may not be led astray by it. I have heard Luther, with whom I have sometimes talked in the spiritual world, execrating faith alone, and saying that when he established it he was warned by an angel of the Lord not to do it; but that his thought was that unless works were rejected no separation from the Catholic religion could be effected; and therefore, contrary to the warning, he established that faith.

259. (6) *The merely natural man confirms himself against the Divine providence by the fact that there have been and still are so many heresies in the Christian world, such as Quakerism, Moravianism, Anabaptism, and others.* For he may think to himself, If the Divine providence were universal in its least particulars, and had the salvation of all as its end, it would have caused one true religion to exist throughout the world, and that one not divided, still less torn into heresies. But make use of your reason, and think more deeply, if you can, whether a man can be saved unless he is previously reformed. For he is born into the love of self and love of the world; and as these loves do not carry in them anything of love to God or of love towards the neighbor except for the sake of self, he has been born also into evils of every kind. What is there of love or mercy in these loves? Does he [from these loves] think anything of defrauding another, defaming him, hating him even to the death, committing adultery with his wife, being cruel to him when moved by revenge, while cherishing in his mind a wish to be highest of all, and to possess the goods of all others, and while regarding others as insignificant and worthless compared with himself? If such a man is to be saved must he not first be led away from these evils, and thus reformed? This can be done only in accordance with many laws which are laws of the Divine providence, as has been shown above in many places. These laws are for the most part unknown; nevertheless, they are laws of the Divine wisdom and at the same time of the Divine love, and the Lord cannot act contrary to them, because to do so would be to destroy man, not to save him. [2] Let the laws that have been set forth be reviewed and compared, and you will see. And since, then, it is in accordance with these laws that there is no immediate influx from heaven, but only mediate influx through the Word, doctrines, and preaching; also, for the Word to be Divine it must needs be written wholly by correspondences; it follows that discussions and heresies are inevitable, and that permissions of these are also in accord with the laws of the Divine providence. Furthermore, when the church itself has taken as its essentials such things as belong to the understanding alone, that is, to doctrine, and not such as belong to the will, that is, to the life, and the things that belong to the life are not made the essentials of the church, man from his understanding is then in mere darkness, and wanders about like a blind man, everywhere running against something and falling into pits. For the will must see in the understanding, and not the understanding in the will; or what is the same, the life and its love must lead the understanding to think, speak, and act, and not the reverse. If the reverse were true, the understanding, from an evil and even a diabolical love, might seize upon whatever presents itself through the senses, and enjoin the will to do it. From all this the source of dissensions and heresies can be seen. [3] And yet it has been provided that every one, in whatever heresies he may be in respect to the understanding, can be reformed and saved, if only he shuns evils as sins, and does not confirm heretical falsities in himself; for by shunning evils as sins the will is reformed, and through the will the understanding, which then first emerges from darkness into light. There are three essentials of the church, an acknowledgment of the Divine of the Lord, an acknowledgment of the holiness of the Word, and the life that is called charity. According to the life which is charity is every one's faith; from the Word comes the knowledge of what the life must be, and from the Lord are reformation and salvation. If the church had held these three as es-

sentials it would not have been divided, but only varied, by
intellectual dissensions, as light varies the color in beautiful
objects, and as various circlets give beauty in the crown of a
king.

260. (7) *The merely natural man confirms himself against
the Divine providence by the fact that Judaism still continues.*
In other words, the Jews after so many centuries have not
been converted, although they live among Christians, and do
not, as the Word predicts, confess the Lord and acknowledge
Him to be the Messiah, who, as they think, was to lead them
back to the land of Canaan, but constantly persist in denying
Him; and yet it is well with them.   But those who so think,
and who therefore call in question the Divine providence, do
not know that by "Jews" in the Word all who are of the
church and who acknowledge the Lord are meant; and by "the
land of Canaan," into which it is said that they are to be led,
the Lord's church is meant. [2] But the Jews persist in denying the Lord, because they are such that they would profane
the Divinity of the Lord and the holy things of His church if
they were to accept and acknowledge them.   Consequently the
Lord says of them :—

He hath blinded their eyes and hardened their heart, lest they should
see with their eyes and understand with their heart, and should turn
themselves, and I should heal them (*John* xii. 40; *Matt.* xiii. 15; *Mark* iv.
12; *Luke* viii. 10; *Isa.* vi. 9, 10).

It is said "lest they should turn themselves and I should heal
them," because if they had been turned and healed they would
have committed profanation; and it is according to the law of
Divine providence (treated of above, n. 221–233) that no one
is admitted by the Lord interiorly into truths of faith and goods
of charity except so far as he can be kept in them until the end
of his life, and if he were admitted he would profane what is
holy. [3] That nation has been preserved and has been scattered over a great part of the world for the sake of the Word
in its original language, which they, more than Christians, hold
sacred; and the Lord's Divinity is in every particular of the

Word, for that which goes forth from the Lord is Divine truth united to Divine good, and by this the Word becomes a conjunction of the Lord with the church and the presence of heaven [with man], as has been shown in the *Doctrine of the New Jerusalem concerning the Sacred Scripture* (n. 62–69); and there is a presence of the Lord and of heaven wherever the Word is read with reverence. Such is the end in the Divine providence, for the sake of which the Jews have been preserved and scattered over a great part of the world. What their lot is after death may be seen in the *Continuation concerning the Last Judgment and the Spiritual World* (n. 79–82).

261. These now are the points set forth above (n. 238), by which the natural man confirms or may confirm himself against the Divine providence. There are yet other points mentioned above (in n. 239), that may serve the natural man as arguments against the Divine providence, and may occur to the minds of others, and excite some doubts. These will now follow.

262. (1) *A doubt may arise in opposition to the Divine providence from the fact that the whole Christian world worships one God under three persons, which is to worship three Gods, not knowing hitherto that God is one in person and essence, in whom is a trinity, and that the Lord is that God.* One who reasons about the Divine providence may ask, Are not three persons three Gods when each person by Himself is God? Who can think otherwise? Who, indeed, does think otherwise? Athanasius himself could not; therefore in the creed that has its name from him it is said: "Although from Christian verity we ought to acknowledge each person to be God and Lord, yet from the Christian faith it is not allowable to speak of or to name three Gods and three Lords." Nothing else is meant by this than that we ought to acknowledge three Gods and Lords, but that it is not allowable to speak of or name three Gods and three Lords. [2] Who can have any perception of one God unless He is also one in person? If it is said that such a perception is possible if the thought is that the three have one essence, is there or can there be any other perception from this than that they are thus one in mind and feeling, but neverthe-less are three Gods?   And if one thinks more deeply he says to himself, How can the Divine essence, which is infinite, be divided?   And how can the Divine essence from eternity beget another, and still further bring forth another that proceeds from both?   If it is said that this is to be believed but not thought about, who can help thinking about that which he is told must be believed?   From what other source is that ac-knowledgment, which is faith in its essence?   Have not So-cinianism and Arianism, which reign in more hearts than you believe, arisen from the thought of God as three persons?   Be-lief in one God, and that the Lord is the one God, constitutes the church; for the Divine trinity is in Him.   That this is true may be seen in the *Doctrine of the New Jerusalem concerning the Lord*, from beginning to end.   [3] But what is the thought respecting the Lord at the present day?   Is it not a thought that He is God and Man, God from Jehovah the Father from whom He was conceived, and Man from the Virgin Mary of whom He was born?   Who thinks that God and Man in Him, or His Divine and His Human, are one person, and are one as soul and body are one?   Does any one know this?   Ask the doctors of the church, and they will say that they have not known it; and yet it is so stated in the doctrine of the church accepted throughout the Christian world, which is as follows:—

Our Lord Jesus Christ, the Son of God, is God and Man; and although He be God and Man yet there are not two, but one Christ; one because the Divine took to itself the Human; yea, wholly one, for He is one per-son; for as soul and body make one man so God and Man is one Christ.

This is from the Faith or Creed of Athanasius.   They have not known this, for the reason that in reading it they have not thought of the Lord as God, but only as a man.   [4] If such are asked whether they know from whom He was conceived, whether from God the Father or from His own Divine, they will answer that He was conceived from God the Father, for this is according to Scripture.   Then are not the Father and

Himself one, as the soul and the body are one? Who can think that He was conceived from two Divines, and if from His own that that was His Father? If they are asked further what their idea is of the Lord's Divine and of His Human, they will say that His Divine is from the essence of the Father and the Human from the essence of the mother, and that His Divine is with the Father. If you then ask where His Human is they will make no reply; for they separate in their thought His Divine and His Human, and make the Divine equal to the Divine of the Father and the Human like the human of another man, and do not know that they thus separate soul and body; nor do they see the contradiction that He would thus have been born a rational man from a mother alone. [5] From the established idea respecting the Lord's Human, that it was like the human of another man, it has come to pass that a Christian can scarcely be led to think of a Divine Human, even when it is said that the Lord's soul or life from conception was and is Jehovah Himself. Gather up the reasons, then, and consider, whether there is any other God of the universe than the Lord alone, in whom the essential Divine, from which are all things, is that which is called the Father, the Divine Human is that which is called the Son, and the Divine going forth is called the Holy Spirit; thus that God is one in person and in essence, and that the Lord is that God. [6] If you persist in saying that the Lord Himself mentions three in *Matthew* :—

Go ye and make disciples of all nations, baptizing them into the name of the Father, and of the Son, and of the Holy Spirit (xxviii. 19),

yet it is clear from the verse immediately preceding and from that immediately following, that He said this to make known that in Himself now glorified there is a Divine trinity. In the preceding verse He says that all power is given to Him in heaven and upon earth; and in the following verse He says that He would be with them until the end of the age; thus speaking of Himself alone, and not of three. [7] Now as regards Divine providence, why it has permitted Christians to worship one God under three persons, that is, to worship three Gods, and why they have hitherto not known that God is one in person and in essence, in whom is the trinity, and that the Lord is this God. Of this man himself, and not the Lord, is the cause. This truth the Lord has taught clearly in His Word, as can be seen from all the passages quoted in the *Doctrine of the New Jerusalem concerning the Lord*. He has also taught it in the doctrine of all the churches, in which it is stated that His Divine and His Human are not two but one person, united like soul and body. [8] The first cause of their dividing the Divine and the Human, and making the Divine equal to the Divine of Jehovah the Father, and the Human equal to the human of another man, was that the church after its rise degenerated into a Babylon, which transferred to itself the Lord's Divine power, but lest it be called Divine power, and not human power, they made the Lord's Human like the human of another man. Afterwards, when the church was reformed, and faith alone was accepted as the sole means of salvation (the faith that God the Father has mercy for the sake of the Son), the Lord's Human could not be regarded differently, for the reason that no one can go to the Lord and in heart acknowledge Him to be the God of heaven and earth until he is living according to His precepts. In the spiritual world, where all are obliged to speak as they think, no one can even mention the name Jesus unless he has lived in the world as a Christian. This is of His Divine providence, lest His name be profaned.

263. But that all this that has been said may be still more clear, I will add what has been said at the end of the *Doctrine of the New Jerusalem concerning the Lord* (n. 60, 61), which is as follows:—

That God and Man in the Lord, according to the doctrine [of the creed], are not two, but one person, and wholly one as the soul and the body are one, is clearly evident from many things that He said, as, That the Father and He are one; That all things of the Father are His, and all His are the Father's; That He is in the Father, and the Father in Him; That all things have been given into His hand; That He has all power; That he is the God of heaven and earth; That whosoever believes in Him has eternal life; and that whosoever does not believe in Him, upon him the wrath of God abides; and further, that both the Divine and the Human were taken up into heaven, and that in respect to both He sits at the right hand of God, that is, that He is almighty; and many more things that have been cited above in great abundance from the Word respecting His Divine Human; all of which testify that God is one both in person and in essence, in whom is a trinity, and that the Lord is that God. [2] These things respecting the Lord are now for the first time published because it has been foretold in the *Apocalypse* (chapters xxi. and xxii.) that a new church would be instituted at the end of the former church in which this doctrine would be primary. It is this church that is there meant by the New Jerusalem, into which none can enter except those that acknowledge the Lord alone as the God of heaven and earth; and this is why that church is there called the Lamb's wife. And I am able to announce that the entire heaven acknowledges the Lord alone, and that whoever does not acknowledge Him is not admitted into heaven, for heaven is heaven from the Lord. This acknowledgment itself, from love and faith, causes men to be in the Lord and the Lord in them, as He Himself teaches in *John :—*

In that day ye shall know that I am in My Father, and ye in Me, and I in you (xiv. 20):

again, in the same :—

Abide in Me and I in you. I am the Vine, ye are the branches; he that abideth in Me and I in him, the same beareth much fruit, for apart from Me ye can do nothing. If a man abide not in Me he is cast forth (xv. 4–6; xvii, 22, 23).

[3] This has not been seen from the Word before, because even if it had been it would not have been accepted, for the last judgment had not yet been accomplished; and before that the power of hell prevailed over the power of heaven; and man is midway between heaven and hell. If, then, this had been seen before, the devil, that is, hell, would have plucked it out of the hearts of men and would also have profaned it. This state of the power of hell was wholly broken up by the last judgment, which has now been accomplished. Since that judgment, that is, now, every man who wishes to be enlightened and to be wise can be.

264. (2) *A doubt may arise in opposition to Divine providence from the fact that hitherto men have not known that there is a spiritual sense in all the particulars of the Word, and that its holiness is therefrom.* For a doubt may arise in opposition to Divine providence when it is asked why this has now been revealed for the first time, and why it has been revealed through this man or that, and not through some primate of the church. But it is of the Lord's good pleasure whether this is done by a primate or by the servant of a primate; the Lord knows what the one is and what the other. But that sense of the Word has not been revealed before, (1) because if it had been, the church would have profaned it, and thereby have profaned the essential holiness of the Word; (2) because the genuine truths, in which the spiritual sense of the Word resides, were not revealed by the Lord until the last judgment had been accomplished, and the new church that is meant by the Holy Jerusalem was about to be established by the Lord. But let these be examined singly. [2] First: *The spiritual sense of the Word has not been revealed before, because if it had been the church would have profaned it, and thereby have profaned the essential holiness of the Word*. Not long after the establishment of the church it was turned into a Babylon, and afterwards into a Philistia; and while Babylon acknowledges the Word it nevertheless despises it, claiming that they are inspired by the Holy Spirit in their supreme judgment just as much as the prophets were. They acknowledge the Word for the sake of the vicarship established by the Lord's words to Peter; and yet they despise the Word because it does not suit them. For the same reason it is taken away from the people and hidden in monasteries, where few read it. Consequently if the spiritual sense of the Word, in which the Lord and all angelic wisdom are present, had been unveiled, the Word would have been profaned, not alone as it now is in its outmosts, which are the things contained in the sense of the letter, but also in its inmosts. [3] Philistia also, by which is meant faith separate from charity, would have profaned the spiritual sense of the Word, because it places salvation in certain words that they may think and talk about, and not in the good works they should do, as has been shown before; thus making that to be saving that is not saving, and also separating the understanding from the things that are to be believed. What have such to do with that light in which the spiritual sense of the Word is? Would it not be turned into darkness? When the natural sense is turned into darkness what would not be done with the spiritual sense? Does any one of such, who has confirmed himself in faith separate from charity and in justification by that alone, wish to know what good of life is, wish to know what love to the Lord and towards the neighbor is, what charity is, and what the goods of charity are, and what good works are, and doing them, or even what faith is in its essence, or any genuine truth that constitutes it? Such write volumes confirming only that which they call faith, and claiming that all the things just mentioned are included in that faith. From all this it is clear that if the spiritual sense of the Word had been unveiled before, it would have come to pass according to the Lord's words in *Matthew :—*

If thine eye be evil thy whole body shall be darkened. If, therefore, the light that is in thee becomes darkness, how great is that darkness! (vi. 23);

"the eye," in the spiritual sense of the Word, meaning the understanding. [4] Secondly: *The genuine truths in which the spiritual sense of the Word resides were not revealed by the Lord until the last judgment had been accomplished, and the new church that is meant by "the Holy Jerusalem" was about to be established by the Lord.* It was foretold by the Lord in the *Apocalypse* that when the last judgment had been accomplished genuine truths would be unveiled, a new church established, and the spiritual sense of the Word disclosed. That the last judgment has been accomplished is shown in the treatise on the *Last Judgment*, and again in the *Continuation* of it. This, too, is what is meant by "the passing away of the heaven and earth" (*Apoc.* xxi. 1). That genuine truths will then be unveiled is foretold in these words in the *Apocalypse:—*

And He that sat upon the throne said, Behold I make all things new (xxi. 5; also xix. 17, 18; xxi. 18–21; xxii. 1, 2).

That the spiritual sense of the Word is then to be unveiled (xix. 11–16), this being meant by "the white horse," upon which He sat who was called the Word of God, and was Lord of lords and King of kings (see the treatise on *The White Horse*). That the Holy Jerusalem means the new church that would then be established by the Lord may be seen in the *Doctrine of the New Jerusalem concerning the Lord* (n. 62–65), where this is shown. [5] From all this it is now clear that the spiritual sense of the Word was to be revealed for a new church that will acknowledge and worship the Lord alone, and will hold His Word to be holy, will love Divine truths, and will reject faith separate from charity. But in regard to this sense of the Word many things may be seen in the *Doctrine of the New Jerusalem concerning the Sacred Scripture* (n. 5–26, and the following numbers); namely, what the spiritual sense is (n. 5–26); that the spiritual sense is in each thing and in all things of the Word (n. 9–17); that it is from the spiritual sense that the Word is Divinely inspired, and holy in every word (n. 18, 19); that the spiritual sense has been hitherto unknown, and why it has not been revealed before (n. 20–25); that hereafter the spiritual sense will be given only to those who are in genuine truths from the Lord (n. 26). [6] From all this it can now be seen that it is of the Lord's Divine providence that the spiritual sense has been hidden from the world until the present age, and in the mean while has been preserved in heaven among the angels, who derive their wisdom from it. That sense was known to the ancients who lived before Moses, and was carefully studied; but their posterity converted correspondences, of which alone their Word and their religion therefrom consisted, into idolatries of various kinds, and the Egyptians converted them into magic, and consequently in the Lord's Divine providence, the Word was closed up, first with the children of Israel and afterwards with Christians, for the reasons given above; and now it is again opened for the Lord's New Church.

265. (3) *A doubt may arise in opposition to Divine providence from the fact that hitherto men have not known that to*

17

shun evils as sins is the Christian religion itself. That this is
the Christian religion itself has been shown in the *Doctrine of
Life for the New Jerusalem,* from beginning to end; and because faith separate from charity is the only obstacle to its
reception, that also is treated of. It is said that it is unknown
that to shun evils as sins is the Christian religion itself. For
it is unknown to almost every one, and yet is known to every
one, as may be seen above (n. 258). It is unknown to almost
every one because it has been blotted out by faith separated;
for that faith affirms that faith alone saves, and not any good
work or good of charity; also that they are no longer under the
yoke of the law, but free. Those who have often heard such
things no longer give any thought to any evil of life or to any
good of life. Moreover, every man from his own nature in-
clines to embrace this faith, and when he has once embraced
it he gives no further thought to the state of his life. This is
why this truth is unknown. [2] That it is unknown has been
disclosed to me in the spiritual world. I have asked more than
a thousand newcomers from the world whether they know that
to shun evils as sins is religion itself; and they said that they
did not know, and that this was something new, not heard
of before; although they had heard that they cannot do good
of themselves, and that they are not under the yoke of the
law. When I asked whether they did not know that a man
must examine himself, see his sins, repent, and then begin a
new life, and that otherwise sins are not remitted, and if sins
are not remitted men are not saved, and reminded them that
this had been read to them in a loud voice as often as they
went to the Holy Supper, they replied that they gave no attention to these things, but only to this, that they have remission of sins by means of the sacrament of the Supper, and
that faith does the rest without their knowledge. [3] Again I
asked, Why have you taught your children the Decalogue? Is
it not that they might know what evils are sins to be shunned;
or is it only that they might know these things and believe,
and not do? Why, then, do you say that this is new? To

this they have only been able to reply that they know and yet
do not know; and that they never thought about the sixth
commandment when committing adultery, or about the seventh
commandment when stealing or defrauding covertly, and so
on; still less that such things are contrary to the Divine law,
thus against God. [4] When I have mentioned many things
from the doctrines of the churches and from the Word to prove
that shunning and turning away from evils as sins is the
Christian religion itself, and that every one has faith as he
does this, they were silent. But they were convinced that this
is true when they saw that all were examined in regard to
their life, and were judged according to their deeds, and no
one was judged according to faith separate from life, because
every one has faith according to his life. [5] That this has
been for the most part unknown to the Christian world is
from the law of the Divine providence that every one is left
to act from freedom in accordance with reason (see above, n.
71–99, and n. 100–128); also from the law that no one is
taught immediately from heaven, but mediately through the
Word and doctrine and preaching from it (n. 154–174); also
from all the laws of permission, which are likewise laws of the
Divine providence. (More on this above, n. 258).

274. (4) *A doubt may arise in opposition to Divine providence from the fact, that it has not hitherto been known that man
lives as a man after death ; also that this has not been disclosed
before.* This has not been known before for the reason that in
those who do not shun evils as sins there is concealed interiorly a belief that man does not live after death; and therefore
it is a matter of no consequence to them whether it is said that
man lives as a man after death or whether it is said that he is
to rise again at the day of the last judgment; and if by any
chance a belief in the resurrection occurs to him he says to
himself, " It will be no worse for me than for others; if I go to
hell I shall have plenty of company, and the same is true if I
go to heaven." And yet in all that have any religion there is
implanted a knowledge that after death they live as men; while

the idea that they will then live as souls and not as men exists only with those that have been infatuated by their own intelligence, and with no others. That in every one that has any religion there is implanted a knowledge that after death he will live as a man can be seen from the following considerations:—(1) Does any one when dying think otherwise? (2) [2] What eulogist, when lamenting the dead, does not exalt them to heaven, and place them among angels as talking with them and enjoying their happiness? Some, moreover, are deified. (3) [3] Who among the common people does not believe that when he dies, if he has lived well, he will go to a heavenly paradise, be clothed in white raiment, and enjoy eternal life? (4) [4] What clergyman is there who does not say the same or like things to one about to die? And when he says it he also believes it, unless he is at the same time thinking about the last judgment. (5) [5] Who does not believe that his little children are in heaven, and that after death he will see his wife whom he has loved? Who thinks that they are ghosts, still less that they are souls or minds flitting about the universe? (6) [6] Who objects when anything is said about the lot or state of those who have passed from time into the eternal life? I have said to many that such is the state and lot of these and of those, and I have never heard any one say that they have not yet had their lot, but will have it at the time of the judgment. (7) [7] When one sees angels painted or sculptured does he not recognize them to be such? Who thinks at such a time that they are spirits without bodies, or are air or clouds, as some of the learned do? (8) [8] The papists believe that their saints are human beings in heaven, and that the rest are somewhere else; the Mohammedans believe the same of their dead; the Africans believe this more than others, and many other nations believe it;—why do not Reformed Christians who know it from the Word? (9) [9] From this knowledge implanted in every one there are some that aspire to immortality of fame; for this knowledge is turned into such an aspiration with some, and makes them heroes or brave in war. (10) [**10**] Inquiry was made in the spiritual world whether this knowledge is implanted in all, and it was found to be implanted in all, not however in the natural ideas belonging to their external thought, but in the spiritual ideas belonging to their internal thought. From all this it can be seen that no doubt in opposition to a Divine providence ought to arise from the fact that it is supposed to be now first disclosed that man lives as a man after death. It is only man's sensual part that wishes to see and to touch what it is to believe; and whoever does not think above that is in the darkness of night regarding the state of his life.

EVILS ARE PERMITTED FOR THE SAKE OF THE END, WHICH IS SALVATION.

275. If man were born into the love into which he was created he would not be in any evil, nor would he even know what evil is; for one who has not been in evil, and consequently is not in evil, cannot know what evil is; and if told that this or that is evil would not believe it possible. Such was the state of innocence in which Adam and Eve his wife were, the "nakedness" that they were not ashamed of signifying that state. A knowledge of evil after the fall is meant by eating from the tree of the knowledge of good and evil. The love into which man was created is love of the neighbor, to the end that he may wish as well to the neighbor as to himself and even better, and may be in the delight of that love when he is doing good to the neighbor; nearly the same as a parent's love for his children. This love is truly human, for there is in it a spiritual [element] that distinguishes it from the natural love that belongs to brute animals. If man were born into that love he would not be born into the thick darkness of ignorance, as every man now is, but into a certain light of knowledge and intelligence therefrom; and into these he would quickly come

At first, of course, he would creep like a quadruped, but with an inherent endeavor to raise himself up upon his feet; for however much like a quadruped he would not turn his face downward to the earth but forward towards heaven, and would so raise himself up as to be able also to look upwards.

276. But when love of the neighbor was turned into love of self, and this love increased, human love was turned into animal love, and man from being a man became a beast, with the difference that he was able to think about what he felt in the body, and could rationally discriminate one thing from another, and could be taught, and could become a civil and moral man, and finally a spiritual man. For, as has been said, a man has a spiritual, and by this he is distinguished from a brute; for by this he is able to know what civil evil and civil good are, also what moral evil and moral good are, and also if he will, what spiritual evil and spiritual good are. When love of the neighbor had been turned into love of self man could no longer be born into the light of knowledge and intelligence, but he was born into the darkness of ignorance, because he was born into the very outmost of life called the corporeal-sensual; and from that he could be led into the interiors of the natural mind by means of instruction, the spiritual always accompanying. Why man is born into the outmost of life which is called the corporeal-sensual, and consequently into the thick darkness of ignorance, will be seen in what follows. [2] That love of the neighbor and love of self are opposite loves any one can see; for love of the neighbor wishes well to every one from itself, while love of self wishes well to itself alone from every one, love of the neighbor wishes to serve every one, while love of self wishes every one to serve it; love of the neighbor regards every one as its brother and friend, while love of self regards every one as its servant, or as its enemy if he does not serve it; in a word, it regards itself only, and others scarcely as men, holding them in heart in less estimation than its horses and dogs. And because it regards them as of so little account it thinks nothing of doing evil to them; and this is the source of hatred and revenge, adultery and whoredom, theft and fraud, lying and defamation, violence and cruelty, and other such evils. Such are the evils in which man is from birth. That they are permitted for the sake of the end, which is salvation, will be shown in the following order:—

(1) Every man is in evil, and must be led away from evil in order to be reformed.

(2) Evils cannot be removed unless they appear.

(3) So far as evils are removed they are remitted.

(4) Thus the permission of evil is for the sake of the end, that there may be salvation.

277a. (1) *Every man is in evil, and must be led away from evil in order to be reformed.* It is admitted in the church that every man has hereditary evil, and that from this he is in the lust of many evils; and it is from this that man cannot do good of himself; for evil does not do good except such good as has evil within it. The evil that is within the good is his doing the good for the sake of self, and thus only for the sake of the appearance. It is admitted that this evil is inherited from parents. It is said to be from Adam and his wife, but this is an error; for every one is born into it from his parent, and the parent from his parent, and he from his, and thus it is successively transferred from one to another; so, too, it is increased, and grows as it were to an accumulated mass, and is transmitted to offspring. In consequence of this there is nothing sound in man, but he is altogether evil. Who has any feeling that it is wrong to love himself more than others? Who, then, knows that it is evil? And yet this is the head of all evils. [2] That there is this inheritance from parents, grandfathers, and great-grandfathers, is evident from many things that are known in the world, as that households, families, and even nations, are distinguished from each other merely by the face, and the face is a type of the mind, and the mind is in accord with the affections which belong to the love. Sometimes, too, the features of a grandfather reappear in those of a grandson or a great-grandson. From the features alone I know whether a man is a Jew or not, and also from what stock some are; and others doubtless know the same. If affections, which belong to the love, are thus derived and handed down from parents, it follows that evils are, for they belong to the affections. But the origin of this resemblance shall now be explained. [3] Every one's soul is from the father, and from the mother it is merely clothed with a body. That the soul is from the father follows not only from the things mentioned above, but also from many other indications; also from the fact that a child of a black or Moorish father by a white or European woman is black, and *vice versa;* also chiefly from this, that the soul is in the seed, for from the seed is impregnation, and the seed is what is clothed with a body by the mother. The seed is the primal form of the love in which the father is; it is the form of his ruling love with its nearest derivations, which are the inmost affections of that love. [4] In every one these affections are encompassed with the honesties that belong to moral life and with the goodnesses that belong partly to the civil and partly to the spiritual life. These constitute the external of life even with the wicked. Into this external of life every infant is born, and consequently is loveable; but as the child grows to boyhood or to youth he passes from that external to what is interior, and finally to the ruling love of his father; and if this has been evil, and has not by various means been tempered and bent by his teachers, it becomes his love as it was the father's. And yet the evil is not eradicated but only removed; of which in what follows. Evidently, then, every man is in evil.

277b. That man must be led away from evil in order to be reformed is evident without explanation; for he that is in evil in the world is in evil after he has left the world; consequently if evil is not removed in the world it cannot be removed afterwards. Where the tree falls there it lies. So, too, does a man's life when he dies remain such as it has been. Every one is judged according to his deeds; not that these are enumerated, but because he returns to them and acts in the same way; for death is a continuation of life, with the difference that man cannot then be reformed. All reformation is effected in completeness, that is, simultaneously in first principles and in outmosts; and outmosts are reformed in agreement with first principles while man is in the world, and cannot be reformed afterwards, because the outmosts of life that man carries with him after death become quiescent, and are in agreement with his interiors, that is, they act as one.

278a. (2) *Evils cannot be removed unless they appear.* This does not mean that man must do evils in order that they may appear, but that he must examine himself,—not his deeds alone but also his thoughts, and what he would do if he did not fear the laws and disrepute, especially what evils he regards in his spirit as allowable and does not account as sins; for these he still does. It is to enable man to examine himself that an understanding has been given him, and this is separated from the will to the end that he may know, understand, and acknowledge what is good and what is evil, also that he may see what his will is, that is, what he loves and what he longs for. In order that man may see this there has been given to his understanding higher and lower thought, or interior and exterior thought, to enable him to see from the higher or interior thought what the will is doing in the lower and exterior thought; this he sees as a man sees his face in a mirror; and when he sees it and knows what sin is, he is able, if he implores the Lord's help, to cease willing it, to shun it, and afterwards to act against it, if not freely, still to coerce it by combat, and finally to turn away from it and hate it; and then, and not before, he perceives and also feels that evil is evil and that good is good. This, then, is examining one's self, seeing one's evils, acknowledging them, and afterwards refraining from them. But as there are few who know that this is the Christian religion itself (because such only have charity and faith, and they alone are led by the Lord and do good from Him), so something shall be said of those who do not do this and nevertheless think that they have religion. They are these: (1) Those who confess themselves guilty of all sins, and do not search out any one sin in themselves.

(2) Those who neglect the search from religious reasons. (3) Those who for worldly reasons think nothing about sins, and are therefore ignorant of them. (4) Those who favor them and in consequence are ignorant of them. (5) To all such sins are not apparent, and therefore cannot be removed. (6) Lastly, the reason, hitherto hidden, will be made evident, why evils cannot be removed unless they are sought out, discovered, acknowledged, confessed, and resisted.

278b. But these points must be examined one by one, because they are the primary things on man's part of the Christian religion. First: *Of those who confess themselves guilty of all sins, and do not search out any one sin in themselves.* Such a one says, "I am a sinner; I was born in sin; there is nothing sound in me from head to foot, I am nothing but evil: good God, be gracious unto me, pardon me, cleanse me, save me, make me to walk in purity and the way of righteousness," and so on; and yet he does not examine himself, and consequently is ignorant of any evil; and no one can shun that of which he is ignorant, still less can he fight against it. He also believes himself to be clean and washed after his confessions, and yet he is unclean and unwashed from the head to the sole of the foot; for a confession of all sin lulls one to sleep, and at length brings blindness. It is like a universal apart from any particular, which is nothing. [2] Secondly: *Of those who neglect the search from religious reasons.* These are especially such as separate charity from faith; for they say to themselves, "Why should I search whether there is evil or good? Why search for evil, when it does not condemn me; or why for good, when it does not save me? It is faith alone, thought and declared with trust and confidence, that justifies and purifies from all sin; and when once I am justified I am whole before God. I am indeed in evil, but God wipes this away as soon as it is done, and thus it no longer appears;" and other like things. But who does not see, if he will open his eyes, that such things are empty words, in which there is no reality, because there is no good in them? Who cannot so think and speak, even with trust and confidence, when at the same time he is thinking about hell and eternal damnation? Does such a one wish to know anything further, either what is true or what is good? Respecting truth he says, "What is truth but that which confirms this faith?" And respecting good he says, "What is good but that which is in me from this faith? But that it may be in me I must not do it as from myself, since this is meritorious; and good for which merit is claimed is not good." Thus he ignores everything until he ceases to know what evil is. What then shall he examine and see in himself? Does not his state then become such that the pent-up fires of the lusts of evil consume the interiors of his mind and lay them waste to the very gate? Only this gate does he guard that the burning may not appear; but after death this is opened, and then it is evident to all. [3] Thirdly: *Of those who for worldly reasons think nothing about sins and are therefore ignorant of them.* These are such as love the world above all things, and admit no truth that would lead them away from any falsity of their religion, saying to themselves, "What is that to me? It is not for me to think of." Thus they reject the truth the moment it is heard, and if they listen to it they stifle it. They do much the same when they hear preaching; they retain nothing of it except some few phrases,—nothing real. Dealing thus with truths they do not know what good is; for good and truth act as one; and from any good that is not from truth evil is not recognized, unless it be to call it good, and this is done by means of reasonings from falsities. Such are meant by the seed that fell among thorns, of whom the Lord says:—

Others fell among the thorns, and the thorns grew up and choked them. These are they that hear the Word, and the care of this world and the deceitfulness of riches so choke the Word that it becometh unfruitful (*Matt.* xiii. 7, 22; *Mark* iv. 7, 19; *Luke* viii. 7, 14).

[4] Fourthly: *Of those that favor sins, and in consequence cannot know them.* These are such as acknowledge God and worship Him in accordance with established ceremonies, and convince themselves that any evil that is a sin is not a sin, painting it over with fallacies and appearances, and thus hiding its

enormity; and having done this they favor it, and make it their friend and familiar. It is said that those do this who acknowledge God, for others do not regard any evil as a sin, for all sin is against God. But let examples illustrate. One that is greedy for wealth makes evil to be no sin when, from reasons that he devises, he makes certain kinds of fraud allowable. He does the same who justifies in himself a spirit of revenge against enemies; or who in war justifies the plundering of those who are not enemies. [5] Fifthly: *To all such sins are not apparent and therefore cannot be removed.* Every evil that is not seen nourishes itself. It is like fire in wood covered with ashes, or like matter in a wound that is not opened. For all evil that is shut in grows and does not stop till the end is reached. That no evil, therefore, may be shut up, every one is permitted to think in favor of God or against God, and in favor of the holy things of the church or against them, and not be punished therefor in the world. Of this the Lord thus speaks in *Isaiah:*—

From the sole of the foot even unto the head there is no soundness in it; the wound, the bruise, and the fresh stripe, they have not been pressed out, nor bound up, nor mollified with oil. Wash you, make you clean; put away the evil of your doings from before Mine eyes, cease to do evil; learn to do well. Then, although your sins have been as scarlet they shall become white as snow; although they have been red as crimson they shall be as wool. But if ye refuse and rebel ye shall be devoured by the sword (i. 6, 16–18, 20).

"To be devoured by the sword" signifies to perish by the falsity of evil. [6] Sixthly: *The reason hitherto hidden why evils cannot be removed unless they are sought out, discovered, acknowledged, confessed and resisted.* It has been remarked in the preceding pages that the entire heaven is arranged in societies according to [the affections of good, and the entire hell according to] the lusts of evil opposite to the affections of good. As to his spirit every man is in some society; in a heavenly society if he is in an affection for good, but in an infernal society if he is in a lust of evil. This is unknown to man so long as he lives in the world; nevertheless he is in respect to his spirit in some society, and without this he cannot live, and by means of it he is governed by the Lord. If he is in an infernal society he can be led out of it by the Lord only in accordance with the laws of His Divine providence, among which is this, that the man must see that he is there, must wish to go out of it, and must try to do this of himself. This he can do while he is in the world, but not after death; for he then remains forever in the society into which he has inserted himself while in the world. This is the reason why man must examine himself, must recognize and acknowledge his sins and repent, and then must persevere even to the end of his life. That this is true I could prove by much experience, sufficient for complete belief; but this is not the place to set forth the proofs of experience.

279. (3) *So far as evils are removed they are remitted.* It is an error of the age to believe that evils have been separated from man, and even cast out, when they have been remitted; and that the state of a man's life can be changed instantly, even to its opposite, and thus from being evil a man can become good, and in consequence be led out of hell and transferred straightway into heaven, and this by the Lord's mercy apart from means. But those who hold this belief and opinion know nothing whatever about what evil is or what good is, and nothing whatever about the state of man's life, and are wholly ignorant of the fact that affections, which belong to the will, are nothing but changes and variations of state of the purely organic substances of the mind, and that thoughts, which belong to the understanding, are nothing but changes and variations in the form of these substances, and that memory is the state of those changes that remains permanent. When all this is known it can be clearly seen that no evil can be removed except by successive steps, and that the remission of evil is not its removal. But these are summary statements, and unless they are demonstrated may be acknowledged but can not be comprehended; and what is not comprehended is [seen indistinctly] like a wheel turned round by the hand; therefore these statements must be demonstrated one by one, in the order in which they are presented. [2] First: *It is an error of the age to believe that evils have been separated, and even cast out, when they have been remitted.* It has been granted me to know from heaven that no evil into which man is born and that he himself actually imbibes is separated from him, but is so removed as not to appear. I formerly held the belief that is held by most in the world, that when evils are remitted they are cast out, and are washed and wiped away, as dirt is washed from the face by water. But this is not true of evils or sins, they all remain; and when after repentance they are remitted they are moved from the center to the sides; and then what is in the center, because it is directly under view, appears as in the light of day, and what is at the sides is in the shade, and sometimes as it were in the darkness of night. And as evils are not separated but only removed, that is, dismissed to the sides, and as man can pass from the center to the parts round about, it is possible for him to return into his evils which he supposed had been cast out. For man is such that he can pass from one affection into another, and sometimes into an opposite one, thus from one center to another, his affection, so long as he is in it, making the center, for then he is in its delight and in its light. [3] There are some who are raised up by the Lord after death into heaven because they have lived well, but who have carried with them a belief that they are clean and pure from sins, and therefore are free from all guilt. These at first are clothed in white garments, in accordance with their belief, for white garments signify a state cleansed from evil. But afterwards they begin to think as they did in the world that they are as it were washed from all evil, and to glory therefore in the idea that they are no longer sinners like others, which can hardly be separated from a kind of elation of mind and a kind of contempt of others compared with themselves. Then, in order to remove them from their imaginary belief they are sent away from heaven and let down into their evils which they contracted in the world; and at the same time they are shown that they are also in hereditary evils, of which they had been ignorant before. When they have thus been compelled to acknowledge that their evils have not been separated from them but only removed, consequently that of themselves they are impure and in fact nothing but evil, and that they are withheld from evils and kept in goods by the Lord, although there is an appearance that this is from themselves, they are again raised up by the Lord into heaven. [4] Secondly: *It is an error of the age to believe that the state of man's life can be changed instantly, and thus from being evil man can become good, and in consequence can be led out of hell, and transferred straightway into heaven, and this by the Lord's mercy apart from means.* Those are in this error who separate charity from faith, and place salvation in faith alone; for they imagine that merely thinking about and uttering the statements of that faith, if it is done with trust and confidence, is what justifies and saves; and many imagine that this may be done instantly, and, if not before, at about the last hour of man's life. Such must needs believe that the state of a man's life can be changed instantly, and man be saved by mercy apart from means. But that the Lord's mercy is not apart from means, and that man cannot from being evil become good in a moment, and can be led out of hell and transferred into heaven only by the unceasing operations of the Divine providence from infancy even to the end of his life, will be seen in the last chapter of this work. Here this only need be said, that all the laws of the Divine providence have for their end the reformation and consequent salvation of man, thus the reversal of his state, which by birth is infernal, into the opposite state which is heavenly; and that this can be done only step by step, as man withdraws from evil and its delight and enters into good and its delight. [5] Thirdly: *Those who so believe know nothing whatever about what evil is or what good is.* For they do not know that evil is the delight of the lust of acting and thinking contrary to Divine order, and that good is the delight of the affection of acting and thinking in accordance with Divine order, and that there are myriads of lusts that enter into and compose every single evil, and myriads of affections in like manner that enter into and compose every single good, and that these myriads are in such order and connection in man's interiors that no one can be changed unless at the same time all are changed. Those who do not know this may hold the belief or opinion that evil, which seems also to them to be a single thing, can easily be removed; and good, which also appears to be a single thing, can be brought in in its place. As such do not know what evil is and what good is they must needs be of the opinion that instant salvation and mercy apart from means are possible; but that they are not will be seen in the last chapter of this work. [6] Fourthly: *Those who believe in instant salvation and mercy apart from means do not know that affections, which belong to the will, are nothing but changes of the state of the purely organic substances of the mind; and that thoughts, which belong to the understanding, are nothing but changes and variations in the form of these substances; and that memory is the state of these changes and variations that remains permanent.* Who does not acknowledge, when it is stated, that affections and thoughts are possible only in substances and their forms, which are subjects? And as these exist in the brains, which are full of substances and forms, the forms are called purely organic. No one who thinks rationally can help laughing at the fancies of some that affections and thoughts do not exist in substantiated subjects, but are exhalations modified by heat and light, like images appearing in the air and ether; and yet thought can no more exist apart from a substantial form than sight apart from its form which is the eye, or hearing apart from its form which is the ear, or taste apart from its form which is the tongue. Examine the brain, and you will see innumerable substances, and fibers likewise, and that there is nothing there that is not organized. What other evidence than this ocular proof is needed? [7] But it is asked, What is affection there, and what is thought there? This may be inferred from all things and each thing in the body; in it are many viscera, each fixed in its place, and these perform their functions by changes and variations of state and form. That each is engaged in its own operations is known—the stomach in its own, the intestines in theirs, the kidneys in theirs, the liver, pancreas, and spleen in theirs, and the heart and lungs in theirs; and all of these are moved to their work solely from within, and to be moved from within is to be moved by changes and variations of state and form. All this makes clear that the operations of the purely organic substances of the mind must resemble these, with the difference that the operations of the organic substances of the body are natural, while those of the mind are spiritual; and that the two make one by correspondences. [8] The nature of the changes and variations of state and form in the organic substances of the mind, which are affections and thoughts, cannot be shown to the eye; nevertheless they may be seen as in a mirror in the changes and variations in the state of the lungs in speaking and singing. There is also a correspondence; for the tone of the voice in speaking and singing, and also its articulations, which are the words of speech and the modulations of singing, are made by the lungs, and tone corresponds to affection and speech to thought. They are also produced therefrom; and this is done by changes and variations in the state and form of the organic substances in the lungs, and from the lungs through the trachea or windpipe in the larynx and glottis, and then in the tongue, and finally in the lips. The first changes and variations of the state and form of the tone take place in the lungs, the second in the trachea and larynx, the third in the glottis by the varied openings of its orifices, the fourth in the tongue by its various adaptations to the palate and the teeth, the fifth in the lips by their varied forms. All this makes clear that mere changes and variations, successively continued, in the state of organic forms, produce tones and their articulations, which are speech and singing. Inasmuch, then, as tone and speech are produced from no other source than the affections and thoughts of the mind (for they exist from these, and never apart from them), it is evident that the affections of the will are changes and variations in the state of the purely

18

organic substances of the mind, and that the thoughts of the understanding are changes and variations in the form of those substances, the same as in the pulmonary substances. [9] As affections and thoughts are mere changes in the state of the forms of the mind it follows that memory is nothing else than the state of these changes that is permanent. For all changes and variations of state in organic substances are such that having once become habitual they are permanent. Thus the lungs are habituated to produce various sounds in the trachea, and to vary them in the glottis, to articulate them with the tongue, and to modify them with the mouth; and these organic activities, having once become habitual, are in the organs and can be reproduced. That these changes and variations are infinitely more perfect in the organic structures of the mind than in those of the body is evident from what has been said in *The Divine Love and the Divine Wisdom* (n. 199–204), where it has been shown that all perfections increase and ascend with degrees and according to degrees. More about this may be seen below (n. 319).

280. Another error of the age is that when sins have been remitted they are removed. Those are in this error who believe that sins are remitted to them by the sacrament of the Supper, although they have not removed them from themselves by repentance. Those also are in it who believe that they are saved by faith alone; also those who believe that they are saved by papal dispensations. All of these believe in mercy apart from means and in instant salvation. Yet when this is reversed it becomes a truth, namely, that when sins have been removed they have also been remitted; for repentance precedes remission, and without repentance there is no remission. Therefore the Lord commanded the disciples

To preach repentance for the remission of sins (*Luke* xxiv. 47).

And John preached the baptism of repentance for the remission of sins (*Luke* iii. 3).

To every one the Lord remits sins. He does not accuse and impute. And yet He can take them away only in accordance

with the laws of His Divine providence; for when to Peter
(who asked how often he should forgive a brother sinning
against him, whether seven times), the Lord said

That he should forgive not only seven times but until seventy times
seven (*Matt.* xviii. 21, 22),

what will not He forgive who is mercy itself?

281. (4) *Thus the permission of evil is for the sake of the
end, that there may be salvation.* It is admitted that man has
full liberty to think and will, but not full liberty to say and to
do whatever he thinks and wills. For he can think like an
atheist, can deny God, and blaspheme the holy things of the
Word and the church; and can even desire to destroy them by
word and deed to their utter extermination, but this is prevented by civil, moral and ecclesiastical laws; consequently he
cherishes inwardly these wicked and impious things, by thinking and willing and also purposing them, but not doing them.
One who is not an atheist has also full liberty to think about
many things that pertain to evil, such as things fraudulent,
lascivious, revengeful, and other insanities; and at times he
does them. Who can believe that unless man had full liberty
he not only could not be saved but would even perish utterly?
[2] Now let the reason be heard: Every man is from birth in
evils of many kinds; these evils are in his will; and whatever
is in the will is loved; for that which a man wills from the interior he loves, and that which he loves he wills, and the will's
love flows into the understanding and makes its delight to be
felt therein, and from that it comes into the thoughts, and also
into the intentions. If, therefore, man were not permitted to
think in accordance with his will's love, which is implanted in
him by inheritance, that love would remain shut in, and would
never be seen by him, and a love of evil that is not seen is like
an enemy in ambush, like matter in an ulcer, like poison in the
blood, or corruption in the breast, which, if they are kept shut
in, induce death. But on the other hand, if man is permitted
to think about the evils of his life's love, even so far as to in-

tend them, they can be cured by spiritual means, as diseases are by natural means. [3] What a man would be if he were not permitted to think in accordance with the delights of his life's love shall now be told. He would no longer be a man. His two faculties called liberty and rationality, in which the essential humanity consists, would be destroyed. The delights of these evils would occupy the interiors of his mind, even to the extent that the door would be closed; and in that case he could speak and act only in accordance with those delights, thus he would act insanely, not only in his own sight but also before the world, and at last he would not know enough to cover his shame. But that he may not become such he is indeed permitted to think about and to will the evils of his inherited nature, but not to talk about and do them; and in the meantime he learns civil, moral, and spiritual things, and these also enter into his thoughts and remove the insanities, and by means of this knowledge he is healed by the Lord; and yet no further than to know how to guard the door, unless he also acknowledges God and implores His help that he may be able to resist the insanities. Then so far as he resists them so far he refuses them admittance into his intentions, and finally into his thoughts. [4] Since, then, man is free to think as he pleases, to the end that his life's love may come forth from its lurking-places into the light of his understanding, and since otherwise he would know nothing about his evil, and therefore would not shun it, it follows that the evil would so grow in him that no spot for restoration would be left in him, and scarcely any in his children if he should beget any, for the parent's evil is transmitted to the offspring. But the Lord provides that this shall not take place.

282. It would have been possible for the Lord to heal the understanding in every man, and thus cause him to think what is good and not what is evil, and this by fears of various kinds, by miracles, by conversations with the dead, and by visions and dreams. But to heal the understanding alone is to heal man only from without; for the understanding with its thought

is the external of man's life, while the will with its affection
is the internal of his life; consequently the healing of the understanding alone would be like palliative healing, whereby the
interior malignity, shut in and wholly prevented from going
out, would destroy first the near and then the remote parts,
even till the whole would become dead. It is the will itself
that must be healed, not by means of an influx into it of the
understanding, for that is not possible, but by means of instruction, and exhortation by the understanding. If the understanding alone were healed man would become like a dead body
embalmed or encased in fragrant aromatics and roses, which
would soon draw from the corpse so foul a stench that they
could not be brought near to any one's nostrils. So would it
be with heavenly truths in the understanding if the will's evil
love were shut in.

283. Man is permitted to think about evils, as has been
said, even so far as to purpose to do them, in order that they
may be removed by means of civil, moral, and spiritual things;
and this is done when he thinks that a thing is contrary to what
is just and equitable, to what is honorable and becoming, and
to good and truth; thus contrary to the tranquillity, the joy,
and the blessedness of life. By means of these three, civil and
moral and spiritual things, the Lord heals the love of man's
will, first by means of fears, and afterwards by means of loves.
Nevertheless, evils are not separated and cast out from man,
but are only removed and transferred to the sides; and when
they are there and good is at the center, evils do not appear;
for whatever is at the center is directly under view, and is seen
and perceived. But it must be known that although good is at
the center man is not therefore in good unless the evils that are
at the sides bend downward or outward; if they look upward
or inward they have not been removed, for they are still striv-
ing to return to the center. They bend and look downward
or outward when man is shunning his evils as sins, and still
more when he turns away from them; for he then condemns
and assigns them to hell, and makes them look hellwards.

284. Man's understanding is a recipient of both good and evil and of both truth and falsity, but his will itself is not; this must be either in evil or in good, it cannot be in both, for the will is the man himself, and his life's love is there. In the understanding, however, good and evil are separated, like what is internal and what is external, and in consequence man can be interiorly in evil and exteriorly in good; and yet during his reformation good and evil meet, and then conflict and combat arise; this, if severe, is called temptation, but if not severe it goes on like the fermentation of wine or liquor. If good then conquers, evil with its falsity is removed to the sides, comparatively as dregs fall to the bottom of a vessel; and the good is like wine that becomes generous after fermentation, or liquor that becomes clear. But if evil conquers, good with its truth is removed to the sides, and becomes turbid and offensive, like unfermented wine or liquor. This process is compared to fermentation because "ferment" [leaven] signifies in the Word the falsity of evil (as in *Hosea* vii. 4; *Luke* xii. 1; and elsewhere).

THE DIVINE PROVIDENCE IS EQUALLY WITH THE EVIL AND WITH THE GOOD.

285. In every man, both good and evil, there are two faculties, one of which constitutes the understanding, and the other the will. The faculty that constitutes the understanding is an ability to understand and think; this faculty is therefore called rationality. The faculty that constitutes the will is an ability to do these things freely, that is, to think and consequently to speak and to act in any way not contrary to reason or rationality; for to act freely is to act whenever one pleases and as he pleases. Since these two faculties never cease, and are continuous from firsts to lasts in all things and in each thing that man thinks and does, and as they are not in man from himself but are present with him from the Lord, it follows that the

Lord's presence, when in them, is in the particulars and even
in the least particulars of man's understanding and thought, and
also of his will and affection, and therefore in the least particulars of his speech and action. Remove these faculties from
any least particular and you will not be able to think or speak
of it as a man. [2] It has been abundantly shown already that
it is through these two faculties that man is a man, that he is
able to think and speak, to perceive what is good and to understand truths, not only civil and moral but also spiritual, also
to be reformed and regenerated—in a word, that he is able to
be conjoined with the Lord and thereby live for ever; and furthermore, that evil men as well as good men possess these
two faculties. Since, then, these faculties are in man from the
Lord, and are not appropriated to man as his (for what is Divine
cannot be appropriated to man as his, but can be adjoined to
him and thereby appear as his), and since this Divine with man
is in the least particulars of his life, it follows that the Lord
governs every least particular, in an evil man as well as in a
good man, and the Lord's government is what is called the Divine providence.

286. And since it is a law of the Divine providence that
man shall be able to act from freedom in accordance with reason, that is, from the two faculties, liberty and rationality, and
since it is also a law of the Divine providence that what a man
does shall appear to him to be as if from himself, and therefore
to be as if it were his own, also that it is a law that evils must
be permitted in order that man may be led out of them, it follows that man has the ability to misuse these faculties, and
from freedom in accordance with reason to confirm whatever
he pleases; for he is able to make whatever he pleases to be
reasonable, whether it is in itself reasonable or not. Consequently some say, "What is truth? Am I not able to make
anything I wish to be true?" And does not the world do this?
And whoever does this does it by reasonings. Assume the fals-
est proposition and ask an ingenious man to prove it, and he
will prove it. Ask him, for instance, to prove that man is a

beast; or that the soul is like a little spider in its web, and governs the body as the spider governs by means of its threads; or tell him that religion is nothing but a mere restraint—and he will prove any one of the things proposed until it looks as if it were true. What is easier? For he knows nothing about the nature of appearances, or of falsity assumed as truth from a blind faith. [2] It is for this reason that man is unable to see this truth, namely, that the Divine providence is in the least particulars of the understanding and will, or what is the same, in the least particulars of thought and affection in every man, whether bad or good. He confuses himself especially by the thought that then evils also would be from the Lord; but it will be seen in what now follows that not the least fraction of evil is from the Lord, but that evil is from man, through his confirming in himself the appearance that he thinks, wills, speaks, and acts from himself. That this may be seen clearly it will be set forth in the following order:—

(1) The Divine providence, not only with the good but with the evil as well, is universal in every least particular; and yet it is not in their evils.

(2) The evil are continually leading themselves into evils, but the Lord is continually leading them away from evils.

(3) The evil cannot be wholly led by the Lord away from evil and into good so long as they believe their own intelligence to be everything and the Divine providence nothing.

(4) The Lord governs hell by means of opposites; and He governs in hell the evil who are in the world in respect to their interiors, but not in respect to their exteriors.

287. (1) *The Divine providence, not only with the good but with the evil as well, is universal in every least particular; and yet it is not in their evils.* It is shown above that the Divine providence is in the least particulars of man's thought and affections; and this means that man can think and will nothing from himself, but that every thing that he thinks and wills, and says and does therefrom, is from influx; if good from influx out of heaven, and if evil from influx from hell; or what is the same, that good is from influx from the Lord, and evil from what is man's own (*proprium*). But I am aware that this can scarcely be comprehended, because a distinction is made between that which flows in out of heaven or from the Lord and that which flows in out of hell or from what is man's own; and yet it is said that the Divine providence is in the least particulars of man's thoughts and affections, even to the extent that man can think and will nothing from himself. But when it is added that he can also do this from hell, also from what is his own, there appears to be a contradiction, and yet there is not. That there is no contradiction will be seen in what follows, when some things have been premised that will illustrate the matter.

288. That no one can think from himself, but can think only from the Lord, all the angels of heaven confess; while all the spirits of hell declare that no one can think from any other than himself. It has often been shown to these spirits, but in vain, for they were unwilling to accept it, that no one of them thinks or can think from himself, but that it is from influx. But experience will teach, in the first place, that every thing of thought and affection, even with the spirits of hell, flows in out of heaven; but that this inflowing good is there turned into evil and this truth into falsity, thus every thing into its opposite. This has been shown thus: A certain truth from the Word was sent down out of heaven, and was received by those who were in the upper part of hell, and by them it was sent down into the lower parts, even to the lowest; and on the way it was gradually turned into falsity and at last into a falsity wholly opposite to the truth; and those in whom this change was made were thinking the falsity as if from themselves, and did not know otherwise, although the truth thus falsified and perverted was a truth flowing down out of heaven on its way to the lowest hell. I have heard three or four times that it was so done. The same is true of good; this flowing down out of heaven is changed as it goes into the evil opposite to the good. Thus has it been made clear that truth and good going forth from the Lord and received by those who are in falsity and in evil are wholly changed, and pass into another form, so different that the first form is not apparent. The same thing takes place with every evil man, for he in respect to his spirit is in hell.

289. It has been shown to me frequently that no one in hell thinks from himself, but he thinks from others about him; and that these others do not think from themselves, but they, too, from others; and that thoughts and affections pass in order from one society to another, and no one is aware that they are not from himself. Some who believed that they thought and willed from themselves were sent into a society and were detained in it, and communication with the neighboring societies to which their thoughts were usually extended was cut off. They were then told to think differently from the spirits of that society and to compel themselves to think in an opposite way, but they confessed that it was impossible. [2] This was done with many; and even with Leibnitz, and he, too, was convinced that no one thinks from himself, but only from others; and that neither do these others think from themselves, but that all think by influx out of heaven, and heaven by influx from the Lord. Some that thought carefully about this have declared it to be astounding, and that scarcely any one could be brought to believe it, because it is wholly contrary to the appearance, and yet they could not deny it, because it was fully shown. Nevertheless, even while they were wondering about it, they said that they were not to blame for thinking evil, also that this made evil seem to be from the Lord; also that they did not comprehend how the Lord alone could cause all to think so diversely. But these three points shall be unfolded in what follows.

290. To the experiences already presented let this be added: When it was granted me by the Lord to speak with spirits and angels this arcanum was at once disclosed to me; for I was told from heaven that, like others, I believed that I thought and that I willed from myself, yet in fact nothing was from myself, but if good it was from the Lord, and if evil it was from hell. That this was true I had a living proof in various thoughts and affections induced upon me, and gradually it was granted me to perceive and to feel it; and thereafter as soon as any evil glided into my will, or any falsity into my thought, I inquired into its source, and this was disclosed to me, and I was permitted to speak with those from whom it came, to reprove them, and to compel them to withdraw, and thus to take back their evil and their falsity and to keep them to themselves, and no longer to infuse any such thing into my thought. This I have done a thousand times; and I have now continued in this state for several years, and continue in it still; and yet I seem to myself to think and to will from myself, like others, with no difference; for it is of the Lord's providence that it should so appear to every one, as has been shown above in its proper place. Novitiate spirits wonder at this state of mine, for it seems to them that I have no thought or will at all from myself, and am therefore like an empty something. But I laid open the mystery to them, showing that while I think interiorly and perceive what flows into my exterior thoughts, and whether it is from heaven or from hell, and reject what is from hell and receive what is from heaven, I still seem to myself to think and to will from myself, as it seems to them.

291. That all good is from heaven and all evil from hell, is not among the things unknown in the world; for it is known to every one in the church. Who in the church that has been inaugurated into the priesthood does not teach that all good is from God, and that man is unable from himself to accept anything except what has been given him from heaven; also that it is the devil who infuses evils into the thoughts of men and leads them astray, and excites them to do evils? Therefore the priest who believes that he preaches from a holy zeal prays that the Holy Spirit may teach him and direct his thoughts and his words, and some declare that they have sensibly perceived that they have been so actuated, and when their preaching is praised they piously reply that they have spoken from God and not from themselves. Moreover, when they see any one speaking well or doing well they say that he has been led to it by God; and on the other hand, when they see any one talking or acting wickedly they say that he has been led to it by the devil. That there is such a mode of speaking in the church is well known; but who believes it to be true?

292. That everything that a man thinks and wills and speaks and does therefrom flows in from the one fountain of life, and yet that the one fountain of life, that is, the Lord, is not the cause of man's thinking evil and falsity, can be illustrated in this way from the natural world: That from its sun heat and light go forth, and these two flow into all subjects and objects that appear before the eyes, both into good subjects and beautiful objects and into evil subjects and unbeautiful objects, and produce in these a variety of effects; for they flow both into trees that bear good fruits and also into trees that bear evil fruits, and even into the fruits themselves and cause them to grow. They flow likewise into good seed and into tares; also into shrubs that have a good use or are wholesome, and into shrubs that have an evil use or are poisonous; and yet it is the same heat and the same light, in which there is no cause of evil; but the cause is in the recipient subjects and objects. [2] The heat that hatches eggs containing the screech-owl, the horned owl, or the viper, acts in the same way as when it hatches eggs in which lie hidden the dove, the beautiful bird, or the swan. Put eggs of the two kinds under a hen, and they will be hatched by her heat, which in itself is free from harm. What, then, has the heat in common with these evil and noxious things? The heat that flows into marshy, stercoraceous, putrid, and cadaverous substances acts in the same way as when it flows into things vinous, fragrant, active and living. Who does not see that the cause is not in the heat but in the recipient subject? Again, the same light presents pleasing colors in one object and disagreeable colors in another; it even grows bright and glows in objects of shining whiteness, and becomes dim and dusky in those verging to black. [3] The same is true in the spiritual world. There, too, there are heat and light, from its sun, which is the Lord; and from that sun these flow into their subjects and objects. The subjects and objects there are angels and spirits, particularly their voluntary and intellectual capacities. The heat there is the Divine love going forth, and the light there is the Divine wisdom going forth; and these are not the cause of the difference in their reception by one and by another, for the Lord says that

He makes His sun to rise on the evil and on the good, and sends rain on the just and on the unjust (*Matt.* v. 45).

In the highest spiritual sense "the sun" means the Divine love, and "rain" the Divine wisdom.

293. To this I will add the angelic view of will and intelligence in man, which is, that not a grain of will or of prudence that is his own is possible in any man. They say that if a grain were possible in any one neither heaven nor hell would continue to exist, and the whole human race would perish; and the reason given is that myriads of myriads of men, as many as have been born since the creation of the world, constitute heaven and hell; which are arranged in such an order, one under another, that on either side they make a one, heaven forming one beautiful Man, and hell one monstrous Man. If any one of these had a grain of will or intelligence of his own that oneness would not be possible, but would be rent asunder; and with it would perish that Divine form, which can have consistence and permanence only when the Lord is the All in all things, and these are utterly nothing. They say further, that this is so because the essential Divine is to think and to will from itself, while the essential human is to think and to will from God; and the essential Divine cannot be appropriated to any man, for if it were man would be God. Keep this in mind, and if you wish you will have it corroborated by the angels when after death you go to the spiritual world.

294. It has been stated above (n. 289) that when some were convinced that no one thinks from himself but only from others, and that all these others think not from themselves but from influx through heaven from the Lord, they said in their wonder that they could not then be blamed for doing evil; also that this made evil seem to be from the Lord; also that they did not comprehend how the Lord alone can cause all to think so diversely.   As these three opinions must needs flow into the thoughts of those who think of effects only from effects, and not of effects from causes, it is necessary to take them up and explain them from causes. [2] First: *They could not then be blamed for doing evil.* For if every thing that a man thinks flows into him from others the blame would seem to rest on those from whom it comes; and yet the blame itself rests on him who receives, for he receives it as his, and he does not know and is unwilling to know anything to the contrary. For every one wishes to be his own and to be led by himself, and especially to think and to will from himself; for this is freedom itself, which appears as the own (*proprium*) in which every man is. If, then, he knew that what he thinks and wills flows in from another he would seem to himself like one bound and captive, and no longer his own master; and thus all the delight of his life would perish, and finally the human itself. [3] That this is so I have often seen proved. It has been granted to some to perceive and feel that they were led by others; they then became so enraged as to lose all self-control, and declared that they would rather be kept bound in hell than not be allowed to think in accordance with their will and to will in accordance with their thought. Not to be allowed to do this they called being bound in their very life, which is harder and more intolerable than being bound in body. Not to be allowed to speak and act in accordance with their thought and will they did not call being bound; because the delight in civil and moral life, which consists in speaking and doing, checks and as it were soothes this feeling. [4] Since, then, man is not willing to know that he is led to think by others, but wishes to think from himself, and believes that he does so, it follows that he is blameable; nor can he rid himself of blame so long as he loves to think what he is thinking; but as soon as he ceases to love this he releases himself from this bond to others. This takes place when he knows that a thing is evil, and wishes in consequence to shun it and refrain from it. And then he is taken away by the Lord from the society that is in that evil, and is transferred to a society that is not in that evil. But if he knows that evil and does not shun it the blame is imputed to him and he becomes guilty of that evil. Anything, therefore, that a man believes that he does from himself is said to be done from him, and not from the Lord. [5] Secondly: *This makes evil to seem to be from the Lord.* This may be thought to be a conclusion from what has been shown above (n. 288), namely, that good flowing in from the Lord is turned in hell into evil, and truth into falsity. But any one can see that evil and falsity are not from good and truth, and thus from the Lord, but are from the recipient subject and object, which is in evil and falsity, and which perverts and inverts that which flows in, as is also fully shown above (n. 292). But it has been frequently shown in the preceding pages what the source of evil and falsity is in man. In the spiritual world an experiment was made with those who believed that the Lord could remove evils in the wicked and could put goods in their place, and thus transfer all hell into heaven and save all. But that this is impossible will be shown near the close of this work, where instant salvation and mercy apart from means are to be treated of. [6] Thirdly: *They do not comprehend how the Lord alone can cause all to think so diversely.* The Lord's Divine love is infinite and His Divine wisdom is infinite, and infinite things of love and of wisdom go forth from the Lord, and these flow into all in heaven, and therefrom into all in hell, and from both of these into all in the world; therefore thinking and willing fail in no one, for infinite things are all things without limit. Those infinite things that go forth from the Lord flow in both universally and also most particularly; for the Divine is universal from its least particulars; and it is these Divine least particulars that are called the universal, as has been shown above; and every Divine least particular is also infinite. From this it can be seen that the Lord alone causes every one to think and to will in accordance with his quality and in accordance with the laws of the Divine providence. That all things that are in the Lord and go forth from the Lord are infinite has been shown above (n. 46–69); and also in the work on *The Divine Love and the Divine Wisdom* (n. 17–22).

295. (2) *The evil are continually leading themselves into evils, but the Lord is continually leading them away from evils.* What the Lord's Divine providence is with the good is more easily comprehended than what it is with the evil; but as the latter is now treated of it shall be told in the following order: (1) In every evil there are things innumerable. (2) An evil man from himself continually leads himself more deeply into his evils. (3) The Divine providence with the evil is a continual permission of evil, to the end that there may be a continual withdrawal from it. (4) The withdrawal from evil is effected by the Lord in a thousand ways, and even in most secret ways.

296. Therefore that the Divine providence with the evil may be more clearly seen and thus comprehended the points that have been stated above shall be explained in the order of their presentation. First: *In every evil there are things innumerable.* In man's sight every evil appears as one simple thing,— hatred and revenge, theft and fraud, adultery and whoredom, pride and haughtiness, and other evils, so appear,—and it is not known that in every evil there are things innumerable, more than there are fibers and vessels in a man's body. For an evil man is hell in the least form; and hell consists of myriads of myriads, and every one there is in form like a man, though monstrous, in which all the fibers and vessels are inverted. The spirit is itself an evil, appearing to itself as a one; but as many as are the innumerable things in a spirit so many are the lusts of that evil; for every man is his own evil or his own good from the head to the sole of the foot. Since, then, an evil man is such, it is evident that he is one evil composed of innumerable different ones, each of which is a distinct evil; and these are called lusts of evil. From all this it follows

that all these, in the order in which they are, must be restored
and turned about by the Lord that man may be reformed;
and that this can be done only by the Lord's Divine providence, step by step, from the earliest period of man's life to
the last. [2] Every lust of evil in hell, when it is represented, appears like some noxious animal, as a dragon, or a
basilisk, or a viper, or a horned owl, or a screech-owl, and so
on; the lusts of evil in an evil man have a like appearance
when he is looked at by angels. All these forms of lusts must
be changed, one by one; the man himself who appears in respect to his spirit as a monster man or as a devil, must be
so changed as to be like a beautiful angel; and every evil lust
must be so changed as to appear like a lamb or a sheep, or like
a pigeon or turtle-dove, which is the way in which the good
affections of the angels appear in heaven when they are represented ; and to change a dragon into a lamb, a basilisk into a
sheep, or an owl into a pigeon, can only be done gradually by
eradicating evil from its seed and implanting good seed in
place of it. This can only be done comparatively as in the
grafting of trees, the roots and some of the trunk of which
remain, and yet the ingrafted branch turns the sap drawn up
through the old root into a sap that makes good fruit. The
branch to be ingrafted can be taken from no other source than
the Lord who is the Tree of Life. This is in accordance with
the Lord's words (*John* xv. 1–7). [3] Secondly: *An evil man
from himself continually leads himself more deeply into his evils*.
The expression, *from himself*, is used because all evil is from
man, for man turns good that is from the Lord into evil, as has
been said above. The essential cause of the evil man's leading
himself more deeply into evil is that as he wills and does evil
he advances more and more interiorly, and also more and more
deeply, into infernal societies, and in consequence the delight
of evil grows; and this so occupies his thoughts that at length
nothing is sweeter to his sense. And he who has advanced
more interiorly and deeply into infernal societies becomes as
if he were bound with cords; although so long as he lives in

19

the world he does not feel the cords, they are as if made of soft wool or smooth threads of silk, which he loves because they titillate. But after death these cords from being soft become hard, and instead of titillating they become galling. [4] That the delight of evil is augmented is known from thefts, robberies, depredations, revenge, tyranny, money-getting, and other evils. Who does not feel the exaltation of delight in these things in the measure of his success and unrestrained indulgence? It is known that a thief feels such delight in thefts that he is unable to refrain, and what is wonderful, that he has more love for one coin that is stolen than for ten received as a gift. The same would be true of adultery, if it had not been provided that this evil decreases in potency in the measure of the abuse; although with many a delight in thinking and talking about it remains, and if nothing more there is still the lust of touch. [5] But it is not known that this increase of delight comes of man's advancing into infernal societies more and more interiorly and more and more deeply, as from will and at the same time from thought he commits the evils. So long as the evils are in thought alone, and not in the will, man is not in an infernal society with the evil, but he enters it as soon as the evils are also in the will. And if he then thinks that this evil is contrary to the commandments of the Decalogue, and regards the commandments as Divine, he commits the evil designedly and thereby sinks himself to a depth from which he can be led forth only by actual repentance. [6] It must be understood that in respect to his spirit every man is in the spiritual world, in some society there—an evil man in an infernal society, and a good man in a heavenly society, and sometimes when in deep meditation he also appears there; also that as the sound of the voice with the spoken words spreads itself all about in the air of the natural world, so affection with thought spreads itself into societies in the spiritual world; and this is a correspondence, for affection corresponds to sound and thought to speech. [7] Thirdly: *The Divine providence with the evil is a continual permission of evil,*

to the end that there may be a continual withdrawal from it.
The Divine providence with evil men is a continual permission,
because nothing but evil can go forth from their life; for man
whether he be in good or in evil, cannot be in both at the same
time, nor alternately unless he is lukewarm; and it is not the
Lord but man that introduces evil of life into the will and
through the will into the thought. This is what is called permission. [8] Since, then, all things that an evil man wills and
thinks are of permission, it may be asked what the Divine providence therein is which is said to be in the least particulars
in every man, whether evil or good. But it consists in this, that
it continually permits for the sake of the end, and permits such
things as pertain to the end and nothing else; and the evils
that go forth from permission it continually surveys, separates,
and purifies, sending away things discordant and discharging
them by unknown ways. These processes take place especially
in man's interior will, and from this in his interior thought.
The Divine providence is also unceasing in keeping watch that
what must be sent away and discharged be not received again
by the will; since all things that are received by the will are
appropriated to man, while whatever is received by the thought
and not by the will is separated and banished. Such is the
Lord's continual providence with the evil, which is, as has been
said, a continual permission, to the end that there may be an
unceasing withdrawal. [9] Of all this man knows scarcely anything, because he has no perception of it. The primary reason
that he has no perception of it is that these evils are the evils
pertaining to the lusts of his life's love; and these evils are
not felt as evils but as delights to which no one gives attention.
Who attends to the delights of his love? His thought floats
on in them like a boat borne by the current of a river, and there
is a perception as it were of a fragrant atmosphere which is
inhaled with a full breath. Only in his external thought can he
feel something of them, and even there he gives no attention to
them unless he knows well that they are evils. But of this more
in what follows. [10] Fourthly: *The withdrawal from evil is*

effected by the Lord in a thousand ways, and even in most secret ways. Only some of these have been disclosed to me, and none but the most general, which are these: The delights of lusts of which man has no knowledge are emitted in companies or in bundles into the interior thoughts that belong to man's spirit, and therefrom into his exterior thoughts, in which they appear under a kind of feeling of satisfaction or pleasure or longing; and there they are mingled with his natural and sensual delights. There, too, are the means of separation and purification, and also the ways of withdrawal and discharge. The means are chiefly the delights of meditation, of thought, and of reflection for the sake of certain ends which are uses; and the ends, which are uses, are as many as are the particulars and least particulars of one's business and office. Or again, they are as many as the delights of reflection, to the end that he may appear like a civil and moral man and also like a spiritual man; besides the undelightful things that insert themselves. These delights, because they belong to one's love in the external man, are the means of separation, purification, excretion, and withdrawal of the delights of the lusts of evil belonging to the internal man. [11] Take, for example, an unjust judge who regards gains or friendship as ends or as uses of his office; inwardly he is continually in these things, but outwardly he aims to act like a skilled lawyer and a just man. He is constantly in the delight of meditation, thought, reflection, and purpose, that he may so bend, turn, adapt, and adjust the right that there may still appear to be a conformity with the laws and a semblance of justice, not knowing that his internal delight consists of cunning, frauds, deceits, clandestine thefts, and many other things, and that this delight, made up of so many delights of the lusts of evil, rules in all things and each thing of his external thought, wherein are the delights of appearing to be just and sincere. The internal delights are let down into these external delights, and they are mixed together like various kinds of food in the stomach; and there they are separated, purified, and conducted away; nevertheless, this is done only

with the more grievous delights of the lusts of evil. [12] For
with an evil man no separation, purification, and withdrawal
is possible except of the more grievous evils from the less
grievous; while with a good man there can be not only a separation, purification, and withdrawal of the more grievous evils,
but also of the less grievous; and this is done by means of the
delights of affections for what is good and true and for what is
just and sincere, into which he comes so far as he regards evils
as sins and in consequence shuns them and turns away from
them, and still more if he fights against them.   Such are the
means by which the Lord purifies all who are saved.   These
He also purifies by external means, which have respect to fame
and honor, and sometimes to wealth; nevertheless there are implanted in these by the Lord the delights of affections for good
and truth, by which they are so regulated and fitted as to
become delights of love of the neighbor. [13] If one could see
the delights of the lusts of evil together in some form, or if he
could clearly perceive them by any sense, he would see and perceive them to be too numerous to be defined; for all hell is
nothing but a form of all the lusts of evil, and there no lust
of evil is exactly like another or the same as another, neither
can there be to eternity.   And of these numberless lusts man
knows scarcely anything, still less how they are connected.
Nevertheless, the Lord through His Divine providence continually permits them to come forth, to the end that they may be
taken away, which is done in every order and series.   An evil
man is a hell in the least form, as a good man is a heaven in
the least form. [14] That this withdrawal from evils is effected
by the Lord in a thousand ways, even the most secret ways,
one can best see and be convinced of by comparison with the
secret operations of the soul in the body.   Those that man has
knowledge of are the following: The food that he is about to
eat he looks at, perceives the odor of, hungers for, tastes, chews
with his teeth, rolls to the œsophagus with his tongue, and
thus into the stomach.   But the soul's secret workings, of which
man knows nothing because he has no sensation of them, are

these: That the stomach rolls about the food received, opens and separates it by means of solvents, that is, digests it, and offers fitting portions of it to the little mouths there opening and to the veins that drink them in, sends some to the blood, some to the lymphatic vessels, some to the lacteal vessels of the mesentery, and some it sends away down the intestines; and finally the chyle, conveyed through the thoracic duct from its receptacle in the mesentery, is carried into the vena cava, and so into the heart, and from the heart into the lungs, from them through the left ventricle of the heart into the aorta, and from this by its branches into the viscera of the whole body and also to the kidneys; and in every one of these organs a separation of the blood, a purification and a withdrawal of heterogeneous substances is effected; not to speak of how the heart presents its blood, when defecated in the lungs, to the brain, which is done through the arteries called carotids, and how the brain returns the blood vivified to the vena cava (just above where the thoracic duct brings in the chyle), and so back again to the heart. [15] These and innumerable others are the secret operations of the soul in the body. These operations are not felt by man, and he who is not versed in the science of anatomy knows nothing about them. And yet similar things take place in the interiors of man's mind; for nothing can take place in the body except from the mind; for man's mind is his spirit, and his spirit is equally a man, with the difference only that whatever is done in the body is done naturally, and whatever is done in the mind is done spiritually; the similitude is complete. From all this it is evident that the Divine providence works in every man in a thousand ways, even to the most secret, and that its unceasing end is to purify him, because its end is to save him; and that nothing is incumbent on man except to remove evils in the external man. All the rest the Lord provides if He is appealed to.

297. (3) *The evil cannot be wholly led by the Lord away from evil and into good so long as they believe their own intelligence to be everything, and the Divine providence nothing.* The appearance is that man has the ability to withdraw himself from evil, provided he thinks this or that to be contrary to the common good, contrary to what is useful, and contrary to the law of the nation and of nations. This an evil man can do as well as a good man, provided he is such by birth or by practice as to be able inwardly in himself to think clearly, analytically and rationally. Nevertheless he is not able to withdraw himself from evil. And the reason of this is that while the Lord gives to every man, the good and the evil alike, the capacity to understand and perceive things, even abstractly, as has been shown above throughout, yet man from that capacity is not able to deliver himself from evil, because evil belongs to the will, and the understanding flows into the will only as with light, enlightening and teaching; and if the heat of the will, that is, man's life's love, is glowing with a lust of evil it is frigid in affection for good; and in consequence, he does not receive [that light], but either rejects or extinguishes it, or by some contrived falsity turns it into evil. It is in this as with the light of winter, which is equally clear with the summer's light, and acts in a like manner as it flows in upon the frozen trees. But this can be seen more fully in the following order: (1) One's own intelligence, when the will is in evil, sees nothing but falsity, and has no desire or ability to see anything else. (2) If one's own intelligence then sees truth it either turns itself away or it falsifies the truth. (3) The Divine providence continually causes man to see truth, and also gives an affection for perceiving it and for receiving it. (4) By this means man is withdrawn from evil, not by himself, but by the Lord.

298. But that these things may be made evident to the rational man, whether he be an evil or a good man, thus whether he be in the light of winter or of summer (for colors appear the same in both), they shall be explained in their order. First: *One's own intelligence, when the will is in evil, sees nothing but falsity, and has no desire or ability to see any thing else.* This has often been shown in the spiritual world. Every man when he becomes a spirit, which takes place after death (for he then puts off the material body and puts on the spiritual), is admitted by turns into the two states of his life, the external and the internal. While he is in the external state he speaks and acts rationally and wisely, just as a rational and wise man does in the world; he can also teach others many things that pertain to moral and civil life; and if he has been a preacher he can teach things pertaining to spiritual life. But when from this external state he is let into his internal, and the external is put to sleep and the internal is awakened, if he is an evil man the scene is changed; from being rational he becomes sensual, and from being wise he becomes insane, for he then thinks from the evil of his will and its delight, thus from his own intelligence, and he sees nothing but falsity and does nothing but evil, believing that shrewdness is wisdom and that cunning is prudence; and from his own intelligence he believes himself to be a deity, and with his whole mind drinks in nefarious schemes. [2] Such insanities I have often seen; I have also seen spirits let into these alternate states two or three times within an hour; and they were then permitted to see their insanities and to acknowledge them; nevertheless they were unwilling to remain in a rational and moral state, but turned themselves back of their own accord into their internal state, which was sensual and insane, for they loved this more than the other, because the delight of their life's love was in it. Who can believe that an evil man is such behind his outward appearance, and that he undergoes such a transformation when he enters into what is within? From this experience alone it can be seen what one's own intelligence is when he thinks and acts from the evil of his will. It is otherwise with the good: when these from the external state are admitted into the internal they become still wiser and better behaved. [3] Secondly: *If one's own intelligence then sees truth it either turns itself away or it falsifies the truth.* Man has a voluntary self (*proprium*) and an intellectual self; the voluntary self is evil, and the intellectual self is falsity therefrom; the latter is meant by "the will of man," and the former by "the will of the flesh" (*John* i. 13). The voluntary self in its essence is love of self, and the intellectual is conceit from that love; these two are like two consorts, and their marriage is called the marriage of evil and falsity. Every evil spirit is admitted into this marriage before he comes into hell, and when he is in it he does not know what good is, for he calls his evil good because he feels it to be delightful; and he then also turns away from the truth and is unwilling to see it, because he sees the falsity that is in harmony with his evil as the eye sees what is beautiful, and he hears it as the ear hears what is harmonious. [4] Thirdly: *The Divine providence continually causes man to see truth, and also gives an affection for perceiving it and receiving it.* This is done because the Divine providence acts from the interior, and through it flows into exteriors, that is, from the spiritual into the things that are in the natural man; and by the light of heaven enlightens the understanding, and by the heat of heaven vivifies the will. The light of heaven in its essence is Divine wisdom, and the heat of heaven in its essence is Divine love, and from the Divine wisdom nothing else can flow in but truth, and from the Divine love nothing else can flow in but good; and from this the Lord gives in the understanding an affection for seeing truth and also for perceiving and receiving it. Thus man becomes a man both in external and in internal aspect. Does not every one wish to appear a rational and spiritual man? And does not every one know that he wishes so to appear, that he may be believed by others to be a true man? If, therefore, he is rational and spiritual in external form only, and not also in internal form, is he a man? Is he anything but as a player upon the stage or as an ape with a face almost human? From this can it not be known that he alone is a man who is interiorly what he wishes to seem to others to be? He who acknowledges the one must acknowledge the other. One's own intelligence can induce the human form on externals only; but the Divine providence induces that form on the internals, and through these in the externals; and when it has been so induced man does not merely appear to be a man but he is a man. [5] Fourthly: *By this means man is withdrawn from evil, not by himself but by the Lord.* When the Divine providence enables man to see truth, and at the same time gives him an affection for it, man can be withdrawn from evil, because truth instructs and prescribes, and when the will does accordingly it conjoins itself with the truth, and in itself it turns the truth into good; for the truth comes to be of its love, and what is of the love is good. All reformation is effected by means of truth, and not without it; for without truth the will is continually in its own evil, and if it consults the understanding it is not instructed, but the evil is confirmed by falsities. [6] In respect to intelligence, it appears both to the good man and to the evil man to be his, even his own; moreover, a good man is bound to act from intelligence as if it were his own just as much as an evil man; but he that believes in the Divine providence is withdrawn from evil, while he that does not believe is not withdrawn; and he believes who acknowledges evil to be sin and wishes to be withdrawn from it, while he does not believe who does not so acknowledge and wish. The difference between these two kinds of intelligence is like the difference between that which is believed to be in itself, and that which is believed not to be in itself and yet as if in itself; or it is like the difference between an external without a correlative internal and an external with a correlative internal; thus it is like the difference between the words and gestures of mimics and actors who personate kings, princes, and generals, and the kings, princes, and generals themselves; the latter are such both inwardly and outwardly, while the others are such only outwardly, and when this outward is put off they are called comedians, performers, and players.

299. (4) *The Lord governs hell by opposites; and He governs in hell the evil who are in the world in respect to their interiors, but not in respect to their exteriors.* He that does not know what heaven is and what hell is can know nothing whatever about what man's mind is. The mind of man is his spirit that lives after death. This is because the mind or spirit of

man is wholly in the form in which heaven is or in which hell
is; there is not the slightest difference, except that one is the
greatest and the other the least, or that one is the effigy and
the other the type. Consequently in respect to his mind or
spirit man is either a heaven or a hell in the least form. He
that is led by the Lord is a heaven, and he that is led by what
is his own is a hell. Since, then, it has been granted me to
know what heaven is and what hell is, and it is important
to know what man is in respect to his mind or spirit, I will
describe both briefly.

300. All that are in heaven are nothing but affections for
good and thoughts of truth therefrom, and all that are in
hell are nothing but lusts of evil and imaginations of falsity
therefrom; and these are so arranged on either side that the
lusts of evil and the imaginations of falsity in hell are directly
opposed to the affections for good and the thoughts of truth
in heaven. Consequently hell is under heaven, diametrically
opposite to it; that is, diametrically opposite like two men lying
in opposite ways, or standing as antipodes, thus inversely to
each other and meeting at the soles of the feet, or with the
heels together. Sometimes hell is seen to be so situated or reversed in respect to heaven. This is because those that are in
hell make lusts of evil the head and affections for good the
feet, while those who are in heaven make affections for good
the head and lusts of evil the soles of the feet; hence the mutual opposition. When it is said that in heaven there are affections for good and consequent thoughts of truth, and in hell
there are lusts of evil and consequent imaginations of falsity,
it is meant that there are spirits and angels there who are such;
for every one is his own affection or his own lust, an angel of
heaven is his own affection and a spirit of hell is his own lust.

301. The angels of heaven are affections for good and consequent thoughts of truth, because they are recipients of Divine
love and Divine wisdom from the Lord. All affections for good
are from the Divine love, and all thoughts of truth are from
the Divine wisdom. But the spirits of hell are lusts of evil and

consequent imaginations of falsity, because they are in the love of self and in their own intelligence, and all lusts of evil are from the love of self, and the imaginations of falsity are from one's own intelligence.

302. The arrangement of affections in heaven and of lusts in hell is wonderful, and is known to the Lord alone. In each they are distinguished into genera and species, and are so conjoined as to act as one. And because they are distinguished into genera and species they are distinguished into societies greater and less; and because they are so conjoined as to act as one they are conjoined like all the things that are in man. Consequently heaven in its form is like a beautiful man, whose soul is the Divine love and Divine wisdom, thus the Lord; and hell in its form is like a monstrous man, whose soul is the love of self and self-intelligence, thus the devil; for there is no devil who is sole lord there, but the love of self is called the devil.

303. But in order to make it better known what heaven is and what hell is, let delights of good be substituted for affections for good, and delights of evil for lusts of evil; for there is no affection or lust without delight, since these make the life of every one. These delights are what are distinguished and conjoined in the way described above respecting affections for good and lusts of evil. The delight of his affection fills and surrounds every angel of heaven, and also a general delight fills and surrounds every society of heaven, and the delight of all together or a most general delight fills and surrounds the universal heaven. In like manner the delight of his lust fills and surrounds every spirit of hell, and a general delight every society of hell, and the delight of all or a most general delight fills and surrounds the entire hell. Because, as said above, the affections of heaven and the lusts of hell are diametrically opposed to each other, it is clear that the delight of heaven is so undelightful in hell that it cannot be endured, and on the other hand, that the delight of hell is so undelightful in heaven that it cannot be endured. This is the cause of the antipathy, aversion, and separation.

304. Inasmuch as these delights constitute the life of every one in particular and of all in general, they are not felt by those who are in them, but their opposites are felt when they approach, especially when they are turned into odors; for every delight corresponds to an odor, and in the spiritual world may be converted into an odor; and then the general delight in heaven is sensed as the odor of a garden, with variety according to the varieties of fragrance there from flowers and fruits, while the general delight in hell is sensed as stagnant water into which different kinds of filth have been thrown, with variety according to the bad odors from putrid and offensive things therein. How the delight of each affection for good in heaven and the delight of the lust of evil in hell is felt it has been granted me to know; but it would require too much space to explain it here.

305. I have heard many newcomers from the world complain that they had not known that their life's lot would be in accordance with the affections of their love, saying that in the world they had not thought about these affections, still less about their delights, because they had loved whatever was delightful to them, and had merely believed that every one's lot would be in accordance with their thoughts from intelligence, especially in accordance with the thoughts arising from their piety and also from their faith. But it was replied that they could have known if they had wished, that evil of life is disagreeable to heaven and displeasing to God, but is agreeable to hell and pleasing to the devil, and on the other hand, that good of life is agreeable to heaven and pleasing to God, and disagreeable to hell and displeasing to the devil; consequently that evil in itself is a stench, while good in itself is fragrant. And as they might have known this if they would, why had they not shunned evil as infernal and diabolical and why had they favored evils merely because they were delightful? And as they were now aware that the delights of evil have so foul a smell, they might also know that those who exhale such smells cannot enter heaven. After this reply they betook themselves to those who were in like delights, because there and not elsewhere they could breathe.

306. From the idea here given of heaven and hell it can be seen what man's mind is; for, as has been said, man's mind or spirit is either a heaven or a hell in the least form, that is, its interiors are mere affections and thoughts therefrom, distinguished into genera and species, as into greater and less societies, and so conjoined as to act as one, and that the Lord rules them in the same manner as He rules heaven and hell. That man is either a heaven or a hell in the least form can be seen in the work on *Heaven and Hell*, published in London in the year 1758 (n. 51–87).

307. Now in regard to the subject proposed: That the Lord governs hell by means of opposites, and that the evil who are in the world He governs in hell, in respect to their interiors but not in respect to their exteriors. As to the first: *That the Lord governs hell by means of opposites.* It has been shown above (n. 288, 289), that the angels of heaven are not in love and wisdom, or in affection for good and the consequent thought of truth from themselves, but from the Lord; also that good and truth flow out of heaven into hell, and that good is there turned into evil, and truth into falsity, because the interiors of the minds of those in heaven and in hell are turned in opposite directions. Since, then, all things in hell are opposite to all things in heaven it follows that the Lord governs hell by means of opposites. [2] Secondly: *The evil who are in the world the Lord governs in hell.* This is true because man as to his spirit is in the spiritual world and in some society there, in an infernal society if he is evil, and in a heavenly society if he is good; for man's mind, which in itself is spiritual, must needs be among the spiritual, and he comes among such after death. That this is true has also been said and shown above. But a man is not there in the same way as a spirit is who has been assigned to the society, for a man is constantly in a state to be reformed, and if he is evil he is transferred by the Lord from one society of hell to another in accordance with his life and its changes.

But if he suffers himself to be reformed he is led out of hell, and is led up into heaven, and there he is transferred from one society to another, and this even until death. But after death he is no longer borne from one society to another there, because he is then no longer in any state to be reformed, but remains in the state in which he is in accordance with his life. When, therefore, a man dies he is assigned to his own place. [3] Thirdly: *The Lord in this way governs the evil in the world in respect to their interiors, but otherwise in respect to their exteriors.* The Lord governs the interiors of man's mind, as has now been told; but the exteriors He governs in the world of spirits, which is intermediate between heaven and hell. The reason of this is that in externals man is for the most part different from what he is in internals, for in externals he can feign himself an angel of light while in internals he is a spirit of darkness; therefore his external is governed in one way and his internal in another. As long as he is in the world his external is governed in the world of spirits, but his internal is governed in heaven or in hell; therefore when he dies he first enters the world of spirits, and there comes into his external, which is there put off; and when this has been put off he is borne into his own place to which he has been assigned. What the world of spirits is and the nature of it may be seen in the work on *Heaven and Hell*, published at London in the year 1758 (n. 421–535).

THE DIVINE PROVIDENCE APPROPRIATES NEITHER EVIL NOR GOOD TO ANY ONE; BUT MAN'S OWN PRUDENCE APPROPRIATES BOTH.

308. Nearly every one believes that man thinks and wills from himself, and consequently speaks and acts from himself. And who from himself can believe otherwise, when the appearance that it is so is so strong that it does not differ in the least from an actual thinking, willing, speaking, and acting from one's self? Nevertheless, that is impossible. In *Angelic Wisdom* *concerning the Divine Love and the Divine Wisdom* it has been shown that there is only one life, and that men are recipients of life; also that man's will is the receptacle of love, and his understanding the receptacle of wisdom, and these two are that only life. It has also been shown there that it is from creation, and therefore from an unceasing Divine providence, that in man this life should manifest itself in the similitude of belonging to him, consequently as if it were his own life; this, however, being an appearance, to the end that man may be a receptacle. It has also been shown above (n. 288–294) that man never thinks from himself, but always from others, nor these others from themselves, but all from the Lord, and that this is true both of the evil man and of the good; furthermore, that this is recognized in the Christian world, especially by those who not only say but believe that all good and truth are from the Lord, also all wisdom, thus all faith and charity, while all evil and falsity are from the devil, or from hell. [2] From all this no other conclusion can follow than that every thing that man thinks and wills flows in. And since all speech flows from thought as an effect from its cause, and all action flows from will in like manner, it follows that everything also that a man says and does flows in, although derivatively or mediately. That every thing that a man sees, hears, smells, tastes, and feels, flows in cannot be denied; why not, then, every thing that a man thinks and wills? Can there be any other difference than that what flows into the organs of the external senses, or those of the body, are such things as are in the natural world, while what flows into the organic substances of the internal senses or those of the mind are such things as are in the spiritual world? Consequently as the organs of the external senses or those of the body are receptacles of natural objects, so the organic substances of the internal senses or of the mind are receptacles of spiritual objects. Such being the state of man, what has he that is his own? His being this or that kind of receptacle is not what is his own, since this own is simply what he is in respect to reception, and is not his life's own, for by one's own nothing else is meant by any one except that one lives from himself, and therefore thinks and wills from himself. But that such an own is not in man, and cannot possibly exist in any man, follows from what has been said above.

309. But I will relate what I have heard from some in the spiritual world. They were among those who believed their own prudence to be everything, and the Divine providence to be nothing. I said that man has nothing that is his own unless you choose to say that his being this or that kind of a subject, or his being this or that kind of an organ, or this or that kind of a form, is his own. But this is not the own that is meant, for this is merely what he is. In fact, no man, according to the common understanding of his own has any thing his own. Those who had ascribed all things to their own prudence, and who might be called owners in their very image, so blazed up at this that flame appeared from their nostrils, saying, "You are uttering contradictions and insanities; would not a man thus be nothing and emptiness, or an idea or fantasy, or a graven image or statue?" [2] But I could only answer that it is absurd and insane to believe that man is life from himself, and that wisdom and prudence do not flow in from God, but are in man, as well as the good that belongs to charity and the truth that belongs to faith. To attribute these to oneself is called by every wise man an insanity, consequently it is absurd; moreover, those who do this are like those who occupy the house and property of another, and as soon as they are in possession persuade themselves that they are the owners; or they are like overseers and stewards who believe all things belonging to their lord to be theirs; or like business servants to whom their lord has given talents and pounds to trade with, and who render no account but keep them as their own, and thus act as thieves. [3] Of all these it can be said that they are insane, and even that they are nothings and vanities, and are merely creatures of thought (*idealistæ*), since they do not have in them from the Lord that good which is the very being of life, thus neither the truth. Therefore such are called "dead," and "nothings and

20

vanities" (*Isaiah* xl. 17, 23), and elsewhere, "formers of an image," and "graven images," and "statues." But of all this more in what follows, which will be considered in this order:—

(1) What one's own prudence is, and what prudence not one's own is.

(2) Man from his own prudence persuades himself and corroborates in himself that all good and truth are from himself and in himself; likewise all evil and falsity.

(3) Everything that a man has adopted by persuasion and confirmation remains in him as his own.

(4) If man believed, as is the truth, that all good and truth are from the Lord, and all evil and falsity from hell, he would not appropriate good to himself and make it meritorious, nor appropriate evil to himself and make himself guilty of it.

310. (1) *What one's own prudence is, and what prudence not one's own is.* Those are in their own prudence who corroborate appearances in themselves and make them truths, especially the appearance that one's own prudence is everything, and the Divine providence nothing unless something universal; and this is impossible without the particulars that constitute it, as has been shown above. Such are in fallacies also, for every appearance confirmed as a truth becomes a fallacy; and as far as they confirm themselves by fallacies they become naturalists, and to that extent they believe nothing but what they are able also to perceive by some bodily sense, especially by the sense of sight, because that sense especially acts as one with thought. Such at last become sensual. When such confirm themselves in favor of nature against God, they close up the interiors of their minds, interposing a veil, as it were, and afterwards they think below the veil, but not of any thing that is above it. The ancients called such sensual men serpents of the tree of knowledge; and in the spiritual world it is said of them that as they confirm themselves they close up the interiors of their minds, at length even to the nose; for the "nose" signifies perception of truth, and this means that they have no perception. What such are shall now be told. [2] They are above others shrewd

and cunning, and ingenious reasoners; and they call shrewdness and cunning intelligence and wisdom, nor do they know
otherwise. Those not like themselves they regard as simple
and stupid, especially those who worship God and acknowledge
the Divine providence. In respect to the interior principles
of their minds, about which they have little knowledge, they
are like those called Machiavelians, who regard murder, adultery, theft, and false witness, viewed in themselves, as of no
account; and if they reason against them it is merely from
prudence, lest they should appear such themselves. [3] Of
man's life in the world they think only that it is like the life
of a beast; and of man's life after death that it is like a living
vapor that after rising out of the corpse or the grave settles
back again and thus dies. From this madness arises the idea
that spirits and angels are made of air, and with such as have
been trained to believe in eternal life, that the souls of men are
of the same nature, and thus cannot see, hear, or speak, and
therefore are blind, deaf, and dumb, and can merely think in
some part of their air. They say, How can the soul be any thing
else? Did not the external senses die with the body; and how
can the soul again resume them until it is reunited with the
body? And this belief has been maintained because they have
been able to comprehend the state of the soul after death only
in this sensual way and not spiritually; and except for this the
belief in an eternal life would have perished. Such have especially confirmed in themselves the love of self, calling it the fire
of life and the incentive to the various uses in the kingdom.
And being such they are idols of self; and as their thoughts
are fallacies and from fallacies they are images of falsity; and
as they favor the delights of lusts they are satans and devils.
Those who confirm in themselves the lusts of evil are called
satans, and those who live those lusts are called devils. [4]
What the most cunning sensual men are it has been granted
me to know. Their hell is deep down behind, and they wish to
be invisible; therefore they appear there flying about like spec-
ters, which are their fantasies. They are called genii. Some

of them were once let out of that hell that I might know their character. They immediately applied themselves to my neck, beneath the occiput, and thus entered into my affections, not wishing to enter my thoughts—these they skilfully avoided; and they varied my affections one after another for the purpose of bending them insensibly into their opposites, which are lusts of evil; and as they did not touch my thoughts they would have bent and inverted the affections without my knowledge if the Lord had not prevented it. [5] Such do those become who in the world do not believe that there is any such thing as Divine providence, and who seek out in others nothing but their cupidities and desires, thus leading them on until they rule over them. And as they do this so secretly and cunningly that the other does not know it, and as after death they become like themselves, as soon as they enter the spiritual world they are cast down into that hell. Such when seen in the light of heaven appear without noses, and what is wonderful, although they are so crafty they are nevertheless more sensual than others. As the ancients called a sensual man a serpent, and as such a man is shrewd, crafty, and an ingenious reasoner above others, therefore it is said that,

> The serpent was made more crafty than any wild beast of the field (*Gen.* iii. 1);

and the Lord says:—

> Be ye therefore prudent as serpents and simple as doves (*Matt.* x. 16);

and also the dragon, which is likewise called "the old serpent," "the devil," and "satan," is described as,

> Having seven heads and ten horns, and seven crowns upon his heads (*Apoc.* xii. 3, 9);

"seven heads" signifying craftiness; "the ten horns" the power of persuading by fallacies; and "the seven crowns" the holy things of the Word and of the church profaned.

311. This description of one's own prudence and of those who are in it makes clear what prudence that is not one's own is, and the character of those who are in it, namely, that pru-

dence not one's own is the prudence of those who do not persuade themselves that intelligence and wisdom are from man;
for they say, How can one be wise from himself, or how can
one do good from himself? And when they say this they see
in themselves that it is so, for they think interiorly; and they
also believe that others think in the same way, especially the
learned, not knowing that any one can think in a purely exterior way. [2] Such are not in fallacies through any confirmations of appearances, and therefore they know and perceive
that murder, adultery, theft, and false witness are sins, and
consequently shun them. They know also that shrewdness is
not wisdom, and that cunning is not intelligence. When they
listen to ingenious reasonings from fallacies they wonder and
inwardly smile. This is because with them there is no veil
between interiors and exteriors, or between the spiritual and
the natural things of the mind, as there is with the sensual;
therefore they receive influx from heaven, by which they interiorly see these things. [3] Such speak more simply and sincerely
than others, and place wisdom in the life, and not in talking.
They are comparatively like lambs and sheep, while those who
are in their own prudence are like wolves and foxes. They
are like those who live in a house and see heaven through the
windows; while those who are in their own prudence are like
those who live in the cellar of a house, and through their windows see only what is below the level of the ground. They
are like those who stand on a mountain, and they see those
who are in their own prudence like persons wandering in the
valleys and forests. [4] From all this it can be seen that the
prudence that is not one's own is prudence from the Lord,
having the same appearance in externals as one's own prudence but wholly unlike it in internals. In the spiritual world
prudence not one's own appears in internals like a man, while
one's own prudence appears like an effigy, seemingly alive
merely from this, that those who are in that prudence have
nevertheless rationality and liberty, or a capacity to understand and will, and consequently to speak and act, and by

means of these capacities they can feign themselves men also.
They are such effigies because evils and falsities have no life,
but goods and truths only are living; and knowing this from
their rationality (for if they did not know it they would not
counterfeit goods and truths) they endow their effigies with
human vitality.　[5] Who cannot know that a man is such as
he is interiorly?　Consequently, is not he a man who is interiorly what he wishes to seem to be outwardly?　And is not he
an effigy who is a man only outwardly, and not interiorly?
Think as you talk, in favor of God and religion, and justice
and sincerity, and you will be a man, and the Divine providence will then be your prudence, and you will see in others
that one's own prudence is insanity.

312. (2) *Man from his own prudence persuades himself and
corroborates in himself that all good and truth are from himself and in himself; likewise all evil and falsity.*　Let an argument be drawn from the analogy between natural good and
truth and spiritual good and truth.　It is asked what the true
and the good are in the sight of the eye?　Is not the true
there that which is called beautiful, and good there that which
is called delightful?　For delight is felt in seeing what is
beautiful.　What are the true and the good in the hearing?　Is
not the true there that which is called harmonious, and the good
that which is called pleasing? for pleasure is felt in hearing
harmonious sounds.　So of the other senses.　This makes clear
what natural truth and good are.　Consider now what spiritual truth and good are.　Is spiritual truth any thing except
the beautiful and harmonious in spiritual things and objects?
And is spiritual good any thing except the delight and pleasure that are derived from what is perceived of their beauty or
harmony?　[2] And now observe whether anything can be said
of the one different from what may be said of the other, that
is, of the spiritual different from what may be said of the natural.　Of the natural it is said that beauty and delight flow
from objects into the eye, and that what is harmonious and
pleasing flows from musical instruments into the ear.　What

is there different in the organic substances of the mind? Of these it is said that their contents reside in them, of natural organs that they flow in. But if it is asked why they are said to flow in, there can be no other answer than that it is because there is a manifest distance between them. But why in the other case are they said to be contained in them? There can be no other answer than that it is because there is no manifest distance between them. Consequently it is the appearance of distance that causes one kind of belief about what man thinks and perceives and another about what he sees and hears. But this falls to the ground as soon as it is known that the spiritual is not in distance as the natural is. Think of the sun and the moon, or of Rome and Constantinople—in the thought is there any distance between them, provided this thought is not joined with experience acquired through sight or hearing? Why then persuade yourself that because there is no manifest distance in the thought, good and truth and also evil and falsity reside within and do not flow in? [3] To this I will add this experience, which is common in the spiritual world. One spirit can infuse his thoughts and affections into another spirit, and the latter be unaware that it is not a part of his own thought and affection. This is there called thinking from another and thinking in another. I have seen this a thousand times, and I have myself done it a hundred times, even when there was an appearance of considerable distance. But as soon as they knew that another had introduced these thoughts and affections they were indignant and turned themselves away, acknowledging, however, that in the internal sight or the thought there is no appearance of distance, except when it is detected, as it may be by the external sight or the eye; and from that it may be believed that there is an inflowing. [4] To this I will add my own daily experience. Evil spirits have often infused into my thoughts evils and falsities which appeared to me to be in me and from me, that is, as if I myself thought them; but as I knew them to be evils and falsities I tried to discover who had infused them, and they who did so were detected and driven away. These had been at a very great distance from me. All this makes clear that all evil with its falsity flows in from hell, and that all good with its truth flows in from the Lord, and that they both appear to be in man.

313. The character of those who are in their own prudence and of those who are in prudence not their own, and who are thus in the Divine providence, is described in the Word by "Adam and his wife Eve," in "the garden of Eden," where there were two trees, one of life and the other of the knowledge of good and evil, and by their eating of the latter tree. That by "Adam and his wife Eve," in the internal or spiritual sense, the Most Ancient Church of the Lord on this earth, which was more noble and heavenly than the succeeding churches, is meant and depicted, can be seen above (n. 241); the signification of the other things is as follows. [2] "The garden of Eden" signifies the wisdom of the men of that church; "the tree of life" the Lord in respect to the Divine providence; and "the tree of knowledge" man in respect to his own prudence; the "serpent" signifies the sensual of man and what is his own (*proprium*), which in itself is the love of self and the pride of self-intelligence, thus the devil and satan; "eating from the tree of knowledge" signifies the appropriation of good and truth, as being from man and consequently man's, and not from the Lord and consequently the Lord's. And as good and truth are the Divine things themselves with man (for by good everything of love is meant and by truth everything of wisdom), so when man claims these to himself as his he cannot but believe that he is as God; therefore the serpent said:—

In the day ye eat thereof your eyes shall be opened, and ye shall be as God, knowing good and evil (*Gen.* iii. 5).

Thus do those do in hell who are in the love of self and in the conceit of their own intelligence therefrom. [3] The condemnation of the serpent signifies the condemnation of one's own love and one's own intelligence; the condemnation of Eve signifies the condemnation of the voluntary self (*proprium*), and

Adam's condemnation signifies the condemnation of the intellectual self (*proprium*); "the thorn and the thistle" that the earth would bring forth to him signify pure falsity and evil; the expulsion from the garden signifies the deprivation of wisdom; "the guarding of the way to the tree of life" the Lord's care lest the holy things of the Word and the church be violated; "the fig leaves with which they covered their nakedness" signify moral truths by which the things of their love and pride were veiled; and "the coats of skin" in which they were afterwards clothed signify the appearances of truth, which were all that they had. Such is the spiritual meaning of these things. But let him who wishes remain in the sense of the letter; only let him know that in heaven this is the meaning.

314. The character of those who are infatuated by their own intelligence can be seen from their fancies in matters of interior judgment; for example, respecting influx, thought, and life. Respecting influx their thought is inverted, as that the sight of the eye flows into the internal sight of the mind, which is the understanding; and the hearing of the ear flows into the internal hearing, which also is the understanding; and they fail to perceive that the understanding from the will flows into the eye and the ear, and not only makes those senses but also uses them as its instruments in the natural world. But as this is not in accordance with the appearance they fail to perceive what is meant when it is simply said that the natural does not flow into the spiritual but that the spiritual flows into the natural, still thinking, "What is the spiritual but a purer natural?" also, "Is it not evident that when the eye sees any thing beautiful, or the ear hears any thing harmonious, the mind, which is the understanding and the will, is delighted?" And they are not aware that the eye does not see from itself, nor the tongue taste from itself, nor the nose smell from itself, nor the skin feel from itself; but that it is man's mind or spirit that there perceives things by the sense, and is affected by the sense in accordance with its nature; and still these things are not felt by man's mind or spirit from itself, but from the Lord; and to think otherwise is to think from appearances, and if these are confirmed, from fallacies. [2] Of *Thought* they say that it is something modified in the air, varied according to its objects and enlarged according to culture, thus that the ideas of the thoughts are images like meteors appearing in the air, while the memory is the tablet on which they have been impressed; and they are not aware that thoughts are as much in substances purely organic as the sight and the hearing are in theirs. Only let them examine the brain and they will see that it is full of such substances; injure them and you become delirious, destroy them and you will die. But what thought is and what memory is can be seen above (near the end of n. 279). [3] Of *Life* they know nothing else than that it is a certain activity of nature that makes itself felt in various ways, as a living body moves itself organically. If it is asserted that if this be so nature is alive, they deny it, and say that nature imparts life. If it is asked, Then is not life dissipated when the body dies? they answer that life remains in that body of air that is called the soul. If it is asked, What is God then? is He not Life itself? they are silent, and are unwilling to declare what they think. If it is asked, Would you admit that Divine love and Divine wisdom are life itself? they answer, "What are love and wisdom?" For in their fallacies they fail to see what these are or what God is. These things are adduced to make clear how man is infatuated by his own prudence, for the reason that he draws all conclusions from appearances and consequent fallacies.

316. One's own prudence persuades and corroborates that every good and truth is from man and in man, because man's own prudence is his intellectual self (*proprium*) flowing in from the love of self which is his voluntary self (*proprium*); and self cannot do otherwise than make all things its own, for it cannot be raised above that. All who are led by the Lord's Divine providence are raised above the self, and they then see that all good and truth are from the Lord; they even see that what is in man from the Lord is ever the Lord's and never man's. He who believes otherwise is like one who has his master's goods under his care, and claims them for himself or appropriates them as his—he is not a steward, but a thief. And as man's self (*proprium*) is nothing but evil, he also immerses them in his evil, whereby they are destroyed like pearls cast into dung or into acid.

317. (3) *Every thing that a man has adopted by persuasion and confirmation remains in him as his own.* Many believe that no truth can be seen by man except when it has been confirmed; but this is a falsity. In the civil and economical affairs of a kingdom or republic what is useful and good can be seen only by a knowledge of many statutes and ordinances there; or in judicial matters only by a knowledge of the laws; or in the things of nature, like physics, chemistry, anatomy, mechanics, and so on, only when man has been well instructed in the sciences. But in things purely rational, moral, and spiritual, truths are seen from the light of truth itself, provided man has from a right education become somewhat rational, moral, and spiritual. This is because every man, in respect to his spirit, which is that which thinks, is in the spiritual world, and is one among those who are there; and consequently is in spiritual light, which enlightens the interiors of his understanding, and as it were dictates. For spiritual light in its essence is the Divine truth of the Lord's Divine wisdom. From this it is that man can think analytically, can form conclusions about what is just and right in judicial affairs, can see what is honorable in moral life and good in spiritual life, and many other truths, which are sunk in darkness only by confirmed falsities. These are seen by man comparatively almost as he sees another's disposition from his face, and perceives his affections from the tone of his voice, with no other knowledge than what is inherent in every one. Why should not man see in some measure from influx the interiors of his life, which are spiritual and moral, when there is no animal that does not know from influx its own necessities, which are natural? A bird knows how to build its nest, lay its eggs, hatch its young, and distinguish its food, besides other wonderful things which are called instincts.

318. But how man's state is changed by confirmations and consequent persuasions shall now be told, and in the following order: (1) There is nothing that cannot be confirmed; and falsity is confirmed more readily than the truth. (2) When falsity has been confirmed the truth is not seen; but from confirmed truth falsity is seen. (3) An ability to confirm whatever one pleases is not intelligence, but only ingenuity, which may exist even in the worst of men. (4) There is confirmation that is intellectual and not at the same time voluntary; but all voluntary confirmation is also intellectual. (5) The confirmation of evil that is voluntary and also intellectual causes man to believe that his own prudence is everything and the Divine providence nothing; but this is not true of intellectual confirmation alone. (6) Every thing confirmed by the will and also by the understanding remains to eternity; but not what has been confirmed by the understanding only. [2] As regards the first: *There is nothing that cannot be confirmed, and falsity is confirmed more readily than the truth.* What is there that cannot be confirmed, when it is confirmed by atheists that God is not the Creator of the universe, but that nature is the creator of itself; that religion is merely a restraint, and for the simple and the common people; that man is like a beast, and dies like one; also when it is confirmed that adulteries are allowable, likewise clandestine thefts, frauds, and deceitful contrivances; that cunning is intelligence and shrewdness is wisdom? Does not every one confirm his own heresy? Are there not volumes filled with the confirmations of the two heresies that reign in the Christian world? Make up ten heresies, however abstruse, ask an ingenious man to confirm them, and he will confirm them all. If afterwards you look at them solely from the confirmations will you not see the falsities as truths? As all falsity is visible in the natural man from its appearances and fallacies, and truth is visible in the spiritual man only, it is clear that falsity can be confirmed more readily than truth. [3] To make clear that every falsity and every evil can be so confirmed as to make the falsity appear like truth and the

evil like good, let it be proved, for example, that light is darkness and darkness light. May it not be asked, What is light
in itself? Is it anything more than a something that appears
to the eye according to its state? What is light to the closed
eye? Have not bats and birds of night such eyes that they
see light as darkness and darkness as light? I have been told
that some men see in this way; and that the infernals, although
they are in darkness, still see each other. Does not man have
light in his dreams in the middle of the night? Thus is not
darkness light, and light darkness? But it may be answered:
What of this? Light is light as truth is truth; and darkness
is darkness as falsity is falsity. [4] Take another example:
It is to be proved that a raven is white. May it not be said
that its blackness is only a shade that is not its real self? Its
feathers are white within, so is its body; and these are the substances of which the bird is formed. As its blackness is a
shade, so the raven grows white when it gets old—such have
been seen. What is black in itself but white? Pulverize black
glass, and you will see that the powder is white; therefore when
you call the raven black you speak from the shadow and not
from the reality. But the reply may be, What of this? In
this way all birds might be called white. Although all this is
contrary to sound reason it has been presented to show how
confirmations can be found for falsity that is directly opposite
to the truth, and for evil that is wholly opposite to the good.
[5] Secondly: *When falsity has been confirmed the truth is not
seen, but from confirmed truth falsity is seen.* All falsity is in
darkness, and all truth is in light; and in darkness nothing is
seen, and what any thing is is known only by handling it; in
light it is otherwise. For this reason, in the Word falsities are
called darkness, and thus those that are in falsities are said to
walk in darkness and in the shadow of death. On the other
hand, truths are there called light, and therefore those who are
in truths are said to walk in the light, and are called children
of light. [6] There are many things to show that when falsity has been confirmed truth is not seen, and that from con-

firmed truth falsity is seen. For example, who could see any spiritual truth if it were not taught in the Word? Would there not be merely thick darkness that could be dispelled only by means of the light in which the Word is, and only in him who is willing to be enlightened? What heretic can see his falsities unless he admits the genuine truths of the church? He does not see them before. I have spoken with those who have confirmed themselves in faith separate from charity; and when asked whether they saw how much is said in the Word about love and charity, about works and deeds, and keeping the commandments, and that he is called blessed and wise who does them, and foolish who does them not, they said, that while reading all this they saw it only as a matter of faith, and thus they passed it by with their eyes shut, as it were. [7] Those that have confirmed themselves in falsities are like those who see cracks in a wall; and in the shades of evening they see them in their fancies as a horseman or a man, but this fanciful image is dispelled by the inflowing light of day. Who can have a sense of the spiritual uncleanness of adultery except one who is in the spiritual cleanness of chastity? Who can have a sense of the cruelty of revenge except one who is in good from love of the neighbor? Who that is an adulterer, or that is eager for revenge, does not sneer at those who call the delights of such things infernal, and on the other hand, call the delights of conjugial love and of love for the neighbor heavenly? And so on. [8] Thirdly: *An ability to confirm whatever one pleases is not intelligence, but only ingenuity, which may exist even in the worst of men.* There are some who are very skilful in confirming, who have no knowledge of any truth and yet are able to confirm both truth and falsity; and some of them ask, What is truth? Is there any? Is not that true that I make true? And yet such are believed in the world to be intelligent; although they are but wall plasterers. Only those who perceive truth to be truth are intelligent, and they confirm truth by verities continually perceived. There is little discernible difference between these two classes, because there is little discernible

difference between the light of confirmation and the light of
the perception of truth; and those who are in the light of
confirmation seem to be also in the light of the perception
of truth; and yet the difference between them is like that
between illusive light and genuine light; and illusive light is
such that in the spiritual world it is turned into darkness
when genuine light flows in   Such illusive light prevails with
many in hell, and when these are brought into genuine light
they see nothing at all. From all this it is clear that the
ability to confirm whatever one pleases is mere ingenuity, and
may exist even in the worst of men. [9] Fourthly: *There is
confirmation that is intellectual and not at the same time voluntary; but all voluntary confirmation is also intellectual.* This
may be illustrated by examples. Those who confirm the doctrine of faith separate from charity and yet live a life of charity, or in general those who confirm falsity of doctrine and yet
do not live according to it, are those that are in intellectual
confirmation and not at the same time in voluntary, while
those that confirm falsity of doctrine and live according to it
are those that are in both voluntary and intellectual confirmation. The reason of this is that the understanding does not
flow into the will, but the will flows into the understanding.
This also shows what falsity of evil is, and what falsity not of
evil is. Falsity not of evil can be conjoined with good, but falsity of evil cannot, for the reason that falsity not of evil is
falsity in the understanding and not in the will; while falsity
of evil is falsity in the understanding from evil in the will;
[10] Fifthly: *The confirmation of evil that is voluntary and
also intellectual causes man to believe that his own prudence is
everything and the Divine providence nothing; but this is not
true of intellectual confirmation alone.* There are many who
by worldly appearances confirm in themselves, their own prudence and yet do not deny the Divine providence; with such
there exists only intellectual confirmation; while with those
who at the same time deny the Divine providence there exists
also voluntary confirmation; but this, together with persua-

sion, exists chiefly with those who are worshipers of nature and also worshipers of self. [11] Sixthly: *Every thing confirmed by the will and also by the understanding remains to eternity, but not what has been confirmed by the understanding only.* For that which pertains to the understanding alone is not within the man but is outside of him; it is merely in the thought; and nothing enters into man and is appropriated to him except what is accepted by the will, for it then comes to be of his life's love. That this remains to eternity will be considered in the following number.

319. Every thing confirmed by the will and also by the understanding remains to eternity, because every one is his own love, and his love belongs to his will; also because every man is his own good or his own evil, for every thing that is called good, and likewise evil, belongs to the love. As man is his own love he is also a form of his love, and may be called the organ of his life's love. It has been said above (n. 279), that the affections of the love and consequent thoughts of man are changes and variations of the state and form of the organic substances of his mind. What these changes and variations are and their nature shall now be explained. Some idea of them may be gathered from the heart and lungs, where there are alternate expansions and compressions or dilations and contractions, which in the heart are called systole and diastole and in the lungs respirations; these are a reciprocal distension and retraction or reciprocal stretching apart and closing together of their lobes. Such are the changes and variations of the state of the heart and lungs. There are like changes in the other viscera of the body, and changes more similar in their parts, by which the blood and the animal juice are received and carried onward. [2] Like things are to be found in the organic forms of the mind, which are the subjects of man's affections and thoughts, as has been shown above; with the difference that their expansions and compressions, or reciprocations, are relatively in such higher perfection as cannot be expressed in the words of natural language, but only in those of spiritual language, and these can be defined in no other way than that they are vortex-like circlings inward and outward, after the manner of perpetual and incurving spirals wonderfully bundled together into forms receptive of life. [3] The nature of these purely organic substances and forms in the evil and in the good shall now be stated. In the good these spiral forms are turned forward, but in the evil backward; and the spiral forms turning forward are turned towards the Lord and receive influx from Him, while those turning backward are turned towards hell and receive influx therefrom. It is to be known that so far as they are turned backward they are open behind and closed in front; and on the other hand, so far as they are turned forward they are opened in front and closed behind. [4] From all this it is evident what kind of a form or organ an evil man is, and what kind of a form or organ a good man is, namely, that they are turned in contrary directions; and as the turning when once fixed cannot be reversed it is clear that such as man is when he dies such he remains to eternity. It is the love of man's will that makes the turning, that is, that converts and inverts, for, as has been said above, every man is his own love. It is from this that every man after death goes the way of his own love—he that is in a good love to heaven, and he that is in an evil love to hell, and he finds rest only in that society where his reigning love is; and what is wonderful, every one knows the way; it is like following a scent with the nose.

320. (4) *If man believed, as is the truth, that all good and truth are from the Lord and all evil and falsity from hell, he would not appropriate good to himself and make it meritorious, nor appropriate evil to himself and make himself guilty of it.* But as this is contrary to the belief of those who have confirmed in themselves the appearance that wisdom and prudence are from man, and do not flow in according to the state of the organization of men's minds (of which just above, n. 319), it must now be made clear; and for the sake of distinctness this shall be done in the following order: (1) To one who confirms in himself the appearance that wisdom and prudence are from

21

man, and are therefore in him as his, it must needs seem that otherwise he would not be a man, but a beast or a statue; and yet the contrary is the truth. (2) To believe and think, as is the truth, that every good and truth is from the Lord and every evil and falsity from hell, appears like an impossibility; and yet it is the truly human principle, and therefore the angelic. (3) To believe and think thus is impossible to those who do not acknowledge the Divinity of the Lord, and who do not acknowledge that evils are sins; but it is possible to those who do acknowledge these two things. (4) Those that are in these two acknowledgments, so far as they shun and turn away from evils as sins need only to reflect upon the evils in themselves and cast them away from themselves to the hell from whence they are. (5) Thus the Divine providence does not appropriate evil to any one, nor good to any one, but his own prudence appropriates both.

321. These things shall now be explained in the proposed order. First: *To one who confirms in himself the appearance that wisdom and prudence are from man and are in man as his, it must needs seem that otherwise he would not be a man, but a beast or a statue ; and yet the contrary is the truth.* It is from a law of the Divine providence that man should think as if from himself, and should act prudently as if from himself, but should nevertheless acknowledge that he does it from the Lord. From this it follows that he who thinks and acts prudently as if from himself and at the same time acknowledges that he does it from the Lord is a man; while he who confirms in himself that every thing he thinks and does is from himself is not a man; neither is he a man who, because he knows that wisdom and prudence are from God, still waits for influx; for the latter becomes like a statue, and the former like a beast. It is evident that one who simply waits for influx will become like a statue, for he must needs stand or sit motionless, with hands hanging down, and eyes either shut or open without winking, with neither thought nor animation. What is there, then, of life in him? [2] It is also evident that he who believes that

every thing that he thinks and does is from himself is not unlike a beast, for he thinks only from the natural mind which is
common to man and beast, and not from the spiritual rational
mind which is the truly human mind; for this mind recognizes
that God alone thinks from Himself, and that man thinks from
God. Consequently such a man knows no difference between
a man and a beast except that a man talks and a beast makes
sounds; and he believes that they both die in like manner.
[3] Of those who await influx there is something more to be
said. They receive no such influx [as they expect] with the
exception that a few, who from the heart desire it, occasion-
ally receive a kind of response through a vivid perception in
thought, or by a tacit speech therein, and rarely by clear speech,
to the effect that they should think and act as they wish and
thus as they can, and that he who acts wisely is wise and he
who acts foolishly is foolish; but they are never thus instructed
what to believe or to do; and this in order that human rationality and liberty may not perish; which are given that every
one may act from freedom in accordance with reason, to all appearance as if from himself. Those who are taught by influx
what to believe or what to do are not taught by the Lord or by
any angel of heaven, but by some enthusiastic spirit, Quaker
or Moravian, and are led astray. All influx from the Lord takes
place by enlightenment of the understanding, and by an affection for truth, and through this affection into the understanding. [4] Secondly: *To believe and think, as is the truth, that
every good and truth is from the Lord and every evil and falsity from hell appears like an impossibility; and yet it is the
truly human principle, and therefore the angelic.* To believe
and think that every good and truth is from God seems possible, provided nothing further is said, for the reason that this
is in accordance with theological faith, contrary to which it is
not allowable to think. But to believe and think that every
evil and falsity is from hell appears impossible, since man must
then believe also that he cannot think at all. Yet man does
think as if from himself even though from hell, because the

Lord gives to every one the appearance that his thought is in him as his own, from whatever source it may be. Otherwise man would not live as a man, nor could he be led out of hell and led into heaven, that is, reformed, as has been frequently shown above. [5] So, too, the Lord enables man to know, and from that to have the thought, that he is in hell when he is in evil, and that he thinks from hell when he thinks from evil; He also enables him to think about the means by which he may come out of hell and not think from it, and may come into heaven and think there from the Lord; and He also gives man freedom of choice. From all this it can be seen that man is able to think evil and falsity as if from himself, also to think that this or that is evil or false; consequently that it is only an appearance that he does this from himself, without which appearance man would not be a man. To think from the truth is the truly human principle and therefore the angelic; and this truth is that man does not think from himself, but that it is granted him by the Lord to think to all appearance as if from himself. [6] Thirdly: *To believe and think thus is impossible to those who do not acknowledge the Divinity of the Lord and who do not acknowledge that evils are sins; but it is possible to those who do acknowledge these two things.* It is impossible to those who do not acknowledge the Lord's Divinity because it is the Lord alone that enables man to think and to will; and those who do not acknowledge the Lord's Divinity, being disjoined from Him, believe that they think from themselves. It is also impossible to those who do not acknowledge evils as sins, because such think from hell; and in hell every one imagines that he thinks from himself. But that it is possible to those who do acknowledge these two things can be seen from what has been fully set forth above (n. 288–294). [7] Fourthly: *Those that are in these two acknowledgments, so far as they shun and turn away from evils as sins need only to reflect upon the evils in themselves, and to cast them away to the hell from whence they are.* Every one knows or is capable of knowing that evil is from hell and good from heaven; therefore every one can know that so far as a man shuns and turns away from evil so far he shuns and turns away from hell. So, too, every one can know that so far as any one shuns and turns away from evil so far he wills and loves good; consequently so far he is delivered from hell by the Lord and led to heaven. All this every rational man can see, provided he knows that there is a heaven and a hell, and that evil is from its own origin, and good from its own origin. If, then, a man reflects upon the evils in himself (which is the same thing as examining himself) and shuns them, he then frees himself from hell and casts it behind him; and introduces himself into heaven, and there beholds the Lord face to face. It is said that man does this, but he does it as if from himself, but in fact from the Lord. When from a good heart and from a pious faith man acknowledges this truth it lies inwardly hidden in all that he afterwards thinks and does as if from himself, like the prolific principle in a seed, which inwardly accompanies its growth even to new seed; or like the pleasure in the appetite for food that a man has once recognized to be wholesome for him; in a word, it is like heart and soul in all that he thinks and does.

[8] Fifthly: *Thus the Divine providence does not appropriate evil to any one nor good to any one, but his own prudence appropriates both.* This follows from all that has now been said. Good is the end of the Divine providence; this it therefore purposes in all its workings. Consequently it does not appropriate good to any one, for good would thus be made meritorious; nor does it appropriate evil to any one, for thus man would be made guilty of the evil. Nevertheless, man does both of these from what is his own (*proprium*) because this is nothing but evil, that of his will that is his own being the love of self, and that of his understanding that is his own being the conceit in his own intelligence; and from this is his own prudence.

EVERY MAN MAY BE REFORMED, AND THERE IS NO SUCH THING
AS PREDESTINATION.

322. Sound reason declares that all men were predestined
to heaven, and no one to hell; for all are born men, and in consequence the image of God is in them.   The image of God in
them is the ability to understand truth and to do good.   The
ability to understand truth is from the Divine wisdom, and the
ability to do good is from the Divine love.   This ability is the
image of God, which remains in every sane man, and is not
eradicated.   From this comes his ability to become a civil and
moral man; and the civil and moral man can also become spiritual, for the civil and moral is a receptacle of the spiritual.
He is called a civil man who knows the laws of the kingdom
wherein he is a citizen and lives according to them; and he is
called a moral man who makes these laws his morals and his
virtues, and from reason lives them.   [**2**] It shall now be told
how a civil and moral life is a receptacle of spiritual life: Live
these laws, not only as civil and moral laws, but also as Divine
laws, and you will be a spiritual man.   Scarcely a nation exists so barbarous as not to have prohibited by laws murder,
adultery with the wife of another, theft, false-witness, and injury to what is another's.   The civil and moral man observes
these laws, that he may be, or may seem to be, a good citizen;
but if he does not also regard these laws as Divine he is
merely a civil and moral natural man; while if he does also
regard them as Divine he becomes a civil and moral spiritual
man.   The difference is that the latter is both a good citizen
of the earthly kingdom and a good citizen of the heavenly
kingdom; while the former is a good citizen of the earthly
kingdom only, and not of the heavenly kingdom.   The difference is seen in the goods they do; the goods done by civil and
moral natural men are not in themselves good, for the man
and the world are in them; the goods done by civil and moral
spiritual men are good in themselves, because the Lord and
heaven are in them.   [**3**] From all this it can be seen that as

every man was born that he might become a civil and moral natural man, so, too, he was born that he might become a civil and moral spiritual man; and this is done simply by his acknowledging God and not doing evil because it is against God, but doing good because it is accordant with God, whereby a spirit enters into his civil and moral activities, and they live; otherwise there is no spirit in them, and therefore they are not living. And this is why the natural man, however civilly and morally he may act, is called dead; but the spiritual man is called living. [4] It is of the Lord's Divine providence that every nation has some religion; and the primary thing in every religion is to acknowledge that there is a God, otherwise it is not called a religion; and every nation that lives according to its religion, that is, that refrains from doing evil because it is contrary to its god, receives something of the spiritual in its natural. When one hears some Gentile say that he is unwilling to do this or that evil because it is contrary to his god, does he not say to himself, Is not this man saved? it seems as if it could not be otherwise. Sound reason declares this to him. On the other hand, when he hears a Christian say, I make no account of this or that evil; why is it said to be contrary to God? does he not say to himself, Is this man saved? it seems impossible. Sound reason declares this also. [5] If such an one says, I was born a Christian, I have been baptized, I have known about the Lord, I have read the Word, I have attended the sacrament of the Supper—does this amount to anything if he does not regard murders, or the revenge that breathes them, adulteries, secret thefts, false testimony or lies, and various kinds of violence, as sins? Does such a man think about God or any eternal life? Does he believe that there is any God or any eternal life? Does not sound reason declare that such a person cannot be saved? All this has been said respecting a Christian, because a Gentile thinks about God from religion in his life more than a Christian does. But on this more shall be said in what follows, and in this order:—

(1) The end of creation is a heaven from the human race.

(2) Therefore it is of the Divine providence that every man can be saved; and that those are saved who acknowledge God and live well.

(3) Man himself is to blame if he is not saved.

(4) Thus all men were predestined to heaven, and no one to hell.

323. (1) *The end of creation is a heaven from the human race.* That heaven consists of none but those that were born men is shown in the work on *Heaven and Hell* (published at London in the year 1758), and also above; and as heaven consists of no others it follows that the end of creation is a heaven from the human race. That this was the end of creation has been shown previously (n. 27–45); but it will be made still clearer by an explanation of these points: (1) Every man was created to live to eternity. (2) Every man was created to live to eternity in a state of blessedness. (3) Thus every man was created to come into heaven. (4) The Divine love must needs will this; and the Divine wisdom must needs provide for it.

324. Since from all this it can be seen that the Divine providence is a predestination to heaven only, and cannot be changed into any other, it shall now be shown, in the proposed order, that the end of creation is a heaven from the human race. First: *Every man was created to live forever.* In the treatise on *The Divine Love and the Divine Wisdom*, Parts Third and Fifth, it has been shown that there are three degrees of life in man, called the natural, the spiritual, and the celestial, and that these degrees are actually in every man; while in beasts there is only one degree of life, which is like the lowest degree in man, which is called the natural. From this it follows that by the elevation of his life to the Lord man is above the beasts, in such a state as to be able to understand what pertains to the Divine wisdom, and to will what pertains to the Divine love, thus to receive the Divine; and a being that is capable of so receiving the Divine as to see and perceive it in himself cannot but be conjoined with the Lord, and by that conjunction live

forever. [2] What would the Lord be in relation to the entire
creation of the universe, if He had not also created images and
likenesses of Himself, to whom He could communicate His
Divine? Otherwise, what would He be but a causing something to be or not to be, or to exist or not to exist, and this for
no other purpose than that He might be able from afar to con-
template mere vicissitudes and continual changes as upon a
stage? What of the Divine would there be in these things,
unless they had as their end to be serviceable to subjects that
could receive the Divine more nearly, and see and feel it? And
as the Divine is of glory inexhaustible, would He keep this to
Himself alone, or would it be possible for Him to do so? For
love desires to communicate its own to another, and even to
give from its own as much as it can. Must not the Divine
love, then, which is infinite, do this? Can that give and take
away again? Would not that be to give what must perish?
and inwardly in itself this is nothing, because when it perishes
it comes to naught. That which *is* is not in it. But the Divine love gives what *is*, or what does not cease to be; and that
is eternal. [3] In order that every man may live to eternity
that which is mortal in him is taken away. The mortal in him
is his material body, and this is taken away by its death. Thus
what is immortal in man, which is his mind, is unveiled, and
he then becomes a spirit in human form; his mind is that
spirit. That man's mind cannot die the sages or wise men of
old saw; for they said, How can the mind (*animus seu mens*)
die, when it has the capacity to be wise? What their interior
idea of this was few at this day know; but it was an idea that
descended from heaven into their general perception, namely,
that God is wisdom itself, and of this man is a partaker, and
God is immortal or eternal. [4] As it has been granted me to
talk with angels I will also say something from experience. I
have talked with those who lived many ages ago, with those
who lived before the flood, and with some who lived after it,
with those who lived in the time of the Lord, and with one of
His apostles, and with many who lived in later ages, and they

all appeared like men of middle age, and they said that they knew nothing about death except that it is damnation. All that have lived well, when they enter heaven come into an age like that of their early manhood in the world and continue in it to eternity, even those that had been old and decrepit in the world. Women also, although they had been old and wrinkled, return into the flower of their age and beauty. [5] That man after death lives to eternity is clear from the Word, where life in heaven is called "eternal life" (as in *Matt.* xix. 29; xxv. 46; *Mark* x. 17; *Luke* x. 25; xviii. 30; *John* iii. 15, 16, 36; v. 24, 25, 39; vi. 27, 40, 68; xii. 50); also simply "life" (in *Matt.* xviii. 8, 9; *John* v. 40; xx. 31); also the Lord said to the disciples:—

> Because I live ye shall live also (*John* xiv. 19);

and of the resurrection, that:—

> God is not a God of the dead but of the living; and that they cannot die any more (*Luke* xx. 36, 38).

[6] Secondly: *Every man was created to live to eternity in a state of blessedness.* This follows as a consequence; for He who wills that man should live to eternity also wills that he should live in a state of blessedness. What would eternal life be without that? All love desires the good of another—the love of parents desires the good of their children; the love of bridegroom and husband desires the good of his bride and wife; and friendship's love desires the good of friends;—why not, then, the Divine love? And what else is this good but delight? And what is Divine good but eternal blessedness? Every good is called good from its delight or its blessedness. What is given or possessed is indeed called goods; but unless these are delightful they are barren goods that in themselves are not good. From all this it is clear that eternal life is also eternal blessedness. This state of man is the end of creation; and that only those who come into heaven are in that state is not the Lord's fault, but man's. That it is man's fault will be seen in what follows. [7] Thirdly: *Thus every man was created to come into heaven.* This is the end of creation. But the reason why

all do not come into heaven is that they imbibe the delights of hell, which are opposite to the blessedness of heaven; and those that are not in the blessedness of heaven cannot enter heaven, for they cannot endure it. It is denied to no one who comes into the spiritual world to ascend into heaven; but when one who is in the delight of hell enters it he is seized with palpitation of the heart and labored breathing, his life begins to fail, he is in anguish, he is in torment, and he writhes like a serpent put near a fire; and this is so because opposite acts against opposite. [8] And yet such cannot die, because they were born men and thereby have the capacity to think and will, and consequently to speak and do; but as they can live only with those who are in a like delight of life to such they are sent; consequently those who are in the delights of evil are sent to their own, and those who are in the delights of good to their own. Every one, in fact, is permitted to be in the delight of his evil provided he refrains from infesting those who are in the delight of good; but as evil cannot do otherwise than infest good—for there is in evil a hatred against good—to prevent their doing harm they are taken away and cast into their own places in hell, where their delight is turned into what is undelightful. [9] But this does not gainsay the truth that man from creation is such, and therefore is born such, that he can enter heaven; for every one who dies in infancy enters heaven, is there brought up and instructed as a man is in the world, and through an affection for good and truth imbibes wisdom and becomes an angel. And the same might be true of the man who is brought up and instructed in the world; for there is the same in him as in the infant. Respecting infants in the spiritual world see the work on *Heaven and Hell* (published at London in the year 1758, n. 329–345). [10] But the reason why many in the world are not prepared for heaven is that they love the first degree of their life, which is called the natural, and are unwilling to withdraw from it and become spiritual; and the natural degree of life viewed in itself loves nothing but self and the world, for it clings to the senses of the body, and these reach out towards the world; while the spiritual degree of life viewed in itself loves the Lord and heaven, and also self and the world, but God and heaven as higher, chief and dominant, and self and the world as lower, instrumental, and subservient. [11] Fourthly: *The Divine love must needs will this, and the Divine wisdom must needs provide for it.* That the Divine essence is Divine love and Divine wisdom has been fully shown in the work on *The Divine Love and the Divine Wisdom.* It is also shown there (n. 358–370) that in every human embryo the Lord forms two receptacles, one for the Divine love and the other for the Divine wisdom, the receptacle of the Divine love for the future will of the man, and the receptacle of the Divine wisdom for his future understanding; and that thus the Lord has endowed every man with a capacity to will good and a capacity to understand truth. [12] Since, then, man from his birth is endowed with these two capacities by the Lord, and consequently the Lord is in these capacities as in His own with man, it is clear that His Divine love must needs will that man should come into heaven, and there enjoy eternal blessedness; also that the Divine wisdom must needs provide for it. But since it is from the Lord's Divine love that man should feel heavenly blessedness in himself as his own, and this is impossible unless man is kept fully in the appearance that he thinks, wills, speaks and acts from himself, therefore the Lord can lead man only in accordance with the laws of His Divine providence.

325. (2) *Therefore it is of the Divine providence that every man can be saved, and that those are saved who acknowledge God and live well.* It is clear from what has been shown above that every man can be saved. Some hold the opinion that the Lord's church is only in the Christian world, because there alone is the Lord known, and there alone is the Word. Nevertheless there are many who believe that the church of God is general, that is, is spread and dispersed throughout the world, and thus exists with such as are ignorant of the Lord and do not have the Word; and they claim that this is not the fault of

such, and that they have no means of overcoming their ignorance, and that it is contrary to God's love and mercy that any
should be born for hell who equally with others are men.   [2]
Since, then, many, if not all, Christians believe that the church,
which is also called a communion, is general, it follows that
there are most general principles of the church which enter into
all religions and constitute that communion.   That these most
general principles are the acknowledgment of God and good of
life will be seen in the following order : (1) The acknowledgment of God causes a conjunction of God with man and of man
with God; and the denial of God causes disjunction.   (2) Every
one acknowledges God and is conjoined with Him according to
his good of life.   (3) Good of life, or living rightly, is shunning
evils because they are against religion, thus against God.   (4)
These are the general principles of all religions, whereby every
one can be saved.

326. But these must be examined and shown one by one.
First: *The acknowledgment of God causes a conjunction of God
with man and of man with God ; and the denial of God causes
severance.*   Some may think that those who do not acknowledge
God can be saved just as well as those who do acknowledge
Him, provided they lead a moral life.   They say, What does
acknowledgment accomplish?   Is it not mere thought?   Can I
not easily acknowledge God when I come to know with cer-
tainty that there is a God?   I have heard of Him, but I have not
seen Him.   Make me see and I will believe.   Such is the language
of many who deny God when they are allowed to reason freely
with one who acknowledges God.   But that the acknowledgment of God conjoins and the denial of Him separates will be
made clear by certain things made known to me in the spiritual
world.   When any one there thinks about another and wishes to
speak with him, the other immediately appears present.   This
is a common occurrence there, and never fails.   And the reason
is that in the spiritual world there is no distance as in the natural world, but only an appearance of distance.   [2] Again, As
thought from any knowledge of another causes presence, so love

from any affection for another causes conjunction; and from this it results that such come together and converse in a friendly way, dwell in the same house or in the same society, meet frequently, and render mutual services. The opposite also occurs, as that he who does not love another, or still more, he who hates another, does not see or meet him, but they are distant in the degree of their hatred or absence of their love; and even if he is present and recalls the hatred he becomes invisible. [3] From these few examples the ground of presence and of conjunction in the spiritual world can be seen, namely, that presence comes from the remembrance of another with a desire to see him, and conjunction from an affection that springs from love. The same is true of all things in the human mind; in it are things without number, and the particulars are there associated and conjoined according to affections, or as one thing loves another. [4] This conjunction is spiritual conjunction, which is like itself in things general and particular. This spiritual conjunction has its origin from the conjunction of the Lord with the spiritual world and with the natural world, in general and in particular. From all this it is evident that so far as any one knows the Lord, and from his knowledge thinks about Him, so far the Lord is present; and so far as any one acknowledges the Lord from an affection of love so far the Lord is conjoined with him; and on the other hand, so far as one does not know the Lord the Lord is absent; and so far as one denies the Lord he is separated from Him. [5] Conjunction causes the Lord to turn the man's face to Himself, and then He leads him. Severance causes hell to turn the man's face to itself, and he is then led by hell. Therefore all the angels of heaven turn their faces to the Lord as a sun; and all the spirits of hell turn their faces away from Him. This makes clear what acknowledgment of God accomplishes, and what the denial of God accomplishes. And those who deny God in the world deny Him after death; and they acquire an organization such as is described above (n. 319), and the organization taken on in the world remains to eternity. [6] Secondly: *Every one acknowl-*

edges God and is conjoined with Him according to his good of life. All who know anything from religion can know God, and from knowledge or memory they can talk about God and some from the understanding can also think about Him; but if they do not live well this effects nothing but presence; for with all this they can turn themselves away from God and turn towards hell, and this they do if they live wickedly. But only those who live well can acknowledge God in heart; and these, according to their good of life, the Lord turns away from hell and towards Himself. This is because these alone love God, for they love the Divine things that are from Him in that they do them. The Divine things that are from God are the commandments of His law; these are God because He is Himself His own proceeding Divine; and this is loving God, for the Lord says :—

He that keepeth My commandments, he it is that loveth Me; but he that keepeth not My commandments loveth Me not (*John* xiv. 21–24).

[7] For this reason there are two tables of the Decalogue, one relating to God and the other relating to man. God works unceasingly to the end that man may receive what is in man's table; but if man fails to do the things that are in his table he does not accept with acknowledgment of heart the things that are in God's table; and if he does not accept he is not conjoined. This is why the two tables were so conjoined as to be one, and were called the tables of the covenant, "covenant" signifying conjunction. Every one acknowledges God and is conjoined with Him according to the good of his life, for the reason that good of life is like the good that is in the Lord, and that thus comes from the Lord; consequently when man is in good of life a conjunction is effected. With evil of life the opposite is true. This rejects the Lord. [8] Thirdly: *Good of life, or living rightly, is shunning evils because they are against religion, thus against God.* That this is good of life, or living rightly, is fully shown in the *Doctrine of Life for the New Jerusalem,* from beginning to end. To which I will merely add,

that if you do good to the fullest extent—for example, building temples, decorating them and filling them with offerings, sustaining hospitals and asylums, giving alms every day, succoring widows and orphans, observing diligently the holy things of worship, and even thinking and talking and preaching about them as if from the heart, and yet do not shun evils as sins against God, none of these goods are good; they are either hypocritical or meritorious, for evil is still inwardly in them. For one's life is in all things and in each one of the things that he does; and goods can become goods only by the removal of evil from them. All this makes clear that living rightly is shunning evils because they are against religion, and thus against God. [9] Fourthly: *These are the general principles of all religions, whereby every one can be saved.* To acknowledge God and to refrain from doing evil because it is against God are the two things that make a religion to be a religion; and if one of these is lacking it cannot be called a religion, for to acknowledge God and to do evil is a contradiction; also to do good and not acknowledge God; for one is not possible without the other. The Lord provides that there shall be some religion nearly everywhere, and that there shall be these two things in every religion. The Lord also provides that every one who acknowledges God and refrains from doing evil because it is against God should have a place in heaven. For heaven in the complex resembles a single man, whose life or soul is the Lord. In that heavenly Man are all things that are in a natural man, with a difference like that between heavenly and natural things. [10] It is known that in man, in addition to forms organized of blood-vessels and nervous fibers, which are called viscera, there are also skins, membranes, tendons, cartilages, bones, nails, and teeth; these are living in a less degree than the organized forms themselves to which they are subservient as ligaments, coverings, and supports. So the heavenly Man, which is heaven, if all these things are to be in it, must be composed not of men of a single religion but of men of many religions; therefore all who make these two universals of the church to enter into their life have a place in that heavenly Man, that is, in heaven, and enjoy happiness in their degree. But more on this subject may be seen above (n. 254). [11] That these two are the primary principles in every religion is shown by the fact that they are what the Decalogue teaches; and the Decalogue was the first thing of the Word, was promulgated by Jehovah by a living voice from Mount Sinai, was written by the finger of God on two tables of stone, and when placed in the ark was called "Jehovah," and constituted the Holy of Holies in the tabernacle, and the sanctuary in the temple at Jerusalem, and from its presence alone all things there were holy; besides other things in the Word respecting the Decalogue in the ark, cited in the *Doctrine of Life for the New Jerusalem* (n. 53–61); to which the following may here be added: It is known from the Word that the ark containing the two tables on which the Decalogue was written was taken by the Philistines and placed in the temple of Dagon in Ashdod, and that Dagon fell to the earth before it, and afterward his head and the palms of the hands torn from the body lay upon the threshold of the house; and that the people of Ashdod and Ekron, to the number of many thousands, were smitten with emerods on account of the ark, and their land was laid waste by mice; also that the Philistines, by the advice of the lords of their nation, made five golden emerods and five golden mice and a new cart, and placed the ark upon it, and near the ark the golden emerods and mice, and by two cows that lowed in the way before the cart they sent back the ark to the children of Israel, who offered the cows and the cart in sacrifice (1 *Sam.* v., and vi.). [12] It shall now be told what all these things signified. "The Philistines" signified those who are in faith separated from charity; "Dagon" represented that religion; the "emerods" with which they were smitten signified natural loves, which are unclean when separated from spiritual love; the "mice" signified the devastation of the church by means of falsifications of truth; the "new cart" upon which they sent back the ark signified new but natural doctrine (a "chariot" signifying in the Word doctrine from spiritual

22

truths); the "cows" signified good natural affections; the "golden emerods" signified natural loves purified and made good; the "golden mice" signified the vastation of the church removed by good ("gold" in the Word signifying good), "the lowing of the cows on the way" signified the difficult conversion of the lusts of evil of the natural man into good affections; "the offering of the cows and the cart as a burnt offering" signified that the Lord was thus propitiated. [13] Such is the spiritual meaning of these historical statements. Join them together into one idea, and make the application. That the "Philistines" represented those who are in faith separated from charity may be seen in the *Doctrine of the New Jerusalem concerning Faith* (n. 49–54); and that the ark, because of its containing the Decalogue, was the holiest thing of the church, may be seen in the *Doctrine of Life for the New Jerusalem* (n. 53–61).

327. (3) *Man himself is to blame if he is not saved.* Every rational man, as soon as he hears it, acknowledges the truth that evil cannot flow from good or good flow from evil, because they are opposites; consequently that from good nothing but good can flow, and from evil nothing but evil. When this truth is acknowledged it is also acknowledged that good can be turned into evil, but by an evil recipient not by a good recipient; for every form turns into its own quality that which flows into it (as may be seen above, n. 292). Since, then, the Lord is good in its very essence, or good itself, it is evident that evil cannot flow from Him or be produced by Him, but that the good may be turned into evil by a recipient subject whose form is a form of evil. Such a subject is man in respect to what is his own (*proprium*). This continually receives good from the Lord and continually turns it to the quality of its own form, which is a form of evil. From this it follows that man is to blame if he is not saved. It is true that evil is from hell; but as man accepts it therefrom as his own, and thereby appropriates it to himself, it is the same thing whether evil is said to be from man or from hell. But how evil comes to be appropriated, even to the extent that religion is destroyed, shall be told in this order: (1) In process of time every religion declines and is consummated. (2) Every religion declines and is consummated by the inversion of God's image in man. (3) This comes from the continual increase of hereditary evil from generation to generation. (4) Nevertheless the Lord provides that every one may be saved. (5) It is provided also that a new church should follow the previous devastated church.

328. But these points are to be made clear in their series. First: *In process of time every religion declines and is consummated.* On this earth there have been several churches, one after another; for wherever the human race exists there a church exists, because heaven, which is the end of creation, is from the human race (as has been shown above), and no one can come into heaven unless he is in the two universals of the church, acknowledgment of God and a good life (as has been shown just above, n. 326). It follows that on this earth there have been churches from the most ancient times down to the present. These churches are described in the Word, but not historically, except the church of Israel and Judah; but there were several previous to that, and these are described only by the names of nations and persons, and by a few things respecting them. [2] The Most Ancient Church, which was the first, is depicted by "Adam and his wife Eve." The church that followed, which shall be called the Ancient Church, is depicted by "Noah and his three sons," and by their posterity. This was a wide-spread church extending through many kingdoms of Asia,—the land of Canaan on both sides of the Jordan, Syria, Assyria, and Chaldea, Mesopotamia, Egypt, Arabia, and Tyre and Sidon. These had the ancient Word treated of in the *Doctrine of the New Jerusalem concerning the Sacred Scripture* (n. 101–103). That this church existed in those kingdoms is evident from various things said of them in the prophetical parts of the Word. But this church was notably changed by Heber, from whom arose the Hebraic Church, in which worship by

sacrifices was first instituted. From the Hebrew Church sprang
the Church of Israel and Judah; and this was solemnly established for the sake of the Word, which was there to be com-
piled. [3] These four churches are meant by

The statue seen by Nebuchadnezzar in a dream, the head of which was
of pure gold, the breast and arms of silver, the belly and thighs of brass,
and the legs and feet of iron and clay (*Dan.* ii. 32, 33).

Nor is any thing else meant by the golden, the silver, the brazen, and the iron ages, mentioned by ancient writers. It is well
known that the Christian Church followed the Jewish. From
the Word it may also be seen that all these churches in process
of time declined until they reached their end, which is called
their consummation. [4] The consummation of the Most Ancient Church, which came from their "eating of the tree of
knowledge" (which signifies the conceit of self-intelligence), is
depicted by the flood. The consummation of the Ancient Church
is depicted in the various devastations of the nations, treated
of both in the historical and in the prophetical parts of the
Word, especially in the expulsion of the nations from the land
of Canaan by the children of Israel. The consummation of the
Church of Israel and Judah is meant by the destruction of the
temple at Jerusalem, and by the carrying away of the people
of Israel into perpetual captivity, and of the Jewish nation to
Babylon, and again by the second destruction of the temple
together with Jerusalem, and the dispersion of that nation.
This consummation is foretold in the prophets in many places
and in *Daniel* (ix. 24–27). The gradual devastation of the
Christian Church until its end is depicted by the Lord in *Matthew* xxiv., in *Mark* xiii., and in *Luke* xxi., but the consummation itself in the *Apocalypse*. From all this it can be seen that
a church in process of time—and religion also—declines and is
consummated. [5] Secondly: *Every religion declines and is
consummated by the inversion of God's image in man.* It is
known that man was created into God's image, after God's
likeness (*Gen.* i. 26). It shall now be told what the "image"

and what the "likeness" of God is. God alone is love and wisdom. Man was created to be a receptacle of both, that his will might be a receptacle of the Divine love and his understanding a receptacle of the Divine wisdom. It has already been shown that these two receptacles are in man from creation, and that they constitute man, and are formed in every one in the womb. Therefore man's being an "image" of God means that he is a recipient of the Divine wisdom, his being a "likeness" of God means that he is a recipient of the Divine love; thus the receptacle called the understanding is an image of God, and the receptacle called the will is a likeness of God. As man, then, was created and formed to be a receptacle, it follows that he was so created and formed that his will might receive love from God, and his understanding might receive wisdom from God; and these man does receive when he acknowledges God and lives according to His commandments, but in a less or greater degree as from religion he has knowledge of God and of His commandments, consequently according to his knowledge of truths; since it is truths that teach what God is and how He must be acknowledged, also what His commandments are and how to live according to them. [6] God's image and God's likeness are not destroyed in man, but are seemingly destroyed; for they remain implanted in his two capacities called liberty and rationality (which have been frequently treated of above). They became seemingly destroyed when man made the receptacle of Divine love, which is his will, a receptacle of love of self, and the receptacle of Divine wisdom, which is his understanding, a receptacle of self-intelligence. In this way he inverted the image and likeness of God, for he turned these receptacles away from God and turned them towards self. Thus they were closed above and opened below, or closed in front and opened behind, although by creation they had been opened in front and closed behind. When these have been thus opened inversely and closed inversely the receptacle of love, or the will, receives influx from hell, or from what is its own (*proprium*); and the receptacle of wisdom, or the understanding, likewise.

From this there has sprung up in the churches a worship of men in place of the worship of God, and a worship from doctrines of falsity in place of a worship from doctrines of truth; the latter from self-intelligence, the former from love of self. This makes clear how in process of time religion declines and is consummated by the inversion of God's image in man. [7] Thirdly: *This comes from the continual increase of hereditary evil from generation to generation.* It was stated and explained above that hereditary evil did not come from Adam and his wife Eve by their eating of the tree of knowledge, but is gradually derived and is transplanted from parents into offspring, and thus by continual increase grows worse from generation to generation. When evil thus grows worse among many it scatters evil from itself among others still; for there is a lust of seducing in all evil, and in some this burns with rage against good; hence the contagiousness of evil. When in the church this has taken possession of the leaders, the rulers, and the champions, religion becomes perverted, and the means of cure, which are truths, become corrupted by falsification. From these there is then a gradual vastation of good and desolation of truth in the church, until its consummation is reached. [8] Fourthly: *Nevertheless the Lord provides that every one may be saved.* The Lord provides that there shall be everywhere a religion; and that in every religion there shall be the two essentials of salvation, which are, to acknowledge God and to refrain from doing evil because it is against God. All other things, which belong to the understanding and to thought therefrom, and which are called matters of faith, are provided for every one according to his life, for they are accessories of the life; and yet if they are put before [the essentials] they receive no life. It is also provided that all that have lived well and have acknowledged God shall be instructed after death by angels; and then those that had been while they lived in the world in these two essentials of religion, accept the truths of the church such as they are in the Word and acknowledge the Lord as the God of heaven and of the church. And this they accept more readily than Christians, who have brought with them from the world an idea of the Lord's Human as separated from His Divine. The Lord also provides that all who die in infancy shall be saved, wherever born. [9] Moreover, there is granted to every man after death ample means of amending his life, if that be possible. All are taught and led by the Lord by means of angels; and as they then know that they are living after death, and that there is a heaven and a hell, they at first receive truths; but those that in the world did not acknowledge God and shun evils as sins soon weary of truths and withdraw; while those that acknowledged truths with the lips but not with the heart are like the foolish virgins who had lamps but no oil, and who begged oil of others, and who went away and bought, and yet were not admitted to the wedding. "Lamps" signify truths of faith, and "oil" signifies the good of charity. From this it can be seen that the Divine providence makes it possible for every one to be saved, and that man himself is to blame if he is not saved. [10] Fifthly: *It is provided also that a new church should follow the previous devastated church*. This has been done from the earliest times, that when a former church has been devastated a new church has followed. The Ancient Church followed the Most Ancient; after the Ancient Church the Israelitish or Jewish Church followed; and after this the Christian. It is foretold in the *Apocalypse* that this also will be followed by a new church, which is there meant by "the New Jerusalem coming down out of heaven." Why the Lord is providing a new church to follow the former devastated church is explained in the *Doctrine of the New Jerusalem concerning the Sacred Scripture* (n. 104–113).

329. (4) *Thus all men were predestined to heaven, and no one to hell.* That the Lord casts no one into hell, but that the spirit does this of his own accord, is shown in the work on *Heaven and Hell* (published at London in 1758, n. 545–550). This every evil and impious person does after death, and the evil and impious man in the world does the same, with the difference that so long as he is in the world he is capable of being reformed and of accepting and being instructed in the means of salvation, but not after his departure from the world. The means of salvation relate to these two points, that evils must be shunned because they are contrary to the Divine laws in the Decalogue, and there must be an acknowledgment that there is a God. This every one can do provided he does not love evils; for the Lord is continually flowing into his will with a power that enables him to shun evils, and into his understanding with a power that enables him to think that there is a God. Nevertheless, no one can do the one apart from the other; the two are joined together like the two tables of the Decalogue, one of which relates to the Lord, and the other to man. The Lord from His table enlightens every man and gives him power, but man receives the power and enlightenment only so far as he does the things commanded in his table; before this these two appear to be lying one upon the other, and closed up with seals; but as man does the things commanded in his table they are unsealed and opened. [2] What is the Decalogue at the present day but like a little sealed book or writing, opened only in the hands of children and youth? Say to any one of mature age that a thing should not be done because it is contrary to the Decalogue, and who listens? But if you say that it should not be done because it is contrary to the Divine laws, he might listen. And yet the commandments of the Decalogue are the Divine laws themselves. An experiment was made with several in the spiritual world, and when the Decalogue or catechism was mentioned they rejected it with contempt. This was because the Decalogue in its second table, which is man's, teaches that evils must be shunned ; and he who does not shun them (whether from impiety or from the religious tenet that works effect nothing, but faith only) can hear the Decalogue or catechism mentioned only with some degree of contempt, as he might some book for little children which is no longer of any use to him. [3] All this has been said to make clear that no. one who wishes to be saved is left without a knowledge of the means, or without the power by which he may be saved. And from this it follows that all men were predestined to heaven and no one to hell. But as a belief about predestination to non-salvation, which is damnation, has been held by some, and as this belief is pernicious, and can be dispelled only when the madness and cruelty in it are recognized by the reason, it shall be considered in the following order: (1) Any predestination except to heaven is contrary to the Divine love and its infinitude. (2) Any predestination except to heaven is contrary to the Divine wisdom and its infinitude. (3) That only those born within the church are saved is an insane heresy. (4) That any of the human race are damned by predestination is a cruel heresy.

330. To make clear how pernicious the belief in predestination is as generally understood these four propositions must be taken up and established. First: *Any predestination except to heaven is contrary to the Divine love, which is infinite.* That Jehovah or the Lord is Divine love, and that He is infinite and the Being (*Esse*) of all life, and that man was created into the image of God after the likeness of God, has been shown in the work on *The Divine Love and the Divine Wisdom.* And as every man is formed by the Lord in the womb into that image after that likeness (as has also been shown), it follows that the Lord is the heavenly Father of all men, and that men are His spiritual children. Thus is Jehovah or the Lord called in the Word, and men likewise; for He says:—

Call no man your father upon the earth, for One is your Father, who is in the heavens (*Matt.* xxiii. 9);

which means that He alone is the Father in respect to the life; and that the earthly father is the father only in respect to the life's covering, which is the body; therefore in heaven no father is mentioned except the Lord. That men who do not pervert that life are said to be His sons and to be born of Him is also evident from many passages in the Word. [2] Thus it can be seen that the Divine love is in every man, both the evil and the good; consequently that the Lord who is Divine love can not act towards them otherwise than as a father on the earth acts towards his children, and infinitely more so, because the Divine love is infinite; and again, that He cannot withdraw from any one because every one's life is from Him.   He appears to withdraw from the evil; but the evil withdraw from Him, while He from love still leads them.   So the Lord says:—

Ask and it shall be given you; seek and ye shall find; knock and it shall be opened unto you.   What man is there of you who if his son ask for a loaf will give him a stone?   If ye, then, being evil, know how to give good gifts unto your children, how much more shall your Father who is in the heavens give good things to them that ask Him? (*Matt.* vii. 7–11).

And elsewhere that

He maketh His sun to rise on the evil and on the good, and sendeth rain on the just and on the unjust (*Matt.* v. 45).

Moreover, it is admitted in the church that the Lord wills the salvation of all, and the death of no one.   All this shows that any predestination except to heaven is contrary to the Divine love.   [3] Secondly: *Any predestination except to heaven is contrary to the Divine wisdom, which is infinite.*   The Divine love through its Divine wisdom provides the means whereby every man can be saved; consequently to say that there is any predestination except to heaven is to say that the Divine love is unable to provide the means by which there is salvation.   Nevertheless, as has been shown above, all have the means, and they are from the Divine providence, which is infinite.   But the reason why there are some that are not saved is that the Divine love wills that man should feel in himself the happiness and blessedness of heaven, since otherwise it would not be heaven to him; and this is impossible unless man's thinking and willing is made to appear to him to be from himself.   For without this appearance nothing could be appropriated to him, nor would he be a man.   This is the purpose of the Divine providence, which is of the Divine wisdom from the Divine love.   [4] But this does not invalidate the truth that all are predestined to heaven and none to hell; and yet it would if the means of salvation were lacking. But that means of salvation have been provided for every one, and that heaven is such that all who live well, of whatever religion they may be, have a place there, has been shown above. Man is like the earth, which produces fruits of every kind, and it is because of this power that the earth is the earth; and that it produces bad fruits also does not preclude its ability to produce good fruits also, but this would be precluded if the earth had never had the ability to produce any thing except bad fruits. Again, man is like an object that variegates in itself the rays of light; if the object presents nothing but disagreeable colors the light is not the cause, for rays of light are also capable of being variegated in pleasing colors. [5] Thirdly: *That only those born within the church are saved is an insane heresy.* Those born out of the church are men equally with those born within it, they are from the same heavenly origin, and are equally living and immortal souls. They also have a religion from which they acknowledge that there is a God, and that they must live rightly; and he who acknowledges God and lives rightly becomes spiritual in his degree and is saved, as has been shown above. It may be said that such have not been baptized; but baptizing saves none except those that are spiritually washed, that is, regenerated; for baptism is for a sign and a memorial of this. [6] Such, it may be said, have no knowledge of the Lord, and without the Lord there is no salvation. But no one is saved for the reason that the Lord is known to him, but because he lives in accordance with the Lord's commandments; and the Lord is known to every one who acknowledges God, for He is the God of heaven and earth, as He Himself teaches (*Matt.* xxviii. 18, and elsewhere). Furthermore, those outside of the church have the idea of God as a man more than Christians have; and those that have the idea of God as a man and live well are accepted by the Lord. Such also acknowledge God as one in person and essence, as Christians do not. They also think of God in their life, for they make evils to be sins against God; and those who do this think of God in their life. Christians have the precepts of religion from the Word, but there are few who draw from it any precepts of life. [7] The Papists do not read it; and the Reformed, who are in faith separated from charity, pay no attention to what relates to life in it, but only to what relates to faith; and yet the whole Word is nothing but a doctrine of life. Christianity exists only in Europe; Mohammedanism and Gentilism exist in Asia, in the Indies, in Africa and America, and the human race in those parts of the globe is ten times more numerous than in the Christian portion; and in the latter there are few who place religion in life. What more insane belief, then, can there be than to hold that only these latter are saved and the former are damned, and that man gains heaven by his birth and not by his life? Therefore the Lord says :—

I say unto you that many shall come from the east and west, and shall recline with Abraham and Isaac and Jacob in the kingdom of the heavens; but the children of the kingdom shall be cast out (*Matt.* viii. 11, 12).

[8] Fourthly : *That any of the human race are damned by predestination is a cruel heresy.* For it is cruel to believe that the Lord, who is love itself and mercy itself, suffers so immense a multitude of men to be born for hell, or so many myriads of myriads to be born condemned and doomed, that is, born devils and satans, and that He does not from His Divine wisdom provide that those who live well and acknowledge God shall not be cast into eternal fire and torment. And yet He is the Lord, the Creator and Saviour of all, and He alone leads all and wills not the death of any. It is therefore cruel to believe and think that so great a multitude of nations and peoples under His auspices and oversight have been handed over by predestination as a prey to the devil.

THE LORD CANNOT ACT CONTRARY TO THE LAWS OF THE
DIVINE PROVIDENCE, BECAUSE ACTING CONTRARY TO THEM
WOULD BE ACTING CONTRARY TO HIS DIVINE LOVE AND
CONTRARY TO HIS DIVINE WISDOM, THUS CONTRARY TO
HIMSELF.

331. It has been shown in the *Angelic Wisdom concerning
the Divine Love and the Divine Wisdom* that the Lord is Divine love and Divine Wisdom, and that these two are Being
(*Esse*) itself and life itself, from which every thing has being
and life. It is also there shown that this same goes forth from
Him, also that the Divine that goes forth is Himself. Of all
that goes forth the Divine providence is primary, for this is
continually in the end for the sake of which the universe was
created. The operation and progress of the end through means
is what is called the Divine providence. Since, then, the Divine
that goes forth is Himself, and the Divine providence is the
primary thing that goes forth, it follows that to act contrary to
the laws of His Divine providence is to act contrary to Himself.
[2] It may be said furthermore, that the Lord is Providence,
as it is said that God is Order, for the Divine providence is
Divine order with primary regard to the salvation of men; and
as there is no order possible without laws, for laws are what
constitute order, and every law derives from order that it is
order, it follows that as God is order so is He the Law of His
order. The same is to be said of the Divine providence, that
as the Lord is His providence He is also the law of His providence. From this it is evident that the Lord cannot act contrary to the laws of His providence, for to act contrary to them
would be to act contrary to Himself. [3] Again, there can be
no operation except upon a subject and upon it through means;
operation except upon a subject and upon it through means is
impossible. The subject of the Divine providence is man; the
means are the Divine truths whereby man gains wisdom and
the Divine good whereby he gains love. The Divine providence through these means works out its end, which is man's

salvation; for he that wills an end wills the means also, consequently in willing to accomplish an end he accomplishes it through means. But all this will become more evident when examined in the following order:—

(1) The operation of the Divine providence for the salvation of man begins at his birth and continues until the end of his life and afterwards to eternity.

(2) The operation of the Divine providence goes on unceasingly through means, out of pure mercy.

(3) Instantaneous salvation from mercy apart from means is impossible.

(4) Instantaneous salvation from mercy apart from means is "the fiery flying serpent" in the church.

332. (1) *The operation of the Divine providence for the salvation of man begins at his birth and continues until the end of his life and afterwards to eternity.* It has been shown above that a heaven from the human race is the essential end of the creation of the universe, and that this end in its operation and progress is the Divine providence for the salvation of men; also that all things exterior to man, and that are serviceable to him in the way of use, are secondary ends of creation, which in brief have relation to all things in the three kingdoms, the animal, the vegetable, and the mineral. When these things go forth regularly in accordance with the laws of Divine order established in their first creation, how is it possible for the primary end, which is the salvation of the human race, not to go forth regularly in accordance with the laws of its order, which are the laws of the Divine providence? [2] Watch a fruit tree. Does it not first have birth as a slender shoot from a small seed, and does it not afterwards gradually grow to a trunk and spread forth branches, which are covered with leaves, and then put forth blossoms, and bring forth fruit, depositing therein new seeds by which it provides for its perpetuity? The same thing occurs with every shrub, and with every herb of the field. In these do not each thing and all things go forth regularly and wonderfully from end to end in accordance with the laws of its order? Why not likewise the primary end, which is a heaven from the human race? Can there be any thing in its progress that does not go on most regularly in accordance with the laws of the Divine providence? [3] As there is a correspondence between man's life and the growth of a tree, let a parallel or comparison be drawn between them. Man's infancy is comparatively like the tender shoot of a tree sprouting up out of the ground from the seed; his childhood and youth are like that shoot growing into a trunk with its little branches; the natural truths that every one first imbibes are like the leaves with which the branches are covered ("leaves" in the Word signifying nothing else); the man's initiation into the marriage of good and truth, that is, the spiritual marriage, is like the blossoms that the tree brings forth in the spring time; spiritual truths are the petals of these flowers; the primary activities of the spiritual marriage are like the beginnings of the fruit; spiritual goods, which are the goods of charity, are like the fruit (and these are signified by "fruit" in the Word); the procreations of wisdom from love are like the seeds, and by these procreations man becomes like a garden or a paradise. Moreover, man is depicted in the Word by a "tree;" and his wisdom originating in love by a "garden" ("the garden of Eden" signifies nothing else). [4] In fact, man is a corrupt tree from the seed; nevertheless, a grafting or budding with shoots taken from the tree of life is possible, whereby the sap drawn from the old root is turned into sap forming good fruit. This comparison has been made to show that when there is so regular a progression of the Divine providence in the growth and regeneration of trees, there must needs be a regular progression in the reformation and regeneration of men, who are of much more value than trees, according to these words of the Lord:—

Are not five sparrows sold for two farthings, and not one of them is forgotten in the sight of God? But the very hairs of your head are all numbered. Fear not, therefore; ye are of more value than many sparrows. And which of you by being anxious can add to his stature one cubit? If ye, then, be not able to do that which is least, why are ye anxious concerning the rest? Consider the lilies how they grow. If, then, God so clothe the grass, which is today in the field and tomorrow is cast into the oven, how much more will He clothe you, O ye men of little faith? (*Luke* xii. 6, 7, 25–28).

333. The operation of the Divine providence for the salvation of man is said to begin at his birth and to continue unto the end of his life. To understand this it must be known that the Lord sees what man is, and foresees what he wills to be, thus what he will be; and that he may be a man and therefore immortal the freedom of his will must not be taken away, as has been frequently shown before. Consequently the Lord foresees man's state after death, and provides for it from his birth until the end of his life. With the evil the Lord provides by permitting evils and continually withdrawing them from evils; while with the good He provides by leading to good. Thus the Divine providence is unceasingly in the work of saving men. But no more can be saved than are willing to be saved, and those are willing to be saved who acknowledge God and are led by Him; and those are unwilling who do not acknowledge God and who lead themselves; for such do not think about eternal life or about salvation, while the others do. This the Lord sees and still He leads them, and leads them in accordance with the laws of His Divine providence, contrary to which laws He cannot act, since to act contrary to them would be to act contrary to His Divine love and contrary to His Divine wisdom, which is to act contrary to Himself. [2] Since, then, the Lord foresees the states of all after death, and also foresees the places in hell of those who are not willing to be saved, and the places in heaven of those who are willing to be saved, it follows that for the evil, as has been said, the Lord provides their places by permitting and by withdrawing, and for the good by leading; and unless this were done unceasingly from every one's birth until the end of his life neither heaven nor hell would continue to exist, for without that foresight and providence together neither heaven nor hell would be anything but confusion. That the Lord from foresight has provided for every one his place may be seen above (n. 202, 203). [3] This may be illustrated by this comparison. If an archer or a marksman should aim at a mark, and behind the mark a straight line were drawn for a mile, and if he should err only by a finger's breadth in his aim, his missile or ball keeping on to the end of the mile would depart very far from the line. So would it be if the Lord did not every moment, and even every least fraction of a moment, regard the eternal in His foreseeing and providing every one's place after death. But this the Lord does because the entire future is present to Him and the entire present is to Him the eternal. That the Divine providence in every thing it does has regard to the infinite and eternal may be seen above (n. 46–69, 214, *seq.*).

334. It is also said that the operation of the Divine providence will continue to eternity, since every angel is perfecting in wisdom to eternity, but each according to the degree of that affection for good and truth in which he was when he left the world. It is this degree that is being perfected to eternity. Anything beyond this degree is outside of the angel and not within him, and that which is outside of him cannot be perfected within him. This is meant by the

Good measure, pressed down and shaken together and running over, that shall be given into the bosom of those who forgive and give to others (*Luke* vi. 37, 38),

that is, who are in good of charity.

335. (2) *The operation of the Divine providence goes on unceasingly, through means, out of pure mercy.* There are means and modes of the Divine providence. Its means are the things whereby man becomes a man and is perfected in respect to his understanding and his will; its modes are the ways whereby these things are accomplished. The means whereby man becomes a man and is perfected in respect to his understanding in general are called truths, which in the thought become ideas, and in the memory are called things. In themselves they are knowledges, of which sciences consist. All these means, viewed

23

in themselves, are spiritual; but as they are in natural things, from their covering or clothing they appear as if natural, and some of them as if material. These means are infinite in number and infinite in variety; they are more or less simple or compound, also more or less imperfect or perfect. There are means for forming and perfecting natural civil life, for forming and perfecting rational moral life, and for forming and perfecting heavenly spiritual life. [2] These means follow in succession, one kind after another, from infancy to the last period of man's life, and after that to eternity; and as they follow in their growth, so the prior become the means of those that come after, for they enter into every thing that is formed as mediate causes, since from these causes every effect or every conclusion becomes effective, and thus becomes a cause. Thus in succession the posterior [or last] become means; and as this process goes on to eternity no last or outmost which brings to an end is possible. For as the eternal is without end so the wisdom that increases to eternity is without end. If wisdom with a wise man were to come to an end, the delight of his wisdom, which consists in the perpetual multiplication and fructification of wisdom, would perish, and thus the delight of his life would perish; and the delight of glory, in which alone there is no heavenly life, would take its place, and the wise man is then no longer like a youth, but like an old man, and finally like one decrepit. [3] Although the wisdom of a wise man increases to eternity in heaven there is still no such approximation of angelic wisdom to the Divine wisdom as to touch it. It may be compared to a straight line drawn near a hyperbola which is said to approach it continually but never to touch it; also to what is said about squaring the circle. All this makes clear what is meant by the means whereby the Divine providence operates in order that man may be a man, and may be perfected in respect to his understanding, and that these means are what are commonly called truths. Equally numerous are the means whereby man is formed and perfected in respect to his will; but these are what are commonly called goodnesses. From these man has love, while from the former he has wisdom. Their conjunction makes the man, for such as the conjunction is such is the man. This conjunction is what is called the marriage of good and truth.

336. The modes, however, by which the Divine providence operates upon the means and by the means to form man and to perfect him are also infinite in number and infinite in variety; they are as numerous as the operations of the Divine wisdom from the Divine love to save man, thus as numerous as the operations of the Divine providence in accordance with its laws, which have been treated of above. How secret these modes are has been illustrated above by the operations of the soul upon the body, of which man knows so little as to amount to scarcely anything; as how the eye sees, the ear hears, the nose smells, the tongue tastes, and the skin feels, how the stomach digests, the mesentery elaborates the chyle, and the liver the blood; how the pancreas and spleen purify the blood, the kidneys separate it from impure humors, the heart collects and distributes it, the lungs clarify it; and how the brain refines the blood and vivifies it anew; besides innumerable other things, all of which are secrets into which scarcely any science can penetrate. Evidently then it can penetrate still less into the secret operations of the Divine providence; it is enough to know its laws.

337. The Divine providence does all things out of pure mercy, because the Divine essence itself is pure love, and it is this that works by means of the Divine wisdom; and it is this operation that is called the Divine providence. This pure love is pure mercy, for these reasons: (1) It is operative with all men throughout the whole world, who are such that they have no ability of their own. (2) It is equally operative with the evil and unjust, and with the good and just. (3) It leads the former in hell and rescues them from it. (4) It there perpetually strives with them and fights for them against the devil, that is, against the evils of hell. (5) To this end it came into the world, and endured temptations even to the last of them, which was the passion of the cross. (6) It unceasingly acts with the unclean to make them clean and with the insane to make them sane; thus it labors unceasingly out of pure mercy.

338. (3) *Instantaneous salvation from mercy apart from means is impossible.* It has been shown in what precedes that the operation of the Divine providence to save man begins at his birth and continues until the end of his life, and afterwards to eternity; also that this operation goes on unceasingly, through means, out of pure mercy. From this it follows that neither instantaneous salvation nor mercy apart from means is possible. But as many who do not think about matters pertaining to the church or to religion from the understanding believe that they are saved by mercy apart from means, and therefore that salvation is instantaneous; and as this is contrary to the truth, and is a pernicious belief, it is important that it should be considered in its proper order: (1) The belief in instantaneous salvation out of mercy apart from means has been adopted from the natural state of man. (2) This belief comes from an ignorance of the spiritual state, which is wholly different from the natural state. (3) The doctrines of all the churches in the Christian world, viewed interiorly, are opposed to instantaneous salvation out of mercy apart from means, but it is upheld, nevertheless, by the external men of the church. [2] First: *The belief in instantaneous salvation out of mercy apart from means has been adopted from the natural state of man.* The natural man from his state does not know otherwise than that heavenly joy is like worldly joy, and that it flows in and is received in the same way; for example, that it is like the experience of a poor man becoming rich, who thus passes from the sad state of poverty into a happy state of opulence; or like one of low standing who becomes honored, and who thus passes from disdain to glory; or like one who goes from a house of mourning to the joy of a wedding. As these states may be changed in a day, and there is no other idea of man's condition after death, the source of the belief in instantaneous salvation out of mercy apart from means is evident. [3] Moreover, in the world, many may be together in one company or in one civil community, and may enjoy themselves together, and yet all differ in mind; this occurs in man's natural state, and the reason is that the external of one man can be accommodated to the external of another, however unlike their internals may be. From this natural state another conclusion is drawn, that salvation is merely admission into heaven among the angels, and that this admission is from mercy apart from means. Consequently it is believed also that heaven can be granted to the evil as well as to the good, and that their association is then like that in the world, with the difference that it is full of joy. [4] Secondly: *This belief comes from an ignorance of the spiritual state, which is wholly different from the natural state.* The spiritual state, that is, the state of man after death, has been treated of above in many places; and it has been shown that every one is his own love, and that no one can live with any except those who are in a like love, and if he comes among others he cannot breathe his own life. It is from this that every one after death comes into the society of his own, that is, of those who are in a like love, and that he recognizes these as relatives and as friends; and what is wonderful, when he meets them and sees them it is as if he had been acquainted with them from infancy. Spiritual relationship and friendship are the cause of this. And what is more, no one in a society can occupy any house but his own, each one in a society has his own house, and this he finds ready for him as soon as he enters the society. Outside of his house he may be in close companionship with others, and yet he can stay nowhere except in his own house. And still further, in another's apartment no one can sit any where except in his own place; if he sits elsewhere he becomes like one who has no command of his mind and is dumb; and what is wonderful, whenever one enters a room he knows his own place. The same is true in places of worship, and of those who come together in public assemblies. [5] All this makes clear that the spiritual state is wholly different from the natural, and is such that no one can be any where but where his ruling love is, for there the delight of his life is, and every one wishes to be in the delight of his life, and a man's spirit cannot be elsewhere because that delight is what constitutes his life, even his very breathing and the motion of his heart. In the natural world it is different. In this world man's external is thoroughly taught from infancy to simulate in countenance, word, and gesture, other delights than those that belong to his internal. Consequently from a man's state in the natural world no conclusion can be formed about what his state will be after death; for every one's state after death is a spiritual state, which is, that he can be nowhere except in the delight of his own love, which delight he acquired by his life in the natural world. [6] All this makes clear that no one can be admitted into the delight of heaven, which is commonly called heavenly joy, who is in the delight of hell; or what is the same, no one who is in the delight of evil can be admitted into the delight of good; and this may be still more clearly concluded from this, that after death no one is forbidden to ascend into heaven; the way is shown him, opportunity is given him, and he is admitted; but as soon as he enters heaven and breathes in its delight he begins to suffer pain in his chest, to be tortured in his heart, to feel as if swooning, under which he writhes like a serpent brought near the fire; and with his face turned away from heaven and turned towards hell he flees precipitately, and does not rest until he has entered the society belonging to his own love. Evidently, therefore, no one enters heaven out of mercy apart from means; consequently mere admittance does not, as many in the world suppose, amount to anything, neither is there any such thing as instantaneous salvation, for this supposes mercy apart from means. [7] There were some who had believed in the world in instantaneous salvation by mercy apart from means, and when they became spirits they desired to have their infernal delight, or their delight in evil, changed by Divine omnipotence and also by Divine mercy into heavenly delight or delight in good. And because they greatly desired this the angels were permitted to do it; but as soon as the angels had taken away their infernal delight, since it was the delight of

their life's love, consequently their life, they lay as if dead,
deprived of all sense and all motion; and it was impossible to
breathe into them any other life than their own, because all
things of their mind and body had been turned backward and
could not be reversed. They were therefore resuscitated by admitting again the delight of their life's love. After this they
said that in that state they interiorly had felt something awful
and horrible which they were unwilling to divulge. For this
reason it is said in heaven that it is easier to change an owl into
a turtle-dove, or a serpent into a lamb, than any infernal spirit
into an angel of heaven. [8] Thirdly: *The doctrines of the
churches in the Christian world, viewed interiorly, are opposed
to instantaneous salvation out of mercy apart from means; but
it is upheld, nevertheless, by the external men of the church.*
The doctrines of all churches, viewed interiorly, teach life.
What church is there the doctrine of which does not teach that
man ought to examine himself, to see and acknowledge his sins,
confess them, repent, and finally live a new life? Who is admitted to the Holy Communion without this admonition and
instruction? Inquire and you will be convinced. What church
is there the doctrine of which is not founded on the commandments of the Decalogue? and the commandments of the Decalogue are the commandments of life. What man of the church
is there in whom there is anything of the church who does not
acknowledge, as soon as he hears it, that he who lives well is
saved and he who lives wickedly is condemned? Therefore in
the Athanasian Creed (which is also the doctrine accepted in
the whole Christian world) it is stated:—

That the Lord will come to judge the living and the dead; and then
those that have done good will enter into life eternal, and those that have
done evil into eternal fire.

[9] This shows clearly that the doctrines of all churches, viewed
interiorly, teach life; and because they teach life they teach
that salvation is in accordance with the life; and the life of a
man is not breathed into him in a moment, but is gradually

formed, and is reformed by his shunning evils as sins; consequently, by his learning what sin is, recognizing and acknowledging it, and not willing it, and thus refraining from it, also by
gaining a knowledge of those means that have reference to a
knowledge of God.   By all these is man's life formed and reformed; and these cannot be poured into him in a moment, for
hereditary evil, which in itself is infernal, must be removed,
and in its place good, which in itself is heavenly, must be implanted.   From his hereditary evil man may be likened in
understanding to an owl and in will to a serpent; but when he
has been reformed he may be likened in understanding to a dove
and in will to a sheep.   Therefore instantaneous reformation
and salvation thereby would be comparatively like the instantaneous conversion of an owl into a dove, and of a serpent into
a sheep.   Who that has any knowledge of human life does not
see that this is impossible, except by the removal of the owl and
serpent nature and the implantation in its place of the dove and
sheep nature?   [**10**] It is also admitted that every one who is
intelligent can become more intelligent, and every one who is a
wise man can become wiser, and that intelligence and wisdom
may grow in man, and with some do grow, from infancy until
the end of life, and that man is thus perfected continually.   Is
this not still more true of spiritual intelligence and wisdom?
These ascend above natural intelligence and wisdom by two
degrees, and as they ascend they become angelic intelligence
and wisdom, which are ineffable.   That these increase to eternity with the angels has been stated above.   Cannot any one
who is willing understand that it is impossible for that which
is perfecting to eternity to be made perfect in an instant?

339. From all this it is clear that no one who from life thinks
about salvation thinks of any instantaneous salvation out of
mercy apart from means; but he thinks about the means of salvation into which and through which the Lord operates in
accordance with the laws of His Divine providence, and by
which, therefore, man is led by the Lord out of pure mercy.
But those who do not think of salvation from life ascribe in-

stantaneousness to salvation and absence of means to mercy, as those do who separate faith from charity (for charity is life); they also ascribe instantaneousness to faith at the closing hour of death, if not before. Those also do this who believe remission of sins without repentance to be an absolution from sins and thus salvation, and who go to the Holy Supper; also those that have faith in the indulgences of the monks and in their prayers for the dead and in the dispensations they grant because of the power they claim over the souls of men.

340. (4) *Instantaneous salvation out of mercy apart from means is the "fiery flying serpent" in the church.* By the "fiery flying serpent" evil glowing from infernal fire is meant, the same as by the "fiery flying serpent" spoken of in *Isaiah:*—

Rejoice not thou, Philistia, all of thee, because the rod that smote thee is broken; for out of the serpent's root shall go forth a basilisk; whose fruit shall be a fiery flying serpent (xiv. 29).

Such evil is flying abroad in the church when there is belief in instantaneous salvation out of mercy apart from means; for thereby: (1) Religion is abolished. (2) Security is induced. (3) Damnation is attributed to the Lord. [2] As to the first: *Religion is abolished thereby.* There are two things that are at once the essentials and the universals of religion, namely, acknowledgment of God and repentance. These two are void of meaning to those who believe that men are saved out of mere mercy, howsoever they live; for what need is there more than to say, "Have mercy on me, O God?" About all other things belonging to religion they are in thick darkness, and they even love this darkness. Of the first essential of the church, which is acknowledgment of God, they merely think, "What is God? Who has seen Him?" If it is said that there is a God and that He is one, they admit that He is one; if it is said that there are three, they admit that there are, but claim that the three must be called one. This is their acknowledgment of God. [3] To the other essential of the church, which is repentance, they give no thought, consequently they give no thought to any sin, and at last they do not know that there is any such thing as sin. And then they hear, and drink in with pleasure, that "The law does not condemn, because the Christian is not under its yoke; you have merely to say, 'God have mercy upon me for the sake of the Son,' and you will be saved." This with them is repentance of life. But take away repentance, or what is the same thing, separate life from religion, and what is left but the mere words, "Have mercy upon me?" For this reason they could not do otherwise than claim that salvation is instantaneous by means of these words, even near the hour of death if not before. What, then, is the Word to them but an obscure and enigmatical voice uttered from a tripod in a cave, or an unintelligible response from the oracle of an idol? In a word, when you take away repentance, that is, separate life from religion, what is man but evil glowing with infernal fire, or a " fiery flying serpent" in the church? For without repentance man is in evil, and evil is hell. [4] Secondly: *A belief in instantaneous salvation out of pure mercy alone induces security of life.* Security of life arises either from the impious man's belief that there is no life after death, or from the belief of him who separates life from salvation. The latter, although believing in eternal life, still thinks, " Whether I live well or ill I can be saved, since salvation is pure mercy, and God's mercy is universal because He desires not the death of any one." And if perchance the thought occurs that mercy ought to be implored in the words of the accepted faith, he may think that this, if not done previously, can be done just before death. Any man in such a state of security makes nothing of adultery, frauds, injustice, violence, defamation, and revenge, but lets his flesh and his spirit run riot in them all; nor does he know what spiritual evil and its lust are. If he listens to anything about this from the Word it is comparatively like something striking against ebony and rebounding, or like what falls into a ditch and is swallowed up. [5] Thirdly: *By that belief damnation is attributed to the Lord.* Who can help concluding that not man but the Lord is to blame if man is not saved, when the Lord is able to save every one out of pure mercy? If it be said that faith is the means of salvation, what man is there to whom that faith cannot be given? For it is nothing but a thought that may be imparted, even with confidence, in any state of the spirit withdrawn from worldly things. It may also be claimed that man cannot of himself acquire that faith; if, therefore, it is not given and the man is damned, must not he that is damned think that the Lord, who had the power to give it and would not, is to blame? And would not this be to call Him unmerciful? Moreover, in the glow of his faith he would say, "How can He see so many damned in hell when He is able out of pure mercy to save them all in a moment?" Other like things he may say that must be called abominable accusations against the Divine. From all this it can now be seen that a belief in instantaneous salvation out of pure mercy is the "fiery flying serpent" in the church.

* * *

Excuse the addition of what follows to fill out the rest of the sheet.

Certain spirits by permission ascended from hell, and said to me, "You have written many things from the Lord; write something from us, too."

I replied, "What shall I write?"

They said, "Write that every spirit, whether good or evil, is in his own delight; a good spirit in the delight of his good, and an evil spirit in the delight of his evil."

I asked, "What is your delight?"

They said, "It is a delight in committing adultery, stealing, cheating, and lying."

Again I asked, "What sort of delights are these?"

They said, "To the senses of others they are like the fetid smell from excrement, the putrid smell from dead bodies, and the odor from stagnant urine."

I said, "Are these things delightful to you?"

They answered, "Most delightful."

I said, " Then you are like the unclean beasts that live in such things."

They replied, " If we are we are; but such things are delicious to our nostrils."

I asked, " What more shall I write from you?"

They said, " Write this: that every one is permitted to be in his own delight, even that which is most unclean, as they call it, provided he does not infest good spirits and angels; but as we could not do otherwise than infest them we were driven away and cast into hell, where we suffer dreadful things."

I said, " Why did you infest the good?"

They replied that they could not do otherwise, that a sort of fury came upon them when they saw any angel and felt the Divine sphere around him.

Then I said, " Thus you are even like wild beasts."

When they heard this a fury came upon them that appeared like the fire of hatred; and to prevent their doing harm they were drawn back into hell.

Of delights perceived as odors and as foul smells in the spiritual world see above (n. 303–305).

INDEX OF SCRIPTURE PASSAGES

INDEX OF WORDS

THE DIVINE PROVIDENCE

AARON,

Although he made the golden calf and commanded the worship of it, could represent the Lord and His salvation (n. 132 [2]).

ABEL

Means love and charity (n. 242). (*See* CAIN.)

ABODE.

The Lord can have an *abode* in man or angel and dwell with them only in His own, and not in what is their own (*proprium*), for that is evil (n. 53 [3]).

ABOMINATE (TO).

So far as one shuns evils as diabolical and as obstacles to the Lord's entrance he is more and more nearly conjoined with the Lord, and he the most nearly who *abominates* them as so many dusky and fiery devils (n. 33 [3]).

ABSTRACT.

In one sense the finite can comprehend (the infinite) because there are *abstract* ideas by means of which the existence of things can be seen, if not the nature of them (n. 46).

ABUSE.

It is by the *abuse* of these powers (liberty and rationality) that man can seem in externals to be different from what he is in internals (n. 15). Man has the ability to misuse these faculties, and from freedom in accordance with reason to confirm whatever he pleases (n. 286).

ACCIDENTAL AND CASUAL

Are idle words (n. 70).

ACKNOWLEDGE.

Nothing can be *acknowledged* except by consent of the will (n. 231 [2]). Every one *acknowledges* God and is conjoined with Him according to his good of life (n. 325 [2], 326 [6]). All who lead an evil life interiorly *acknowledge* nature and human prudence alone (n. 205). Those who *acknowledge* God and His Divine providence are like the angels of heaven. . . . . But those who *acknowledge* nature and their own prudence are like spirits of hell (n. 208). He who does not *acknowledge* God cannot be saved (n. 91 [3]).

ACKNOWLEDGMENT OF GOD.

There can be an *acknowledgment* of the Lord from wisdom, and there can be an *acknowledgment* of the Lord from love. *Acknowledgment* of the Lord from wisdom is effected by doctrine; while *acknowledgment* of the Lord from love is effected by a life in accordance with doctrine. This produces conjunction, but the other presence (n. 91 [2]). The *acknowledgment* of God causes a conjunction of God with man and of man with God, and the denial of God causes severance (n. 326).

ACTING

From an enjoyment of love is *acting* from freedom, and since reason favors the love this is also *acting* in accordance with reason (n. 85).

ACTORS.

Of some who do not believe in the Divine at all, but play with Divine things outwardly like *actors* (n. 222 [2]).

ADAM.

By *Adam* and his wife the first of all mankind that were created on this earth are not meant, but the men of the Most Ancient Church and their new creation or their regeneration is thus described (n. 241, 313, 328 [2]). The state of innocence in which *Adam* and Eve his wife were (n. 275). Hereditary evil . . . is said to be from *Adam* and his wife, but this is an error, for every one is born into it from his parents (n. 277, 328 [7]). *Adam's* condemnation signifies the condemnation of the intellectual self (*proprium*) (n. 313 [3]). (*See also* n. 236, 251, 328.)

ADMISSION INTO HEAVEN.

No one enters *heaven* out of mercy apart from means, consequently mere *admittance* does not amount to anything (n. 338 [6]). After death no one is forbidden to ascend into *heaven;* the way is shown him, opportunity is given him, and he is *admitted* (n. 338 [6]).

ADULT.

(*See* MATURE MAN.)

ADULTERATION OF GOOD.

He that upholds evil loves does violence to Divine goods, and this violence is called *adulteration of good* (n. 231 [3]).

ADULTERY,

Its horrible nature. The love of *adultery* communicates with the lowest hell (n. 144 [3]).

AFFECTION.

Every *affection*, which in its essence is a subordinate love derived from the life's love, as a stream from its fountain, . . . has its delights (n. 195). They are derivations from the life's love of every one (n. 28 [3]). No one can perceive or think anything apart from *affection*, and every one perceives and thinks according to *affection* (n. 28 [4], 106). The affections of a man's life's love are known to the Lord alone (n. 197). By means of His Divine providence the Lord lead the *affections* of a man's life's love (n. 200). By means of His Divine providence the Lord combines the *affections* of the whole human race into one form, which is the human form (n. 201). Every *affection* for good and at the same time for truth is in its form a man (n. 66). External *affections* of thought manifest themselves in bodily sensation, but rarely in the thought of the mind. The internal *affections* of thought, from which the external *affections* have their existence, never manifest themselves before man (n. 199 [2]). Interior *affections* (join to themselves) mates called perceptions, and the exterior *affections* mates called thoughts (n. 194). Every *affection* has its mate, which is like a spouse—*affection* from natural love has knowledge, *affection* from spiritual love understanding, and *affection* from celestial love wisdom (n. 74 [2]). In beasts there is a marriage of *affection* and knowledge, the *affection* in them pertaining to natural good, and knowledge to natural truth (n. 74 [2]). With man it is otherwise. He has not only *affection* from natural love, but also *affection* from spiritual love, and *affection* from celestial love (n. 75). It is an *affection* from the love of good that makes heaven in man (n. 63). The derivatives of this love (of evil), which are its *affections*, are as many as are the evils into which it has determined itself (n. 33).

AFFECTIONS AND THOUGHT.

All *affection* is in heat, and *thought* is in light (n. 199). Every particular *affection* has its delight, and every particular perception and *thought* therefrom has its enjoyment (n. 195). No *affection* is possible apart from its *thought*, nor any *thought* apart from its *affection* (n. 194, 196). The *affections* of heaven and the lusts of hell are diametrically opposed to each other (n. 303). *Affection* corresponds to sound, and *thought* to speech (n. 296 [6]). As the sound of the voice with the spoken words spreads itself all about in the air of the natural world, so *affection and thought* spreads itself into societies in the spiritual world (n. 296 [6]). *Affections* associated with perceptions constitute man's internal, and the enjoyments of *affections* associated with *thoughts* constitute his external (n. 106). By means of His Divine providence the

Lord leads the *affections* of a man's life's love, and at the same time leads his *thoughts*, from which human prudence is derived (n. 200). *Affections and thoughts* exist in substantiated subjects (n. 279 [6]). *Affections*, which belong to the will, are nothing but changes and variations of state of the purely organic substances of the mind, and *thoughts*, which belong to the understanding, are nothing but changes and variations in the form of these substances (n. 279). The organic forms of the mind are the subjects of man's *affections and thoughts* (n. 319 [2]). *Affection* and the *thought* from it are not in space and time (n. 50 [2]).

AFRICANS (THE),

Believe more than others that their dead are human beings in the other life (n. 274[8]).

AGE.

All that have lived well, when they enter heaven come into an *age* like that of their early manhood in the world, and continue in it to eternity, even those that had been old and decrepit in the world. Women also, although they had been old and wrinkled, return into the flower of their *age* and beauty (n. 324[4]).

AGES.

The four churches—the Most Ancient, the Ancient, the Hebraic, and that of Israel and Judah—are meant by the golden, the silver, the brazen, and the iron *ages* mentioned by ancient writers (n. 328 [3]).

AGREEMENT

Is equivalent to doing the thing (n. 111 [2]).

ALLOWABLE.

Whatever is made *allowable* in the thought comes from the will, for there is then consent (n. 81). When a man believes any evil to be *allowable* he continually does it in his spirit (n. 81, 278*a*). Man must examine himself, not his deeds alone but his thoughts, especially what

evils he regards in his spirit as *allowabl*₄ (n. 278*a*). Such evils as a man believes to be *allowable*, even though he does not do them, are appropriated to him (n. 81).

ALPHABET.

In the spiritual world each letter in its *alphabet* signifies a single thing, and the several letters joined into a single word or making a person's name involve the entire state of the thing (n. 230).

AMBASSADOR.

Disputing with two priests about human prudence, whether it is from God or from man (n. 197 [2]).

AMERICA.

Gentilism exists in Asia, in the Indies, in Africa and *America* (n. 330 [7]).

AMMONITES (THE).

Each nation with which the children of Israel waged war signified some particular kind of evil (n. 251 [3]).

AMORITES (THE),

(As above, n. 251 [3].)

ANABAPTISM

Named amongst heresies (n. 259, 238).

ANALYTICALLY.

Whence man's power to think *analytically* (n. 317).

ANATOMICAL DETAILS.

(N. 164, 165, 174, 180, 181, 199, 279, 296, 319, 336.)

ANCIENT CHURCH (THE),

Is depicted (in the Word) by Noah and his three sons and by their posterity (n. 328 [2]).

ANGELS.

Love and wisdom constitute the life of *angels* (n. 28). *Angels* confess that they live from the Lord (n. 28, 158). *Angels* and spirits are affections that belong to love, and thoughts from affection (n. 50, 300, 301). All *angels* turn their faces to the Lord (n. 29 [2]). *An-*

gels do not from themselves turn their faces to the Lord, but the Lord turns them to Himself (n. 29 [2]). To their sight the Lord is above them in the sun there (n. 31). The *angels* of the third heaven perceive the influx of Divine love and Divine wisdom from the Lord (n. 158). Sometimes the Lord so fills an *angel* with His Divine that the *angel* does not know that he is not the Lord (n. 96 [6]). No one becomes an *angel*, that is, comes into heaven, unless he carries with him from the world what is *angelic* (n. 60).

ANSWERS BY INFLUX,

What results from it (n. 321 [3]).

ANTIPATHY.

Aversion and separation between heaven and hell (n. 303).

ANTIPODES.

Heaven and hell are diametrically opposite, as *antipodes* (n. 300).

AORTA

(N. 296 [14].)

APPEAR (TO).

Whatever one does from freedom, whether it be of reason or not, provided it is in accordance with his reason, *appears* to him to be his (n. 76 [2], 73 [6]). Sometimes, when in deep meditation, a man *appears* in his society in the spiritual world (n. 296 [6]). The Lord *appears* to angels at a distance like a sun; the reason (n. 162).

APPEARANCES.

Every *appearance* confirmed as a truth is converted into a fallacy (n. 220 [6], 310). When a man confirms *appearances* it is the same as asserting that the clothes are the man (n. 220 [6]). They who confirm themselves in *appearances* become natural (n. 187 [2]). Every man is permitted to speak from *appearance*, nor can he do otherwise (n. 162 [2]). Angels of the higher heavens, while they speak from *appearance* think from the truth (n. 162 [2]). To the an-

gels there is an *appearance* of space and time in accord with their states of affections and thoughts therefrom (n. 50). In the spiritual world the spaces are merely *appearances* (n. 29[1]). Why man is kept fully in the *appearance* that he thinks, wills, speaks, and acts from himself (n. 324 [12]). *Appearances* and fallacies (n. 213).

APPROPRIATE (TO).

The Divine providence appropriates neither evil nor good to any one; but man's own prudence *appropriates* both (n. 308). Whatever a man thinks, says and does from his will, whether good or evil, is *appropriated* to him and remains (n. 226). Whatever a man does from freedom in accordance with his thought is *appropriated* to him as his, and remains (n. 78). Nothing that a man merely thinks, nor even that which he thinks to will, is *appropriated* to him, unless at the same time he so far wills it as to do it if opportunity offers (n. 80). Such evils as a man believes to be allowable, even though he does not do them, are *appropriated* to him (n. 81). Nothing that a man has *appropriated* to himself can be eradicated; for it has come to be of his love and at the same time of his reason, and consequently of his life (n. 79). If man believed, as is the truth, that all good and truth are from the Lord and all evil and falsity from hell, he would not *appropriate* good to himself and make it meritorious, nor *appropriate* evil to himself and make himself guilty of it (n. 320). Goods are *appropriated* to man only in the sense that they are always the Lord's in man (n. 79 [3]).

APPROPRIATION

Of good and evil (n. 78–81, 320, 321). All things that a man thinks, says and does from the will are *appropriated* to him and remain (n. 227 [3]).

ARABIA

Was one of the countries where the Ancient Church existed, and in which the Ancient Word was known (n. 328 [2]).

ARCANA.

The *arcana* of heaven are innumerable, with scarcely one of which man is acquainted (n. 254). Man possesses the ability to understand the *secrets* of wisdom like the angels themselves (n. 223). Devils and satans understand the *arcana* of wisdom as well as angels, but only while they heard them from others (n. 99). *Arcana* of angelic wisdom cannot be comprehended by man unless his spiritual mind has been opened (n. 164). Angelic *arcana* (n. 4 [4], 124, 125, 163, 164, 254). The *arcanum* of *arcana* of angelic wisdom (n. 172 [6]).

ARGUMENTS.

Ordinary *arguments* against the Divine providence (n. 236–239); refuted (n. 241-274).

ARIANISM,

Its origin (n. 262 [2]). It reigns in the hearts of more people than is imagined (n. 262 [2]).

ARIANS,

Their final condition in the other life (n. 231 [6], *see also* n. 257 [4]).

ARK (THE),

Because of its containing the Decalogue, was the holiest thing of the (Israelitish) church (n. 326 [13]).

ARRANGEMENT (THE),

Of affections in heaven and of lusts in hell is wonderful, and is known to the Lord alone (n. 302).

ARROGATE.

To declare that one can open and close heaven, remit and retain sins, and therefore save and condemn men, is to *arrogate* to one's self Divine power (n. 257).

ARTERIES.

(N. 296 [14].)

AS IF BY HIMSELF.

(N. 164 [5].)

AS IF FROM HIMSELF.

(N. 76, 88 [2], 90, 92 [2], 95, 96 [2], 210, 321.)

AS IF IN HIMSELF.

(N. 54.)

AS IF OF HIMSELF.

(N. 102.)

ASSYRIA

Signifies the profanation of what is holy (n. 251 [3]). *Assyria* was one of the countries where the Ancient Church existed, and in which the Ancient Word was known (n. 328 [2]).

ATHANASIAN CREED.

(N. 127, 202 [2], 258 [4], 262, 338 [8].)

ATHANASIUS

Himself could not think otherwise than that three persons are three Gods when each person by Himself is God (n. 262). The Faith that takes its name from *Athanasius* (n. 127).

ATHEISTS.

Those who attribute all things to nature and nothing to the Divine, and who have made this to be their belief by reasonings from things visible, are *atheists* (n. 98 [4]). Those who confirm in themselves the appearance apart from the truth become worshipers of nature and thus *atheists* (n. 154 [2]). *Atheists* who have become devils and satans can understand the arcana of wisdom as well as angels, but only while they hear them from others (n. 99).

ATMOSPHERE.

The delight of the affections of their life's love encompasses every one as his *atmosphere* (n. 196).

AVARICE

Is the root of evils (n. 220 [11]).

BABEL, BABYLON,

Mentioned in many places in the Word, means the profanation of good in such as attribute to themselves what is Divine (n. 231 [5]). Those who claim for themselves Divine power and wish to be worshiped as gods, declare that they can open and close heaven, remit and retain sins, and therefore save and condemn men, are described in the *Apocalypse* and the prophets by *Babylon* (n. 257). Not long after the establishment of the church it was turned into a *Babylon*, and afterwards into a Philistia; and while *Babylon* acknowledges the Word it nevertheless despises it, claiming that they are inspired by the Holy Spirit in their supreme judgment just as much as the prophets were (n. 264 [2]).

BACK.

To see the Divine providence in the *back* and not in the face is to see it after it occurs and not before (n. 187).

BAPTISM.

Baptizing saves none except those that are spiritually washed, that is, regenerated; for *baptism* is for a sign and a memorial of this (n. 330 [5]). (*See* To REGENERATE.)

BASILISK.

(N. 296 [2].)

BATS

See light as darkness and darkness as light (n. 318 [3]).

BEASTS.

Difference between their faculties and those of men (n. 74, 96). Natural affection, which in itself is desire, with its mate knowledge, is alone what leads and moves *beasts* to do what they do (n. 96 [4]). How man is differentiated from the *beasts* (n. 16). From the abuse of rationality and liberty men become worse than *beasts* (n. 75 [3]). He who believes that everything that he thinks and does is from himself is not unlike a *beast* (n. 321 [2]). Such a man knows no difference between a man and a *beast* except that a man talks and a *beast* makes sounds, and he believes that both die in like manner (n. 321 [2]). Difference between a *beast* and a

man who has become a *beast* (n. 276). In *beasts* there is only one degree of life, which is like the lowest degree in man (n. 324).

BEATITUDES.

The *happinesses* of heaven cannot be described in words, though in heaven they are perceptible to the feeling (n. 39).

BEAUTIFUL.

The true in the sight of the eye is that which is called *beautiful* (n. 312).

BELIEF.

In the spiritual world it is not asked what your *belief* or what your doctrine has been, but what your life has been (n. 101 [3]).

BIRD,

Its instincts (n. 317). *Birds* of night see light as darkness and darkness as light (n. 318 [3]).

BLAME.

If man knows an evil and does not shun it the *blame* is imputed to him, and he becomes guilty of that evil (n. 294 [4]). If everything that a man thinks flows into him from others the *blame* would seem to rest on those from whom it comes; and yet the *blame* itself rests on him who receives, for he receives it as his (n. 294 [2]). Man himself is to *blame* if he is not saved (n. 327).

BLESSINGS.

When honors and possessions are *blessings* and when curses (n. 217 [1–6]).

BLINDNESS.

Why those who are in a state of *blindness* of the understanding cannot be reformed (n. 144). *Blindness* from a misunderstanding of *Rom.* iii, 28 (n. 115).

BLOOD

Signifies Divine truth (n. 231 [9]). "*Bloods*," in the Word, signify the violence called the falsification of truth, and that called the adulteration of good (n. 231 [3]).

BODY (THE).

At first man puts on the grosser things of nature; these constitute his *body;* but by death he puts these off and retains the purer things of nature which are nearest to spiritual things (n. 220[3]). When the *body* is sick the mind is also sick (n. 142). In the whole *body* and in every part there are both externals and internals; the externals are called skins, membranes and sheaths; the internals are forms variously composed and interwoven of nerve fibers and blood vessels (n. 180 [2]). The *body* is obedience (n. 124 [2]).

BONES (THE).

The Divine Man (that is, heaven) is a man in complete form, not only in respect to external members and organs, but also in respect to internal members and organs, which are many, and even with respect to the skins, membranes, cartilages and *bones* (n. 254 [3]). It has been provided by the Lord that those who could not be reached by the Gospel, but only by a religion, should also be able to have a place in that Divine Man, that is, heaven, constituting those parts that are called skins, membranes, cartilages and *bones* (n. 254 [3]).

BORN (TO BE).

Why man is *born* into the outmost of life which is called the corporeal-sensual, and consequently into the thick darkness of ignorance (n. 276). Into the external of life every infant is *born* and consequently is loveable; but as the child grows to boyhood or to youth he passes from that external to what is interior, and finally to the ruling love of his father (n. 277*a* [4]). Man, by inheritance from his parents, is *born* into the love of self and love of the world, and from these as fountains, into evils of every kind (n. 83). If man were *born* into the love into which he was created he would not be in any evil, nor would he even know what evil is (n. 275). No one can come into the kingdom of God unless he has been *born* again (n. 83).

From being natural to become spiritual is to be *born* again (n. 83, 126).

BOUNDARY.

Man can pass from the natural to the spiritual only through a *boundary,* such a *boundary* as may be likened to a door that must be first unfastened and opened (n. 71).

BRAIN (THE),

Composed of innumerable substances and fibers (n. 279 [6]). The *brain* refines the blood and vivifies it anew (n. 336).

BRANCHES.

The life's love is the tree, the *branches* with its leaves are affections for good and truth with their perceptions, and the fruits are the enjoyments of affections with their thoughts (n. 107).

BRIDE.

Why heaven and the church are called "the *Bride*" in the Word (n. 8).

BRIDEGROOM.

Why the Lord is called in the Word "the *Bridegroom*" (n. 8).

BUSINESS

Is a good when that is the final love, and money is a mediate and subservient love, provided the *business* man shuns and turns away from frauds and evil devices as sins (n. 220 [11]). There are *business* transactions and consequent possessions in heaven, since there are societies and communities there (n. 217 [4]).

CAIN

Signifies wisdom and faith; strictly, wisdom separated from love, or faith separated from charity. "*Cain* who slew Abel" is this separated faith which rejects love and charity and even annihilates them (n. 242). What is meant by the cursing and the marking of *Cain* (n. 242 [2]; *see also* 236). (*See* ABEL.)

CALF OF GOLD.

Why its worship was permitted in the wilderness (n. 243).

CALVIN.

(N. 50 [4].)

CANAAN.

By "the Land of *Canaan*" is meant the Lord's church (n. 132, 260).

CANCER.

If evils were prevented they would remain shut in and, like *cancers*, would spread and consume all that is vital in man (n. 251).

CAPACITIES.

The origin of evil is from the abuse of the *capacities* peculiar to man that are called rationality and liberty. These two *capacities* are in the evil as well as in the good (n. 15). (*See* FACULTY.)

CAPTIVITY (THE)

Of the people of Judah in Babylonia represents the devastation of the church (n. 246).

CAROTID ARTERIES.

(N. 296 [14].)

CART (THE NEW),

Upon which the ark was returned by the Philistines signified new but natural doctrines (n. 326 [12]).

CARTILAGES (THE).

All the members and organs of the Grand Man are spiritual, not material; and it has been provided by the Lord that those also who could not be reached by the Gospel but only by a religion should also be able to have a place in the Divine Man, that is, heaven, constituting those parts that are called skins, membranes, *cartilages* and bones (n. 254 [3], 326).

CATECHISM, DECALOGUE,

Is at the present day but like a little sealed book or writing opened only in the hands of children and youth (n. 329 [2]).

CATHOLICISM (ROMAN),

Its dominion (n. 215 [5]). Why such things have been permitted (n. 257 [3]).

To prevent the profaning the most Holy Supper they were permitted under the Divine providence to divide it, and to give the bread only to the people; also, to make it corporeal and material and to adopt this as the primary principle of religion (n. 257 [6]).

CATHOLICS (ROMAN).

Many suffer themselves to be compelled in respect to religion; but this takes place with those in whose worship there is nothing internal but all is external (n. 136 [4]).

CAUSE.

Whatever is done from any *cause* is done from the Divine providence according to some law of it (n. 246). A thing cannot exist and operate without a *cause* (n. 212). The *causes* of permissions are the laws of Divine providence (n. 249 [3]). If you withdraw the *cause* from the effect the effect would perish (n. 3 [2]). The *cause* is called the mediate end (n. 108[2]). The Lord is not the *cause* of a man's thinking evil and falsity (n. 292).

CELLAR.

Those who are in their own prudence are like those who live in the *cellar* of a house, and through their windows see only what is below the level of the ground (n. 311 [3]).

CENTER.

Evils transferred from the *center* to the circumference (n. 79). That which is at the *center* flows out even to the circumferences (n. 86). In the wicked, evil with falsities are, as it were, in the *center*, while goods with truths are in the circumferences; but in the good, goods with truths are in the *center* and evils with falsities are in the circumferences (n. 86). Thus in the evil the goods in the circumferences are defiled by the evils at the *center;* while in the good, the evils in the circumferences are moderated by the goods at the *center* (n. 86). Whatever is at the *center* is directly under view, and is seen and perceived (n. 283).

CHALDEA

Signifies the profanation of truth in those who attribute to themselves what is Divine (n. 231 [5]). Also the profanation of what is holy (n. 251 [3]). *Chaldea* was one of the countries in which the Ancient Church existed and where the Ancient Word was known (n. 328).

CHANGES.

Goods and truths are *changes* and variations of state in the forms of the mind (n. 195 [3]). Affections are *changes* and variations of state of the purely organic substances of the mind, and thoughts are *changes* and variations in the form of these substances. Memory is the state of those *changes* that remain permanent (n. 279 [1,9]). All *changes* and variations of state in organic substances are such that having once become habitual they are permanent (n. 279 [9]). *Changes* and variations are infinitely more perfect in the organic structures of the mind than in those of the body (n. 279 [9]). Of the nature and quality of these *changes* (n. 319 [3]).

CHARIOT

In the Word signifies doctrine from spiritual truths (n. 326 [12]).

CHILDREN.

In the spiritual world all *children* are led by the Lord into angelic wisdom, and through that into heavenly love by means of things enjoyable and pleasing (n. 136 [6]). (*See* INFANCY.)

CHRIST.

No one can even mention the Lord or His names, "Jesus" and "*Christ*," except from Him (n. 53 [2]).

CHRISTIANS

Do not comprehend that God, the Creator of the universe, came into the world and assumed the Human; and in their thought they separate His Divine from His Human (n. 255 [4]). Those who deny the holiness of the Word are not regarded as *Christians* (n. 256 [3]).

CHRISTIAN RELIGION (THE),

Why it is accepted only in the smaller division of the habitable globe called Europe, and is there divided (n. 256). Why in many kingdoms where *the Christian religion* is accepted there are some who claim for themselves Divine power, and wish to be worshiped as gods, and invoke the dead (n. 257). Why among those who profess *the Christian religion* there are some who place salvation in certain phrases which they must think and talk about, making no account of the good works they must do (n. 258). Why hitherto men have not known that to shun evils as sins is *the Christian religion* itself (n. 265).

CHRISTIAN WORLD.

Why the whole *Christian world* worships one God under three persons, which is to worship three Gods, not knowing hitherto that God is one in person and essence, in whom is a trinity, and that the Lord is that God (n. 262). Why there have been and still are so many heresies in the *Christian world* (n. 259). (*See* HERESIES.)

CHURCH.

There are most general principles of the *church* which enter into all religions and constitute that communion; these are the acknowledgment of God and good of life (n. 325 [2]). The Lord's *church* is not in the Christian world only, but is spread and dispersed throughout the world, and thus exists with such as are ignorant of the Lord and do not have the Word (n. 325). On this earth there have been *churches* from the most ancient times. These are described in the Word; first, the Most Ancient *Church;* second, the Ancient *Church;* third, the Hebraic *Church*, from which sprang the *Church* of Israel and Judah (n. 328). The *churches* previous to that of Israel and Judah are described only by the names of nations and persons and by a few things respecting them (n. 328). The Christian *Church* followed the Jewish (n. 328). The *churches* before the coming of the Lord were all representative *churches* (n. 255 [2]). The Christian *Church* after its rise degenerated into a Babylon which transferred to itself the Lord's Divine power; but lest it be called Divine power, and not human power, they made the Lord's Human like the human of another man (n. 262 [8]). From the earliest times when a former *church* has been devastated a new *church* has taken its place (n. 328 [10]). It is foretold in the *Apocalypse* that the Christian *Church* will be followed by a new *church* which is there meant by "the New Jerusalem coming down out of heaven" (n. 328 [10]).

CHYLE.

Man borne through infinite turnings much as the *chyle* is carried to its destination (n. 164 [6]).

CIRCLE.

A *circle* of love to thoughts and from thoughts to love from love, is in all things of the human mind. This *circle* may be called the *circle* of life (n. 29 [3]).

CIVIL.

The *civil* and moral man can also become spiritual, for the *civil* and moral is a receptacle of the spiritual. He is called a *civil* man who knows the laws of the kingdom wherein he is a citizen and lives according to them (n. 322). (*See* MORAL.)

CLEANSING.

All *cleansing* from evils is from the Lord (n. 151 [2]). So long as man from himself holds the outmosts closed there can be no *cleansing*, but only such operation by the Lord in man's interior as the Lord carries on in hell (n. 119). Among the Jews washing represented *cleansing* from evils. Washing the head and hands means to *cleanse* the internal man, and washing the feet the *cleansing* of the natural or external man (n. 151 [2]). How a man is *cleansed* from evil (n. 121). (*See* PURIFICATION.)

COATS OF SKINS (THE),

In which Adam and Eve were clothed, signify the appearances of truth, which were all they had (n. 313 [3]).

COGNITIONS.

(*See* KNOWLEDGES.)

COLORS.

There could be no variety in *color* unless the light were constant (n. 190 [2]). Various *colors* according to the forms into which light flows (n. 160). *Colors* appear the same in the light of winter or of summer (n. 298).

COMBAT.

A *combat* of the internal man with the external arises when one refrains from sins (n. 146). *Combat* arises when a man thinks that evils are sins and therefore resolves to refrain from them (n. 145 [2], 146). From contrariety a *combat* arises, and when this becomes severe it is called temptation (n. 145 [2]). In those who have indulged much in the enjoyments of evil, *combats* appear as temptations (n. 147, 284). These *combats* are against the things that are in the man himself, and that he feels to be his own (n. 147). The hardest struggle of all is with the love of rule from the love of self (n. 146).

COMMANDMENTS.

(*See* PRECEPTS.)

COMMERCE.

(*See* BUSINESS.)

COMMUNICATION.

In the spiritual world there is a *communication* of affections and of consequent thoughts (n. 224 [3]).

COMPARISONS REGARDING

Evil that is not seen (n. 278 [5]). Heavenly love, with its affections, perceptions, and thoughts (n. 107, 207). Infernal love, with its affections, lusts, and thoughts (n. 107). Joy in the highest and the lowest heaven (n. 254 [3]). Lusts with their enjoyments (n. 112). One who denies the Divine providence *compared* to one who sees a magnificent temple and hears an enlightened preacher, but afterwards declares that he has only seen a house of stone and heard nothing but articulate sound (n. 189 [2]). Piety without repentance (n.

121). Pleasures of affections for good (n. 40). Pleasures of lusts for evil (n. 40). The combat when good and evil meet during man's reformation (n. 284). The conjunction of the will with the understanding (n. 165). The life of the evil; its origin (n. 160). The natural rational and the spiritual rational (n. 154 [2]). Those who attribute to themselves the good that belongs to charity and the truth that belongs to faith (n. 309 [2]). Wisdom conjoined with love (n. 35). Wisdom in its progression (n. 335 [2]). Wisdom not conjoined with love (n. 35).

COMPARISONS AND ILLUSTRATIONS.

Acid (n. 316, 298 [6]). Affections (n. 40). Actor (n. 121 [2], 217 [6]). Apes (n. 121 [2], 298). Arrow (n. 202 [3]). Ashes (n. 278 [5]). Atmosphere (n. 195). Basement (n. 311 [3]). Basilisk (n. 296). Beast (n. 176, 321). Besieged city (n. 113). Birds of night (n. 117[2]). Blood (n. 195 [2]). Bow (n. 202 [3]). Cards (n. 212). Carved image (n. 176 [2]). Camp (n. 233 [2]). Chyle (n. 164 [6]). Clouds (n. 137 [4]). Cold (n. 86). Consorts (n. 298). Cords (n. 296 [3]). Current (n. 186, 200, 296). Dead body (n. 282). Dice (n. 212). Diseases (n. 281 [2]). Disease of the heart (n. 184). Door (n. 71). Dove (n. 292 [2], 338 [9]). Dragon (n. 296). Dross (n. 14 [2], 215 [13]). Dung (n. 14 [2], 316). Eagles (n. 20). Eggs (n. 292 [2]). Enemy (n. 233 [2]). Excrement (n. 164 [7]). Faces (n. 168 [5]). Falling star (n. 35). Fire (n. 112, 136 [5], 278 [5].) Fishes (n. 56 [3]). Fixed star (n. 35). Floods (n. 112). Flower bed (n. 40). Flowers (perishable) (n. 205). Food in the stomach (n. 296). Fortifications (n. 233 [2]). Fruit (n. 215 [13]). Gardens (n. 40). Garments (borrowed) (n. 205). Gold (n. 14 [2], 215 [13]). Grafting (n. 296). Harlot (n. 121 [2], 199). Heaps (scattered) (n. 204 [2]). Heat (n. 86). Hen (n. 292). Hinge (n. 235). Human body (n. 4 [5]). Lamb (n. 296 [2]). Leaven (n. 25, 284). Light (n. 168[4], 297). Marksman (n. 333 [3]). Meteor (n. 35). Mimics (n. 121

[2]). Mirror (n. 52, 130 [2], 298). Near sighted person (n. 189 [2]). Noses (n. 310 [5]). Owl (n. 338 [9]); Horned owl (n. 292 [2]). Palace (n. 203 [2]). Pearls (n. 316). Pigeon (n. 296 [2]). Pirate (n. 199). Player (n. 298 [4]). Poison (n. 184, 281). Red lead (n. 153). River (n. 73 [2]). Robber (n. 199). Sail (n. 235). Screech owl (n. 292 [2], 296). Screws (n. 211 [2]). Seeds (n. 3 [2], 56 [3], 98 [6]). Serpents (n. 40, 324 [7], 338 [6]). Sheep (n. 296, 338 [9]). Ship (n. 198, 200). Sores (n. 113). Spider (n. 107, 286). Sponge (n. 17). Statue (n. 176, 321). Sun (n. 35, 160, 162). Surface (n. 217 [6]). Swan (n. 292 [2]). Talent (n. 210 [2]). Tide (favoring) (n. 186). Tree (n. 3 [2], 107, 160). Tools (n. 96 [3]). Turtle dove (n. 296 [2], 338 [7]). Ulcers (n. 113, 281). Urine (n. 165[7]). Viper (n. 292 [2], 296). Virgin (n. 130 [2]). Wall (cracked) (n. 318). Water (n. 195 [2]). Water from an impure fountain (n. 84 [6]). Water (stagnant) (n. 117). Wave (n. 195, 200). Wheel (n. 279). Windows (n. 207). Wine (n. 284). Wound (n. 278 [5]). Youth (n. 130 [2]).

COMPEL.

The external cannot *compel* the internal, but the internal can *compel* the external. The internal is so averse to compulsion by the external that it turns itself away (n. 136, 129). Being *compelled* is not from freedom in accordance with reason, and not from oneself, but is from what is not freedom, and from another (n. 129). The Lord in no case *compels* any one (n. 43). It is impossible to *compel* any one to think what he is not willing to think and to will what his thought forbids him to will, or to love what he does not love (n. 129). One can no more be *compelled* to believe than to think that a thing is so when he thinks it is not so; and one can no more be *compelled* to love than to will what he does not will (n. 136 [2]). There is an internal that man has in common with beasts, and this can be *compelled* (n. 136 [2]). To be *compelled* by love and a fear of losing it is to compel oneself (n. 136 [9]). It is not contrary to rationality and liberty to *compel* oneself (n. 129 [3], 136 [9], 147, 148, 145 [3]). Man's spirit has full liberty by influx from the spiritual world, which does not *compel* (n. 129). A *compelled* internal and a free internal are possible (n. 136 [9]). What *compelled* worship is and what worship not *compelled* is (n. 137). To *compel* men to Divine worship by threats and punishments is pernicious (n. 136 [4]). *Compelled* worship shuts in evils (n. 136 [4]).

CONCUBINE

In the Word signifies a religion. The three hundred *concubines* of Solomon represent various religions in the world (n. 245).

CONCUPISCENCES.

(*See* LUSTS.)

CONFESSION

Is a primary thing on man's part of the Christian religion (n. 278*b*). Of those who *confess* themselves guilty of all sins and do not search out any sin in themselves (n. 278*b*). *Confession* of all sin lulls one to sleep, and at length brings blindness. It is like a universal apart from any particular, which is nothing (n. 278*b*).

CONFIRM.

Every thing that a man has adopted by persuasion and *confirmation* remains in him as his own (n. 317). There is nothing that cannot be confirmed, and falsity is *confirmed* more readily than the truth (n. 318 [2]). Every falsity and every evil can be so *confirmed* as to make the falsity appear like truth, and every evil like good (n. 318 [3], 286 [1]). When falsity has been *confirmed* truth is not seen; but from *confirmed* truth falsity is seen (n. 318 [6]). Ability to *confirm* whatever one pleases is not intelligence, but only ingenuity, which may exist in the worst of men (n. 318 [8]). Every thing *confirmed* by the will and also by the understanding remains to eternity; but not what has been *confirmed* by the understanding only (n. 318 [11]). He that upholds evil loves does violence to Divine goods, and he that upholds false principles does violence to Divine truths (n. 231 [3]). The *confirmation* of falsity is a denial of truth, and the *confirmation* of evil is a rejection of good (n. 231 [3]). There is a *confirmation* that is intellectual and not at the same time voluntary; but all voluntary *confirmation* is also intellectual (n. 318 [9]). The *confirmation* of evil that is voluntary and also intellectual causes man to believe that his own prudence is everything and the Divine providence nothing; but this is not true of intellectual *confirmation* alone (n. 318 [10]). There are some who are very skilful in *confirming*, who have no knowledge of any truth and yet are able to *confirm* both truth and falsity (n. 318 [8]).

CONFLICT. COMBAT.

During man's reformation good and evil meet, and then *conflict* and *combat* arise; this if severe is called temptation (n. 284).

CONJOIN (TO).

How a man can be more nearly *conjoined* with the Lord (n. 33). Every one acknowledges God and is *conjoined* with Him according to the good of his life (n. 326 [7]). The conjunction of the Lord with a man or a spirit or an angel is such that every thing that has relation to the Divine is not from them, but from the Lord (n. 53 [2]). Love is conjunction itself (n. 34). The more nearly a man is *conjoined* with the Lord the wiser he becomes (n. 34); and the happier (n. 41); and the more distinctly does he seem to himself as if he were his own, and the more clearly does he recognize that he is the Lord's (n. 42). The Lord *conjoins* man with Himself by means of appearances (n. 219 [5]); and by means of correspondences (n. 219 [6]). Through His Divine providence the Lord *conjoins* Himself with natural things by means of spiritual things, and with temporal things by means of eternal things according to uses (n. 220 [4]). The Lord *conjoins* Himself with uses by means of correspondences, and thus by means of appearances in accordance with the confirmations of these by man (n. 220 [6]). The understanding does not *conjoin* itself with the will, or the thought of the understanding with the affection of the will, but the will with its affection *conjoins* itself with the understanding and its thought (n. 80). (*See* CONJUNCTION.)

CONJUGIAL LOVE

Is the spiritual heavenly love itself, an image of love of the Lord and of the church, and derived from that love (n. 144 [2]). Love truly *conjugial* communicates with the inmost heaven (n. 144 [3]).

CONJUNCTION

With the Lord is according to the reception of love and wisdom from Him (n. 162). *Conjunction* with the Lord and regeneration are one (n. 92). The *conjunction* is more and more near or more and more remote (n. 28, 32 [3]). So far as one shuns evils as diabolical and as obstacles to the Lord's entrance he is more and more nearly conjoined with the Lord (n. 33 [3]). The end of the Lord's Divine providence is the *conjunction* of the human race with Himself (n. 45). The more nearly any one is conjoined with the Lord, the more distinctly does he appear to himself to be his own, and the more clearly does he recognize that he is the Lord's (n. 158). *Conjunction* of the Lord with man and the reciprocal *conjunction* of man with the Lord are effected by means of the two faculties, rationality and liberty (n. 92); and by loving the neighbor as oneself and loving the Lord above all things (n. 94, 326). The reciprocal *conjunction* of angels with the Lord is not from the angels but is as if it were from them (n. 28 [4]). By means of the two faculties, rationality and liberty, there is a *conjunction* of the Lord with every man, both the evil and the good, therefore man has immortality. But eternal life, that is, the life of heaven, is given to him in whom there is a reciprocal *conjunction* from inmosts to outmosts (n. 96 [7]). Upon the *conjunction* of the Creator with man both the connection of all things and the conservation of all

things depend (n. 3 [3]). Love does nothing except in *conjunction* with wisdom (n.4). All *conjunction* in the spiritual word is effected by means of looking to another (n. 29). Examples of presence and *conjunction* in the spiritual world (n. 326). The acknowledgment of God causes a *conjunction* of God with man and of man with God (n. 326). In the spiritual world *conjunction* is from an affection that springs from love in. 326 [3]). The several particulars in the human mind are associated and conjoined according to affections, or as one thing loves another. This *conjunction* is spiritual *conjunction*, which is like itself in things general and particular. Its origin is from the *conjunction* of the Lord with the spiritual world and with the natural world, in general and in particular (n. 326 [4]). The *conjunction* of the will with the understanding is like the inflow of the blood from the heart into the lungs (n. 165). The *conjunction* of all things of the will and understanding, that is, of the mind of man with his life's love (n. 108). There is no *conjunction* of minds unless it is reciprocal, and the reciprocation is what conjoins (n. 92 [2]). If one loves another and is not loved in return, then as the one approaches the other withdraws; but if he is loved in return then as one approaches the other approaches and *conjunction* takes place (n. 92 [2]).

CONSERVATION (THE).

Upon the conjunction of the Creator with man both the connection of all things and *conservation* of all things depend (n. 3 [3]).

CONSTANT.

There are many *constant* things created in order that things not *constant* may have existence; some named and described (n. 190).

CONSUMMATION.

The end of a church is called its *consummation* (n. 328 [3]). The *consummation* of the Most Ancient Church, the Ancient Church, the Hebraic Church and the Church of Israel and Judah are described in the Word. The decline and *consummation* of the Christian Church is described in the *Apocalypse* (n. 328 [4]).

CONTAGIOUSNESS OF EVIL,

Whence it arises (n. 328 [7]).

CONTAINANTS.

Extremes and outmosts are *containants*, and these are in the natural world (n. 220 [2]). By death the grosser things of nature are put off, while the purer things of nature which are nearest to spiritual things are retained; and these then become his *containants* (n. 220 [3]).

CONTIGUITY.

Whatever is living in man or angel is from the Divine going forth conjoined with him by *contiguity*, and appearing to him as if it were his (n. 57).

CONTINUITY.

The natural does not communicate with the spiritual by *continuity* but by correspondences; how felt (n. 41).

CONVERSATION WITH SPIRITS

Is possible (though rarely with the angels of heaven); and this has been granted to many for ages (n. 135). *Conversation with the dead* would have the same effect as miracles, namely, man would be persuaded and forced (n. 134*b*).

CORDS.

The evil man, so long as he lives in the world, does not feel the *cords* that bind him; they are as if of soft wool or smooth threads of silk, which he loves because they titillate. But after death they become hard and galling (n. 296 [3]).

CORRESPONDENCES.

All things of the mind *correspond* to all things of the body (n. 181). The Lord conjoins Himself with uses by means of *correspondences* and thus by means of appearances (n. 220). All things of the Word are pure *correspondences* of spiritual and celestial things, and because they are *correspondences* they are also appearances (n. 220 [6]).

Correspondences are in great part appearances of truth, enclosed within which, however, genuine truths lie hidden (n. 256 [3]). The Word is written throughout wholly in *correspondences* (n. 256 [4]). Among the ancients there was a knowledge of *correspondences* (which includes a knowledge of representatives), the essential knowledge of the wise. This was especially cultivated in Egypt (n. 255 [2]).

COUNCIL OF TRENT.

Of a papal bull confirming the decree of the (n. 257 [2]).

COUNTENANCE.

The internal is hidden interiorly in the tone, in the speech, in the *countenance*, and in the gestures of the external (n. 224 [3]).

COVENANT.

Why the two tables of the law are called the *covenant* (n. 326 [7]).

COVERINGS.

Man after death is just as much a man as he was in the world, with this difference only, that he has cast off the *coverings* that formed his body in the world (n. 124).

COWS (THAT CARRIED BACK THE ARK),

Signified good natural affections (n. 326 [12]).

CREATE.

The universe, with each thing and all things therein, was *created* from Divine love by means of Divine wisdom (n. 3). The Divine love and the Divine wisdom, which are a one in the Lord, are in every *created* thing in a certain image (n. 5). In every thing *created* there is something that is referable to the marriage of good and truth (n. 74 [2]). No angel or spirit was *created* such immediately, but they were all born first as men (n. 220 [2]). Every man was *created* to live to eternity in a state of blessedness (n. 324 [6]). Man was *created* to be a receptacle of the Divine love and of the Divine wisdom (n. 328 [5]). The difference between *creating* and proceeding from (n. 219 [2]).

CREATION.

The end of *creation* is a heaven from the human race (n. 323). All things exterior to man and that are serviceable to him in the way of use are secondary ends of *creation* (n. 332). The Lord *created* the universe that an infinite and eternal *creation* from Himself might exist in it (n. 202, 203 [2]). The new *creation*, that is, the regeneration of the men of the Most Ancient Church, is described in the first chapter of *Genesis* by the *creation* of heaven and earth (n. 241). The laws of Divine order established in the first *creation* (n. 332). All things of the universe are *creations* from Divine love and Divine wisdom (n. 1, 3).

CROWNS.

"The seven *crowns* upon the heads of the dragon" (*Apoc.* xii. 3) signify the holy things of the Word and the church profaned (n. 310 [5]).

CRUCIFY.

Why the Jewish nation was permitted to *crucify* the Lord (n. 247).

CRUELTY

Originates in love of self (n. 276 [2]).

CUNNING (THE),

Their fate in the other life (n. 310).

CUP OF COLD WATER,

(*Matt.* x. 42) means something of truth (n. 230 [3]).

CURE (TO).

The evils of a man's life's love can be *cured* by spiritual means as diseases are by natural means (n. 281 [2]). (*See* HEAL.)

CURSE.

The *cursing* of Cain involves the spiritual state into which those come after death who separate faith from charity or wisdom from love (n. 242 [2]). What are real *curses* (n. 217, 250).

DAGON

Represented the religion of the Philistines (n. 326 [12]).

DAMNATION.

Predestination to non-salvation is *damnation* (n. 329 [3]). Man's first state is a state of *damnation* (n. 83). By a belief in instantaneous salvation out of pure mercy *damnation* is attributed to the Lord (n. 340 [5]). That any of the human race have been *damned* from predestination is a cruel heresy (n. 330 [8]).

DANES.

What they teach in their exhortation to the holy communion (n. 114).

DARKNESS (*tenebræ*).

In the Word falsities are called "*darkness*," and thus those in falsities are said to "walk in *darkness* and in the shadow of death" (n. 318 [5]). Hypocrites sent into outer *darkness* (n. 231 [4]).

THICK DARKNESS (*caligo*).

When an angel of heaven looks into hell he sees nothing but mere *thick darkness*, and when a spirit of hell looks into heaven he sees nothing there but *thick darkness;* the reason (n. 167 [3]). Those who are sent into outer *darkness* (n. 231 [4]).

DAVID

Represents the Lord who was to come into the world (n. 244, 245).

DEAD.

The natural man, however civilly and morally he may act, is called *dead* (n. 322 [3]; *see also* n. 236).

DEATH

Is a continuation of life, with the difference that man cannot then be reformed (n. 277*b*). By *death* man puts off the grosser things of nature, and retains the purer things of nature which are nearest to spiritual things, and these then become his containants (n. 220 [3]). By *death* man puts off what is natural and temporal, and puts on the spiritual and eternal things that correspond to them (n. 220 [4, 2]). In the spiritual world, into which every man comes after *death*, it is not asked what your belief or what your doctrine has been, but what your life has been (n. 101 [3]). The natural man, however civilly and morally he may act, is called *dead*, but the spiritual man is called living (n. 322 [3]). After *death* a man is no longer borne from one society to another in the spiritual world, because he is then no longer in any state to be reformed (n. 307 [2]).

DECALOGUE (THE),

Was the first thing of the Word, and, when placed in the ark, was called "Jehovah," and constituted the Holy of Holies in the tabernacle and in the sanctuary in the temple of Jerusalem (n. 326 [11]). There are two tables of *The Decalogue*, one relating to God and the other to man (n. 326 [7]). *The Decalogue* taught to children (n. 258 [4], 265 [3]). *The Decalogue* at the present day is like a little sealed book or writing opened only in the hands of children and youth (n. 329 [2]).

DEEDS.

(*See* WORKS.)

DEGREES.

There are two kinds of *degrees*, discrete *degrees*, that is, *degrees* of height; and continuous *degrees*, that is, *degrees* of breadth (n. 32 [2]). There are three discrete *degrees* or *degrees* of height in man from creation (n. 32). Every man by his creation and consequently by birth has three discrete *degrees* or *degrees* of height; the first *degree* is called the natural, the second the spiritual, the third the celestial (n. 32 [2], 324). These *degrees* the Lord opens in man according to his life actually in this world, but not perceptibly and sensibly till after he leaves this world (n. 32 [3]). There are three *degrees* of wisdom in man; these are opened in the measure of his conjunction with the Lord. Since love is conjunction itself they are opened in the measure of love (n. 34). These *degrees* are not connected continuously, but are conjoined by correspondences

(n. 34 [2]). Wisdom can be elevated in a triplicate ratio, and in each *degree* in a simple ratio to its highest point (n. 34 [2]). There are three *degrees* of life in man. In beasts there is only one, which is like the lowest *degree* in man called the natural (n. 324). The reason why many in the world are not prepared for heaven is that they love the first *degree* of their life which is called the natural, and are unwilling to withdraw from it and become spiritual (n. 324 [10]). The natural *degree* of life viewed in itself loves nothing but self and the world; the spiritual *degree* loves the Lord and heaven, and also self and the world, but God and heaven as higher, chief, and dominant, and self and the world as lower, instrumental, and subservient (n. 324 [10]). The Lord alone opens the spiritual *degree* and the celestial *degree* and opens them in those only who are wise from Him (n. 34 [3]). Every angel is perfecting in wisdom to eternity, but each according to the *degree* of that affection in good and truth in which he was when he left the world (n. 334).

DELIGHTS.

There is no affection or lust without *delight*, since these make the life of every one (n. 303). The *delight* of his affection fills and surrounds every angel of heaven, and also a general *delight* of all together, or a most general *delight*, fills and surrounds the universal heaven. In like manner the *delight* of his lust fills and surrounds every spirit of hell, and a general *delight* every society of hell, and the *delight* of all, or a most general *delight*, fills and surrounds the entire hell (n. 303). What *delight* and pleasure are (n. 312). The *delights* belonging to the lusts are evils, and the thoughts belonging to the *delights* are falsities (n. 206 [2]). The *delight* of evil grows with the evil man as he wills and does evil (n. 296 [3]). The *delight* of the affection of their life's love encompasses every one as his atmosphere (n. 196). What and how great the *delight* of the love of ruling from the love of self (n. 215 [9]). (*See* ENJOYMENTS.)

DELUGE.

The consummation of the Most Ancient Church which came from their eating of the tree of knowledge is depicted by the *flood* (n. 328 [4]).

DENY (TO).

Those who *deny* God in the world *deny* Him after death (n. 326 [5]). Those who *deny* the Divinity of the Lord cannot be admitted into heaven and be in the Lord (n. 231 [6]). So far as one *denies* the Lord he is separated from Him (n. 326 [4]).

DERIVATIVES OF THE LOVE OF EVIL.

(N. 33.) The *derivations of infernal love* are affections for evil and falsity, which, strictly speaking, are lusts; and the derivations of heavenly love are affections for good and truth, which, strictly speaking, are dilections (n. 106 [2]). The lusts of evil, which are *derivatives* of that love, have their life from it (n. 206 [2]).

DESCRIPTION (A SHORT),

Of heaven and hell (n. 299–306).

DESOLATION.

The causes leading to a gradual vastation of good and *desolation* of truth in the church, until its consummation is reached (n. 328 [7]).

DETERMINATION.

Every power must have a supply that must be imparted to it and thus a *determination* from what is more internal or higher than itself (n. 88). The mind has not from itself the power to think and to will one thing or another apart from something more internal or higher that *determines* the mind to it (n. 88).

DEVASTATION.

The essential *devastation* of the church was represented by the destruction of the temple itself, and by the carrying away of the people of Israel, and by the captivity of the people of Judah in Babylonia (n. 246).

25

DEVICES.

The perceptions belonging to lusts of evil are *devices* (n. 206 [2]).

DEVIL.

By the *"devil"* is meant hell in the whole complex (n. 204). There is no *devil* who is sole lord in hell, but the love of self is called the *"devil"* (n. 302). Hell in its form is like a monstrous man, whose soul is the love of self and self-intelligence, thus the *devil* (n. 302). Whether you say evil or the *devil* it is the same; the *devil* is within all evil n. 233 [3]). Evil is the *devil* (n. 215) [13]). Evil and the *devil* are one and the falsity of evil and Satan are one (n. 33 [3]). Those who confirm in themselves the lusts of evil are called satans, and those who live those lusts are called *devils* (n. 310 [3]). I have seen fiery *devils* who, while they were hearing the secrets of wisdom, not only understood them but from their rationality talked about them; but as soon as they returned to their diabolical love they ceased to understand them (n. 223). (*See* HELL *and* SATAN.)

DIASTOLE,

What it is (n. 319).

DIFFERENCE

Between those who believe all good to be from the Lord and those who believe good to be from themselves (n. 93); between man and beasts (n. 74, 96 [4], 276): between enlightenment from the Lord and enlightenment from man (n. 168, 169); between the love of dignities and riches for their own sake, and the love of them for the sake of uses (n. 215).

DIGESTION,

The process of (n. 296 [14]).

DIGNITIES.

What *dignities* and riches are and whence they are (n. 215 [2]). Natural and temporal in external form, but spiritual and eternal in internal form (n. 220 [8]). *Dignities* and wealth to the wicked are but stumbling-blocks (n.

250). What spiritual *dignities* and possessions are (n. 217 [4]). *Dignities* in the earliest times were such only as were accorded by children to parents. They were *dignities* of love, full of respect and veneration (n. 215 [2]). (*See* HONORS.)

DISCIPLE.

By a "*disciple*" (*Matt.* x. 42) is meant the state of those who are in some of the spiritual things of the church (n. 230 [3]).

DISSENSIONS. HERESIES.

There must needs spring up in the church disputes, controversies and *dissensions*, especially in regard to the understanding of the Word (n. 256 [3], 259 [2]). Permissions of these are in accord with the laws of the Divine providence (n. 259 [2]). If the church had held to the three essentials it would not have been divided, but only varied by intellectual *dissensions*, as light varies its color in beautiful objects (n. 259 [3]).

DISTANCE

Is an appearance according to conjunction with the Lord (n. 162). The Lord appears to angels at a *distance* like a sun (n. 162). *Distances* appear in the spiritual world in accord with the dissimilarity of affections and of thoughts therefrom (n. 162 [3]). The spiritual is not in *distance* as the natural is (n. 312 [2]). It is the appearance of *distance* that causes one kind of belief about what man thinks and perceives, and another about what he sees and hears (n. 312 [2]).

DISTINCT.

What is not *distinct* is mixed up, giving rise to every imperfection of form (n. 4 [4]).

DIVIDED.

The Lord does not suffer any thing to be *divided* (n. 16). (*See* DIVISION.)

DIVINE.

The *Divine* looks to what is eternal in every man, both in the evil and in the good (n. 59). The *Divine* is in every created thing because the sun of the spiritual world which is from the Lord, and from which all things are, is in every created thing, but with infinite variety according to uses (n. 5). The *Divine* in itself is in the Lord, while the *Divine* from itself is the *Divine* from the Lord in created things (n. 52). What is *Divine* cannot be appropriated to man as his, but can be adjoined to him and thereby appear as his (n. 285 [2]).

DIVINE ESSENCE (THE),

Is love and wisdom (n. 46). (*See* ESSENCE.)

DIVINE GOING FORTH (THE),

Is called the Holy Spirit (n. 262 [5]).

DIVINE HUMAN (THE),

Is that which is called the Son (n. 262 [5]). It has come to pass that a Christian can scarcely be led to think of a *Divine Human* (n. 262 [5]).

DIVINE ITSELF (THE).

The essential *Divine*, from which are all things, is that which is called the Father (n. 262 [5]). By the Infinite and Eternal in itself *the Divine Itself* is meant (n. 52).

DIVINE LOVE AND WISDOM (THE),

Go forth from the Lord as a one (n. 4). The *Divine love and Divine wisdom* are substance and are form (n. 4 [3], 46 [3]). *Divine love* is of *Divine wisdom*, and *Divine Wisdom* is of *Divine love* (n. 4). *Divine love* created all things, but nothing apart from *Divine wisdom* (n. 3 [3]). *Divine love* has as its end a heaven consisting of men who have become or are becoming angels (n. 27 [2]).

DIVISION.

A man can be, while he is living in the world, in good and in falsity at the same time, and thus be as it were a double man, and inasmuch as this *division* destroys the man, the Lord's Divine providence in each and every particular of it, has as its end that this *division* shall not be (n. 16). (*See* DIVIDED.)

DOGMA.

Where there is conversation with the dead, *dogmas* of religion are sometimes imposed upon the mind by spirits. This is never done by any good spirit, still less by any angel of heaven (n. 134*b*).

DOING.

When love is taken away there is no longer any willing and thus no *doing* (n. 3).

DOMINION (LOVE OF).

When the *love of rule* from the mere delight of that love gradually came in (n. 215 [3]). (*See* RULE.)

DOOR.

The *"door"* (*John* x. 2, 3) means the Lord (n. 230 [4]). When the *door* stands open and when shut (n. 71). The love of self guards the *door* lest man should open it, and the Lord should thereby cast it out (n. 210 [2]). Evils obstruct and close the *door* (n. 119). This *door* cannot be opened by the Lord but by means of the man (n. 116, 119). When man refrains from evils as sins a *door* is opened and the Lord casts out the lusts of evil that have occupied the internal of thought (n. 145 [2]). Man opens this *door* by shunning evils as sins as if from himself with the acknowledgment that he does it from the Lord (n. 210 [2]). The *door* is opened by man's removing evil by shunning and turning away from it as infernal and diabolical (n. 233 [3]). When man as if of himself opens the *door*, the Lord roots out the lusts and the evils together (n. 119). The Lord continually solicits and urges man to open the *door* to Him (n. 119).

DRAGON (THE).

By *the "dragon"* in the Word are meant those who separate faith from charity (n. 258).

DWELLING PLACE.

(*See* ABODE.)

EAGLES

Signify rapacious men who are endowed with intellectual sight (n. 20).

EAR (THE).

There cannot be hearing apart from its form which is the *ear* (n. 279 [6]). Very little is known as to how the *ear* hears (n. 336, 174, 180). The understanding from the will flows into the eye and the *ear*, and not only makes those senses but also uses them as its instruments in the natural world; this is not in accordance with the appearance (n. 314). It is the understanding that sees in the eye and hears in the *ear*, and not the reverse (n. 150 [2]).

EAT.

"*Eating* from the tree of knowledge" signifies the appropriation of good and truth as being from man and consequently man's, and not from the Lord and consequently the Lord's (n. 313 [2], 241). "*Eating* of the tree of knowledge" signifies the conceit of self-intelligence (n. 328 [4]). A knowledge of evil after the fall is meant by "*eating* from the tree of the knowledge of good and evil" (n. 275). The end of the Most Ancient Church is signified by the "*eating* from the tree of knowledge" (n. 241).

EBER.

The Ancient Church was notably changed by *Eber* (or Heber) from whom arose the Hebraic Church (n. 328 [2]).

EDEN (THE GARDEN OF).

The wisdom and intelligence of the Most Ancient Church are described by "*the garden of Eden*" (n. 241, 313). Man's wisdom originating in love is depicted by a *garden* (n. 332 [3]).

EFFECT.

Withdraw the cause from the *effect* and the *effect* would perish (n. 3 [2]). *Effect* is called the outmost end (n. 108 [2]). (*See* END.)

EFFORT.

Withdraw *effort* from movement, movement would stop (n. 3 [2]).

EGYPT

Was one of the kingdoms in which the Ancient Church existed and in which the Ancient Word was known (n. 328 [2]). (Here and in other places where the same statement is made, *Egypt* is named as in Asia, in which it had extensive dominion.) Why the sons of Israel were led out of *Egypt* (n. 243).

EGYPTIANS (THE),

Represent a particular kind of evil (n. 251 [3]). They converted correspondences into magic (n. 264 [6]).

ELEVATION. ASCENT.

The *ascent* of love according to degrees is perceived by man only in an obscure way, while the *ascent* of wisdom is clearly perceived by such as know and see what wisdom is (n. 34). *Exaltation* in respect to affection would not be possible unless man had from rationality an ability to raise the understanding, and from liberty an ability to will this (n. 75).

EMBRYO.

In every human *embryo* the Lord forms two receptacles, one for the Divine love and the other for the Divine wisdom; a receptacle of the Divine love for the future will of the man, and a receptacle of the Divine wisdom for his future understanding (n. 324 [11]).

EMERODS.

The "*emerods*" with which the Philistines were smitten signified natural loves, which are unclean when separated from spiritual love; and the "golden *emerods*" signified spiritual loves purified and made good (n. 326 [12]).

END.

There are everywhere three things together that make one; these are called *end*, cause, and effect (n. 108). As *end* conjoins itself with the cause, and through the cause with the effect, so does the life's love conjoin itself with the internal of thought, and through this with its external (n. 108 [2]). The *end* imparts itself wholly to the cause, and through the cause to the effect (n. 108 [2]). There is nothing essential in the effect except what is in the cause, and through the cause in the *end* (n. 108 [2]). As the *end* is the very essential which enters into the cause and the effect, so cause and effect are called mediate and outmost *ends* (n. 108 [2]). He that wills an *end* wills the means also (n. 331 [3]). The operation and progress of the *end* for the sake of which the universe was created through means, is what is called the Divine providence (n. 331). The Lord is willing that a man should think and talk about Divine things provided the *end* is to see the truth (n. 219 [3]). The *end* of the Divine providence (n. 16, 27, 45). The *end* in creation (n. 27 [2], 45, 323, 332). Secondary *ends* of creation (n. 332). (*See* CAUSE, EFFECT.)

ENGLAND.

The teaching in the churches to those who are coming to the Lord's Supper (n. 258 [3]).

ENGLISH.

Of those who do not suffer themselves to be compelled (in respect to religion) there are many of the *English* nation (n. 136 [4]). The *English* hold the doctrine of faith alone, and yet in their exhortation to the holy communion they plainly teach self-examination, acknowledgment, confession of sins, repentance and renewal of life (n. 114).

ENJOYMENT (*jocundum*).

Man is in the *enjoyment* of self-love, and that *enjoyment* constitutes his very life (n. 186). Every *enjoyment* that man has is from his love; no *enjoyment* is possible from any other source (n. 73 [2]). Every *enjoyment* and pleasure, and therefore every thing of the will, is from affection, which belongs to love (n. 76). The *enjoyments* of good are what are called goods of charity (n. 145 [2]). Acting from love's *enjoyment* is acting from freedom (n. 73 [2]). Acting from an *enjoyment* of love is acting from freedom; and since reason favors the love this is also acting in accordance with reason (n. 85). There are two kinds of *enjoyments*, *enjoyments* of the understanding and *enjoyments* of the will; those of the understanding are also *enjoyments* of wisdom, and those of the will are also *enjoyments* of love (n. 136 [5]). The varieties of delight and *enjoyment* constitute man's life (n. 195). The life's love has its delight, and the wisdom thereof has its *enjoyment* (n. 195). Vital heat is from the delights of the affections and from the *enjoyment* of the perceptions and thoughts (n. 195 [2]). External *enjoyments* allure the internal to consent and love (n. 136). *Enjoyments* direct the thoughts and banish reflection (n. 113). After death, when they have become spirits, the evil are incapable of any other *enjoyment* than that which they had in spirit while in the world; and that *enjoyment* is the *enjoyment* of infernal love, which is then turned into what is undelightful, painful, and terrible; and this is what is meant in the Word by "torment" and "hell" (n. 83 [3]). *Enjoyments* of infernal spirits (n. 340 [5]). Lusts with their *enjoyment* block the way and close the doors before the Lord (n. 33 [2]). (*See* DELIGHTS.)

ENLIGHTEN. ENLIGHTENMENT.

Man is taught by the Lord by means of *enlightenment*, because teaching and *enlightenment* are predicated only of wisdom and the understanding (n. 165). There is an interior and an exterior *enlightenment* from the Lord, and there is an interior and an exterior *enlightenment* from man (n. 168). By interior *enlightenment* from the Lord a man perceives at the first hearing whether what is said is true or not true. Exterior *enlightenment* is from this in the thought (n. 168). Interior *enlightenment* from man is from mere confirmation; and exterior *enlightenment* from man is from mere knowledge (n. 168). There is another kind of *enlightenment*, by which it is revealed to man in what faith and

what intelligence and wisdom he is (n. 170). The *enlightenment* of Swedenborg (n. 135). Since the last judgment, that is, now, every man who wishes to be *enlightened* and to be wise can be (n. 263 [3]).

ENMITY.

"The *enmity* put between the serpent and the woman and between the seed of the serpent and the seed of the woman" (*Gen.* iii. 15) is between the love belonging to man's own and the Lord, and thus between man's own prudence and the Lord's Divine providence (n. 211). Man's own has an inborn *enmity* against the Divine providence (n. 211).

ENTHUSIASTIC SPIRITS.

Diabolical visions have sometimes appeared, induced by *enthusiastic* and visionary *spirits*, who from the delirium that possessed them called themselves the Holy Spirit (n. 134a [3]). Those who are taught by influx what to believe or what to do are not taught by the Lord or by any angel of heaven, but by some *enthusiastic spirit*, Quaker or Moravian, and are led astray (n. 321 [3]).

EQUILIBRIUM

Between heaven and hell (n. 23). In this *equilibrium* every man is held as long as he lives in the world, and by means of it he is held in freedom to think, to will, to speak, and to do; and in this it is possible for him to be reformed (n. 23). Those who have joined evil and falsity in themselves made of service for the conjunction of good and truth in others (n. 22).

ERROR OF THE AGE,

To believe that evils have been separated from man, and even cast out, when they have been remitted (n. 279); that the state of a man's life can be changed instantly, and thus from being evil man can become good (n. 279 [4]); that when sins have been remitted they are removed (n. 280).

ESSE

Is nothing apart from *existere* (n. 11). Love is the being (*esse*) of a thing (n. 11). (*See* EXISTERE.)

ESSENCE.

There is an only *essence* from which has come all the *essences* that have been created. That only *essence* is the Divine love and the Divine wisdom (n. 157). The Divine *essence* itself is pure love, and it is this that works by means of the Divine wisdom (n. 337).

ESSENTIALS.

There are three *essentials* of the church, an acknowledgment of the Divine of the Lord, an acknowledgment of the holiness of the Word, and the life that is called charity (n. 259 [3]). There are two things that are at once the *essentials* and the universals of religion, namely, acknowledgment of God and repentance (n. 340 [2]).

ETERNAL.

The image of the Infinite and *Eternal* is in man exclusively in the marriage of good and truth (n. 58). The Infinite and *Eternal*, that is, the Divine, is not in time (n. 59). An image of the Infinite and *Eternal* is presented in the angelic heaven (n. 62). The angels understand by the Infinite nothing else than the Divine being (*esse*), and by the *Eternal* the Divine manifestation (*existere*) (n. 48). *Eternal* things relate to spiritual honors and possessions, which pertain to love and wisdom in heaven (n. 216). (*See* INFINITE, IMAGE.)

ETERNAL LIFE.

Difference between immortality and *eternal life* (n. 96 [7]).

ETHER.

Varieties in sight would be impossible unless the *ether* in its laws and the eye in its form were constant (n. 190 [2]).

EUROPE.

The Christian religion is accepted only in the smaller division of the habitable globe, *Europe*, and is there divided (n. 256).

EVE.

The condemnation of *Eve* signifies the condemnation of the voluntary self (*proprium*) (n. 313 [3]). (*See* ADAM.)

EVIL AND FALSITY.

Every *evil* and *falsity* is from hell (n. 321 [4]). *Evil* cannot exist without its *falsity* (n. 233). *Evil* from its delight and *falsity* from its enjoyment may be called, and may be believed to be, good and truth (n. 195 [3]). *Evil* is confirmed by means of fallacies and appearances which become *falsities* when they are confirmed (n. 87). That is *evil* to a man that destroys the delight of his affection, and that is *falsity* that destroys the enjoyment of his thought therefrom (n. 195 [3]). *Evil and falsity* are both made serviceable in the way of equilibrium, of relation, and of purification, and thus in the conjunction of good and truth in others (n. 21).

EVIL (HEREDITARY).

(*See* HEREDITARY.)

EVIL

Is the delight of the lust of acting and thinking contrary to Divine order (n. 279 [5]). There are myriads of lusts that enter into and compose every single *evil* (n. 279 [5]). In every *evil* there are things innumerable (n. 296). Because they do not do them outwardly many are not aware that they are in *evils* (n. 117). All cleansing from *evils* is from the Lord (n. 151 [2]). *Evil* can be confirmed as easily as good (n. 87). *Evils* that have been appropriated cannot be eliminated, but may be removed from the center to the circumference (n. 79). An *evil* man is hell in the least form (n. 296). The love of self and love of the world are as fountains from which are *evils* of every kind (n. 83 [2]). *Evil* and the devil are one (n. 33 [3]). Its own punishment follows every *evil* (n. 249 [3]). It is better for a man to be in *evil* and in falsity at the same time than to be in good and in *evil* at the same time (n. 16). *Evils* cannot be prevented by any providence; the reason (n. 251). *Evils* are permitted for the end, which is salvation (n. 249 [3], 281). All who lead an *evil* life interiorly acknowledge nature and human prudence only (n. 205). There is inherent in all *evil* a hatred of good (n. 233 [2]). *Evil* cannot be taken away from any one until it becomes evident and is seen and acknowledged (n. 183 [2], 277). Unless *evils* were permitted to break out man would not see them (n. 251). Except *evils* in the external man are put away no exit is open for the lusts; for they are shut in like a besieged city or like a closed ulcer (n. 113). So long as *evils* continue in the lusts of their love and the consequent enjoyments, there is no faith, charity, piety, or worship, except in mere externals (n. 84 [5]). The *evils* pertaining to the lusts of a man's life's love are not felt as *evils* but as delight (n. 296 [9]). *Evils* that are not removed are like fire in wood covered with ashes, or like matter in a wound that is not opened (n. 278 [5]). With an *evil* man no separation, purification, and withdrawal is possible, except of the more noxious *evils* from the less noxious (n. 296 [12]). So far as *evils* are removed they are remitted (n. 279). The *evil* are continually leading themselves into *evils*, but the Lord is continually leading them away from *evils* (n. 295). No *evil* can be removed except by successive steps (n. 279). The *evil* who are in the world the Lord governs in hell in respect to their interiors, but not in respect to their exteriors (n. 307 [2]). The Divine providence with the *evil* is a continual permission of *evil*, to the end that there may be a continual withdrawal from it (n. 296 [7]). The withdrawal from *evil* is effected by the Lord in a thousand ways, and even in most secret ways (n. 296 [10]). Those who give no thought to the *evils* in themselves, that is, do not examine themselves and afterwards refrain from *evils*, must needs be ignorant of what *evil* is (n. 101 [2]). (*See* EVIL AND FALSITY, HEREDITARY.)

EXALTATION

In respect to affection would not be possible unless man had from rationality an ability to raise the understanding, and from liberty an ability to will this (n. 75).

EXAMINATION (SELF),

What it is (n. 278). No one can be reformed unless he *examines* himself, sees and acknowledges his evils, and afterwards refrains from them (n. 152). Not only the external but also the internal must be *examined* (n. 152). If the external only is *examined* a man sees only what he has actually done (n. 152). One cannot be reformed unless the evils of the spirit are *examined* (n. 152). By the *examination* of the internal man the external man is essentially *examined* (n. 152). Those who do not *examine* themselves and afterwards refrain from evils must needs be ignorant of what evil is (n. 101 [2]).

EXISTERE

Is nothing apart from *esse* (n. 11). (*See* ESSE.)

EXPULSION.

"The *expulsion* from the garden of Eden" signifies the deprivation of wisdom (n. 313 [3]).

EXTERNAL (THE),

Springs from the internal, and consequently has its essence from the internal (n. 224). *The external* can present an appearance not in accordance with its essence from the internal, as in the case of hypocrites, flatterers, and pretenders (n. 224). *The external* man must be reformed by means of the internal, and not the reverse (n. 150). The appearance is that *the external* flows into the internal, when the contrary is true (n. 150 [2]). *The external* of man's thought is in itself of the same character as its internal (n. 106). *Externals* are so connected with internals as to make one in every operation (n. 180 [2]). If man does not shun and turn away from evils as sins, not only does *the external* of the thought and will become vitiated and destroyed, but the internals of them at the same time (n. 180 [5]).

EYE (THE),

In the spiritual sense of the Word means the understanding (n. 264 [3]). Sight cannot exist apart from its form, which is *the eye* (n. 279 [6]). In the spiritual world, where all are spiritual even in respect to their bodies, each one's *eyes* are formed to see from their light, not being able to see in any other (n. 167). *The eye* does not see from itself but it is man's mind or spirit that there perceives things by the sense, and is affected by the sense in accordance with its nature (n. 314). Man knows very little as to how *the eye* sees (n. 336, 174, 180). The understanding from the will flows into *the eye*, and not only makes that sense but also uses it as its instrument in the natural world (n. 314). *The eyes* correspond to wisdom and its perceptions (n. 29 [2]). It is the understanding that sees in *the eye* and hears in the ear, and not the reverse (n. 150 [2]).

FACE (THE),

Is a type of the mind (n. 56 [2], 277*a* [2]). In the spiritual world every one's *face* is changed and becomes like his affections, so that what he is is apparent even from his *face* (n. 224 [3]). To see the Divine providence in the back, and not in *the face*, is to see it after it occurs and not before (n. 187). Angels constantly turn their *faces* to the Lord as a sun (n. 29 [3]). When a man turns his *face* to the Lord love and wisdom are given him. These enter man by *the face* and not by the back of the neck (n. 95).

FACULTY.

Every man possesses the *faculty* to will that is called liberty, and the *faculty* to understand that is called rationality; these *faculties* are as it were innate in man, for his human itself is in them (n. 98). Man possesses reason and freedom, or rationality and liberty, and these two *faculties* are in man from the Lord (n. 73). Unless man possessed a

will from the *faculty* that is called liberty, and an understanding from the *faculty* that is called rationality, he would not be a man (n. 96 [4]). Without these two *faculties* man could not be conjoined with the Lord, and thus could not be reformed and regenerated (n. 96 [5]). Without these two *faculties* man could not have immortality and eternal life (n. 96 [7]). These two *capacities* are in the evil as well as in the good (n. 15, 96 [5], 99, 285 [1, 2]). The Lord preserves these two *faculties* in man inviolate and as sacred in the whole course of His Divine providence (n. 96). The Lord has His residence in every man in these *faculties* (n. 96 [5]). (*See* Capacity, Freedom, Reason, Liberty, Rationality.)

FAITH

Separate from charity (n. 264 [3]); is the only obstacle to the reception of the Christian religion (n. 265). Those who have confirmed themselves in this from Paul's saying (*Rom.* iii. 28) (n. 115). How great the blindness that has been induced by a wrong understanding of this single passage (n. 115). *Faith* induced by miracles is not *faith*, but persuasion—it is only an external without an internal (n. 131).

FALLACIES

From appearances blind the understanding (n. 175 [2]). Every appearance confirmed as a truth becomes a *fallacy* (n. 310). They who confirm themselves by *fallacies* become naturalists (n. 310). Evil is confirmed by means of *fallacies*, and appearances which become *fallacies* when confirmed (n. 87). Appearances and *fallacies* (n. 213).

FALSIFICATION.

He that upholds false principles does violence to Divine truths, and this violence is called *falsification* of truth (n. 231 [3]). In the Word *falsifications* of truth are depicted by whoredoms (n. 233 [10]). These are effected by reasonings from the natural man, also by proofs drawn from the appearances of the sense of the letter of the Word (n. 233 [10]). (*See* WHOREDOMS.)

FALSITY.

Falsity not of evil can be conjoined with good, but *falsity* of evil cannot. *Falsity* not of evil is *falsity* in the understanding and not in the will; while *falsity* of evil is *falsity* in the understanding from evil in the will (n. 318 [9]). The *falsity* of evil and "Satan" are one (n. 33 [3]). *Falsity* is confirmed more readily than the truth (n. 318 [2]). When *falsity* has been confirmed the truth is not seen, but from confirmed truth *falsity* is seen (n. 318 [5]). Evil is confirmed by means of fallacies, and by appearances which become *falsities* when they are confirmed (n. 87). That is called *falsity* to a man that destroys the enjoyment of his thought from his affection (n. 195 [3]). The thoughts belonging to the delights belonging to the lusts of evil are *falsities* (n. 206 [2]).

FAMILIES

And even nations are distinguished from each other merely by the face (n. 277a [2]).

FANCY.

Nature itself, which in itself is dead, inspires the *fancy* with insanities in those under the dominion of self-love (n. 233 [12]).

FAT

Signifies Divine good (n. 231 [10]).

FATHER.

The Lord is the heavenly *Father* of all men, and men are His spiritual children (n. 330). The Lord alone is the *Father* in respect to the life; the earthly *father* is the *father* only in respect to the life's covering, which is the body (n. 330).

FAULT.

(*See* BLAME.)

FAVOR.

The natural by itself *favors* falsities and evils. *Favoring* evils and falsities is not in accord with doing good (n. 14 [2]).

FEAR (TO).

By "*fearing* God" is meant *fearing* to offend Him, "offending God" meaning to sin. This *fear* is not so much a matter of *fear* as of love (n. 140).

FEAR.

In its true sense the "*fear* of God" is nothing else than *fear* of losing His love (n. 136 [9]). Who they are who have the *fear* of God (n. 253). No one is reformed in a state of *fear* (n. 139). *Fear* can in no wise take possession of the internal of thought, but it can of the external of thought (n. 139 [2]). Various kinds of *fear*, a *fear* of the loss of honor or gain; a *fear* of civil punishments (n. 139 [3]); a *fear* of infernal punishments (n. 139 [4]). *Fear* closes the internal from above against influx from heaven (n. 139 [6]). Such *fear* takes away rationality and liberty, and is a hindrance to man's ability to be reformed (n. 139 [6]).

FEEL.

Everything that a man *feels* flows in (n. 308). Man knows so little as to amount to scarcely anything as to how the eye sees, the ear hears, the nose smells, the tongue tastes, and the skin *feels* (n. 336). Why the operation of the Divine providence is not made evident to man's perceptions and senses (n. 175, 176).

FELICITIES.

(*See* HAPPINESSES.)

FERMENTATION.

Ferment (leaven) signifies in the Word the falsity of evil (n. 284). Spiritual *fermentations* are affected in many ways, both in the heavens and on the earth (n. 25). There are evils and falsities together that do a work, when introduced into societies, like that of leaven put into meal, or *ferment* into new wine, by which heterogeneous things are separated and homogeneous things are conjoined, and purity and clearness are the result (n. 25).

FIBERS.

Every man in hell is in form like a man, though monstrous, in which all the *fibers* and vessels are inverted (n. 296). The workings of both brains into *fibers* and of *fibers* into muscles and of muscle into action (n. 180[6])

FIERY FLYING SERPENT.

The belief in instantaneous salvation out of pure mercy is the "*fiery flying serpent*" in the church (n. 340[5]). The "*fiery flying serpent*" means evil glowing from infernal fire (n. 340).

FIG TREE.

(*See* LEAVES.)

FINITE.

What the Infinite and Eternal is the *finite* cannot comprehend, and yet it can (n. 46, 53). The conjunction between the Infinite and the *finite* (n. 54). How the *finite* being becomes capable of containing what is infinite (n. 54). By things *finite* all things created by the Divine, especially men, spirits, and angels, are meant (n. 52). A man or an angel is *finite*, and purely a receptacle, in itself dead; and whatever is living in him is from the Divine going forth conjoined with him by contiguity, and appearing to him as if it were his (n. 57).

FIRE.

Why there is more of the *fire* and ardor of doing uses in love of self and the world than those have who are not in the love of self and the world (n. 215[12], 250[3] 252[2]).

FIRSTS.

The Lord from eternity, or Jehovah, came into the world and assumed Humanity in outmosts, that He might thus from *firsts* through outmosts rule the whole world. Why the Lord is called "The *First* and the Last" (n. 124[4]). (*See* ULTIMATES, INMOSTS.)

FLAME.

Some in the spiritual world who ascribed all things to their own prudence, when instructed, so blazed up that *flame* appeared from their nostrils (n. 309).

FLATTERERS.

(N. 14, 89, 104, 224.)

FLESH.

Man has a voluntary self (*proprium*), which is evil, and is meant by "the will of the *flesh*" in *John* i. 13 (n. 298[3]).

FLOOD.

The consummation of the Most Ancient Church is described in the Word by the "*flood*" (n. 328[3]).

FLOW IN (TO).

No part whatever of the plan or preparation (of successful war) is from (man) himself; it all *flows in* either from heaven or from hell—from hell by permission, from heaven by providence (n. 251[6]). Every thing of thought and affection, even with the spirits of hell, *flows in* out of heaven; but that this *inflowing* good is there turned into evil and this truth into falsity, thus every thing into its opposite (n. 288, 294[6], 307). The natural does not *flow into* the spiritual, but the spiritual *flows into* the natural (n. 314). Every thing that a man thinks, and wills, and speaks, and does therefrom *flows in* from one fountain of life (n. 292). All evil with its falsity *flows in* from hell, and all good with its truth *flows in* from the Lord (n. 312[4])

FLOWERS.

Man's initiation into the marriage of good and truth, that is, the spiritual marriage, is like the blossoms that the tree brings forth in the spring time; spiritual truths are the petals of these *flowers* (n. 332[3]).

FORCED.

(*See* COMPEL.)

FOREHEAD.

The Lord's look is upon the *forehead*, because the *forehead* corresponds to love and the affections (n. 29[2]).

FOREKNOWLEDGE.

Knowledge of future events is not granted to man; the reason (n. 178). As a knowledge of future events takes away the human itself, which is to act from freedom in accordance with reason, a knowledge of the future is granted to no one (n. 179).

FORESIGHT (THE),

Of the Lord is like His Divine providence, continual; one does not exist without the other (n. 67, 333). Without the Lord's *foresight* and providence together neither heaven nor hell would be anything but confusion (n. 333 [2]). The Lord's *foresight* has provided for every one his place (n. 333 [2]). (*See* FUTURE.)

FORM.

There is an only *form* from which has come all the *forms* that have been created (n. 157 [2]). Every *form* turns into its own quality that which flows into it (n. 327, 160). Every *form*, the general and the particular, or the universal and the special, by wonderful conjunction act as one (n. 180 [4]). Whatever has existence derives from *form* that which is called quality, and that which is called predicate, also that which is called change of state, also that which is called relativity, and the like (n. 4 [2]). The *form* makes a one the more perfectly as the things entering into the *form* are distinctly different and yet united (n. 4 [4]). The *form* of a heavenly society is more perfect in proportion as each angel is more distinctly his own, and therefore free (n. 4 [4]). The *form* of heaven (n. 61). The *form* of heaven is perfected to eternity according to the increase of numbers, for the greater the number of those that enter into the *form* of the Divine love, which is the *form* of *forms*, the more perfect the unity becomes (n. 62). Changes and variations of state and *form* in the organic substances of the mind, which are affections and thoughts, cannot be shown to the eye (n. 279 [8]). *Form* of the rule of the life's love (n. 107). (*See* SUBSTANCE.)

TO FORM.

Every thing of the understanding and will must be *formed* by means of what is external before it is *formed* by the means of what is internal; since every thing of the understanding and will is first *formed* by means of what enters through the senses of the body, especially through the sight and hearing (n. 136 [7]).

FORTUNE.

Can the cause have any other possible source than the Divine providence in outmosts, when by constancy and by change it deals wonderfully with human prudence and yet conceals itself? (n. 212). As the Divine providence is in the least particulars of things insignificant and trifling, why should it not be in the least particulars of things not insignificant and trifling, as the affairs of peace and war in the world, or of salvation and life in heaven? (n. 212 [2], 251 [6]). The successes and favorable occurrences of war are called in common language the *fortune* of war; and this is Divine providence, especially in the plans and preparations of the general, even although he then and afterwards may ascribe it all to his own prudence (n. 251 [6]). The heathen formerly acknowledged *Fortune* and built her a temple; so also the Italians at Rome (n. 212 [2]). (*See* ACCIDENTAL.)

FOUNTAIN.

The Lord is the one *fountain* of life (n. 292). All the worship of the ancients was representative, therefore they consecrated *fountains* (n. 255 [2]).

FOXES.

They who are in their own prudence are like wolves and *foxes* (n. 311 [3]).

FRAGRANT.

Good is in itself *fragrant* (n. 305).

FRAUDS,

Their source, and why permitted (n. 276 [2]).

FREEDOM.

Freedom is a property of love, insomuch that love and *freedom* are one. And as love is the life of man, *freedom* also belongs to his life (n. 73 [2]).

Freedom, like love, is inseparable from willing (n. 89). There is infernal *freedom* and there is heavenly *freedom* (n. 43). What one thinks, speaks, and does from each (n. 43). Whatever a man thinks, wills, speaks, and does from *freedom* seems to him to be his own (n. 43, 176). There cannot be two kinds of *freedom,* in themselves opposite, and each *freedom* in itself (n. 43). The *freedom* of sin is infernal *freedom,* and in itself bondage; and from this to see heavenly *freedom,* which is *freedom* itself, is like seeing day when immersed in thick darkness, or; like seeing what is from the sun above when under a dark cloud (n. 149). The difference between heavenly *freedom* and infernal *freedom* is like that between what is alive and what is dead (n. 149). There are many kinds of *freedom,* but in general three, natural, rational, and spiritual (n. 73 [2]).

NATURAL FREEDOM

Every one has by inheritance. From it a man loves nothing but self and the world; his first life is nothing else. Thinking and willing evils is man's *natural freedom* and when he has confirmed evils in himself by reasonings he does evils from *freedom* in accordance with his reason, thus from his faculty that is called liberty. It is from the Lord's Divine providence that man is permitted to do this. Man is in this kind of *freedom* by nature because by inheritance; and all those are in it who by means of reasonings have confirmed it in themselves from the enjoyment of the love of self and the world (n. 73 [3, 4]).

RATIONAL FREEDOM

Is from the love of reputation with a view to honor or gain. The enjoyment of this love lies in appearing externally as a moral man; and because man loves such a reputation he does not defraud, commit adultery, take revenge, or blaspheme; and because he makes this a matter of reason he acts from *freedom* in accordance with his reason in sincere, just, chaste, and friendly ways; and from his reason he can advocate such conduct; still the good deeds that he does are not

in themselves good. His *freedom* derives nothing from a love for the public welfare, neither does his reason, since this assents to his love. Consequently this *rational freedom* is a more internal natural *freedom.* This *freedom,* too, by the Lord's Divine providence remains with every one (n. 73 [5]).

SPIRITUAL FREEDOM

Is from a love for eternal life. Into that love and its enjoyments no one comes except he that thinks evils to be sins and in consequence does not will them, and at the same time looks to the Lord. At first such a *freedom* does not seem to be *freedom,* and yet it is. This *freedom* increases as natural *freedom* decreases and becomes subservient; and it conjoins itself with rational *freedom* and purifies it (n. 73 [6]). Any one may come into this *freedom* if he is but willing, because he has rationality and liberty, and the Lord continually gives the ability (n. 73 [7]). Those who are in a love of evil have no other perception than that infernal *freedom* is *freedom* itself; while those who are in a love of good perceive that heavenly *freedom* is *freedom* itself, and consequently its opposite is slavery, both to the good and to the evil (n. 43). To be led by good is *freedom,* and to be led by evil is slavery, because to be led by good is to be led by the Lord, and to be led by evil is to be led by the devil (n. 43). Every man wishes to be free. All who willingly serve for the sake of liberty compel themselves, and when they compel themselves they act from *freedom* in accordance with reason, but from an interior *freedom* from which exterior *freedom* is looked upon as a servant (n. 148). It is a law of the Divine providence that man should act from *freedom* in accordance with reason; the *freedom* that is here meant is *spiritual freedom* and not natural *freedom,* except when the two are one (n. 71, 176). Man cannot be conjoined with the Lord, and thus reformed, regenerated, and saved unless it is permitted him to act from *freedom* in accordance with reason (n. 123 [4], 97). To act from *freedom* in accordance with reason, to act from liberty and rationality, and to act from the will and the understanding, are the same thing; but it is one thing to act from *freedom* in accordance with reason, or to act from liberty and rationality, and it is another thing to act from *freedom* itself in accordance with reason itself, or to act from liberty itself and from rationality itself (n. 97). A man who does evil from the love of evil and confirms that evil in himself acts from *freedom* in accordance with reason; and yet his *freedom* is not in itself *freedom*, but is an infernal *freedom;* and his reason is not in itself reason, but is either a spurious or false reason (n. 97). Man has *freedom* of reason by his being midway between heaven and the world, and by his ability to think from heaven or from the world (n. 142). Only such as have suffered themselves to be regenerated by the Lord act from *freedom* itself in accordance with reason itself; all others act from *freedom* in accordance with thought, to which they give the semblance of reason. And yet every man, unless born foolish or excessively stupid, is able to attain to reason itself, and through it to *freedom* itself (n. 98). Man is led by the Lord continually in *freedom*, and is also reformed and regenerated in *freedom* (n. 43). (*See* LIBERTY.)

FREELY.

To will *freely* as if from himself is from a faculty continually given him by the Lord that is called liberty (n. 96 [2]). So long as enjoyment from the love of evil rules, man is not able to will *freely* what is good and true, and to make these to be of his reason (n. 85). Every man can *freely*, yea, most *freely*, think as he wishes as well against God as for God; and he that thinks against God is rarely punished in the natural world, because there he is always in a state to be reformed; but he is punished in the spiritual world, This takes place after death because he can there no longer be reformed (n. 249).

FRENCH (THE),

Called a noble nation (n. 257 [4]).

FRIENDSHIP (SPIRITUAL),

And relationship, how shown in the spiritual world (n. 338 [4]).

FRUCTIFICATIONS.

Fructifications and multiplications have not failed from the beginning of creation, nor will ever fail to eternity (n. 56 [3]). Affections may be *fructified* and perceptions multipled without end (n. 57). This ability to *fructify* and multiply without end, that is, infinitely and eternally, men have in natural things, the spiritual angels in spiritual things, and the celestial angels in celestial things (n. 57).

FRUITS.

Spiritual goods, which are the goods of charity, are like *fruit;* and these are signified by *"fruit"* in the Word (n. 332 [3]). The primary activities of the spiritual marriage are like the beginnings of the *fruit* (n. 332 [3]).

FUTURE.

The entire *future* is present to the Lord, and the entire present is to Him the eternal (n. 333 [3]). A knowledge of the *future* is granted to no one; nevertheless every one is permitted to form conclusions about the *future* from reason (n. 179). A longing to know things *future* is innate with most people; but this longing has its origin in a love of evil, and is therefore taken away from those who believe in the Divine providence (n 179). (*See* FORESIGHT.)

GANGRENE.

Evils if prevented by any providence would remain shut in, and like the diseases called cancer and *gangrene*, would spread and consume all that is vital in man (n. 251.)

GARDEN.

"The *garden* of Eden" signifies the wisdom of the men of the Most Ancient Church (n. 241, 313 [2].

GARMENTS (WHITE),

Signify a state cleansed from evil (n 279 [2]).

GENERAL.

A *general* thing exists from its particulars (n. 201 [2]).

GENERATION (THE ORGANS OF),

In either sex correspond to societies of the inmost heaven (n. 144 [3]).

GENESIS.

The learned try to explain the contents of the first chapter, and at length confess that they do not understand it. The new creation itself, that is, the regeneration of the man of the Most Ancient Church, is described therein (n. 241 [1, 2]).

GENII.

The most cunning sensual men are called *Genii*. Their hell described (n. 310 [4]). Those that have done good and have believed it to be from themselves, if after death they do not receive the truth, mingle with infernal *genii* and at length come to be one with them (n. 93).

GENTILES.

The human race is ten times more numerous in Mohammedan and *Gentile* lands than in the Christian portion; and in the latter there are few who place religion in life. What more insane belief, then, can there be than to hold that only these latter are saved and the former are damned, and that man gains heaven by his birth and not by his life? (n. 330 [7]). All that have lived well and have acknowledged God are instructed after death by angels; and then those that had been, while they lived in the world, in the two essentials of religion accept the truths of the church such as they are in the Word, and acknowledge the Lord as the God of heaven and of the church (n. 328 [8]). A *Gentile* thinks about God from religion in his life more than a Christian does (n. 322 [5]).

GERMANS (THE).

What the *Germans* teach in their exhortation to the holy communion (n. 114).

GLOTTIS,

Its functions (n. 279 [8]).

GOATS.

By "*goats*" in the Word are meant those who separate faith from charity (n. 258). By the "*goats*" spoken of by the Lord in *Matt.* xxv. 32–46 are meant such as neglect to think about evil, and because of this are continually in evil (n. 101).

GOD

Is one in person and essence, in whom is a trinity, and the Lord is that *God* (n. 262). If man clearly saw the Divine providence, either he would deny *God* or he would make himself to be *God* (n. 182). There are some who have arrogated to themselves Divine power and wish to be worshiped as *gods* (n. 257). (*See* THE LORD, BABYLON.)

GOOD

Is the delight of the affection of acting and thinking in accordance with Divine order (n. 279 [5]). Myriads of affections enter into and compose every single *good*, and these myriads are in such order and connection in man's interiors that no one can be changed unless at the same time all are changed (n. 279 [5]). There is inherent in all *good* a love of protecting itself against evil and of separating it from itself (n. 233 [2]). By *good* is meant that which universally embraces and involves all things of love (n. 11). What is *good* apart unless related to something? Can it be called *good*, since no affection or perception can be predicated of it? (n. 11). Every *good* is called *good* from its delight or its blessedness (n. 324 [6]). *Good* of life, or living rightly, is shunning evils because they are against religion, thus against God (n. 326 [8]). Terms *good* and truth of *good*, also evil and falsity of evil explained (n. 233). *Good* and use are one (n. 233 [5]).

GOOD AND TRUTH.

All things in the universe have relation to *good and truth* and to their conjunction. *Good* belongs to love and *truth* to wisdom; for love calls all that pertains to it *good*, and wisdom calls all that pertains to it *truth* (n. 5 [2]). Every one calls that *good* which from the love of his will he feels to be delightful; and he calls that *truth* which from the wisdom of his understanding he perceives to be enjoyable therefrom (n. 195 [2]). *Good* is nothing apart from *truth*, and *truth* is nothing apart from *good* (n. 11, 13). After death every one must be in *good* and also in *truth* or must be in evil and also in falsity (n. 18). In angels of heaven and in men on earth *good* is good in itself only so far as it has become joined with *truth;* and *truth* is *truth* in itself only so far as it has become joined with *good* (n. 10). *Good* is not in the least *good* except so far as it has become joined with its *truth*, and that *truth* is not in the least *truth* except so far as it has become joined with its *good* (n. 13). Every *good and truth* is from the Lord (n. 321 [4]). *Good* cannot exist apart from its *truth*, nor evil apart from its falsity; for they are bedfellows or consorts (n. 233). Every one's *good* is that which is delightful to his affection; and *truth* is that which is enjoyable therefrom to his thoughts (n. 195 [2]). *Goods and truths* are changes and variations of state in the forms of mind; but these are perceived and have their life solely by means of their delights and enjoyments (n. 195 [3]). What natural *truth and good* are, and what spiritual *truth and good* are (n. 312). All *good* with its *truth* flows in from the Lord (n. 312 [4]).

GOSPEL.

It has been provided by the Lord that those who could not be reached by the *Gospel*, but only by a religion, should also be able to have a place in the Divine man, that is, in heaven (n. 254 [1, 3]).

GOVERN.

The Lord *governs* hell by means of opposites, and the evil who are in the world He *governs* in hell, in respect to their interiors, but not in respect to their exteriors (n. 307). (*See* Rule.)

GOVERNMENT.

What is called Divine providence is the *government* of the Lord's Divine love and Divine wisdom (n. 2). The Lord governs every least particular, in an evil man as well as in a good man, and the Lord's *government* is what is called the Divine providence (n. 285 [2]).

GOVERNMENTS IN HEAVEN.

There are *governments in heaven*, and consequently administrations and functions (n. 217 [3]). (*See* Heaven.)

GRAFTING.

Man is a corrupt tree from the seed; nevertheless a *grafting* or budding with shoots taken from the tree of life is possible, whereby the sap drawn from the old root is turned into sap forming good fruit (n. 332 [4]). (*See* Ingrafted.)

GRAIN.

Not a *grain* of will or of prudence that is his own is possible in any man (n. 293).

GRANDFATHER.

Sometimes the features of a *grandfather* reappear in those of a grandson or a great-grandson (n. 277a [2]).

GRAVEN IMAGES.

(*See* Idols.)

GREAT AND RICH.

The fate of most of those who have become *great and rich* in the natural world, and in this regarded themselves only (n. 185). Both the evil and the good are exalted to honors and advanced to wealth (n. 217a [2]).

GUARDING.

The *guarding* of the way to the tree of life (in *Gen*. iii. 24) signifies the Lord's care lest the holy things of the Word and the church be violated (n. 313 [3]).

GUILTY.

If a man knows an evil and does not shun it the blame is imputed to him, and he becomes *guilty* of that evil (n. 294 [4]).

HAIR.

A *"hair"* signifies in the Word the least of all things (n. 159).

HAPPINESSES.

The *happinesses* of heaven cannot be described in words, although in heaven they are perceptible to the feeling (n. 39). And yet these *happinesses* enter as man puts away the lusts of the love of evil and falsity as if of himself (n. 39 [2]). *Happinesses* in infinite variety are in every affection for good and truth, especially in an affection for wisdom (n. 39 [2]). *Happinesses*, that is, beatitudes and pleasures, are exalted as the higher degrees of the mind are opened (n. 37).

HAPPY.

The more nearly a man is conjoined with the Lord the *happier* he becomes (n. 37).

HARMONY.

Harmonies of sound are of infinite variety, but they would be impossible unless the atmospheres were constant in their laws and the ears in their form (n. 190 [2]).

HATREDS.

The love of self regards every one as its servant, or as its enemy if he does not serve it, and this is the source of *hatred* (n. 276 [2]).

HEADS.

"The seven *heads* of the dragon" (*Apoc.* xii. 3, 9) signify craftiness (n. 310 [5]). "The serpent's *head*" (*Gen.* iii. 15) signifies the love of self (n. 211, 241).

HEAL.

How the Lord *heals* man (n. 281 [3]). To *heal* the understanding alone is to *heal* man only from without; this would be like palliative *healing*. It is the will itself that must be *healed* by means of instruction and exhortation in the understanding (n. 282). The Lord *heals* the love of man's will, first by means of

fears, and afterwards by means of loves (n. 283).

HEAR.

Every thing that a man *hears* flows in (n. 308 [2]). *Hearing* cannot exist apart from its form, which is the ear (n. 279 [6]).

HEART (THE),

Means, in the spiritual sense, affection which belongs to the love or will (n. 80). What is not in *the heart* perishes in the understanding; *the "heart"* meaning man's love (n. 172 [6]). *The heart* and lungs in the body correspond to the will and understanding (n. 193 [2]). As the pulsation of *the heart*, together with the respiration of the lungs, governs the whole man in respect to his body, so the will together with the understanding governs the whole man in respect to his mind (n. 193 [2]). The natural principle of life is *the heart's* pulsation, and the spiritual principle of life is the mind's volition (n. 193 [2]). *The heart* joins with itself the lungs, and the will joins with itself the understanding (n. 193 [2]). *The heart* collects and distributes the blood (n. 336). Functions of *the heart* (n. 174, 279 [7], 296 [14]).

HEAT.

Spiritual *heat* and spiritual light in their going forth from the Lord as a sun make one (n. 4). The *heat* in the spiritual world is the Divine love going forth (n. 292 [3]). Analogy between the effects produced by spiritual *heat* and those produced by natural *heat* (n. 292, 160). Vital *heat* is from the delights of the affections, and from the enjoyment of the perceptions and thoughts (n. 195 [2]).

HEAVEN

Is from the human race (n. 27). *Heaven* is not the same thing to one as to another (n. 28). *Heaven* is from those who are in the love of good and in the consequent understanding of truth (n. 27). *Heaven* is an abiding with the

Lord to eternity (n. 27 [2]). *Heaven* from the human race was the end in creation and the end of His Divine providence (n. 27 [2], 323). *Heaven* is conjunction with the Lord (n. 28). It is not from the angels but from the Lord that *heaven* is *heaven*, for the love and wisdom in which angels are, and which make *heaven*, are not from the angels but from the Lord, and in fact are the Lord in them (n. 28). *Heaven* is in the human form (n. 204). *Heaven* in the complex resembles a single man, whose life or soul is the Lord. In that *heavenly* man are all things that are in a natural man, with a difference like that between heavenly and natural things (n. 326 [9]). The entire *heaven* is as one man before the Lord, and likewise each society of heaven, and it is from this that each angel is a man in complete form (n. 64, 124 [2], 254 [3]). The entire *heaven* is divided into two kingdoms, one of which is called the celestial kingdom, the other the spiritual kingdom, and each into societies without number (n. 217 [3]). *Heaven* is divided into as many general societies as there are organs, viscera, and membranes in a man, and each general society is divided into as many less general or particular societies as there are larger divisions in each of the viscera and organs (n. 65, 68). The entire *heaven* is arranged into societies according to affections of good (n. 278 [6]). No one becomes an angel, that is, comes into *heaven*, unless he carries with him from the world what is angelic (n. 60). *Heaven* is granted only to those who know the way to it and walk in that way (n. 60). A brief description of *heaven* (n. 60–62). The angelic *heaven* is an image of the Infinite and Eternal (n. 62). It is most important to know what *heaven* is in general or in many, and what it is in particular or in the individual, and what it is in the spiritual world and what it is in the natural world (n. 27 [3]). The Lord's *heaven* in the natural world is called the church; and an angel of that *heaven* is a man of the church who is conjoined with the Lord, and who becomes an angel of the

26

spiritual *heaven* after he leaves this world (n. 30). *Heaven* is made up of myriads of myriads of angels (n. 62). In *heaven* there are both rich and poor and both great and small, and in hell also (n. 217). Each angel is a *heaven* in the least form; and *heaven* in general consists of as many *heavens* as there are angels (n. 31). Man by creation is a *heaven* in the least form (n. 67). Every one who permits himself to be led to *heaven* is prepared for his own place in *heaven* (n. 67). Those that have acknowledged God and His Divine providence constitute *heaven* (n. 205). The entire *heaven* acknowledges the Lord alone, and whoever does not acknowledge Him is not admitted into *heaven*, for *heaven* is *heaven* from the Lord (n. 263 [3]). The Mohammedan *heaven* is divided into three *heavens*, a highest, a middle, and a lowest (n. 255 [5]). (*See* Mohammedans.)

HEBER.

The Ancient Church was notably changed by *Heber* (or Eber), from whom arose the Hebraic Church (n. 328 [2]).

HEBRAIC CHURCH.

In the *Hebraic Church*, which arose from Heber, worship by sacrifices was first instituted (n. 328 [2]).

HELL

Consists of myriads of myriads, and every one there is in form like a man, though monstrous, in which all the fibers and vessels are inverted (n. 296). *Hell* is in the human form, but it is a monstrous human form, like that of the devil, by whom is meant *hell* in the whole complex (n. 204). An evil man is *hell* in the least form (n. 296). The entire *hell* is arranged in societies according to lusts of evil, opposite to the affections of good (in the societies in heaven) (n. 278*b* [6]). Those that have acknowledged nature alone and human prudence alone constitute *hell* (n. 205). Many, especially such as have confirmed themselves in a faith separated from charity, do not know that when they are in evils they are in *hell* (n. 101). The *hells* abound in unclean things (n. 38 [2]). All in *hell* wish to do evil to all, while those in heaven wish to do good to all (n. 215 [8]). (*See* DEVIL, SATAN.)

HEREDITARY EVIL.

It is admitted in the church that every man has *hereditary evil*, and that from this he is in the lust of many evils. This *evil* is said to be from Adam and his wife, but this is an error; for every one is born into it from his parent, and the parent from his parent, and thus it is successively transferred from one to another; so it is increased and grows, as it were, and is transmitted to offspring (n. 277*a*, 328 [7]). Man, because of his *hereditary evil*, is always panting for the lowest hell; but the Lord by His providence is constantly leading and drawing him away from it, first to a milder hell, then out of hell, and finally to Himself in heaven (n. 183). The passion to be greatest and richest lies most deeply hidden in *hereditary evil;* but providence takes it away so quietly and gradually that man knows nothing about it (n. 183 [2]). Spirits shown that they are in *hereditary evils* of which they had been ignorant before (n. 279 [3]).

HERESIES

In the Christian world (n. 238, 239, 259). The confirmations of *heresies* (n. 318 [2]). That only such as are born within the church are saved is an insane *heresy* (n. 329 [3], 330 [5]). That any of the human race are damned by predestination is a cruel *heresy* (n. 329 [3], 330 [8]).

HERETIC.

What *heretic* can see his falsities unless he accepts the genuine truths of the church? (n. 318 [6]).

HIEROGLYPHICS,

Whence derived (n. 255 [2]).

HOLINESS.

A spiritual *holiness*, which is also called the spirit of truth going forth from the Lord, is within each of the particulars of the sense of the letter of the Word. This *holiness* is injured when the Word is falsified and adulterated (n. 231 [3]).

HOLY SPIRIT (THE).

The Divine going forth is called the *Holy Spirit* (n. 262 [5]).

HOME.

(*See* HOUSE.)

HONORS AND POSSESSIONS

May be blessings and also may be curses; when blessings they are from God, and are spiritual and eternal; when curses they are from the devil, and are temporal and perishable (n. 216 [2]). Why the Divine providence permits the impious in heart to be raised to dignities and enriched with *possessions* (n. 250 [3]). The Lord never leads man away from seeking *honors* or from acquiring wealth, but only leads him away from a desire to seek *honors* for the sake of mere eminence, that is, for the sake of himself (n. 183 [4]). (*See* DIGNITIES.)

HOPE.

The source of what is called *hope* (n. 178).

HORNS.

"The ten *horns* of the dragon" (*Apoc.* xii. 3) signify the power of persuading by fallacies (n. 310 [5]).

HOUSE.

No one (in the spiritual world) can occupy any *house* but his own; each one in a society has his own *house*, and this he finds ready for him as soon as he enters the society. Outside of his *house* he may be in close companionship with others, and yet he can stay nowhere except in his own *house* (n. 338 [4]).

HUMAN.

Every one has what is truly *human* from rationality (n. 227 [6]). To think from the truth is the truly *human* principle, and therefore the angelic (n. 321 [5]). The essential *human* is to think and to will from God (n. 293). Christians in their thought separate His Divine from His *Human*, and place the Divine near the Father in heaven, and His *Human* they know not where (n. 255 [4], 262 [4]). They make His *Human* like the *human* of another man, and do not know that they thus separate soul and body (n. 262 [4]). The essential *humanity* consists in the two faculties called liberty and rationality (n. 281 [3]).

HUMBLE.

The Lord constantly *humbles* the proud and exalts the *humble* (n. 183 [4]).

HUSBAND.

Why the Lord is called in the Word "the *Husband*" (n. 8).

HYPERBOLA.

There is no such approximation of angelic wisdom to the Divine wisdom as to touch it. It may be compared to a straight line drawn near a *hyperbola*, which is said to approach it continually but never to touch it (n. 335 [2]).

HYPOCRISY

Is lighter or more grievous in the measure of the confirmations against God and the outward reasonings in favor of God (n. 231 [4]).

HYPOCRITES.

(N. 14, 89, 104 [2], 109, 222 [2], 224, 231 [4].) *Hypocrites* are sometimes permitted to speak otherwise than as they think, but the tone of their speech makes them known (n. 224 [3]).

IDEALISTS

Are visionaries (n. 46 [2]).

IDEAS.

In every one who has any religion there is implanted a knowledge that after death he will live as a man; this, however, is not in the natural *ideas* belonging to their external thought, but in the spiritual *ideas* belonging to their internal thought (n. 274 [10]). There

are abstract *ideas* by means of which the existence of things can be seen, if not the nature of them (n. 46). The two properties of nature, space and time, must needs limit *ideas*, and cause abstract *ideas* to be as nothing; but if these can be withdrawn in man, as they are in an angel, the infinite may be comprehended (n. 46 [2]).

IDOLATERS.

Those who confirm in themselves the appearance and not also the truth are all interior *idolaters*, since they are worshipers of self and the world. If they have no religion they become worshipers of nature, and thus atheists; while if they have a religion they become worshipers of man and also of images (n. 154 [2]).

IDOLATRY.

The origin of *idolatry* (n. 255 [2]). Among the ancients there was a knowledge of correspondences; . . . from that knowledge they knew the signification of animals of every kind, . . . and made graven images of them, . . . to call to remembrance the holy things which they signified (n. 255 [2]). After a time their posterity began to worship the graven images themselves, . . . and from this the *idolatries* arose which filled the whole world (n. 255 [3], 264 [6]).

IDOLS.

There are many, even in the Christian world, who worship *idols* and graven images, to whom these are serviceable as a means of awakening thought about God (n. 254 [5]).

IGNORANCE.

No one is reformed in a state of *ignorance*, because all reformation is effected by means of truths and a life according to them (n. 143).

ILLUMINATION.

(*See* ENLIGHTENMENT.)

IMAGE AND LIKENESS OF GOD.

Terms explained (n. 27, 328 [6]). Man's being an "*image*" of God means that he is a recipient of the Divine wisdom, his being a *"likeness"* of God means that he is a recipient of the Divine love; thus the receptacle called the understanding is an *image of God* and the receptacle called the will is a *likeness of God* (n. 328 [5]). *God's image* and *God's likeness* are not destroyed in man, but are seemingly destroyed; for they remain implanted in his two capacities called liberty and rationality (n. 328 [6]). The angelic heaven is the very *image and likeness* of the Lord (n. 163). In the created universe there is an *image* of man, and this is an *image* of what is infinite and eternal, thus an *image of God* the Creator, that is, of the Lord from eternity (n. 52). The Divine love and the Divine wisdom, which in the Lord are one, and which go forth as one from the Lord, in a certain semblance are in every thing created by Him (n. 8). The Divine providence presents an *image* of the Infinite and Eternal in the variety of all things, and in the fructification and multiplication of all things (n. 57). The *image* of the Infinite and Eternal is in man exclusively in the marriage of good and truth (n. 58). So far as heaven and the church in general, or an angel of heaven and a man of the church individually, are in the marriage of good and truth, they are an *image and likeness* of the Lord (n. 8). The ability to understand truth is from the Divine wisdom, and the ability to do good is from the Divine love. This ability is the *image of God*, which remains in every sane man and is not eradicated (n. 322).

IMAGES.

There are some to whom graven *images* are serviceable as a means of awakening thought about God (n. 254 [5]). (*See* STATUE.)

IMMEDIATE. IMMEDIATELY.

Salvation by *immediate* mercy is impossible (n. 221, 279). Man is not taught *immediately* from heaven, but mediately (n. 254). Man is led and taught by the Lord alone, and is led and taught *immediately* by Him when this is done from the Word (n. 172 [6]). That this is done mediately through preaching does not take away the immediateness (n. 172 [6]).

IMMORTAL.

That which is mortal in man is taken away by death, and what is *immortal* in him, which is his mind, is unveiled, and he then becomes a spirit in human form (n. 324 [3]).

IMMORTALITY.

Man without liberty and rationality could not have *immortality* and eternal life (n. 96 [1, 7]). By means of these two faculties there is a conjunction of the Lord with every man, and every man has *immortality* (n. 96 [7]). Difference between *immortality* and eternal life (n. 96 [7]). The interior idea of the sages or wise men of old in regard to *immortality* (n. 324 [3]). Why some aspire to an *immortality* of fame (n. 274 [9]).

IMPIETIES.

All *impieties* and also the glorying in them are permissions, the causes of which are laws of Divine providence (n. 249).

IMPIOUS.

Why the Divine providence permits the *impious* in heart to be raised to dignities and enriched with possessions (n. 250 [3]).

INFANCY. INFANTS.

Every one who dies in *infancy* enters heaven, is there brought up and instructed as a man is in the world, and through an affection for good and truth imbibes wisdom and becomes an angel (n. 324 [9]). The Lord provides that all who die in *infancy* shall be saved, wherever born (n. 328 [8]). (*See* CHILDREN.)

INFINITE.

(N. 46–49.) The angels understood by the *Infinite* nothing else than the Divine being (*esse*). An infinity of space is impossible, also an infinity of time, because infinity is without end, either first or last, that is, without limits (n. 48 [2]). The *Infinite* and Eternal, thus the Lord, must be thought of apart from space and time (n. 51). The Divine providence in every thing that it does looks to what is *infinite* and eternal from itself (n. 55, 69). The *infinite* and eternal that the Lord looks to in forming His heaven out of men is that it shall be enlarged to infinity and to eternity (n. 202). The Lord's Divine love is *infinite* and His Divine wisdom is *infinite*, and *infinite* things of love and of wisdom go forth from the Lord, and these flow into all in heaven and therefrom into all in hell, and from both of these into all in the world (n. 294 [6]). (*See* FINITE, IMAGE.)

INFLUX.

Everything that a man thinks and wills, and says and does therefrom, is from *influx*—if good from *influx* out of heaven and if evil from *influx* from hell; or what is the same, that good is from *influx* from the Lord, and evil from what is man's own (*proprium*) (n. 287, 288, 291, 294, 307, 308). The Lord's *influx* is into the love of good and into its affections, and through these affections into the perceptions and thoughts; so the *influx* of the devil, that is, of hell, is into the love of evil and into its affections, which are lusts, and through these into the perceptions and thoughts (n. 33 [3]). Those who are taught by *influx* what to believe or what to do are not taught by the Lord or by any angel of heaven, but by some enthusiastic spirit (n. 321 [3]). All *influx* from the Lord takes place by enlightenment of the understanding, and by an affection for truth and through affection into the understanding (n. 321 [3]). By *influx* from the spiritual world, which does not compel, man's spirit has full liberty in thinking, willing, believing, and loving (n. 129). Man must act from freedom, as if from himself, and not let his hands hang down and wait for *influx* (n. 200, 210, 321 [3]). *Influx* is received by the angels in the perception of truth and in thought, for in these the *influx* becomes apparent to them, but not in the affections (n. 28 [3]). It is from an *influx*

from heaven that those who acknowledge God wish to see Him (n. 254 [5]).

INGRAFTED.

The *ingrafted* branch turns the sap drawn up through the old root into a sap that makes good fruit. The branch to be *ingrafted* can be taken from no other source than the Lord, who is the Tree of Life (n. 296 [2]). (*See* GRAFTING.)

INMOST.

The operation of the Lord's Divine providence in conjoining man with the Lord and the Lord with man is from his *inmost* and from his outmost simultaneously (n. 125, 220 [3]). The *inmost* of man is his life's love (n. 125). The Lord acts from man's *inmosts* and upon the unbroken series to outmosts (n. 125). The things that are in man's *inmosts* and in the series from *inmosts* to outmosts are wholly unknown to man; and therefore he knows nothing whatever of the way in which the Lord works these or what He does (n. 125). Intermediates are connected in unbroken series from *inmosts* even to outmosts, and in outmosts they are together (n. 124 [4]). There is a constant connection between the outermosts and the *inmosts* (n. 180 [3]). Looking to what is infinite and eternal in the formation of the angelic heaven, that it may be before the Lord as one man, is the *inmost* of the Divine providence (n. 64, 67, 68). The *inmost* of the Divine providence respecting hell (n. 69).

INNOCENCE.

The state of *innocence* in which Adam and Eve his wife were portrayed by their "nakedness" (n. 275).

INSANITY.

The evil man when after death he becomes a spirit is usually let into alternate states of wisdom and *insanity*, that he may see the latter from the former; but although from wisdom such see that they are insane, yet when the choice is given them they admit themselves into the state of *insanity* and love it (n. 223). The devils call *insanity* wisdom (n. 223).

INSTANTANEOUS.

The impossibility of *instantaneous* reformation and salvation illustrated by the change of an owl to a dove, or of a serpent to a sheep (n. 338 [7]).

INSTINCTS

A result of influx (n. 317).

INSTRUCT.

All that have lived well and have acknowledged God are, after death, *instructed* by the angels (n. 328 [8]).

INTELLIGENCE.

The angelic view of will and *intelligence* in man is that not a grain of will or of prudence that is his own is possible in any man (n. 293). A good man is bound to act from *intelligence* as if it were his own just as much as an evil man (n. 298 [6]). The difference between these two kinds of *intelligence* is like the difference between that which is believed to be in itself, and that which is believed not to be in itself and yet as if in itself (n. 298 [6]). One's own *intelligence* can induce the human form on externals only; but the Divine providence induces that form on the internals and through these in the externals (n. 298 [4]). An ability to confirm whatever one pleases is not *intelligence*, but only ingenuity, which may exist in the worst of men (n. 318 [8]).

INTELLIGENT.

Only those who perceive the truth are *intelligent*, and they confirm truth by verities continually perceived (n. 318 [8]).

INTENTION.

Man knows his thoughts and consequent *intentions* (n. 197). The will's love flows into the understanding and makes its delight to be felt therein, and from that it comes into the thoughts and also into the *intentions* (n. 281 [2]). (*See* PURPOSES.)

INTERIORS.

The *interiors* of man mean the internal of his thought, of which he knows noth-ing until he comes into the spiritual world and its light, which he does after death (n. 233 [1, 3]). Evil with its falsity and good with its truth cannot be in man's *interiors* together (n. 233[2]). Of the *interior* state of his mind, or of his internal man, man knows nothing whatever (n. 120). Good and the truth of good can be brought into a man's *interiors* by the Lord only so far as evil and the falsity of evil there have been removed (n. 233 [3]). That in the *interiors* of man's mind there are things too limitless to be numbered (n. 199 [3], 120). The few externals that come within the view of man's thought are produced from the *interiors*, and the *interiors* are governed by the Lord alone by His Divine providence (n. 199 [2]).

INTERMEDIATES.

Man's *intermediates* are the things that are in the internal of his thought (n. 125). *Intermediates* are connected in unbroken series from inmosts even to outmosts, and in outmosts they are together (n. 124 [4]).

INTERNAL.

By the *internal* man nothing else is meant than the *internal* of the will and understanding (n. 103). A compelled *internal* is possible in such as are in external worship only, also in such as are in the *internal* of worship; it may be an *internal* compelled by fear or an *internal* compelled by love (n. 136 [9]). Such an *internal* is the external of thought, and is called *internal* because it belongs to thought (n. 136 [9]). This *internal* is not the strictly human *internal;* but it is an *internal* that man has in common with beasts. The human *internal* has its seat above this animal *internal* (n. 136 [2]). The appearance is that the external flows into the *internal*, when nevertheless the contrary is true (n. 150 [2]). The external cannot compel the *internal*, but the *internal* can compel the external (n. 136 [2]). The *internal* is so averse to compulsion by the external that it turns itself away (n. 136). Externals are so connected with *inter-*

nals as to make one. in every operation (n. 180). Only in certain externals is man associated with the Lord; and if he were at the same time in the *internals* he would pervert and destroy the whole order and tenor of the course of the Divine providence (n. 180). As man orders the externals so the Lord orders the *internals* (n. 181 [2]). He that does not acknowledge the Lord is unable to receive any *internal* of worship (n. 132 [3]). (*See* BODY, EXTERNALS.)

INTESTINES.

(N. 180 [4], 279 [7], 296 [14].)

INVOKE.

Some *invoke* the dead (n. 257, 257 [5]).

ISRAEL.

The men of Judah and of *Israel* were wholly external men, and were led into the land of Canaan merely that they might represent the church and its internals by means of the externals of worship (n. 132). (*See* CHURCH.)

JEHOVAH.

The Divine Itself, which is called *Jehovah* the Father, is the Lord from eternity (n. 157 [9]). The Lord from eternity, or *Jehovah*, is Life itself, since He is Love itself and Wisdom itself (n. 157 [5, 9]). Angels that were seen by Abraham, Hagar, and Gideon were so filled with the Divine that they called themselves *Jehovah* (n. 96 [6]).

JESTS.

Profanation is committed by those who make *jests* from the Word and about the Word, or from the Divine things of the church and about them (n. 231).

JESUITS.

(N. 222.)

JESUS.

In the spiritual world, where all are obliged to speak as they think, no one can even mention the name "*Jesus*" unless he has lived in the world as a Christian (n. 262 [8]). No one can even mention the Lord, or His names "*Jesus*" and "*Christ*" except from Him (n. 53).

JEWS.

By "*Jews*" in the Word all who are of the church and who acknowledge the Lord are meant (n. 260). The *Jewish* nation has been preserved and has been scattered over a great part of the world for the sake of the Word in its original language, which they, more than Christians, hold sacred (n. 260 [3]). The *Jews* persist in denying the Lord, because they are such that they would profane the Divinity of the Lord and the holy things of His church if they were to accept and acknowledge them (n. 260 [2]). Why the *Jewish* nation was permitted to crucify the Lord (n. 247). What is represented by the carrying away of the people of Israel, and by the captivity of the people of Judah in Babylonia (n. 246). Whether a man is a *Jew* or not known from the features alone (n. 277*a* [2]).

JOY.

Every one who comes into heaven enters into the highest *joy* of his heart; he can bear no higher *joy*, for he would be suffocated thereby (n. 254 [3]). Heavenly happiness for each in his degree illustrated by the surroundings of a peasant and of a king (n. 254 [4]).

JUDAISM.

Why *Judaism* still continues (n. 260).

JUDAS.

(N. 114, 258 [3].)

JUDGE.

Unjust *judges* (n. 109, 168, 296 [11]). Who does not see that the *judge* is for the sake of justice, the magistrate for the sake of the common welfare, and the king for the sake of the kingdom, and not the reverse? (n. 217 [2]).

JUDGMENT (THE LAST).

The power of hell was wholly broken up by *the last judgment*, which has now been accomplished. Since the *judg-*

ment, that is, now, every man who wishes to be enlightened and to be wise can be (n. 263 [3]).

JUDGMENTS.

The church instituted with the nation of Israel and Judah was a representative church, therefore all the *judgments* and statutes of that church represented the spiritual things of the church which are its internals (n. 245).

KIDNEYS (THE).

(N. 174, 180, 279.) In *the kidneys* a separation of the blood, a purification and withdrawal of heterogeneous substances is effected (n. 296 [14]). The *kidneys* separate impure humors from the blood (n. 336, 174).

KING.

In the church with the nation of Israel and Judah the "*King*" represented the Lord; "David" representing the Lord who was to come into the world, and "Solomon" the Lord after His coming (n. 245). Why many *kings* after Solomon were permitted to profane the temple and the holy things of the church (n. 246). Who does not see that the judge is for the sake of justice, the magistrate for the sake of the common welfare, and the *king* for the sake of the kingdom, and not the reverse? (n. 217 [2]).

KINGDOM.

The Lord's *kingdom* is a *kingdom* of uses (n. 26, 250 [3]). Search and see how many there are in the *kingdoms* of the present day who aspire to dignities and who are not loves of self and the world (n. 250 [4]). It is not known in this world what *kingdoms* in Christendom answer to the "Moabites" and "Ammonites," what to the "Syrians" and "Philistines," or what to the "Chaldeans" and "Assyrians," and the others with whom the children of Israel waged war; and yet there are those that do answer to them (n. 251 [4]). The entire heaven is divided into two *kingdoms*, one of which is called the celes-

tial *kingdom*, the other the spiritual *kingdom* (n. 217 [3]).

KNOWING.

All *knowing*, perceiving, or thinking is of the understanding, and has relation to truth (n. 11 [2]).

KNOWLEDGES

Are like tools to the workman (n. 96 [3]). *Knowledge* is inexhaustible (n. 57).

LAMPS

Signify truths of faith; oil the good of charity (n. 328 [9]).

LARYNX (THE).

(N. 180 [3], 279 [8].)

LAWS OF DIVINE PROVIDENCE.

(N. 70–190.) The Lord cannot act contrary to the *laws of Divine providence*, because acting contrary to them would be acting contrary to His Divine love and to His Divine wisdom, thus contrary to Himself (n. 331). There are no laws of permission by themselves or apart from the *laws of the Divine providence*, but the two are the same (n. 234). Whatever is done for the sake of the end, which is salvation, is according to the *laws of the Divine providence* (n. 234). One who does not acknowledge the *Divine providence* at all does not in his heart acknowledge God (n. 235). Things by which a natural man confirms himself against the *Divine providence* (n. 236–239).

LEAVEN

Signifies in the Word the falsity of evil (n. 284, 25). (*See* FERMENTATION.)

LEAVES

Signify the natural truths that every one first imbibes (n. 332 [3]). The fig *leaves* with which Adam and Eve covered their nakedness signify moral truths by which the things of their love and pride were veiled (n. 313 [3]). (*See* TREE.)

LED (TO BE).

The appearance is that man is *led* and taught by himself; but the truth is that he is *led* and taught by the Lord alone (n. 154–157, 174). The angels of heaven are averse to being *led* by themselves and love to be *led* by the Lord (n. 208). It is an evidence that they are *led* by the Lord that they love the neighbor (n. 208). Spirits of hell are averse to being *led* by the Lord and love to be *led* by themselves (n. 208). They who in their life look to God, and do not do evil to the neighbor are *led* by the Lord (n. 253). All who are *led* by the Lord's Divine providence are raised above the self, and they then see that all good and truth are from the Lord (n. 316). Man is *led* and taught by the Lord alone through the angelic heaven and from it (n. 162). Unless man were *led* every moment and fraction of a moment by the Lord he would depart from the way of regeneration and would perish (n. 202 [2]). Each one, from infancy even to the end of his life, is *led* by the Lord in the least particulars (n. 203).

LEIBNITZ

Was convinced that no one thinks from himself (n. 289 [2]).

LIBERTY.

Man has the faculty of thinking, willing, speaking, and doing what he understands, which is *liberty* (n. 73, 15). Unless man possessed a will from the faculty that is called *liberty* he would not be a man (n. 96 [3], 98, 227 [5]), 286). *Liberty* and rationality are from the Lord (n. 73). Man has full *liberty* to think and will, but not full *liberty* to say and to do whatever he thinks and wills (n. 281). Unless man had full *liberty* he not only could not be saved but would even perish utterly (n. 281). Who those are to whom freedom itself or *liberty* itself, together with reason itself or rationality itself, cannot be given; and to whom they can scarcely be given (n. 98).

LIBERTY AND RATIONALITY.

These faculties are, as it were, innate in man, for his human itself is in them (n. 98). By means of *rationality and liberty* man is reformed and regenerated,

and without them he could not be reformed and regenerated (n. 85). *Liberty* itself and *rationality* itself can scarcely be given to those who have strongly confirmed themselves in falsities of religion (n. 98 [5]). Every one can come into *liberty* itself and *rationality* itself, provided he shuns evils as sins (n. 99). A mature man who does not come into *liberty* itself and *rationality* itself in the world can in no wise come into them after death (n. 99). Infants and children cannot come into *liberty* itself and *rationality* itself until they are grown up (n. 98 [6]). To whom these faculties cannot be given (n. 98 [2, 4]). *Liberty* with its *rationality* has been destroyed in those who have mixed good and evil together (n. 227 [5]).

LIFE

The Lord is the one fountain of *life* (n. 292, 159). There is only one *life*, and men are recipients of *life* (n. 308). It is from creation, and therefore from an unceasing Divine providence, that in man this *life* should manifest itself in the similitude of belonging to him (n. 308). The Divine love and the Divine wisdom are the *life*, which is the source of the *life* of all things and of all things of *life* (n. 157). Man's *life* is his love, and love is manifold (n. 33). The Lord flows into the *life's* love of every one, and through its affections into the perceptions and thoughts, and not the reverse (n. 33 [2]). Each one must have his own life; no one lives in another's *life*, still less in an opposite *life* (n. 227 [4]). The *life* makes doctrine for itself and belief for itself (n. 101 [3]). That man after death lives to eternity is clear from the Word, where *life* in heaven is called "eternal *life*" (n. 324 [5]). Eternal *life* is also eternal blessedness (n. 324 [6]). Without liberty and rationality man could not have immortality and eternal *life* (n. 96 [7]). Through conjunction with the Lord man has immortality, and through reformation and regeneration he has eternal *life* (n. 96 [7]). The source of *life* in the evil man illustrated (n. 160). The *life* of animals is a *life* of merely natural affection, with the knowledge that is its mate. It is a mediate *life* corresponding to the *life* of those who are in the spiritual world (n. 161 96 [4], 74). The internal memory is the book of man's *life* which is opened after death, and in accordance with which he is judged (n. 227).

LIGHT.

There is spiritual *light* and natural *light;* these are alike in outward appearance, but inwardly unlike; for natural *light* is from the sun of the natural world, and is therefore in itself dead, while spiritual *light* is from the sun of the spiritual world, and is in itself living (n. 166). Spiritual *light* in its essence is the Divine truth of the Lord's Divine wisdom. It enlightens the interiors of his understanding, and as it were dictates (n. 317, 166). In the spiritual world there are three degrees of *light:* celestial *light*, spiritual *light*, and spiritual-natural *light*. Celestial *light* is a flaming ruddy *light*. This is the *light* of those that are in the third heaven. Spiritual *light* is a shining white *light*. This is the *light* of those that are in the intermediate heaven. Spiritual-natural *light* is like the *light* of day in our world. This is the *light* of those that are in the lowest heaven, also of those that are in the world of spirits (n. 166 [2]). None of the *light* of the spiritual world has anything in common with the *light* of the natural world; they differ as what is living and what is dead (n. 166 [3]). In hell also there are three degrees of *light*. In the lowest hell the *light* is like that from burning charcoal; in the middle hell it is like the *light* from the flame of a hearth fire; while in the uppermost hell it is like the *light* from candles, and to some like the nocturnal *light* of the moon (n. 167). There is little discernible difference between the *light* of confirmation and the *light* of the perception of truth; and those who are in the *light* of confirmation seem to be also in the *light* of the perception of truth; and yet the difference between them is like that between illusive *light* and genuine *light;* and illusive *light* is such that in the spir-

itual world it is turned into darkness when genuine *light* flows in (n. 318 [8]). In the Word those that are in truths are said "to walk in the *light*," and are called "children of *light*" (n. 318 [5]). Who are meant by devils who make themselves angels of *light* (n. 223). It is spiritual *light* and not natural *light* that illumines the human understanding. Natural and rational lumen is from the former, not from the latter. This is called natural and rational lumen because it is spiritual-natural (n. 166). *Light* is turned into various colors according to the forms into which it flows. The same is true of spiritual *light* which in itself is wisdom from the sun of the spiritual world; the forms into which it flows (human minds) cause the diversity (n. 160).

LIKENESS.

There is a *likeness* between the spiritual things of the mind and the natural things of the body (n. 181). (*See* IMAGE.)

LIPS.

Their function in speech (n. 279 [8]).

LIVE.

Man *lives* from the Lord, and not from himself (n. 156, 157). The appearance that a man *lives* from himself is never taken away from him, for without it a man is not a man (n. 156). Man *lives* a man after death (n. 274). Good of life, or living rightly, is shunning evils because they are against religion, thus against God (n. 325 [2], 326 [8]).

LIVER (THE).

Its organization (n. 180, 279 [7]). The *liver* assorts (n. 174).

LIVING.

The spiritual man is called *living*, but the natural man, however civilly and morally he may act, is called dead (n. 322 [3]).

LOBES OF THE LUNGS.

(N. 319.)

LOOK (TO).

The Lord's *look* is upon the forenead of the angels (n. 29 [2]). The more deeply any object is examined the more wonderful, perfect, and beautiful are the things seen in it (n. 6). All conjunction in the spiritual world is effected by means of *looking* (n. 29, 326).

LORD.

The *Lord* is the God of heaven and earth (n. 330 [6]). The *Lord* is the very Man (n. 65). How the *Lord* is the Divine truth of the Divine good (n. 172 [4]). The *Lord* is the Word because the Word is from Him and treats of Him (n. 172 [2]). The *Lord* alone is heaven (n. 29 [3]). Let no one cherish the mistaken idea that the *Lord* dwells among the angels in heaven, or is with them like a king in his kingdom. In respect to their sight He is above them in the sun there; but in respect to the life of their love and wisdom He is in them (n. 31). It is the *Lord's* will, for the sake of reception and conjunction, that whatever a man does freely in accordance with reason should appear to him to be his (n. 77 [3]). The *Lord* alone causes every one to think and to will in accordance with his quality and in accordance with the laws of Divine providence (n. 294 [6]). Man is led by the *Lord* by means of influx, and is taught by the *Lord* by means of enlightenment (n. 165). The man who is taught from the Word is taught by the *Lord* Himself (n. 172 [5]). The *Lord*, who is good itself and truth itself, cannot enter into man unless the evils and falsities in him are put away (n. 100). The *Lord* is within all good, and the devil is within all evil (n. 233 [3]).

LOT.

Most persons when they enter the spiritual world wish to know their *lot* (n. 179 [2]). Every one's life awaits him and from this is his *lot;* for the *lot* is in accordance with the life (n. 179 [2]). A longing to know things future is taken away from those who believe in the Divine providence, and there is

given them a trust that the Lord is directing their *lot.* They have no wish to know beforehand what it will be, lest they should in some way interfere with the Divine providence (n. 179).

LOVE.

Love makes the life of man (n. 13). The *love* that makes man's inmost life is *love* and wisdom together (n. 13). The life's *love* of no one can exist without derivations, which are called affections (n. 106 [2]). *Love* dwells in its affections like a lord in his realm, or like a king in his kingdom. The dominion of these *loves* is over the things of the mind, that is, the things of man's will and understanding (n. 106 [2]). The life's *love*, which is the ruling *love* with every one, continues after death and cannot be taken away (n. 231 [7]). Each one's life's *love* makes an understanding for itself, and thus a light; for *love* is like the fire of life, from which is the light of life (n. 167). *Love* belongs to the will (n. 136 [2]). The will's *love* flows into the understanding and makes its delight to be felt therein, and from that it comes into the thoughts and also into the intentions (n. 281 [2]). The will's *love* inspires the understanding with whatever it desires, and not the reverse (n. 209). The will's *love* makes a faith for itself (n. 136 [8]). *Love* desires to communicate its own to another, and even to give from its own as much as it can (n. 324 [2]). *Love* wills to be loved; this is implanted in it; and so far as *love* is loved in return it is in itself and in its enjoyment (n. 92 [2]). The Divine essence itself is pure *love*, and it is this that works by means of the Divine wisdom (n. 337). *Loves* are manifold; but two of them, heavenly *love* and infernal *love*, are like lords and kings. Heavenly *love* is *love* to the Lord and *love* towards the neighbor; and infernal *love* is *love* of self and of the world. These two kinds of *love* are opposite to each other as hell and heaven are (n. 106, 107). The quality of the *love* of one's will is the quality of the whole man (n. 199 [3]). If man attributes all things to himself and to nature the *love* of self becomes the soul; but if he attributes all things to the Lord *love* to the Lord becomes the soul. This *love* is heavenly, while the other is infernal (n. 199 [3]). It is the nature of the *love* of self to regard self only, and to regard others as of little or of no account (n. 206). The man who is in the *love* of self looks only to himself, and thus immerses his thoughts and affections in what is his own. There is in the *love* of self the *love* of doing evil, for the reason that the man loves not the neighbor but himself alone (n. 215 [7]). The *love* of evil defined (n. 33). What the *love* of riches and dignities for their own sake is, and what the *love* of dignities and riches for the sake of uses is (n. 215 [6, 7]). The *love* of self, which is the head of all evils, surpasses all other *loves* in its ability to adulterate goods and falsify truths (n. 233 [11]). The hardest struggle of all is with the *love* of rule from the *love* of self. He who subdues this, easily subdues the other evil *loves*, for this is their head (n. 146). *Love* of ruling from *love* of self is the fountain head of the pleasures of the lusts of evil (n. 38). Spiritual *love* is such that it wishes to give its own to another, and so far as it can do this it is in its being (*esse*), in its peace, and in its blessedness. Spiritual *love* derives this from the Lord's Divine *love*, which is such infinitely (n. 27 [2]). The *love* into which man was created is *love* of the neighbor, to the end that he may wish as well to the neighbor as to himself, and even better, and may be in the delight of that *love* when he is doing good to the neighbor (n. 275). This *love* is truly human, for there is in it a spiritual (element) that distinguishes it from the natural *love* that belongs to brute animals (n. 275). When *love* to the neighbor was turned into *love* of self, and this *love* increased, human *love* was turned into animal *love* (n. 276). The life's *love* has a vicar called the *love* of means, and enjoins upon it to take heed and watch that nothing from its lusts appear (n. 109. 110). Conjugial *love* is the spiritual heavenly *love* itself, an im-

age of *love* of the Lord and of the church, and derived from that *love* (n. 144 [2]). *Love* truly conjugial communicates with the highest heaven (n. 144 [3]). To act from one's *love* is to act from one's freedom (n. 43). *Love* and freedom are one (n. 73 [2]). (*See* FREEDOM, LIBERTY.)

LOVE (TO).

Only those who are in the good of life *love* God, for they *love* the Divine things that are from Him in that they do them (n. 326 [6]). What it is *to love* the Lord above all things, and the neighbor as one's self (n. 94). Those who shun evils as monstrous sins *love* the Lord above all things. This none can do except those who *love* the neighbor as themselves (n. 94).

LOVE AND WISDOM.

Love can be understood only from its quality, and its quality is *wisdom;* and its quality or *wisdom* can exist only from its being (*esse*), which is *love* (n. 13). *Love* in its form is *wisdom*, and good in its form is truth (n. 13). *Love* can do nothing apart from *wisdom*, and *wisdom* can do nothing apart from *love* (n. 3, 4). *Love* calls all that pertains to it good, and *wisdom* calls all that pertains to it truth (n. 5 [2]). *Wisdom* belongs to the understanding, and *love* to the will (n. 136 [5]). When man turns his face to the Lord *love and wisdom* are given him. These enter man by the face, and not by the back of the neck (n. 95). *Love and wisdom* are not in space and time (n. 49). How *love* conjoins itself with *wisdom* (n. 28 [3]).

LOWING.

The *lowing* of the cows on the way (I *Sam.* v. and vi.), signified the difficult conversion of the lusts of the evil of the natural man into good affections (n. 326 [12]).

LUCIFER,

In the fourteenth chapter of *Isaiah,* means Babylon. "Babylon," mentioned in many places in the Word, meaning the profanation of good in such as attribute to themselves what is Divine (n. 231 [5]). Why called "the Son of the morning" in *Isaiah* xiv. 12 (n. 257 [3]).

LUKEWARM.

The profane who first acknowledge Divine truths and live according to them, but afterwards recede and deny them, are meant by the *"lukewarm,"* described in the *Apoc.* iii. 15, 16 (n. 231 [8], 226).

LUMINOUS.

In the spiritual world those who were in enlightenment from the Lord have sometimes been seen with a *luminous* appearance around the head glowing with the color of the human face. But in the case of those that were in enlightenment from themselves this *luminous* appearance was not about the head, but about the mouth and chin (n. 169).

LUNGS (THE),

Correspond to the understanding (n. 193 [2]). In the *lungs* a separation of the blood, a purification and a withdrawal of heterogeneous substances is effected (n. 296 [14]). The tone of the voice in speaking and singing, and its articulations, which are the words of speech and the modulations of singing, are made by the *lungs* (n. 279 [8]). The first changes and variations of the state and form of the tone take place in the *lungs* (n. 279 [8]). Action of a diseased pleura upon the *lungs* (n. 180 [3]). No one knows how the soul operates to cause the *lungs* to breathe (n. 174).

LUSTS.

The love of evil with its affections are *lusts* (n. 33 [2]). These have their seat in the natural man (n. 33 [2]). As many as are the innumerable things in a spirit so many are the *lusts* of that evil (n. 296). If one could see the delights of the *lusts* of evil together in some form, he would see them to be too numerous to be defined (n. 296 [13]). Hell is nothing but a form of all the *lusts* of evil (n. 296 [13]). No one who is in the pleasures of the *lusts* of evil can know anything about the pleasures of affections for

good in which the angelic heaven is (n. 38). These *lusts* beset the interiors of the mind, and from the interiors they flow down into the body, and there excite the unclean things that titillate the fibers (n. 38). Evils are in the external man and the *lusts* of evil in the internal man, and the two are connected like root and trunk (n. 119). The pent-up fires of the *lusts* of evil consume the interiors of the mind and lay them waste to the very gate (n. 278 [2]). Every *lust* of evil in hell, when it is represented, appears like some noxious animal (n. 296 [2]). *Lusts* with their enjoyments may be likened to fire; the more it is fed the more it burns (n. 112 [2]). Through the external of thought the *lusts* enter the body (n. 112). Man is not able to perceive the *lusts* of his evil; he does perceive their enjoyments, although he does not think much about them. Unless one knew from some other source that his *lusts* are evils he would call them good (n. 113). The perceptions belonging to *lusts* are devices; the delights belonging to *lusts* are evils; the thoughts belonging to the delights are falsities (n. 206 [2]). *Lusts* with their enjoyments block the way and close the doors before the Lord (n. 33 [2]). All *lusts* of evil are from the love of self (n. 301).

LUTHER

In the spiritual world execrated faith alone, saying that when he established it he was warned by an angel of the Lord not to do it; but his thought was that unless works were rejected no separation from the Catholic religion could be effected (n. 258 [6]). (*See* n. 50 [4]).

LYING.

One of the evils in which man is from birth; why permitted (n. 276 [2]).

MACHIAVELIANS.

Cunning, sensual men likened to those called *Machiavelians* (n. 310 [2]).

MAGISTRATE.

The judge is for the sake of justice, the *magistrate* for the sake of the common welfare, and the king for the sake of the kingdom, and not the reverse (n. 217 [2]).

MAINTENANCE

Involves perpetual creation, as permanence involves a perpetual springing forth (n. 3 [2]).

MAMMON.

In the spiritual sense "the *mammon* of unrighteousness" (*Luke* xvi. 8, 9) means the knowledge of truth and good possessed by the evil, which they employ solely in acquiring for themselves dignities and wealth (n. 250 [5]).

MAN.

As *man* is his own love he is also a form of his love, and may be called the organ of his life's love (n. 319). *Man* by creation is a heaven in the least form, and consequently an image of the Lord (n. 67). *Man* from birth is like a little hell, between which and heaven there is perpetual discordance (n. 251 [2], 296). If *man* were born into the love into which he was created he would not be in any evil, nor would he even know what evil is; he would not be born into the thick darkness of ignorance as every *man* now is, but into a certain light of knowledge and intelligence therefrom, and these he would quickly come into after birth (n. 275). He alone is a *man* who is interiorly what he wishes to seem to others to be (n. 298 [4]). An evil *man* is a hell in the least form, as a good *man* is a heaven in the least form (n. 296 [13], 299, 306). Heaven forms one beautiful *Man*, and hell one monstrous *Man* (n. 293). Every *man* is in the spiritual world in some society there—an evil *man* in an infernal society, and a good *man* in a heavenly society—and sometimes when in deep meditation he also appears there (n. 296 [6]), 278 [6]). Heaven in the complex resembles a single *man*, whose life or soul is the Lord. In that heavenly *Man* are all things that are in a natural *man*, with a difference like that between heavenly and natural things (n. 326 [9]). The heavenly *Man*, which is heaven if all these things are

to be in it, must be composed not of men of a single religion but of men of many religions (n. 326 [10]). Every *man* is both in evil and in good, in evil from himself and in good from the Lord; nor can he live unless he is in both (n. 227 [2]). *Man* lives as a *man* after death (n. 274, 324 [4]). Every *man* is held in equilibrium between heaven and hell as long as he lives in the world, and by means of this he is held in freedom to think, to will, to speak, and to do; and in this it is possible for him to be reformed (n. 23). *Man* must put away evils as if of himself, and yet must acknowledge that he does it from the Lord (n. 116). *Man* knows his thoughts and consequent intentions, because he sees them in himself (n. 197). If *man* believed, as is the truth, that all good and truth are from the Lord and all evil and falsity from hell, he would not appropriate good to himself and make it meritorious, nor appropriate evil to himself and make himself guilty of it (n. 320). If *man* clearly saw the Divine providence he would set himself against the order and tenor of its course, and pervert and destroy it (n. 180). *Man* is admitted interiorly into truths of faith and into goods of charity only so far as he can be kept in them until the end of his life (n. 221). It has not been hitherto known that *man* lives as a *man* after death. Why this has not been disclosed before (n. 274). There is a correspondence between *man's* life and the growth of a tree (n. 332). *Man* has a voluntary self (*proprium*) and an intellectual self; the voluntary self is evil, and the intellectual self is falsity therefrom; the latter is meant by "the will of *man*," and the former by "the will of the flesh," in *John* i. 13 (n. 298 [3]). A mature *man* who does not come into liberty itself and into rationality itself in the world can in no wise come into them after death (n. 99). (*See* MEN.)

MARRIAGE.

In this work the expression "the *marriage* of good and truth" is used instead of "the union of love and wisdom" (n.

7). The *marriage* of good and truth is from the *marriage* of the Lord with the church; and this is from the *marriage* of love and wisdom in the Lord (n. 21, 7, 8, 9). From that union heaven is called a *marriage* and the church is called a *marriage;* and in consequence the kingdom of God is likened in the Word to a *marriage* (n. 21). As there was by creation a *marriage* of good and truth in every created thing, and as this *marriage* was afterwards severed, the Lord must be continually working to restore it (n. 9). Many have sundered or are sundering this *marriage*, especially by the separation of faith from charity (n. 22). In each and in all things of the Word there is a *marriage* of good and truth (n. 21). The conjunction of the Lord with the church and of the church with the Lord is called the celestial and spiritual *marriage* (n. 28 [4], 84). There may be a *marriage* of good and truth in the cause, and there may be a *marriage* of good and truth from the cause in the effect. A *marriage* of good and truth in the cause is a *marriage* of will and understanding, that is, of love and wisdom (n. 12). The love of self and the conceit from that love are like two consorts, and their *marriage* is called the *marriage* of evil and falsity (n. 298 [3]).

MASSES,

Not understood by the common people, and other perversions, are of the Divine providence that the holy things of the Word and of the church should not be profaned (n. 257 [5, 6]).

MATURE MAN.

A *mature man* who does not come into liberty itself and rationality itself in the world can in no wise come into them after death, for his state of life then remains forever such as it had been in the world (n. 99).

MEANS.

Instantaneous salvation from mercy apart from *means* is impossible (n. 338). The Divine providence works by *means*, and the *means* operate through man or through the world (n. 187 [2]). The operation of the Divine providence goes on unceasingly through *means*, out of pure mercy (n. 335). Its *means* are the things whereby man becomes a man, and is perfected in respect to his understanding and his will (n. 335). These *means* in respect to his understanding are called truths (n. 335); and in respect to his will these are called goodnesses (n. 335 [2]). The *means* whereby man is led by the Lord are what are called the laws of the Divine providence (n. 221, 249). *Means* of separation, purification, excretion, and withdrawal of the delights of the lusts of evil belonging to the internal man (n. 296 [10]). The *means* of salvation relate to these two points, that evils must be shunned and that there is a God (n. 329). No one who wishes to be saved is left without a knowledge of the *means*, or without the power by which he may be saved (n. 329 [3]). The love of *means* the vicar of the life's love (n. 109 [2], 110). The salvation of man is effected by *means*, and only the Lord is able to lead man in accordance with these *means* (n. 221).

MEDIATELY.

The Word must needs be taught *mediately*, through parents, teachers, preachers, books, and especially by the reading of it. That this is done *mediately* through preaching does not take away the immediateness (n. 172 [6]). (*See* IMMEDIATE.)

MEDITATION.

A man when in deep *meditation* sometimes appears, as to his spirit, in the society of the spiritual world in which he is (n. 296 [6]).

MELANCTHON,

Mentioned (n. 50 [4]).

MEMBRANES.

Of those who constitute *membranes* in the Divine Man, that is, heaven (n. 254 [3], 326 [10]).

MEMORY

Is the state of the changes and variations in the form of the purely organic substances of the mind that remain permanent (n. 279). When truths are in the understanding only, and from it in the *memory*, they are not in the man but outside of him (n. 233 [7]). Man's *memory* may be compared to the ruminating stomach of certain animals, into which they first receive their food; and so long as it is there it is not within but without the body; but when they draw the food out of the stomach and eat it, it becomes a part of their life and the body is nourished. But man's *memory* contains spiritual, not material, foods, that is, truths, which in themselves are knowledges. So far as a man by thinking, or as it were by ruminating, draws these from the *memory* his spiritual mind is nourished (n. 233 [8]). Man has an external or natural *memory* and an internal or spiritual *memory*. Upon his internal *memory* each and every thing that he has thought, spoken, and done in the world has been inscribed, so completely and particularly that not a single thing is lacking (n. 227). This internal *memory* is the "book of man's life" which is opened after death, and in accordance with which he is judged (n. 227).

MEN.

Those born out of the church are *men* equally with those born within it: they are from the same heavenly origin and are equally living and immortal souls (n. 330 [5]).

MERCY.

Immediate *mercy* is impossible, because the salvation of man is effected by means (n. 221). It is an error of the age to believe that the state of a man's life can be changed instantly, even to its opposite, and thus from being evil a man can become good, and in consequence be led out of hell and transferred straightway into heaven, and this by the Lord's *mercy* apart from means (n. 279). No one enters heaven out of *mercy* (n. 338 [6]). (*See* SAFETY, SALVATION.)

MERITORIOUS.

The good that has man in it, provided it has salvation as its end, is a *meritori-*

ous good; but the good that has the Lord in it is not *meritorious* (n. 90). If man believed that all good and truth are from the Lord he would not appropriate good to himself and make it *meritorious* (n. 320).

MESENTERY.

The *mesentery* elaborates the chyle (n. 336, 164 [6], 180 [4], 296 [14]).

MESOPOTAMIA,

One of the countries in which was the Ancient Church, and in which the Ancient Word was known (n. 328 [2]).

MICE (THE),

By which the land of Ashdod and Ekron was laid waste, signified the devastation of the church by means of falsification of truth. The "five golden *mice*" sent by the Philistines with the ark (I *Sam.* vi.) signified the vastation of the church removed by good (n. 326 [12]).

MIND (*animus*).

The face is a type of the *mind* (n. 56 [2]). The affections, perceptions and thoughts constitute the *mind* (n. 56 [2]). Of a kind of elation of *mind* (n. 279 [3]). No one is reformed in unhealthy mental states, because these take away rationality, and consequently the freedom to act in accordance with reason. The *mind* may be sick and unsound, and while a sound *mind* is rational a sick *mind* is not (n. 141). There is a certain quiet and peace of *mind* that especially follows combats against evils (n. 41).

MIND (*mens*).

The *mind* or spirit of man is wholly in the form in which heaven is or in which hell is; there is not the slightest difference, except that one is the greatest and the other the least (n. 299). The human *mind* is of three degrees (n. 75). Man has a natural *mind*, a spiritual *mind*, and a celestial *mind;* and so long as a man is in the lusts of evil and in their enjoyments he is in the natural *mind* alone, and the spiritual *mind* is closed (n. 147). The natural *mind* is common to man and beast; the spiritual rational *mind* is the truly human *mind* (n. 321 [2]). Man's *mind*, which in itself is spiritual, must needs be among the spiritual, and he comes among such after death (n. 307 [2]). As the *mind* is such is the body, thus the whole man (n.112). The *mind* of man is continually in three things called end, cause, and effect. If one of these is lacking the human *mind* is not in its life (n. 178 [2]). How the Lord governs the interiors and exteriors of man's *mind* (n. 307). (*See* MIND (*animus*).)

MIRACLES.

No one is reformed by *miracles* and signs, because they compel (n. 130). A faith induced by *miracles* is not faith but persuasion, for there is nothing rational in it, still less anything spiritual; it is only an external without an internal (n. 131). The effect of *miracles* on the good and on the evil is different (n. 133). The good do not desire *miracles*, but they believe in the *miracles* recorded in the Word, and when they hear anything about a *miracle* they give thought to it only as an argument of no great weight that confirms their faith (n. 133). The evil may be driven and compelled to a belief by *miracles*, and even to worship and piety, but only for a short time (n. 133). Why there were so many *miracles* among the descendants of Jacob (n. 132). Why *miracles* are not wrought at this day (n. 133).

MISFORTUNE.

No one is reformed in a state of *misfortune* (n. 140). By states of *misfortune* are meant states of despair from danger, as in battles, duels, shipwrecks, falls, fires, threatened or unexpected loss of wealth or of office and thus of honors and other like things (n. 140).

MISUSE.

Man has the ability to *misuse* his faculties of liberty and rationality, and from freedom in accordance with reason to confirm whatever he pleases (n. 286).

27

MIXED.

What is not distinct is *mixed* up, giving rise to every imperfection of form (n. 4 [4]).

MOABITES.

Each nation with which the children of Israel waged war signified some particular evil (n. 251 [3]). It is not known in this world what kingdoms in Christendom answer to the *Moabites* and others with whom the children of Israel waged war, and yet there are those who do answer to them (n. 251 [4]).

MODES.

The *modes* of the Divine providence are the ways by which man becomes a man and is perfected in respect to his understanding and will (n. 335). The *modes* by which the Divine providence operates upon the means and by the means to form man and to perfect him are infinite in number and in variety. These *modes* are most secret (n. 336).

MOHAMMEDAN RELIGION (THE),

Was raised up by the Lord's Divine providence to destroy the idolatries of many nations (n. 255 [2, 4]). *The Mohammedan religion* acknowledges the Lord as the Son of God, as the wisest of men, and as the greatest prophet who came into the world to teach men (n. 255 [1, 3]). This *religion* would not have been accepted by so many kingdoms if it had not been adapted and suited to the ideas of thought and to the life of them all (n. 255 [4]). All of that *religion* who acknowledge the Lord as the Son of God and at the same time live according to the commandments of the Decalogue, which they have, by shunning evils as sins, come into a heaven that is called the *Mohammedan* heaven (n. 255 [5]; *see also* n. 238).

MOOR.

The child of a black or *Moorish* father by a white or European woman is black, and *vice versa* (n. 277a [3]).

MORAL.

The civil and *moral* man can also become spiritual, for the civil and *moral* is a receptacle of the spiritual (n. 322). He is called a *moral* man who makes the laws of the kingdom wherein he is a citizen his *morals* and his virtues, and from reason lives them (n. 322).

MORALISTS.

The state after death of natural *moralists* who believe that civil and moral life with its prudence accomplishes everything and Divine providence nothing (n. 117 [2]).

MORAVIANS.

Moravianism mentioned among heresies (n. 259, 238); as enthusiastic spirits (n. 321 [3]).

MORNING.

Why Lucifer is called "the Son of the *morning*" in *Isaiah* xiv. 19 (n. 257 [3]).

MORTAL.

In order that every man may live to eternity that which is *mortal* in him is taken away (n. 324 [3]). The *mortal* in man is his material body, and this is taken away by its death (n. 324 [3]).

MOST ANCIENT CHURCH.

The men of that church were in the beginning the wisest of men (n. 241).

MOUTH.

In *Luke* vi. 45, the "*mouth*" signifies thought which pertains to the understanding (n. 80). In the spiritual sense the "*mouth*" means thought because thought speaks by means of the *mouth* (n. 80).

MOVEMENT.

Withdraw effort from *movement* and *movement* would stop (n. 3 [2]).

MULTIPLICATIONS.

(*See* FRUCTIFICATIONS.)

MUSCLES.

The workings of both brains into fibers, of fibers into *muscles*, and *muscles* into actions (n. 180 [6]).

MYRIADS.

Heaven is composed of *myriads* of *myriads;* and *myriads* enter it each year, and will continue to enter into it to eternity (n. 63).

NAILS.

It is known that in man, in addition to forms organized of blood vessels and nervous fibers, which are called viscera, there are skins, membranes, tendons, cartilages, bones, *nails*, and teeth (n. 326 [10]). (*See* BONES.)

NAKEDNESS.

The "*nakedness*" of Adam and Eve his wife, that they were not ashamed of, signified the state of innocence (n. 275).

NAME.

In the Word "the *name* of God" signifies God with every thing that is in Him and that goes forth from Him. And as the Word is the Divine going forth, which is "the *name* of God," and as all the Divine things that are called the spiritual things of the church are from the Word, they, too, are "the *name* of God" (n. 230 [2]). In the spiritual world each one has a *name* that is in accordance with the quality of his love and wisdom; for as soon as any one enters a society or into association with others, he immediately has a *name* that is in accord with his character (n. 230). "*Name*" signifies the nature of the state of love and wisdom or of good and truth (n. 230 [4]). *Naming* is effected by spiritual language, which is such that it is capable of *naming* every thing (n. 230). A *name* involves the entire state of the thing (n. 230).

NATIONS

Are distinguished from each other merely by the face (n. 277a [2]). The *nation* that regards the precepts of the Decalogue as Divine and lives according to them from a religious motive is saved (n. 254 [2]). Most *nations* remote from Christendom regard these not as civil but as Divine laws, and hold them sacred (n. 254 [2]). In the earliest times tribes, families, and households dwelt apart from one another, and not under general governments as at the present day (n. 215 [2]). When a religion has been once implanted in a *nation* the Lord leads that *nation* according to the precepts and dogmas of its own religion (n. 254 [2]). (*See* GENTILES.)

NATURAL.

The *natural* does not communicate with the spiritual by continuity, but by correspondences (n. 41). *Natural* and temporal things are not only such as are proper to nature but also such as are proper to men in the *natural* world (n. 220[4]). *Natural* things that are proper to nature have relation in general to times and spaces, and in particular to the things that are seen on the earth (n. 220 [4]).

NATURALISTS.

Those who confirm themselves in the appearance that one's own prudence is everything and the Divine providence nothing are in fallacies; and as far as they confirm themselves by fallacies they become *naturalists*, believing nothing but what they are able to perceive by some bodily sense, especially by the sense of sight (n. 310).

NATURE.

The things proper to *nature* are especially spaces and times, both having limit and termination (n. 219). The extremes or outmosts of *nature* are not receptive of the spiritual and eternal things in conformity to which the human mind was formed as these are in themselves (n. 220 [3]).

NEBUCHADNEZZAR.

By the statue seen by *Nebuchadnezzar* in a dream, the first four churches are meant; also the golden, the silver, the brazen, and the iron ages mentioned by ancient writers (n. 328 [3]).

NEIGHBOR.

In what loving the *neighbor* as one's self consists (n. 94).

NOAH.

The Ancient Church is depicted in the Word by *Noah* and his three sons, and by their posterity (n. 328 [2]).

NOSE.

The *nose* signifies perception of truth. The closing of the *nose* in the spiritual world means that they have no perception (n. 310). The *nose* does not smell from itself, but it is man's mind or spirit that there perceives things by the sense, and is affected by the sense in accordance with its nature (n. 314). Man knows scarcely anything as to how the *nose* smells (n. 336).

OBOTFARDIGAS FORBINDER.

(*Hindrances or Stumbling-blocks of the Impenitent* (n. 258 [5]).)

ODORS.

Every delight corresponds to an *odor*, and in the spiritual world may be converted into an *odor*. The general delight in heaven is sensed as the *odor* of a garden, with variety; . . . while the general delight of hell is sensed as stagnant water into which different kinds of filth have been thrown (n. 304).

OFFSPRING.

The parent's evil is transmitted to the *offspring* (n. 281 [4]).

OIL

Signifies the good of charity (n. 328 [9]).

OLD.

All that have lived well, when they enter heaven come into an age like that of their early manhood in the world, and continue in it to eternity, even those that had been *old* and decrepit in the world. Women also, although they had been *old* and wrinkled, return into the flower of their age and beauty (n. 324[4]).

ONE.

Divine love and Divine wisdom go forth from the Lord as a *one* (n. 4). A *one* is impossible apart from a form, the form itself making the *one* (n. 4 [2]). The form makes a *one* the more perfectly as the things entering into the form are distinctly different and yet united (n. 4 [4]). Man is such a *one*, human society is such a *one*, the church is such a *one*, also the whole angelic heaven before the Lord (n. 4 [3]). How perfectly distinct things are united and thus make a *one* (n. 4 [5]).

OPERATION.

The *operation* and progress of the end through means is what is called the Divine providence (n. 331). There can be no *operation* except upon a subject, and upon it through means (n. 331 [3]). The Divine providence has for its end nothing else than reformation and consequent salvation; this is its unceasing *operation* with every one (n. 257). Nothing of the *operation* of the Divine providence should be evident to man's perception or senses, but he should nevertheless know about it and acknowledge it (n. 175). The entire working (*operation*) of the Lord is from first principles and from outmosts simultaneously (n. 220 [3]). If the *operation* of the Divine providence were made evident to man's perception and senses he would not act from freedom in accordance with reason, nor would any thing appear to him to be his (n. 176). The Lord's *operations* in the interior substances and forms of the mind are not manifest to man (n. 174). The *operations* of the organic substances of the body are natural, while those of the mind are spiritual; and the two make one by correspondences (n. 279 [7]). The soul's secret workings (*operations*), of which man knows nothing because he has no sensation of them (n. 296 [14], 336). The *operation* of the Lord's Divine providence in conjoining man with the Lord, and the Lord with man is not upon any particular of man by itself except as it is simultaneously upon all things of man, from his inmost and from his outmost simultaneously (n. 125). The *operation* of the Lord's Divine providence to withdraw man from evils is continuous (n. 177).

OPPOSITES

Fight each other till one destroys the other (n. 18). Two *opposites* cannot exist together in one substance or form without its being torn asunder and destroyed (n. 233 [2]). Every thing is known from its *opposite* (n. 38 [2]). An *opposite* may take away perceptions and sensations or may exalt them; when it mingles itself it takes away, but when it does not mingle itself it exalts (n. 24).

OPPOSITION.

The affections of heaven and the lusts of hell are diametrically *opposed* to each other (n. 303). The quality of a good is known only by its relation to what is less good, and by its contrariety (*opposition*) to evil (n. 24). *Opposition* destroys (n. 11 [4]).

OPULENCE.

Opulence, greater or less, in itself is but an imaginary something (n. 250 [2]). Such as have looked to riches and possessions solely for their own sake and for what can be gained from them, after death, in place of riches have poverty, and in place of possessions wretchedness (n. 220 [10]).

ORDER.

As God is *order*, so is He the law of His *order* (n. 331 [2]). There is no *order* possible without laws (n. 331 [2]).

ORGANIZATION. ORGANIZE.

The *organization* taken on in the world (by those who deny God) remains to eternity (n. 326 [5]). In the brain there are innumerable substances, and there is nothing there that is not *organized* (n. 279 [6]).

ORGANIC. ORGANS.

The operation, the changes, and variations in the state and form of *organic* substances (n. 279). What flows into the *organs* of the external senses, or those of the body, are such things as are in the natural world, while what flows into the *organic* substances of the internal senses, or those of the mind, are such things as are in the spiritual world (n. 308 [2]). As the *organs* of the external senses, or those of the body, are receptacles of natural objects, so the *organic* substances of the internal senses, or of the mind, are receptacles of spiritual objects (n. 308 [2]).

ORIENTALS.

The Christian religion is not adapted to the genius of the *Orientals* like the Mohammedan religion (n. 256).

ORIGIN OF EVIL (THE),

Is from the abuse of the capacities peculiar to man that are called rationality and liberty (n. 15).

OUTERMOST.

There is a constant connection between the *outermosts* and the inmosts; consequently as the *outermost* acts or is acted upon, so the interiors from the inmosts act or are acted upon (n. 180 [3]).

OUTMOSTS.

The Lord acts from man's inmosts and upon the unbroken series to *outmosts*. The things that are in man's inmosts and in the series from inmosts to *outmosts* are wholly unknown to man (n. 125). Man's *outmosts* are the things that are in the external of his thought (n. 125). The Lord acts from inmosts and *outmosts* simultaneously (n. 124, 220 [3]). Intermediates are connected in unbroken series from inmosts even to *outmosts*, and in *outmosts* they are together (n. 124 [4]). The *outmosts* of life that man carries with him after death become quiescent, and are in agreement with his interiors, that is, they act as one (n. 277*b*). *Outmosts* are reformed in agreement with first principles while man is in the world, and cannot be reformed afterward (n. 277*b*).

OWLS.

The eyesight of the spirits of hell is formed for the reception of the light there, and this sight is like that of *owls* and bats, which see objects at night as clearly as other birds see them by day (n. 167 [2]).

OWNERS.

Those who ascribed all things to their own prudence called "*owners*" (n. 309 [2]).

PALACE OF WISDOM.

The angels said they represent *wisdom* to themselves as a *palace*, the twelve steps to which signify goods conjoined with truths and truths conjoined to goods (n. 36).

PANCREAS.

(N. 180 [4], 279 [7]); it purifies the blood (n. 336); it assorts (n. 174).

PARABLES.

Why the Lord spoke in *parables* (n. 231 [9]).

PARTICULAR. PARTICULARS.

In every form, the general and the *particular*, or the universal and the special, by wonderful conjunction act as one (n. 180 [4]). That is called universal which is made up of the most *particular* things taken together, like any general thing that exists from its *particulars* (n. 201 [2]). The Divine providence is in the minutest *particulars* of nature, and in the minutest *particulars* of human prudence; it is from these that it is universal (n. 201 [3]). The Lord's Divine providence is universal because it is in *particulars*, and it is *particular* because it is universal (n. 124 [3]).

PAUL.

Explanation of *Paul's* saying (*Rom.* iii. 28) respecting faith apart from works (n. 115).

PEOPLE.

The Israelitish and Jewish *people* represented the church (n. 245).

PERCEIVE. PERCEPTION.

If the operation of the Divine providence were made evident to man's *perceptions* and senses he would not act from freedom in accordance with reason; nor would any thing appear to him to be his (n. 176). The quality of a good is known only by its relation to what is less good, and by its contrariety to evil. From this comes all power to *perceive* and to feel, since from this comes the quality of these powers (n. 24). *Perceptions* and thoughts are derivatives of spiritual light (n. 173). What the Lord teaches He gives man ability to *perceive* rationally, and this in two ways; in one man sees in himself that a thing is so as soon as he hears it; in the other he understands it by means of reasons (n. 150 [2]). The Divine good of the Divine love and the Divine truth of the Divine wisdom are given to the evil and to the good, to the just and to the unjust; for unless they were given no one would have *perception* and thought (n. 173). *Perception* and thought belong to life, consequently they are from the same fountain from which life is (n. 173). (*See* ENLIGHTENMENT, THOUGHT.)

PERFECT (TO BE).

It is impossible for that which is perfecting to eternity to be made *perfect* in an instant (n. 338 [10]). Each degree of wisdom may be *perfected* to its highest point, but it cannot enter into a superior degree (n. 34 [2]).

PERFECTIONS.

All *perfections* increase and ascend by degrees and according to degrees (n. 279 [9]).

PERIPHERY.

(*See* CENTER.)

PERISH.

Unless man had full liberty he not only could not be saved but would even *perish* utterly (n. 281).

PERITONEUM

Is the general sheath of all the abdominal viscera (n. 180 [4]).

PERMANENCE

Involves a perpetual springing forth (n. 3 [2]).

PERMISSION.

There are no laws of *permission* by themselves, or apart from the laws of the Divine providence (n. 234). The Divine providence with the evil is a continual *permission* of evil, to the end that there may be a continual withdrawal from it (n. 296 [7]). It is not the Lord but man that introduces evil of life into the will, and through the will into the thought. This is what is called *permission* (n. 296 [7]). All things that an evil man wills and thinks are of *permission* (n. 296 [8]). Evils are *permitted* for the sake of the end, which is salvation (n. 249 [3], 275, 276 [2], 281). The laws of Divine providence are the causes of *permissions* (n. 249 [2]). Nothing can be *permitted* without a reason, and the reason can be found only in some law of the Divine providence, which law teaches why it is *permitted* (n. 234). God is said to *permit*, which does not mean that He wills, but that on account of the end, which is salvation, He cannot avert it (n. 234). The Lord *permits* evils of life and many heresies in worship that man may not fall into the most grievous kind of profanation (n. 233 [13]). (*See* PROFANATION.)

PHARISEES.

Those who say with the lips pious and holy things, and counterfeit the affections of love for these in tone and in gesture, and yet in heart do not believe them or love them, are "*Pharisees*," from whom after death all truth and good are taken away (n. 231 [4]).

PHILISTIA.

Not long after the establishment of the church it was turned into a Babylon, and afterwards into a *Philistia* (n. 264 [2]). By "*Philistia*" is meant faith separate from charity (n. 264[3]).

PHILISTINES.

Those that make faith alone saving, and not a life of charity, are meant in the Word by "*Philistines*" (n. 258, 326 [12], 251).

PLACES.

The Lord foresees the *places* in hell of those who are not willing to be saved, and the *places* in heaven of those who are willing to be saved (n. 333 [2]). The Lord provides their *places* for the evil by permitting and by withdrawing, and for the good by leading (n. 333 [2]). In the spiritual world, in another's apartment no one can sit anywhere except in his own *place;* if he sits elsewhere he becomes like one who has no command of his mind, and is become dumb (n. 338 [4]). Whenever one enters another's room there he knows his own *place* (n. 338 [4]).

PLEASANTNESS.

(*See* ENJOYMENT, DELIGHT.)

PLEASURES (THE),

Of lusts for evil and the *pleasures* of affections for good cannot be compared. The devil is inwardly in the *pleasures* of lust for evil, and the Lord is inwardly in the *pleasures* of affections for good (n. 40).

PLEURA,

The general sheath of the chest (n. 180 [3]).

PLEURISY.

(N. 180.)

POISON.

Except for liberty to think and will evils and to put these away as if of himself, combined with the Divine providence, evils would be like *poison* kept in and not expelled, which would soon spread and carry death to the whole system; or like a disease of the heart itself from which the whole body soon dies (n. 184).

POLYGAMISTS.

A religion that makes it unlawful to marry more than one wife is not accepted, but is rejected by those who for ages back have been *polygamists* (n. 256).

POSSESSIONS.

Eternal things relate to spiritual honors and *possessions,* which pertain to love and wisdom in heaven (n. 216). The natural man calls honors and pos-

sessions Divine blessings (n. 216). Honors and *possessions* may be blessings and also may be curses (n. 216 [2]): they are blessings to those who do not set their hearts upon them, and curses to those who do set their hearts upon them (n. 217). When dignities and *possessions* are blessings they are spiritual and eternal, and when they are curses they are temporal and perishable (n. 217 [3]). Riches and *possessions* are natural and temporal with those who look solely to them, and to themselves in them; but these same things are spiritual and eternal with those who look to good uses in them (n. 220 [10]). The love of riches and *possessions* for the sake of riches and *possessions* is the love of the world, strictly, the love of possessing the goods of others by any device whatever (n. 215 [6]). (*See* RICHES, WEALTH.)

POWER.

The *power* (*posse*) to will and the *power* to understand are not from man, but are from Him who possesses *Power* itself, that is, *Power* in its essence (n. 88). Every created thing is endowed with *power* (*vis*); but *power* acts not from itself but from Him who bestowed the *power* (n. 3 [3]). Before the last judgment the *power* (*potentia*) of hell prevailed over the *power* of heaven (n. 263 [3]). The wicked all believe themselves to be *powerful,* while the good all believe themselves to be destitute of *power* (n. 19 [2]). *Power* in the seed is from God the Creator (n. 3 [2]).

PRAYER (THE LORD'S).

The words "Hallowed be Thy Name" mean that this name must not be profaned (n. 230).

PREACHERS.

The Word must needs be taught mediately through *preachers;* nevertheless it is not taught by them but by the Lord through them (n. 172 [6]). A *preacher* can, while in the external state, teach things pertaining to spiritual life, but when from this external state he is let into the internal, if he is an evil man he sees nothing but falsity and does nothing but evil (n. 298).

PRECEPTS.

The Lord has provided that there shall be in every religion *precepts* like those in the Decalogue (n. 254 [2]). "To have the commandments" (*John* xiv. 21, 23) is to know; "and to do them" is to love (n. 33 [5]).

PREDESTINATION.

Any *predestination* except to heaven is contrary to the Divine love (n. 330 [2]). That any of the human race have been damned by *predestination* is a cruel heresy (n. 330 [8]).

PREDESTINED.

All men were *predestined* to heaven and no one to hell (n. 322 [2], 329).

PREDICATE.

Whatever has existence derives from form that which is called quality, and that which is called *predicate* (n. 4 [2]).

PRESENCE.

When any one in the spiritual world is thinking about another from a desire to speak with him, the other immediately becomes *present*, and they see each other face to face (n. 29, 50, 326). He who does not love another, or still more, he who hates another, does not see or meet him. They are distant in the degree of their hatred or absence of their love (n. 326 [2]). *Presence* comes from the remembrance of another with a desire to see him (n. 326 [3]). The reason is that in the spiritual world there is no distance as in the natural world, but only an appearance of distance (n. 326). With every man there are spirits *present*, and they are as really *present* as if the man were included in their society (n. 50 [2]). Space and time have nothing to do with that *presence*, because affection and thought from it are not in space and time; and spirits and angels are affections and thoughts therefrom (n. 50 [2]).

PRESENT.

Who they are who think from what is *present* in the world and not from what is *present* in heaven (n. 59). How any one in the spiritual world shows himself *present* (n. 29, 50). (*See* PRESENCE.)

PRESERVATION.

(*See* CONSERVATION) (n. 3 [3]).

PRIDE IN ONE'S INTELLIGENCE.

(N. 197, 206, 321 [8].)

PRINCE OF THE WORLD.

That honors and possessions are bestowed by the devil is confessed, for from this he is called the *Prince of the world* (n. 216 [2]).

PRINCIPLES.

In every man there are two *principles* of life, the one natural and the other spiritual; the natural *principle* of life being the heart's pulsation, and the spiritual *principle* of life the mind's volition (n. 193 [2]).

PROCEED (TO).

Difference between creating and *proceeding* (n. 219 [2]). Nothing can *proceed* from any one except what is in him (n. 219 [2]). Nothing but what is temporal can *proceed* from man, and nothing but what is eternal from the Lord (n. 219 [2]). Of all that goes forth (from the Lord) the Divine providence is primary (n. 331).

PROCEEDING (THE DIVINE).

The Infinite and Eternal from itself is *the Divine going forth*, that is, the Lord in others created from Himself, thus in men and in angels (n. 55). This *Divine going forth* is the same as the Divine providence (n. 55).

PRODUCE (TO).

What is *produced* does not proceed, but is created (n. 219). (*See* To PROCEED.)

PROFANATION.

In the most general sense *profanation* means all impiety (n. 229). There are several kinds of *profanation* of what is holy (n. 226, 229–233); some lighter and some more grievous, but they may be referred to seven kinds (n. 231). The worst kind of *profanation* (n. 229). He that upholds evil loves does violence to Divine goods, and this violence is called adulteration of good (n. 221 [3]). In the Word, adulterations of good are depicted by adulteries, and falsifications of truth by whoredoms (n. 233 [10]). These adulterations and falsifications are effected by reasonings from the natural man, which is in evil (n. 233 [10]). (*See* To PROFANE.)

PROFANERS

Mean all the impious who in heart deny God, the holiness of the Word and the spiritual things of the church therefrom, which are essentially holy things, and who also speak impiously of these (n. 229). Only those who have a knowledge of holy things can profane them (n. 257 [5]). Difference between *profaners* and the profane (n. 229). (*See* PROFANE.)

PROFANE (THE),

Are those who profess to believe in God, who assert the holiness of the Word, and who acknowledge the spiritual things of the church, the most of whom, however, only with the mouth (n. 229). Such commit profanation for the reason that what is holy from the Word is in them and with them; and this which is in them and which makes some part of their understanding and will they profane; but in the impious who deny the Divine and Divine things there is nothing that can be profaned (n. 229).

PROFANE (TO).

Those who *profane* holy things by mixing them with things *profane* are such as first accept and acknowledge them and afterwards backslide and deny (n. 228). The seventh kind of profanation is committed by those who first acknowledge Divine truths and live according to them, but afterwards recede and deny them. This is the worst kind

of profanation (n. 231 [7], 232). What is meant by *"profaning* the name of God" (n. 230 [2]).

PROGRESSION.

Each thing and all things in the growth of every shrub and every herb of the field goes forth regularly and wonderfully from end to end, according to the laws of their order. There can be nothing that in its *progress* does not go on most regularly in accordance with the laws of the Divine providence (n. 332 [2]). There must needs be a regular *progression* in the reformation and regeneration of men (n. 332 [4]). Every created thing goes forth from a First, which is the Infinite and Eternal, to things last. And from things last to the First from whom it came (n. 56).

PROPHET.

The "name" and "reward of a *prophet"* (*Matt.* x. 41, 42), mean the state and the happiness of those who are in Divine truths (n. 230 [3]).

PROPRIUM (THE).

(*See* SELF (ONE'S OWN).)

PROVIDE (TO).

The Lord *provides* that every one may be saved (n. 328 [8]). It is *provided* by the Lord that a new church should follow the previous devastated church (n. 328 [10]).

PROVIDENCE (THE DIVINE),

Is the government of the Lord's Divine love and Divine wisdom (n. 1, 2, 331, 337). Whence *the Divine providence* is and what it is (n. 207). The restoration of the marriage of good and truth in every created thing, and the consequent conjunction of the created universe with the Lord through man, must be the end of *the Divine providence* (n. 9). *The Divine providence* has as its end a heaven consisting of men who have become or are becoming angels (n. 27 [2], 202). *The Divine providence* looks, in everything that it does, to what is infinite and eternal (n. 46).

The Infinite and Eternal in itself must needs look to what is infinite and eternal from itself in things finite (n. 52, 58). *The Divine providence* in its whole progress with man looks to his eternal state (n. 59). The laws of *the Divine providence* heretofore hidden in the wisdom of angels are now revealed (n. 70 [3]). It is a law of *the Divine providence* that man should act from freedom in accordance with reason (n. 71, 97). It is a law of *the Divine providence* that man should as if from himself put away evils as sins in the external man (n. 100). It is a law of *the Divine providence* that man should not be compelled by external means to think and will, and thus to believe and love the things of religion, but should guide himself and sometimes compel himself (n. 129). It is a law of *the Divine providence* that man should be led and taught by the Lord from heaven by means of the Word and by means of doctrine and preaching from the Word, and this to all appearance as if by himself (n. 154). It is a law of *the Divine providence* that nothing of the operation of *the Divine providence* should be evident to man's perceptions or senses, but that he should, nevertheless, know about it and acknowledge it (n. 175). If the operation of *the Divine providence* were made evident to man's perceptions and senses he would not act from freedom in accordance with reason, nor would any thing appear to him to be his (n. 176). If man clearly saw *the Divine providence* he would set himself against the order and tenor of its course, and would pervert and destroy it (n. 180). If man clearly saw *the Divine providence*, either he would deny God or he would make himself to be God (n. 182). *The Divine providence* never acts in accord with the will's love in man, but constantly against it (n. 183, 234). The Lord in His *Divine providence* leads men as silently as a hidden current or favoring tide bears a vessel (n. 186). It is granted man to see *the Divine providence* in the back and not in the face; also to see it in a spiritual state and not in his natural state. To see *the Divine*

providence in the back and not in the face is to see it after it occurs and not before (n. 187). *The Divine providence* works by means, and the means operate through man or through the world (n. 187 [2]). The man who has become spiritual by the acknowledgment of God, and wise by a rejection of what is his own (*proprium*), sees *the Divine providence* in the whole world and in all and each of the things in it (n. 189). *The Divine providence*, because of its minute particulars, is universal (n. 191, 202). *The Divine providence* is in the minutest particulars of nature and in the minutest particulars of human prudence, and it is from these that it is universal (n. 201 [3]). *The Divine providence*, in order that man may not perish, works so secretly that scarcely any one knows of its existence (n. 211). *The Divine providence* by things constant and things inconstant deals wonderfully with human prudence, and yet conceals itself (n. 212). *The Divine providence* looks to eternal things, and to temporal things only so far as they make one with eternal things (n. 214). The conjunction of temporal things and eternal things in man is the Lord's *Divine providence* (n. 220). All the laws of *the Divine providence* have for their end the reformation and consequent salvation of man (n. 279 [4]). *The Divine providence* is equally with the evil and with the good (n. 285). *The Divine providence*, not only with the good but with the evil as well is universal in every least particular, and yet it is not in their evils (n. 287). *The Divine providence* appropriates neither evil nor good to any one; but man's own prudence appropriates both (n. 308). The Lord cannot act contrary to the laws of *the Divine providence*, because acting contrary to them would be acting contrary to His Divine love and contrary to His Divine wisdom, thus contrary to Himself (n. 331). The subject of *the Divine providence* is man. the means the Divine truths whereby man gains wisdom and the Divine goods whereby he gains love (n. 331 [3]). *The Divine providence* does all things out of pure mercy (n. 337). The operation of *the Divine providence* for the salvation of man begins at his birth and continues until the end of his life and afterwards to eternity (n. 332, 333). Looking to what is infinite and eternal in the formation of the angelic heaven, that it may be before the Lord as one Man which is an image of Himself, is the inmost of *the Divine providence* (n. 64, 67, 68). The inmost of *the Divine providence* respecting hell (n. 69). Who those who acknowledge God and His *Divine providence* are like, and who those who acknowledge nature and their own prudence (n. 208). Man's own (*proprium*) has an inborn enmity against *the Divine providence* (n. 211). Arguments of those who confirm themselves against *the Divine providence* (n. 236–240). Arguments refuted (n. 241–274). (*See* TABLE OF CONTENTS.)

PRUDENCE

Is from God, and not from man (n. 191 [2]). That man's own *prudence* is nothing is contrary to appearance (n. 191). *Prudence* has no other source than intelligence and wisdom (n. 191). Man's own *prudence* is from the love of self and from conceit in his own intelligence (n. 321 [8]). Human *prudence* is nothing (n. 70). Man's own *prudence* is nothing; it merely appears to be something, and should so appear (n. 191). Man from his own *prudence* persuades himself and corroborates in himself that all good and truth are from himself and in himself, likewise all evil and falsity (n. 312). Two priests in the spiritual world disputing with a royal ambassador about human *prudence* (n. 197 [2]). Whence man's *prudence* is and what it is (n. 206, 316, 321 [8]). What one's own *prudence* is and what *prudence* not one's own is (n. 310–326). Who those are who acknowledge nature and their own *prudence* (n. 208). *Prudence* is the "talent" given the servants to trade with (*Luke* xix., *Matt.* xxv.) (n. 210 [2]).

PRUDENTLY.

He who thinks and acts *prudently* as if from himself and at the same time acknowledges that he does it from the Lord is a man, while he who confirms in himself that every thing he thinks and does is from himself is not a man (n. 321).

PUNISHMENT.

Its own *punishment* follows every evil; it is as if its *punishment* were inscribed upon the evil, and this *punishment* the wicked man endures after death (n. 249 [3]). No one is reformed by threats and *punishments*, because they compel (n. 136). (*See* COMPEL.)

PURIFICATION

Is effected in two ways, one by temptations, the other by fermentations (n. 25). All cleansing from evils is from the Lord (n. 151 [2]). The Lord's Divine providence causes both the evil and the falsity to be serviceable in the way of equilibrium, of relation, and of *purification*, and thus in the conjunction of good and truth in others (n. 21, 25). Means of *purification* and withdrawal of the delights of the lusts of evil belonging to the internal man (n. 296 [10]). (*See* CLEANSING.)

PURPOSE.

To think from *purpose* is to will and to do (n. 152). *Purposes* are thoughts from the will (n. 152). (*See* INTENTION.)

QUADRUPED.

At first man would creep like a *quadruped*, but with an inherent endeavor to raise himself upon his feet (n. 275).

QUAKERS

Classed with heretics (n. 259, 238), and enthusiastic spirits (n. 321).

QUALITY.

Whatever has existence derives from form that which is called *quality* (n. 4 [2]). (*See* FORM.)

RAIN.

(In *Matt.* v. 45, as elsewhere in the Word) means the Divine truth of the Divine wisdom (n. 173, 292).

RATIONAL (THE),

Of those who are both in the appearance and in the truth is a spiritual-*rational*, while the *rational* of those who are in the appearance apart from the truth is a natural-*rational* (n. 154 [3]). The natural-*rational* may be likened to a garden as it is in the light of winter, while the spiritual-*rational* may be likened to a garden as it is in the light of spring (n. 154 [3]). Those who are *rationally* blind (n. 168 [5]).

RATIONALITY

Is the faculty of understanding (n. 73 [1, 3]). Unless man possessed a will from the faculty that is called liberty and an understanding from the faculty that is called *rationality* he would not be a man (n. 96 [4], 98, 167, 227, 285). *Rationality* and liberty are in man from the Lord (n. 73). *Rationality* itself is from spiritual light, and not at all from natural light (n. 167). It is the light of heaven which gives enlightenment (n. 168 [2]). By *rationality* a man may be raised up into wisdom almost angelic (n. 222). Those that are in hell have the ability to understand that is called *rationality*, but the spiritual light which these have from *rationality* is changed into infernal light (n. 167). (*See* FACULTY, LIBERTY, RATIONAL (THE).)

RAVEN.

The "*raven*" used to illustrate the confirmation of a falsity (n. 318 [4]).

REASON (TO).

The Lord is willing that a man should think and talk about Divine things and also *reason* about them, for the purpose of seeing a thing to be so or not so (n. 219 [3]).

REASONERS.

Sensual men are above others shrewd and cunning, and ingenious *reasoners*, and they call shrewdness and cunning intelligence and wisdom, nor do they know otherwise (n. 310 [2]).

RECEPTACLE.

Man was created that he might be a *receptacle* of the Divine love and of the Divine wisdom (n. 328 [5]). How a civil and moral life is a *receptacle* of spiritual life (n. 322 [2]).

RECIPIENT.

For good to be good in itself, and for truth to be truth in itself, they must make one in the *recipient*, that is, in an angel of heaven or a man on the earth (n. 10).

RECIPROCAL.

The conjunction of the Lord with man, and the *reciprocal* conjunction of man with the Lord is effected by means of the faculties of rationality and liberty (n. 92, 96 [6]). There is no conjunction of minds unless it is *reciprocal*, and the *reciprocation* is what conjoins (n. 92 [2]). What the *reciprocal* in man is (n. 92 [3]). The *reciprocal* conjunction of angels with the Lord is not from the angels, but is as if it were from them (n. 28 [4]).

REFORM (TO).

The external man must be *reformed* by means of the internal and not the reverse (n. 150). Man is not *reformed* unless the external is *reformed* as well as the internal (n. 151). The external is *reformed* by means of the internal when the external refrains from the evils that the internal does not will because they are infernal, and still more when the external for this reason shuns evils and fights against them (n. 151). It is by means of the faculties called rationality and liberty that man is *reformed* and regenerated by the Lord, and without them he cannot be *reformed* and regenerated (n. 82, 85, 96 [5]). No one is *reformed* by miracles and signs (n. 130); nor by visions or conversations with the dead (n. 134); nor by threats and punishments (n. 136); nor in states that do not spring from rationality and liberty (n. 138). No one is *reformed* in a state of fear (n. 139); or in a state of misfortune (n. 140); nor in unhealthy mental states (n. 141); nor in a state of bodily disease (n. 142); nor in states of ignorance (n. 143). After death man can no longer be *reformed* and regenerated; he remains such as his ruling love has been in this world (n. 17). Without a knowledge and recognition of the evils and falsities, and the goods and truths of his life and doctrine in himself, man cannot be *reformed* (n. 16). How the internal man is *reformed*, and the external by means of it (n. 151).

REFORMATION.

All *reformation* is effected in completeness, that is, simultaneously in first principles and in outmosts; and outmosts are *reformed* in agreement with first principles while man is in the world (n. 277b). Why man cannot be *reformed* afterwards (n. 277b). Man comes into the state of *reformation* when he begins to think that there is such a thing as sin, and still more when he thinks that this or that is a sin, and when he examines it in himself and refrains from willing it (n. 83 [5]). Stages in *reformation* described (n. 151). All *reformation* is effected by means of truth (n. 298 [5]). Principal means of *reformation* (n. 233 [3]). (*See* REGENERATION.)

REGENERATE (TO),

Man is to unite good and truth in him, or love and wisdom, as they are united in the Divine that goes forth from the Lord (n. 58). With one who is *regenerated* the order of life is reversed; from being natural he becomes spiritual (n. 83 [6]). After death man can no longer be reformed and *regenerated* (n. 17). (*See* REFORM (TO), ACKNOWLEDGMENT.)

REGENERATION.

The conjunction of man with the Lord and of the Lord with man is what is called reformation and *regeneration* (n. 123). *Regeneration* begins when man refrains from evils as sins; it progresses as he shuns them, and is perfected as he fights against them; and as he from the Lord conquers them he is *regenerated* (n. 83 [6]). By means of rationality and liberty man is reformed and *regenerated*, and without them he cannot be reformed and *regenerated* (n. 85).

RELATION.

The conjunction of good and truth is provided by the Lord by means of *relation* (n. 24). The quality of a good is known only by its *relation* to what is less good, and by its contrariety to evil (n. 24).

RELIGION.

To shun evils as sins is the Christian *religion* itself (n. 265). Hitherto men have not known that to shun evils as sins is the Christian *religion* itself (n. 265, 278b). The Christian *religion* is accepted only in the smaller division of the habitable globe called Europe, and is there divided (n. 256). All the human beings that are born, however many and in whatever *religion*, can be saved, provided they acknowledge God and live according to the commandments in the Decalogue (n. 253, 254 [2], 322 [4]). The Lord provides that there shall be some *religion* everywhere, and that there shall be these two things in every *religion* (n. 326 [9]). No man gets his *religion* from himself, but through another who has either learned directly from the Word or by transmission from others (n. 254). The Lord has provided that there shall be in every *religion* precepts like those in the Decalogue (n. 254 [2]). There are two things that are at once the essentials and the universals of *religion*, namely, acknowledgment of God and repentance (n. 340 [2]). When a *religion* has been once implanted in a nation the Lord leads that nation according to its precepts and dogmas (n. 254 [2]). Every nation that lives according to its *religion*, that is, that refrains from doing evil because it is contrary to its god, receives something of the spiritual in its natural (n. 322 [4]). In process of time every *religion* declines and is consummated (n. 328). The understanding is blinded not only by ignorance but also by a *religion* that teaches a blind faith, also by false doctrine (n. 144). In every one that has any *religion* there is implanted a knowledge that after death he will live as a man (n. 274). To acknowledge God and to refrain from doing evil because it is against God are the two things that make a *religion* to be a *religion* (n. 326 [9]).

RELIGIOUS SYSTEMS.

Principles of various *religious systems* (n. 253, 254, 139). Solomon's wives, seven hundred in number, represented the various religions in the world. A concubine represents a religion (n. 245). The Mohammedan religion is accepted by more kingdoms than the Christian religion (n. 255). (*See* MOHAMMEDAN.)

REMISSION (THE),

Of sin is not its removal; so far as evils are removed they are *remitted* (n. 279, 280). Repentance precedes *remission*, and without repentance there is no *remission* (n. 280). Man must examine himself, see his sins, acknowledge them, confess them before God, and refrain from them; this is repentance, *remission* of sins, and consequently salvation (n. 127).

REMIT.

To every one the Lord *remits* sins. He does not accuse and impute. And yet He can take them away only in accordance with the laws of the Divine providence (n. 280). When sins have been *remitted* they are not also removed; but when sins have been removed they have also been *remitted* (n. 280). (*See* REMISSION.)

REPENTANCE

Precedes remission, and without *repentance* there is no remission (n. 280). *Repentance* is void of meaning to those who believe that men are saved out of mere mercy, however they live (n. 340 [2]). Without *repentance* man is in evil, and evil is hell (n. 340 [3]). When a man wishes to repent he must look to the Lord alone; if he looks to God the Father only he cannot be cleansed; nor if he looks to the Father for the sake of the Son, nor if he looks to the Son as merely a man (n. 122). *Repentance* from sins is the way to heaven; faith separate from *repentance* is not faith; and those who are not in faith because

they do not repent are in the way to hell (n. 114 [2], 127).

REPRESENT.

The men of Judah and Israel were led into the land of Canaan merely that they might *represent* the church (n. 132). A bad man equally with a good man may *represent* the church and its internals by means of the externals of worship (n. 132).

REPRODUCTION.

The final thing to which the tree aims is seed, in which its *reproductive* power exists anew (n. 3 [2]).

RESIDENCE.

The Lord has His *residence* in man, both in the evil and in the good, in the two faculties called rationality and liberty (n. 96 [5]).

RESTORATION (THE),

Of the marriage of good and truth in every created thing, and the consequent conjunction of the created universe with the Lord through man, must be the end of Divine providence (n. 9).

RESURRECTION.

In every one that has any religion there is implanted a knowledge that after death he will live as a man (n. 274).

REVENGE

Has its source in the love of self (n. 276 [2]).

REWARD.

The *reward* of a prophet (*Matt.* x. 41, 42) means the happiness of those who are in Divine truths; and the *reward* of a righteous man means the happiness of those who are in Divine goods (n. 230 [3]).

RICHES.

What the love of *riches* and dignities for their own sake is, and what the love of dignities and *riches* for the sake of uses is (n. 215 [6]). How the love of *riches* arose (n. 215 [4]). (*See* POSSESSIONS, WEALTH.)

RULE (LOVE OF),

When it gradually came in (n. 215 [3], and the result (n. 215 [5]).

RULE (TO).

The Lord *rules* the whole angelic heaven as one man; the Lord *rules* heaven as the soul *rules* its body; the whole human race is *ruled* by the Lord, not through heaven but from heaven by the Lord, consequently from Himself, because He is heaven (n. 163). (*See* GOVERN.)

RUMINATING.

Man's memory may be compared to the *ruminating* stomach of certain animals. Man's memory contains truths which in themselves are knowledges, and so far as by thinking, or as it were by *ruminating*, he draws these from the memory, his spiritual mind is nourished (n. 233 [8]).

SABBATH (THE),

In the Israelitish church was the most holy thing of worship, for it signified the union of truth with good and of good with truth in man, for thus man is united to the Lord (n. 21).

SACRIFICES.

Worship by *sacrifices* was first instituted in the Hebraic Church which arose from Heber (n. 328 [2]).

SAGES.

That man's mind cannot die the *sages* or wise men of old saw; for they said, "How can the mind die when it has the capacity to be wise?" (n. 324 [3]).

SALVATION.

The Lord wills the *salvation* of all (n. 221). Without the Lord there is no *salvation*. No one is saved for the reason that the Lord is known to him, but because he lives in accordance with the Lord's commandments (n. 330 [6]). The Divine providence has for its end nothing else than reformation and consequent *salvation* (n. 257). *Salvation* can be accomplished only through an acknowledgment of the Divinity of the Lord, and a confidence that the Lord effects *salvation* when man lives according to His commandments. Instantaneous *salvation* from mercy apart from means is impossible (n. 338). Instantaneous *salvation* out of mercy apart from means is the "fiery flying serpent" in the church (n. 340). (*See* SAVE (TO).)

SATAN.

The falsity of evil and *Satan* are one (n. 33 [3]). Those who confirm in themselves the lusts of evil are called *satans* (n. 310 [3]). (*See* HEAVEN AND HELL.)

SAVE.

It is of the Divine providence that every man can be *saved*, and that those are *saved* who acknowledge God and live well (n. 325). No mortal could have been *saved* unless the Lord had come into the world (n. 124 [4]). The operation of the Divine providence for the salvation of man begins at his birth and continues until the end of his life, and afterwards to eternity (n. 332-335). But no more can be *saved* than are willing to be *saved* (n. 333). Those who are willing to be *saved* who acknowledge God and are led by Him (n. 333). Every one, in whatever heresies he may be in respect to the understanding, can be reformed and *saved* if only he shuns evils as sins and does not confirm heretical falsities in himself (n. 259 [3]). That only those born within the church are *saved* is an insane heresy (n. 330 [5]). He who acknowledges God and lives rightly becomes spiritual in his degree and is *saved* (n. 330 [5]).

SECURITY

Of life arises either from the impious man's belief that there is no life after death, or from the belief of him who separates life from salvation (n. 340 [4]).

SEE.

What the Lord teaches He gives man ability to perceive rationally in two ways—*seeing* in himself that it is so, and understanding it by means of reasons. His *seeing* it in himself is in his internal man; his understanding it by means of reasons is in the external man (n. 150 [2]).

SEED (THE),

Is the primal form of the love in which the father is; it is the form of his ruling love with its nearest derivations, which are the inmost affections of that love (n. 277a [3]). The soul is in the *seed*, for from the *seed* is impregnation, and the *seed* is what is clothed with a body by the mother (n. 277a [3]).

SELF (ONE'S OWN).

This *own* is the love of *self* and the love of the world therefrom, or is the love of the world and the love of *self* therefrom (n. 206). Man has a voluntary *self* (*proprium*) and an intellectual *self;* the voluntary *self* is evil, and the intellectual *self* is falsity therefrom (n. 298 [3]). The love of *self* viewed in itself is the love of *one's own* (*proprium*); and man's own in respect to its affections, which are all natural, is not unlike the life of a beast (n. 233 [12]). Not a grain of will or of prudence that is his *own* is possible in any man (n. 293). No man, according to the common understanding of his *own*, has any thing his own (n. 309). The things proper to nature are especially spaces and times, both having limit and termination; the things therefore proper to man are those that belong to his *own* will and his *own* understanding (n. 219). All things proper to the Lord are infinite and eternal, thus without time, consequently without limit and without end. Things therefrom seemingly proper to man are likewise infinite and eternal, yet nothing of them is man's, but they belong to the Lord alone in man (n. 219).

SENSATION.

The quality of a good is known only by its relation to what is less good and by its contrariety to evil. From this comes all power to perceive and to feel (n. 24).

SENSES.

Of the *senses* of the body and their relation to the mind (n. 314). It is man's mind or spirit that perceives things by the *senses* (n. 314).

SENSUAL.

The ancients called men who had confirmed appearances as truths, and had thus become *sensual*, serpents of the tree of knowledge (n. 310). Such a man is shrewd, crafty, and an ingenious reasoner above others (*see Gen.* iii. 1) (n. 310 [2, 5]).

SEPARATION,

(*See* SEVERANCE.)

SERPENT (THE),

Signifies the sensual of man and what is his own (*proprium*), which in itself is the love of self and the pride of self-intelligence, thus the devil and Satan (n. 313 [2], 211). The "serpent" is evil of all kinds (n. 211). The "head of the *serpent*" (*Gen.* iii. 15) is love of self (n. 211). By "the fiery flying *serpent*" (*Isa.* xiv. 29) evil glowing from infernal fire is meant (n. 340). The ancients called those who believed only the things perceived through the senses *serpents* of the tree of knowledge (n. 310). The condemnation of the *serpent* (*Gen.* iii. 14) signifies the condemnation of one's own love and one's own intelligence (n. 313 [3]).

SERVITUDE.

Heavenly freedom is freedom itself, and consequently its opposite is slavery both to the good and to the evil (n. 43). Every man wishes to be free, and to put away from himself non-freedom or *servitude* (n. 148). Man does not know what spiritual *servitude* is and what spiritual liberty is; he does not possess the truths that teach this; and without truths spiritual *servitude* is believed to be freedom, and spiritual freedom to be *servitude* (n. 149). To be led by good is freedom, and to be led by evil is slavery (n. 43). Why man does not wish to come out of spiritual *servitude* into spiritual liberty (n. 149).

SEVERAL. SEVERALLY.

(*See* PARTICULARS.)

SEVERANCE.

So far as one denies the Lord he is separated from Him. *Severance* causes hell to turn the man's face to itself, and he is then led to hell (n. 326 [4,5]).

SHEATH.

The pleura, which is the general *sheath* of the chest (n. 180[3]). The peritoneum, the general *sheath* of the abdominal viscera (n. 180 [4]). *Sheaths* surrounding the several organs, as the stomach, liver, pancreas, spleen, intestines, mesentery, kidneys (n. 180 [4]).

SHEEP.

"To call the *sheep* by name" (*John* x. 2, 3) means to teach and to lead every one who is in the good of charity according to the state of his love and wisdom (n. 230 [4]).

SHEPHERD (THE).

To be saved the Lord Himself must be approached, and whoever goes to Him is a *shepherd* of the sheep (n. 230 [4]).

SHUN.

So far as one *shuns* evils as diabolical and as obstacles to the Lord's entrance he is more and more nearly conjoined with the Lord, and he the most nearly who abominates them as so many dusky and fiery devils (n. 33 [3]).

SICKNESS.

When a man is *sick*, and is thinking about death and the state of his soul after death, he is not in the world, but in spirit he is withdrawn; and in this state no one can be reformed (n. 142). No one is reformed in unhealthy mental states, because they take away rationality. For the mind may be *sick* and unsound; and while a sound mind is rational a *sick* mind is not (n. 141). When the body is *sick* the mind is also *sick* (n. 142). Some unhealthy mental states named (n. 141). It is vain to think that any can repent or receive any faith during *sickness*, for in such repentance there is nothing of action, and in such faith nothing of charity (n. 142 [2]).

28

If men had not been reformed before their *sickness*, if they die they afterwards become such as they were before the *sickness* (n. 142 [2]).

SIDON,

One of the kingdoms in which the Ancient Church existed and where the Ancient Word was known (n. 328 [2]).

SIGHT.

Man has an internal and an external *sight* (n. 166). Internal *sight* is that of the understanding by spiritual objects, and the external *sight* is that of the eye by natural objects (n. 166). The *eyesight* of the angels of heaven is formed for the reception of their light, and the *eyesight* of the spirits of hell for the reception of their light (n. 167).

SIGNS.

No one is reformed by miracles and *signs*, because they compel (n. 130).

SIMPLE.

The *simpler* and purer any thing is, the more and the fuller it is (n. 6). The belief of many that there is an only first substance, the source of all things, so *simple* that nothing is *simpler*, is a fallacy (n. 6).

SIMULTANEOUS.

In the outmost there is a *simultaneous* presence of all things from the first (n. 124 [4]). The Lord acts upon every particular in man singly, but *simultaneously* through all things of his form (n. 124 [3]). The Lord acts from inmosts and from outmosts *simultaneously* (n. 124 [4]). How the *simultaneous* produces the successive (n. 12).

SINGLE. SINGLY.

(*See* PARTICULARS, UNIVERSALS.)

SINS.

When *sins* have been removed they have also been remitted; but not the reverse (n. 280). Of those who confess themselves guilty of all *sins* and do not search out any *sin* in themselves (n.

278*b*). A confession of all *sin* is unconsciousness of all (n. 278*b*).

SKELETONS.

Of profaners who in the light of heaven look like *skeletons;* some like *skeletons* of the color of bone, some as fiery *skeletons*, and others as charred (n. 226).

SKIN (THE),

Does not feel from itself, but it is man's mind or spirit that there perceives things by the sense, and is affected by it in accordance with its nature (n. 314). Man knows so little as to amount to scarcely anything of how *the skin* feels (n. 336). It has been provided by the Lord that those who could not be reached by the Gospel, but only by a religion, should also have a place in the Divine Man, that is, heaven, constituting those parts that are called *skins*, membranes, cartilages, and bones (n. 254 [3], 326 [10]).

SLAVERY.

(*See* SERVITUDE.)

SMELL.

All that a man sees, hears, *smells*, tastes and feels, flows in (n. 308 [2]). Evil in itself is a stench, while good in itself is fragrant (n. 305).

SMOKE,

Like that of a conflagration, through which no spiritual truth in its own light could pass, surrounds the hells of those who are loves of self and the world (n. 250 [4]).

SOCIETY.

The entire heaven is arranged in *societies* according to the affections of good, and the entire hell according to the lusts of evil opposite to the affections of good (n. 278*b* [6]). As to his spirit every man is in some *society;* in a heavenly *society* if he is in an affection for good, but in an infernal *society* if he is in a lust of evil (n. 278*b* [6], 296 [6], 307). Sometimes when in deep meditation he appears there (n. 296 [6]). But a man is

not there in the same way as a spirit who has been assigned to the *society*, for a man is constantly in a state to be reformed, and he is transferred by the Lord from one *society* to another, in accordance with his life and its changes (n. 307 [2]). Each *society* of heaven is as one man before the Lord (n. 64).

SOCINIANISM AND ARIANISM,

Which reign in more hearts than you believe, arose from the thought of God as three persons (n. 262 [2], 256 [3]).

SOCINIANS,

Their final condition in the other life (n. 231 [6]; *also* 257 [4]).

SOLOMON

Represented the Lord after His coming; and because the Lord after the glorification of His Human had power over heaven and earth, so *Solomon* appeared in glory and magnificence, and possessed wisdom above all the kings of the earth (n. 245). Why he was permitted to establish idolatrous worship and to marry so many wives (n. 245; *see also* n. 236).

SOMETHING.

Every thing that perishes and comes to nothing is inwardly in itself nothing; outwardly it is *something*, but it is not so inwardly (n. 217 [6]). There is an appearance that good is *something* apart from truth, and that truth is *something* apart from good; and yet they are not (n. 11). Good is nothing apart from truth, and truth is not any thing apart from good (n. 11). That which is in good and also in truth is *something;* but that which is in evil and also falsity is not anything (n. 19). Unless the Infinite God were the All and were Substance itself and Wisdom itself, man would not be anything (n. 46 [2]).

SOUL.

Every one's *soul* is from the father, and from the mother it is merely clothed with a body (n. 277*a* [3]). The *soul* is in the seed, for from the seed is impregnation, and the seed is what is clothed with a body by the mother (n. 277a [3]). Man's *soul* is nothing else than the love of his will and the love therefrom of his understanding (n. 199 [3]). If man attributes all things to himself and to nature, the love of self becomes the *soul;* but if he attributes all things to the Lord love to the Lord becomes the *soul* (n. 199 [3]). Naturalists have been able to comprehend the state of the *soul* after death only in a sensual way, and not spiritually (n. 310 [3]). Of the secret operations of the *soul* in the body (n. 296 [14], 336.)

SOUND.

Tone corresponds to affection, and speech to thought (n. 279 [8]). The affection of one's love can be recognized from one's tone when speaking; and from the variation of it, which is speech, his thought can be recognized (n. 194). The tone of the voice in speaking and singing, and its articulations which are words of speech, and the modulations of singing, are made by the lungs (n. 279 [8]). Hypocrites are sometimes permitted in the spiritual world to speak otherwise than as they think, and by the discord their hypocrisy is disclosed (n. 224 [3]).

SPACE AND TIME

Are properties of nature (n. 51). *Time* is only an appearance in accord with the state of affection from which the thought springs. The same is true of thought about distance in *space* (n. 49). In the spiritual world there is no *space*, but there distance and presence are appearances in accordance with similarities and dissimilarities of affection (n. 33 [4]). Angels and spirits are not in *space and time*, but only in the appearance of them (n. 50).

SPEAK.

The simple and the wise *speak* alike but do not think alike (n. 162 [3]). In the spiritual world no one can *speak* otherwise than he thinks (n. 224 [3]). All *speech* flows from thought as an effect from its cause (n. 308 [2]). Every-

thing that a man says and does flows in, although derivatively or mediately (n. 308 [2]). Unless man had an external and an internal of thought from liberty and rationality he would not be able to *speak*, but only to utter sounds like a beast (n. 104 [2]).

SPEAKING. SINGING.

How the articulations of *speech* and the modulations of *singing* are produced (n. 279 [8]). (*See* SOUND.)

SPEECH

Corresponds to thought, and tone to the affections (n. 279 [8]). All *speech* flows from thought as an effect from its cause (n. 308 [2]). How *speech* is produced (n. 279 [8]). (*See* SOUND.)

SPHERES.

In the spiritual world all are joined together in accord with the *spheres* that exhale from their affections through their thoughts (n. 196). What each one is is recognized from the *sphere* of his life (n. 196).

SPIDER (THE).

Infernal love with its affections for evil and falsity likened to a *spider* with its surrounding web (n. 107).

SPIRALS.

Changes and variations in the organic forms of the mind cannot be expressed in words of natural language except as vortex-like circlings inward and outward, after the manner of perpetual and curving *spirals*, wonderfully combined into forms receptive of life (n. 319 [2]). In the good these *spiral* forms are turned forward towards the Lord, but with the evil they are turned backward toward hell (n. 319 [3]).

SPIRIT (THE).

Every man's *spirit* is affection and the thought therefrom (n. 61, 196).

SPIRIT (THE HOLY).

What is meant by the sin against *the Holy Spirit* which is not forgiven (n. 98 [3], 231 [6]).

SPIRITS

Are joined together in accord with the spheres that exhale from their affections through their thoughts (n. 196). All in the spiritual world think from the affections of their life's love (n. 196). Conversation with the dead would have the same effect as miracles—one would be persuaded and forced, and thus be deprived of rationality, and at the same time evils are shut in, to break out with blasphemy and profanation. But this takes place only when some dogma of religion has been imposed upon the mind by *spirits*, which is never done by any good *spirit*, still less by any angel of heaven (n. 134*b*). Swedenborg's personal experiences with *spirits* (n. 135).

SPIRITUAL MAN (THE).

The natural man, however civilly and morally he may act, is called dead; but *the spiritual man* is called living (n. 322 [3]). Man becomes *spiritual* by the acknowledgment of God (n. 189); and not doing evil because it is against God (n. 322 [3]). The *spiritual* state (n. 189).

SPIRITUAL SENSE OF THE WORD.

Why that sense has not been revealed before. Now revealed for a new church that will acknowledge and worship the Lord alone and will hold His Word holy (n. 264).

SPLEEN.

(N. 279 [7].) The *spleen* purifies the blood (n. 336).

SPONGE.

When truth has been taken away from a man, after death, he imbibes such falsity as agrees with his evil as a *sponge* imbibes water (n. 17).

SQUARING OF THE CIRCLE.

Comparison between angelic wisdom and Divine wisdom drawn from what is said about *squaring the circle* (n. 335 [2]).

STATES.

Every man when he becomes a spirit is introduced by turns into the two *states*

of his life, the external and the internal (n. 298). The spiritual *state* of man (that after death) is wholly different from the natural *state* (n. 338[4]). A spirit is usually let into alternate *states* of wisdom and insanity that he may see the latter from the former (n. 223). To understand how man is regenerated three things must be considered; his first *state*, which is a *state* of damnation; his second, which is a *state* of reformation; and his third, that of regeneration (n. 83). From a man's *state* in the natural world no conclusion can be formed about what his *state* will be after death (n. 338 [5]). No one is reformed in *states* that do not spring from rationality and liberty (n. 138). These *states* are many: some enumerated (n. 138–144).

STATUE (THE),

Seen by Nebuchadnezzar in a dream (*Dan.* ii. 32, 33), means the four churches —the Most Ancient, the Ancient, the Hebraic, and that of Israel and Judah (n. 328 2]). He who, because he knows that wisdom and prudence are from God, still waits for influx, becomes like a *statue* (n. 321).

STATUTES (THE),

Of the church with the nation of Israel and Judah represented the spiritual things of the church, which are its internals (n. 245).

STOMACH,

Its function and operation (n. 279 [7], 296 [14], 336). Man's memory may be compared to the ruminating *stomach* of certain animals (n. 233 [8]). No one knows how the soul operates to cause the *stomach* to digest (n. 174, 180 [6]).

STUMBLING-BLOCKS.

Hindrances or Stumbling-blocks of the Impenitent (n. 258 [5]).

SUBDUE.

He who *subdues* the love of rule from the love of self easily *subdues* all other evil loves, for this is their head (n. 146).

SUBJECTS.

Affections and thoughts are possible only in substances and their forms, which are *subjects* (n. 279 [6], 319 [2]). It is the form that makes the *subject*, of which quality, state, power to effect and any thing that accords with the perfection of the form, can be predicated (n. 4 [2]).

SUBSISTENCE.

(*See* PERMANENCE.)

SUBSTANCE.

There is an only *substance* which is the first *substance* and the source of all things (n. 6, 157). The sun of the spiritual world, which is from the Lord, and in which the Lord is, is not only the first *substance* but is also the only *substance* from which all things are (n. 5). Affections which belong to the will are nothing but changes and variations of state of the purely organic *substances* of the mind, and thoughts which belong to the understanding are nothing but changes and variations in the form of these *substances* (n. 279, 319).

SUBSTANTIATE.

The spiritual sun is the first and only substance from which all things are; infinitely more things are in that substance than can appear in the substances that spring from it, which are called *substantiate* (or composited), and at length material (n. 6 [2]).

SUCCESSIVE.

How the simultaneous produces what is *successive* (n. 12). (*See* SIMULTANEOUS.)

SUN.

The Lord produced from Himself the *sun* of the spiritual world, and through that *sun* all things of the universe (n. 5). That *sun*, which is from the Lord, is not only the first substance but is also the only substance from which all things are (n. 5). The spiritual *sun*, which is from the Lord, and in which the Lord is, is itself the only substance; and this substance is not in space. It is the all

in all, and is in the greatest and the least of the created universe (n. 6). The Lord appears above the angelic heaven as a *sun* (n. 162). By the "*sun*" in the Word is meant the Divine love (n. 173, 292). In respect to their sight the Lord is above the angels in their *sun*, but in respect to the life of their love and wisdom He is in them (n. 31). From the *sun* of the world heat and light flow in alike into trees that bear evil fruit and good fruit (n. 160).

SUPPER (THE HOLY),

Confirms the remission of sins in those who repent, because that *Supper* or communion every one is kept looking to the Lord alone ( ).

SUPPLY.

Every power must have a *supply* that must be imparted to it, and thus a determination from what is more internal or higher than itself (n. 88).

SWEDENBORG

Talked with many after their death in Europe and its various kingdoms, in Asia and Africa and their various kingdoms, and they were all near *him* (n. 50 [3]). *He* talked with those who lived many ages ago; with those who lived before the flood and with some who lived after it, with those who lived in the time of the Lord and with one of His Apostles, and with many who lived in later ages. They all appeared like men of middle age, and they said that they knew nothing about death except that it is damnation (n. 324 [4]). For several years *he* talked with spirits and with angels, nor did any spirit dare, or any angel wish, to tell *him* anything, still less to instruct *him* about any matter in the Word, or about any matter of doctrine from the Word. *He* was taught by the Lord alone, who was revealed to *him*, and appeared constantly before *his* eyes as a Sun in which He is, in the same way that He appears to the angels, and enlightened *him* (n. 135). When it was granted *him* by the Lord to speak with spirits and angels it was at once revealed to *him* that neither thought nor will was from *himself*, but that if good it was from the Lord, and if evil it was from hell. This was demonstrated to *him* by much experience. Novitiate spirits wondered at this state of mind, but *he* laid open the mystery to them, showing that while *he* thought interiorly and perceived what flowed into *his* exterior thoughts, and whether it was from heaven or from hell, and rejected what was from hell and received what was from heaven, *he* still seemed to *himself* to think and to will from *himself* (n. 290). Evil spirits who infused evil thought into *his* mind detected and driven away (n. 312 [4]).

SWEDES.

Things plainly taught in their exhortation to the holy communion (n. 114, 258 [5]).

SWORD.

"To be devoured by the *sword*" signifies to perish by the falsity of evil (n. 278*b* [5]).

SYRIA,

One of the countries where the Ancient Church existed, and where the Ancient Word was known (n. 328 [2]).

SYRIANS (THE).

Each nation with which the children of Israel waged war signified some particular kind of evil (n. 251 [3]).

SYSTOLE.

Of the dilations and contractions of the heart called *systole* and diastole (n. 319).

TABLES OF THE LAW.

There are two *tables of the law*, one for the Lord and the other for man (n. 95, 326 [7]). So far as man keeps the *law* of his *table* as if from himself, so far the Lord enables him to keep the *laws* of His *table* (n. 95). The *laws* of man's *table* all refer to love to the neighbor, and the *laws* of the Lord's *table* all refer to love to the Lord (n. 95). (*See* DECALOGUE.)

TALENT (THE).

Prudence is the *"talent"* given to the servants to trade with, of which they must render an account (*Luke* xix.; *Matt.* xxv.) (n. 210 [2]).

TASTE

Cannot exist apart from its form, which is the tongue (n. 279 [6]).

TASTE (TO).

Every thing that a man sees, hears, smells, *tastes*, and feels flows in (n. 308 [2]).

TEACH.

The Lord alone *teaches* man, but mediately by means of the Word when in a state of enlightenment (n. 135). The man who is *taught* from the Word is *taught* by the Lord alone (n. 172). How man is *taught* by the Lord (n. 154-174). Every one is *taught* according to the understanding that belongs to his own love; what is beyond this is not permanent (n. 172 [5]). All who are *taught* by the Lord in the Word are *taught* a few truths in the world, but many when they become angels (n. 172 [5]).

TEETH (THE).

It has been provided by the Lord that those who could not be reached by the Gospel, but only by a religion, should have a place in the Divine Man, that is, in heaven, constituting those parts that are called skins, bones, etc. (n. 254 [3], 326 [10]).

TEMPLE (THE),

Built by Solomon signified both the Lord's Divine Human (*John* ii. 19, 21), and the church (n. 245). The destruction of *the temple* represented the essential devastation of the church (n. 246).

TEMPORAL

Things that are proper to men in the natural world have relation in general to dignities and possessions, and in particular to every one's necessities, which are food, clothing and habitation (n. 220 [5], 215). Man puts off natural and *temporal* things by death, and puts on spiritual and eternal things that correspond to them (n. 220 [4]). Nothing but what is *temporal* can proceed from man, and nothing but what is eternal from the Lord (n. 219 [2]). *Temporal* things and eternal things are separated by man, but are conjoined by the Lord (n. 218). The *temporal*, relatively, is nothing, and becomes nothing when it is ended (n. 59).

TEMPTATIONS (SPIRITUAL),

Are nothing else than combats against the evils and falsities that are exhaled from hell and affect man (n. 25). Genuine *temptations* have as their object things spiritual (n. 141). *Temptations* are infestations by the evil who are with men (n. 19 [2]).

TENDONS (THE).

The heavenly Man, which is heaven, if all the organized forms of the human body are to be in it, must be composed not of men of a single religion but of men of many religions (n. 326 [10], 254).

THEFT,

The love of self its source (n. 276 [2]).

THIEF AND ROBBER (THE).

Whoever does not go to the Lord to be saved is "a *thief* and a *robber*" (*John* x. 1) (n. 230 [4]).

THINK.

It was shown to spirits that no one *thinks*, nor can *think*, from himself, but that it is from influx (n. 288). No one *thinks* from himself, but only from others; neither do these others *think* from themselves, but all *think* from influx out of heaven, and heaven by influx from the Lord (n. 289 [2], 294, 308). All *think* from the Lord, and this is true both of the evil man and of the good (n. 308). Whoever does not *think* above the sensual is in the darkness of night regarding the state of his life (n. 274 [10]). What it is, while one is *thinking* from the present, to *think* at the same time from the eternal (n. 59). It

is from a law of the Divine providence that man should *think* as if from himself and should act prudently as if from himself, but should nevertheless acknowledge that he does it from the Lord (n. 321). No one *thinks* from time and space when thinking of those who are in the spiritual world (n. 50 [4]). (*See* THOUGHT.)

THINK AND WILL (TO).

The essential Divine is *to think and to will* from itself, while the essential human is *to think and will* from God (n 293). *Thinking and willing* are spiritual, speaking and doing are natural (n. 71).

THORNS AND THISTLES (THE),

That the earth was to bring forth (*Gen.* iii. 18) signify pure falsity and evil (n. 313 [3]).

THOUGHT.

No *thought* is possible to man except from some affection of his life's love; *thought* is nothing but the form of affection (n. 198). All of man's *thoughts* are from the affection of his life's love; and apart from these there are and can be no *thoughts* whatever (n. 193). *Thoughts*, which belong to the understanding, are nothing but changes and variations in the form of the purely organic substances of the mind (n. 279 [6]). Every man has an external and an internal of *thought* (n. 103, 106-110, 120, 139, 145, 150.) The affections associated with perceptions constitute man's internal, and the enjoyments of affections associated with *thoughts* constitute his external (n. 106). By the external and internal of thought the same is meant as by the external and internal man (n. 103). The external of man's *thought* is in itself of the same character as its internal (n. 106). The internal of *thought* and the external of *thought* are distinct like what is prior and what is posterior, or what is higher and what is lower (n. 145.) The interiors of man mean the internal of his *thought*, of which he knows nothing until he comes into the spiritual world and its light, which he does after death (n. 233). The internal of *thought* in man coheres with the external of *thought* in so close a connection that they cannot be separated (n. 233). That both exterior and interior *thought* are possible to man is clearly evident from his being able from his interior *thought* to look upon his exterior *thought* and to judge of it whether it is evil or not evil (n. 104 [2]). *Thought* from this exterior enlightenment sees a thing on both sides; on the one it sees the reasons that confirm, on the other the appearances that invalidate; the latter it disperses, the former it collects (n. 168 [3]). From *thought* abstracted from time and space a comprehension of the Divine Omnipresence and the Divine Omnipotence, also of the Divine from eternity, is possible (n. 51). If you should withdraw *thought* from speech speech would stop (n. 3 [2]). (*See* AFFECTIONS AND THOUGHT, THINK, AFFECTION, ILLUMINATION.)

THREATS.

No one is reformed by *threats* and punishments, because they compel (n. 136). (*See* COMPEL (To).)

TIME

Is only an appearance in accord with the state of affection from which the thought springs (n. 49). (*See* SPACE AND TIME.)

TONE

Corresponds to affection, and speech to the thought (n. 279 [8]).

TONGUE (THE).

(N. 180 [6], 279 [8], 336.) *The tongue* is the form of taste (n. 279 [6]). *The tongue* does not taste from itself; it is man's mind or spirit that there perceives things by the sense, and is affected by the sense in accordance with its nature (n. 314). Man knows so little as to amount to scarcely anything as to how *the tongue* tastes (n. 336, 174). When it is granted, spirits speak with man in his mother *tongue*, but only a few words (n. 135).

TORMENT (THE)

Of one in the delight of hell who is permitted to approach heaven (n. 324 [7], 338 [6]).

TRACHEA OR WINDPIPE,

Its functions (n. 180 [3], 279 [8,9]).

TRANSFERRED.

Man is constantly in a state to be reformed, and if he is evil he is *transferred* by the Lord from one society of hell to another, or if he suffers himself to be reformed he is *transferred* from one society of heaven to another, and this even until death (n. 307 [2]).

TREE.

There is a correspondence between man's life and the growth of a *tree* (n. 332 [3]). Man is depicted in the Word by a *tree* (n. 332 [3]). Where the *tree* falls there it lies. So, too, does a man's life when he dies remain such as it has been (n. 277*b*). Heavenly love with its affections for good and truth and perfections therefrom, together with the enjoyments from these affections and thoughts therefrom may be likened to a *tree* distinguished for its branches, leaves, and fruits (n. 107). The "*tree* of life" means the Lord in respect to His Divine providence; and the "*tree* of knowledge" means man in respect to his own prudence (n. 241 [3], 313 [2]).

TRIBES.

In the earliest times *tribes*, families, and households dwelt apart, and not under general governments as at this day (n. 215 [2]).

TRINE (THE).

It is in the Lord alone that this *Trine* in One is possible (n. 123 [2]).

TRINITY.

God is one in person and in essence, in whom is the *trinity*, and that the Lord is this God (n. 262 [7], 263).

TRUTH.

By *truth* is meant that which universally embraces and involves all things of wisdom (n. 11). Every thing of the understanding has relation to *truth* (n. 11 [2]). The genuine *truths* in which the spiritual sense of the Word resides were not revealed by the Lord until the last judgment had been accomplished, and the new church that is meant by "The Holy Jerusalem" was about to be established by the Lord (n. 264 [4]). How a *truth* from the Word, sent down out of heaven, was changed into falsity in its descent through the hells (n. 288).

TYRE,

One of the kingdoms in which the Ancient Church existed and in which the Ancient Word was known (n. 328).

ULTIMATES

(*See* OUTMOSTS.)

UNDERSTAND.

Two ways to perceive rationally: in one man sees in himself that a thing is so, and in the other he *understands* it by means of reasons (n. 150 [2]). Understanding is the consort or mate of willing, without which it cannot exist; and in the measure of your willing you have the ability to *understand* (n. 96 [2]).

UNDERSTANDING (THE),

Which is man's internal sight, is illumined by spiritual light, just as the eye, or man's external sight, is illumined by natural light (n. 166). There is an internal *understanding* and an external *understanding* (n. 111 [2]).

UNDERSTANDING AND WILL.

In every man, both good and evil, there are two faculties, one of which constitutes the *understanding*, the other the *will* (n. 285). The faculty that constitutes the *understanding* is an ability to understand and think. The faculty that constitutes the *will* is an ability to do these things freely, that is, to think and consequently to speak and to act in any way not contrary to reason or rationality (n. 285). Without rationality and liberty man would not possess *will and understanding*, and would not be man (n. 96 [2]). An *understanding* has been

given to man, and this is separated from the *will*, to the end that he may know, understand, and acknowledge what is good and what is evil, and see what his *will* is (n. 278a). Man's *understanding* is a recipient of both good and evil and of both truth and falsity, but his *will* itself is not. This must be either in evil or in good; it cannot be in both (n. 284). The *will's* love inspires the *understanding* with whatever it desires, and not the reverse; it even destroys in the *understanding* every thing that is not from itself (n. 209). *Understanding* apart from *will* cannot think anything, or see or feel anything, or say or do anything (n. 3). Man's life's *will* is led and his life's *understanding* is taught by the Lord alone (n. 156).

UNION. UNITY.

The Lord's Divine providence continually labors to unite truth with good and good with truth in man, because such *union* is the church and is heaven (n. 21). The *union* of love and wisdom called the marriage of good and truth (n. 7). The greater the number of those that enter into the form of the Divine love, which is the form of forms, the more perfect the *unity* becomes (n. 62). The *union* of charity and faith and of the will and understanding (n. 82).

UNITE.

To *unite* all affections into the form of heaven is possible only to Him who is love itself and also wisdom itself, and who is at once Infinite and Eternal (n. 63). The unceasing object of the Divine providence is to *unite* good to truth and truth to good in man, for thus man is *united* to the Lord (n. 21).

UNIVERSAL.

In every form, the general and the particular, or the *universal* and the special, by wonderful conjunction act as one (n. 180 [4]). That is called *universal* which is made up of particular things taken together, like any general thing that exists from its particulars (n. 201 [2]). A *universal* apart from any particular is nothing (n. 278b). The

Divine is *universal* from its least particulars, and it is these Divine particulars that are called the *universal* (n. 294 [6]). The Lord's Divine providence is *universal* from the minutest particulars (n. 202). To acknowledge God and to refrain from doing evil because it is against God are the two *universals* of the church (n. 326 [9, 10], 328). (*See* PARTICULAR, PARTICULARS, SINGLE, SINGLY.)

UNIVERSE (THE),

With each thing and all things therein, was created from Divine love by means of Divine wisdom (n. 3). The Lord did not create *the universe* for His own sake but for the sake of those with whom He is to be in heaven (n. 27 [2]). God created *the universe* and all things thereof from Himself and not from nothing (n. 46 [3]).

USE

Is a good, and from the understanding which is conjoined or adjoined to the *use* it has relation to truth; and from that the *use* has its quality (n. 11 [3]). By *uses* goods are meant; and therefore doing *uses* or goods means serving others and ministering to them (n. 215 [11]). *Uses* are the goods that are called the goods of charity (n. 220 [5]). By *uses* are not meant merely the necessaries of life, which have relation to food, clothing, and habitation for the individual and those dependent on him, but also the good of one's country, of society, and of the fellow citizen (n. 220 [11]). They who are in the love of self and of the world perform *uses* for the sake of reputation or gain, thus for the sake of self; while those who perform *uses* do this from the Lord, and not from self (n. 215 [12], 217 [2,5]). One who is led by the devil performs *uses* for the sake of self and the world; but one who is led by the Lord performs *uses* for the sake of the Lord and heaven (n. 215 [13]). All who shun evils as sins perform *uses* from the Lord, while all who do not shun evils as sins perform *uses* from the devil (n. 215 [13]. The Lord's kingdom is a kingdom of *uses* (n. 26, 250 [3]). The Lord provides that there shall

be in hell no person by whom, or no thing by means of which, some *use* is not accomplished (n. 26). Through His Divine providence the Lord conjoins Himself with natural things by means of spiritual things, and with temporal things by means of eternal things according to *uses* (n. 220 [4]). The Lord conjoins Himself with *uses* by means of correspondences, and thus by means of appearances in accordance with the confirmations of these by man (n. 220 [6]). To whatever height the love of self climbs the lust of performing *uses* for the sake of its own glory burns in it (n. 250 [3]). The Lord leads man into a love of *uses* that he may esteem eminence not for his own sake but for the sake of *uses* (n. 183 [4]). The wicked perform *uses* equally with the good, and the evil from their fire with more ardor than the good (n. 252 [2]).

VARIATIONS

Of state in the purely organic substances of the mind (n. 195 [3], 179 [8], 319).

VARIETY.

An image of the Infinite and Eternal in the *variety* of all things is apparent in this, that there is no one thing that is the same as another, nor can there be to eternity (n. 56 [2]). *Variety* is infinite and eternal (n. 56 [2]). In every matter from the greatest to the least of it there must be *variety* (n. 24). The changing can have existence only in the constant, the fixed, and the sure. Examples (n. 190). The changes themselves progress to infinity and have no end (n. 190 [3]).

VASTATION.

There is a gradual *vastation* of good and desolation of truth in the church until its consummation is reached (n. 328 [7]).

VEIL.

The *veil* that is between interiors and exteriors, or between the spiritual and the natural things of the mind, with the sensual (n. 311 [2]). The sensual finally close up the interiors of their minds, interposing a *veil*, as it were, and afterwards they think below the *veil*, but not of any thing that is above it (n. 310).

VENA CAVA.

The brain returns the blood vivified to the *vena cava*, and so back again to the heart (n. 296 [14]).

VENTRICLE (LEFT),

Of the heart (n. 296 [14]).

VESSELS (LYMPHATIC AND LACTEAL).

(N. 296 [14].)

VICAR.

The life's love places a *vicar* below itself, which is called the love of means (n. 109).

VICTORIES

Seem to be on the side of prudence, and sometimes not on the side of justice, because man judges from the appearance (n. 252, 251 [5,6]).

VIOLENCE.

He that upholds evil loves does *violence* to Divine goods; and he who upholds false principles does *violence* to Divine truths (n. 231 [3]).

VIRGINS (THE FOOLISH).

Those that acknowledge truths with the lips but do not with the heart, are like *the foolish virgins* who had lamps but no oil, and were not admitted to the wedding (n. 328 [9]).

VISCERA.

(N. 180 [4], 279 [7], 296 [14].)

VISIONARY.

Diabolical visions have sometimes appeared, induced by enthusiastic and *visionary* spirits, who, from the delirium that possessed them called themselves the Holy Spirit (n. 134a [3]). (*See* VISIONS.)

VISIONS.

No one is reformed by *visions*, or by conversations with the dead, because they compel (n. 134a [1,3]). *Visions* are of two kinds, Divine and diabolical. Divine *visions* are produced by means of representations in heaven, and diabolical *visions* by means of magic in hell (n. 134a). There are also fantastic *visions*, which are delusions of an abstracted mind (n. 134a [1,3]). Divine *visions*, which are produced by means of representation in heaven, are such as the prophets had, who were not in the body but in the spirit when they were in these *visions;* for *visions* cannot appear to any one in the waking states of the mind (n. 134a). Such *visions* do not take place at the present day; if they did they would not be understood, because they are produced by means of representation, each one of which is significative of the internal things of the church and the arcana of heaven (n. 134a [3]). Diabolical *visions* have sometimes appeared, induced by enthusiastic and visionary spirits (n. 134a [3]). It was foretold by Daniel (*Dan.* ix. 24) that *visions* would cease when the Lord came into the world (n. 134a [3]).

VITAL HEAT

Is from the delights of the affections and from the enjoyment of the perceptions and thoughts (n. 195 [2]).

VOLITION.

The *volition* of every good and the understanding of every truth are not from man but from the Lord (n. 88).

WARS.

All *wars*, however much they may belong to civil affairs, represent in heaven the states of the church, and are correspondences (n. 251 [3]. Such were all the *wars* described in the Word, and such also are all *wars* at this day (n. 251 [3]). It is not known in this world what kingdoms in Christendom answer to the Moabites and Ammonites, what to the Syrians and Philistines, or what to the Chaldeans and Assyrians, and the others with whom the children of Israel waged *war*, and yet there are those that do answer to them (n. 251 [4]). Why there are *wars*, and why the Lord does not check them (n. 251 [2,3]).

WASHING.

To "*wash*" means to cleanse from evils. "*Washing* the head and the hands" (*John* xiii. 8–10) means to cleanse the internal man; and "*washing* the feet*" means to cleanse the external man (n. 151 [2]).

WAY.

The Lord enters into man through no other than an internal *way*, which is through the Word and doctrine and preaching from the Word (n. 131). In the spiritual world there are actually *ways* that lead to every society of heaven and to every society of hell (n. 60). There is a *way* there for every love, and the love opens the *way* and leads one to his fellows. Other *ways* than the *way* of his love no one sees (n. 60). Every man after death goes the *way* of his own love, he that is in a good love to heaven, and a he that is in an evil love to hell (n. 319 [4]). In what is angelic there is present a knowledge of the *way* from walking in it, and a walking in the *way* through a knowledge of it (n. 60).

WEALTH.

The Lord never leads man away . . . from acquiring *wealth*, but only leads him away from acquiring *wealth* for the sake of mere opulence, that is, for the sake of riches (n. 183 [4]).

WHOREDOMS

Have their source in the love of self (n. 276 [2]). In the Word falsifications of truth are depicted by *whoredoms* (n. 233 [10]).

WICKED.

(*See* EVIL.)

WIFE.

A *wife* in the Word signifies the church (n. 245). In the Word heaven and the church are called "the bride" and "the *wife*" (n. 8). The seven hundred *wives* of Solomon represented the various religions of the world (n. 245). (*See* MARRIAGE.)

WILL AND LOVE.

The *will* and the *love* act as one (n. 96 [3]). Man's internal *will* is that which is in the lusts, and the external *will* is that which is in the enjoyments of the lusts (n. 111 [2]). If you should withdraw willing from doing work would stop (n. 3 [2]). Man's *will* runs counter to the Lord's *will* (n. 219 [4]). It is the *will* of the Lord that causes the appearance in man that what he thinks, speaks, *wills*, and does is his own (n. 96 [5]). It is the inflow of the Lord's *will* that does this (n. 96 [6]). The internal of the *will* conjoins itself with the internal of the understanding and makes the conjunction to be reciprocal (n. 136 [8]). (*See* UNDERSTANDING AND WILL.)

WILL (TO).

Willing is not possible apart from understanding; understanding is its consort or mate, without which it cannot exist (n. 96 [2]). There is in man an interior and an exterior *willing;* and he can act in accordance with the exterior and not at the same time in accordance with the interior (n. 89). All *willing* is of love and has relation to good (n. 11 [2]. 89). *To will* apart from knowing, perceiving, and thinking what one *wills* is not anything; but together with these it becomes something (n. 11 [2]). (*See* To THINK AND To WILL.)

WINGS

Signify spiritual truths (n. 20).

WISDOM

Is conjunction with the Lord (n. 36). *Wisdom* not conjoined with love is like a vanishing meteor (n. 35). There are three degrees of *wisdom*, the natural, the spiritual and the celestial, and these are opened in the measure of love (n. 34 [1,2]). *Wisdom* can be elevated in a triplicate ratio, and in each degree in a simple ratio to its highest point (n. 34 [2]). These three **degrees** are not connected continuously, but they are conjoined by correspondences (n. 34 [9]). *Wisdom* that comes to perception is a perception of truth from an affection for it (n. 36). *Wisdom* that increases to eternity is without end. If *wisdom* with a wise man were to come to an end the delight of his *wisdom*, which consists in the perpetual multiplication and fructification of *wisdom*, would perish (n. 335 [2]). A man may be admitted into the *wisdom* of spiritual things, and also into a love for them, and yet not be reformed (n. 222). Angelic *wisdom* is ineffable (n. 34 [3]). There is no such approximation of angelic *wisdom* to the Divine *wisdom* as to touch it (n. 335 [3]). (*See* LOVE AND WISDOM.)

WISE.

The more closely a man is conjoined with the Lord the *wiser* he becomes (n. 34). No one is *wise* from himself, but only from the Lord (n. 36). Those are *wise* from the Lord who cast out the devil, that is, evil, from themselves (n. 34 [3]).

WITHDRAWAL FROM EVIL (THE),

Is effected by the Lord in a thousand ways, and even in most secret ways (n. 296 [10]).

WOLVES.

They who are in their own prudence are like *wolves* and foxes (n. 311 [3]).

WOMB.

Every man is formed by the Lord in the *womb* into the image and likeness of God (n. 330).

WORD.

The Lord is the *Word* because the *Word* is from Him and treats of Him; and because it is the Divine truth of the Divine good (n. 172 [2,3]). All doctrine of the church must be drawn from the *Word* (n. 172). When man is taught from the *Word* he is taught from the Lord (n. 172 [5]). No one is taught immediately from heaven, but mediately through the *Word* (n. 265 [5]). All things of the *Word* have communication with heaven, and with the Lord Himself (n. 172 [2]). There is a presence of the Lord and of heaven wherever the *Word* is read with reverence (n. 260 [3]). The whole *Word* is nothing but a doctrine of life (n. 330 [7]). The Papists do not read it; and the Reformed, who are in faith separated from charity, pay no attention to what relates to life in it, but only to what relates to faith (n. 330 [7], 264 [2]). Why hitherto men have not known that there is a spiritual sense in all the particulars of the *Word*, and that its holiness is therefrom (n. 264 [1,6]). Those have light therefrom who are outside of the church and do not have the *Word* (n. 256 [2]). All who are taught by the Lord in the *Word* are taught a few truths in the world, but many when they become angels (n. 172 [5]). The interiors of the *Word*, although implanted in the mind while in the world, are not opened in man until after his death (n. 172 [5]). The *Word* is written throughout wholly in correspondences (n. 256 [4]). Whenever any spirit opens the *Word* and rubs his face or his clothing against it, his face or clothing shines from the mere rubbing as brightly as the moon or a star, and this in sight of all whom he meets (n. 256 [4]).

WORKING.

(*See* OPERATION.)

WORKS.

(*See* DEEDS.)

WORLD.

All things that take place in the natural *world* correspond to spiritual things in the spiritual *world*, and every thing spiritual has relation to the church (n. 251 [4]). There is nothing in the natural *world* unconnected with the spiritual *world* (n. 74 [3]). In the spiritual *world* all are spiritual even in respect to their bodies (n. 167).

WORLD OF SPIRITS (THE),

Is intermediate between heaven and hell (n. 307 [3]). As long as a man lives in the world his external is governed in *the world of spirits* (n. 307 [3]). When a man dies he first enters *the world of spirits* and there comes into his external, which is there put off; and when this has been put off he is borne into his own place, to which he has been assigned (n. 307 [3]).

WORLD (THE CHRISTIAN).

Why the whole *Christian world* worships one God under three persons, which is to worship three Gods, not knowing hitherto that God is one in person and essence, in whom is a trinity, and that the Lord is that God (n. 262). Why there have been and still are so many heresies in *the Christian world* (n. 259).

WORSHIP.

To compel men to Divine *worship* by threats and punishments is pernicious (n. 136 [4]). Compelled *worship* shuts in evils, and evils then lie hidden like fire in wood under ashes, which is continually kindling and spreading till it breaks out in flames (n. 136 [4]). *Worship* not compelled, but spontaneous, does not shut evils in, and in consequence these are like fires that blaze up quickly and are gone (n. 136 [4]). A compelled internal is possible in such as are in the internal of *worship*. It may be an internal compelled by fear, or an internal compelled by love (n. 136 [9]). Com-

pelled *worship* is corporeal, lifeless, darkened, and sad (n. 137). *Worship* not compelled, when it is genuine, is spiritual, living, clear, and joyful (n. 137). Among the ancients all *worship* was representative, consisting of pure correspondences (n. 255 [2]). Of those who *worship* the sun and moon, believing God to be there, and of others who *worship* idols and graven images (n. 254 [5]). In places of *worship* in the spiritual world every one knows his own place (n. 338 [4]).

WORSHIPER.

Things enumerated that confirm every *worshiper* of himself and of nature against the Divine providence (n. 249–253). Of those who are *worshipers* of self and the world; *worshipers* of nature; *worshipers* of men and of images, and *worshipers* of the Lord (n. 154 [2]).

YOKE.

Concerning those who from their religion believe that they are not under the *yoke* of the law (n. 42, 101).

ZEAL.

There are some who seem to be in a blaze of *zeal* for the salvation of souls, and yet this may be from an infernal fire (n. 139 [6]).